NEGIMA!

33

Ken Akamatsu

TRANSLATED AND ADAPTED BY
Alethea Nibley and Athena Nibley

LETTERING AND RETOUCH BY
Scott O. Brown

KC
KODANSHA
COMICS

A word from the author

THIS VOLUME BRINGS US TO THE 300TH CHAPTER AND BEYOND. MAN...I'VE DRAWN A LOT.

CHARACTER-WISE, WE FINALLY LEARN ZAZIE'S TRUE IDEN-TITY. I FEEL LIKE NEGIMA! ITSELF HAS ENTERED ITS FINAL STAGE. (BUT IT WON'T END YET! (^^;))

Presenting *Negima!* volume 33!

Incidentally, we've seen a lot of the classmates' artifacts now. Which is your favorite? Naturally, I like Paru's Imperium Graphices. I'd also like Natsumi's Adiutor Solitarius. I can think of a few uses for that. Mwa ha ha...

Ken Akamatsu's home page address*
http://www.ailove.net/

*Please note the webpage is in Japanese.

NEGIMA!

MAGISTER NEGI MAGI

33

Ken Akamatsu

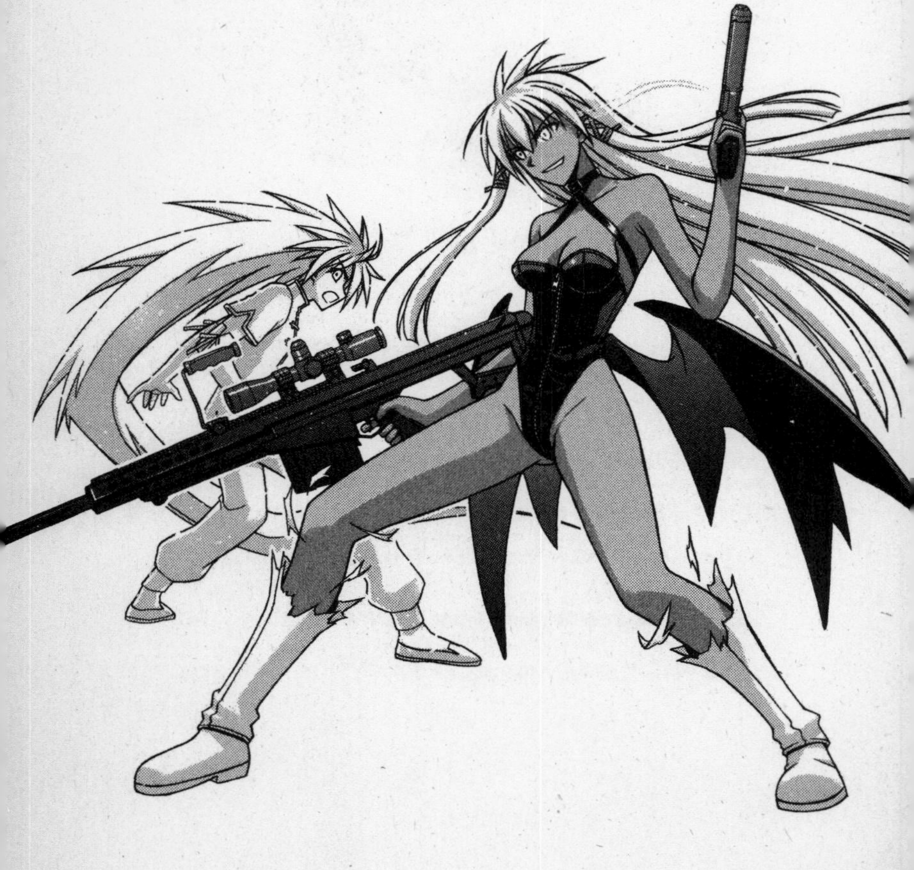

CONTENTS

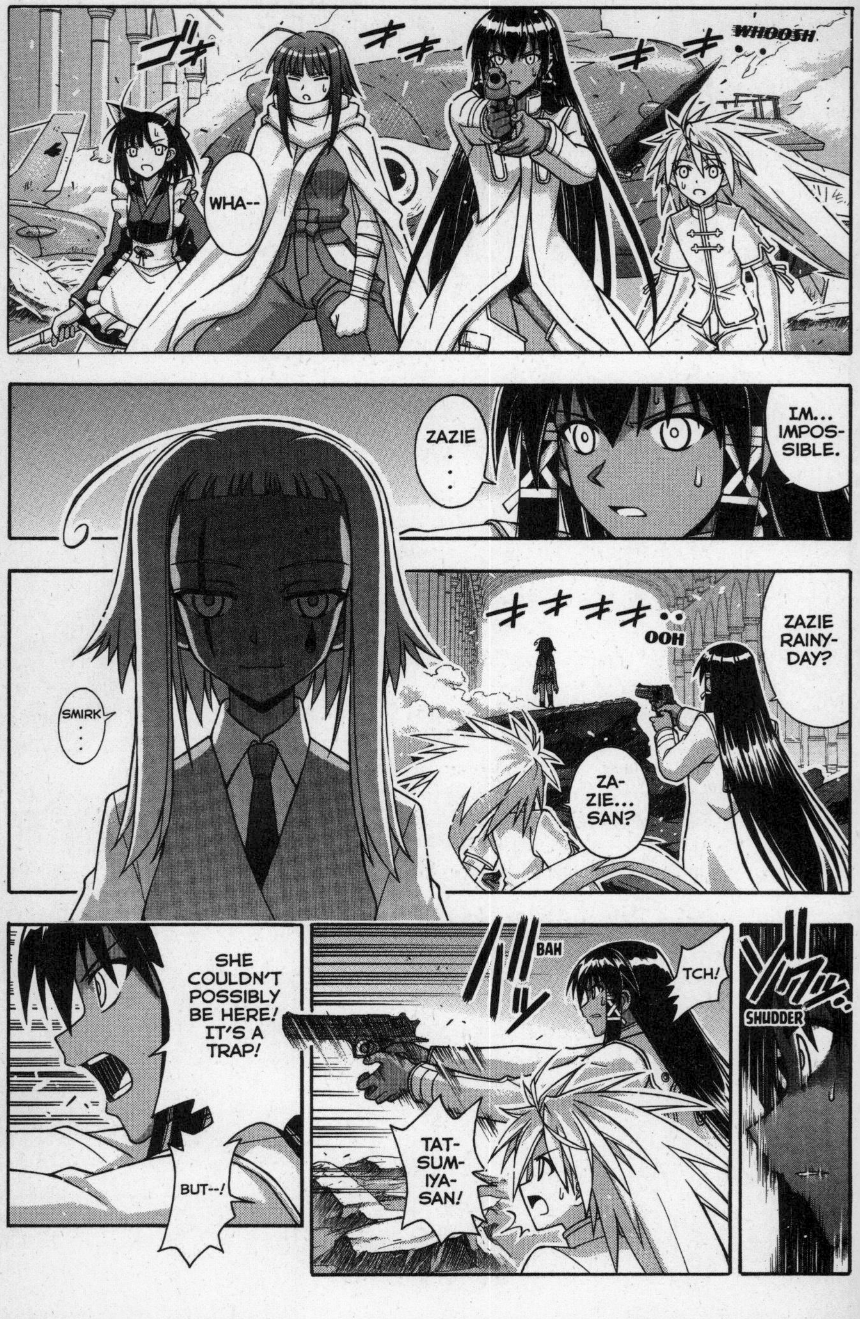
WHOOSH
WHA--
IM... IMPOS-SIBLE.
ZAZIE . . .
ZAZIE RAINY-DAY?
OOH
ZA-ZIE... SAN?
SMIRK . . .
SHUDDER
TCH!
BAH
TAT-SUM-IYA-SAN!
SHE COULDN'T POSSIBLY BE HERE! IT'S A TRAP!
BUT--!

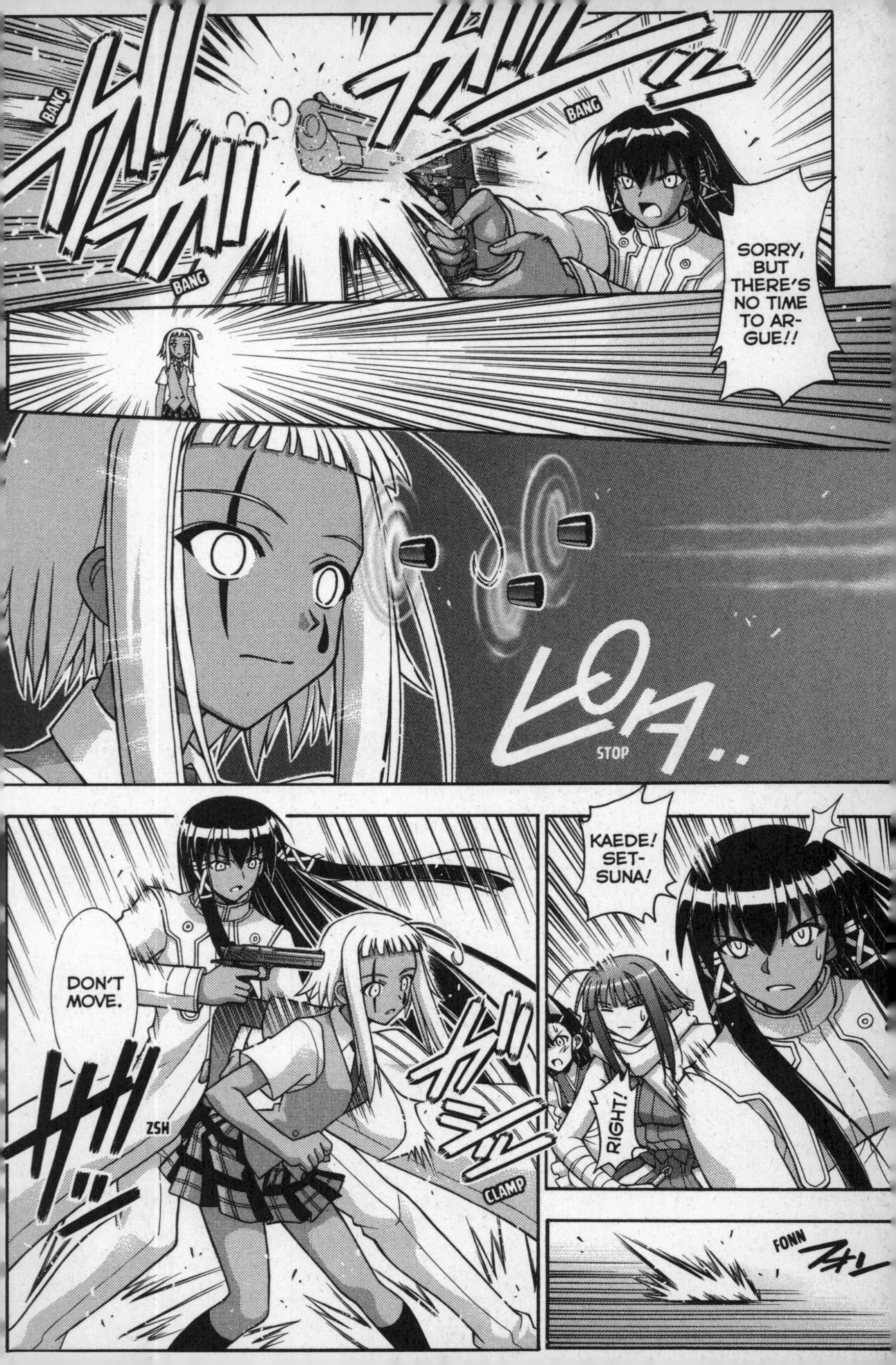
BANG
SORRY, BUT THERE'S NO TIME TO AR-GUE!!
BANG
BANG
STOP
KAEDE! SET-SUNA!
RIGHT!
FONN
DON'T MOVE.
CLAMP
ZSH

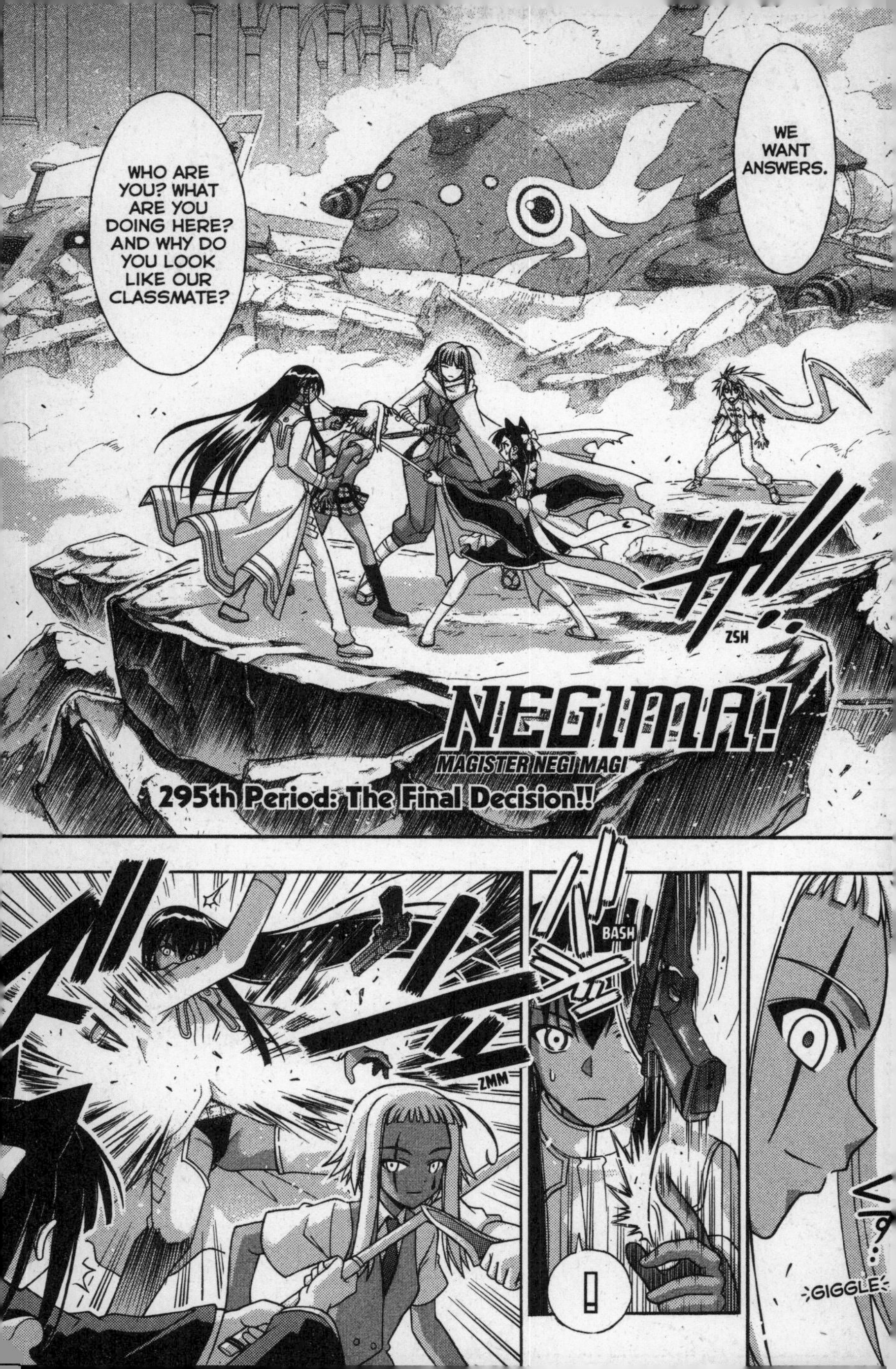
WE WANT ANSWERS.
WHO ARE YOU? WHAT ARE YOU DOING HERE? AND WHY DO YOU LOOK LIKE OUR CLASSMATE?
ZSH
NEGIMA!
MAGISTER NEGI MAGI
295th Period: The Final Decision!!
GIGGLE
BASH
!
ZMM

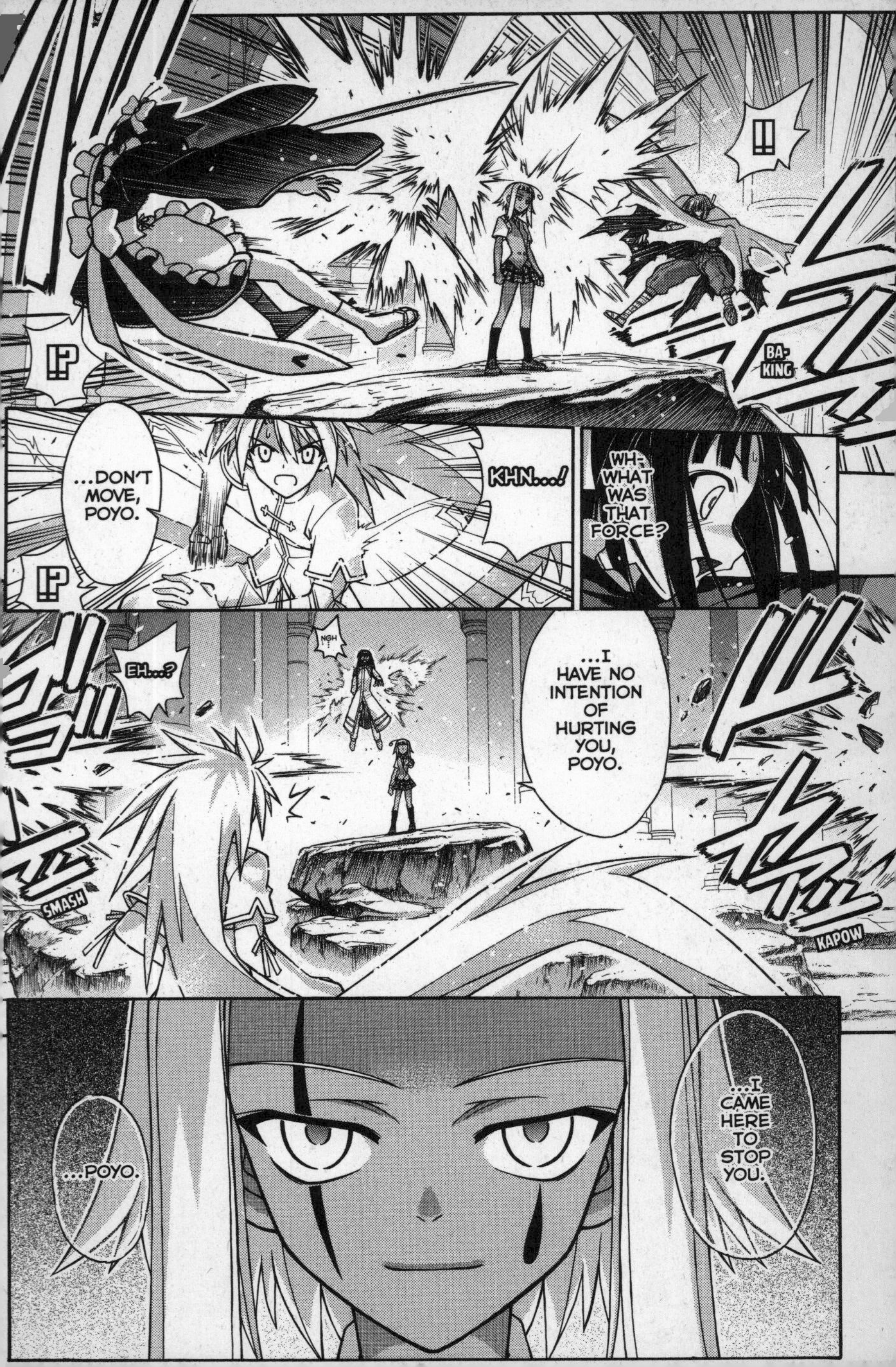
!!
BA-KING
!?
WH-WHAT WAS THAT FORCE?
KHN...!
...DON'T MOVE, POYO.
!?
KAPOW
...I HAVE NO INTENTION OF HURTING YOU, POYO.
NGH !
EH...?
SMASH
...I CAME HERE TO STOP YOU.
...POYO.

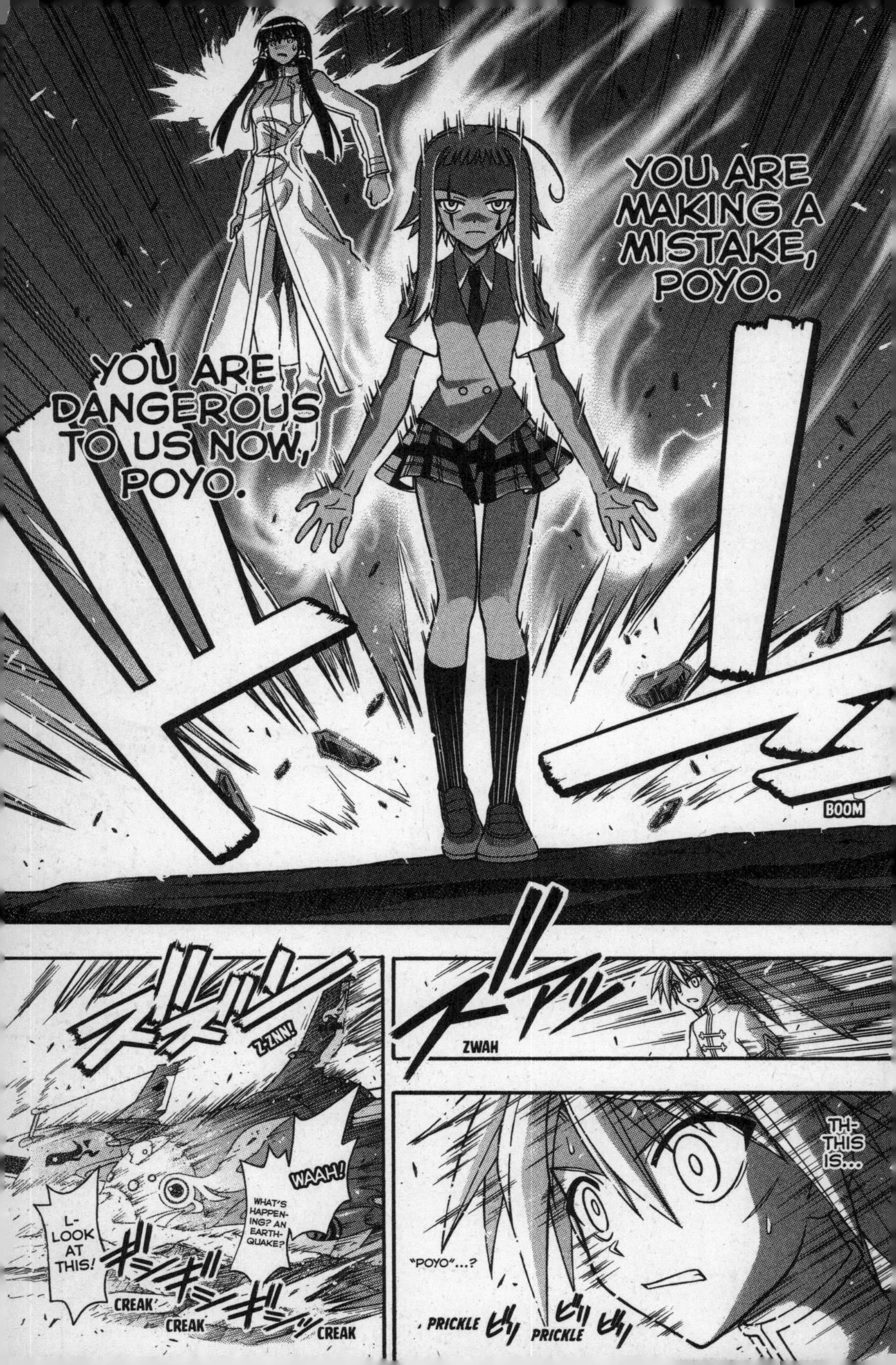
YOU ARE MAKING A MISTAKE, POYO.
YOU ARE DANGEROUS TO US NOW, POYO.
BOOM
ZWAH
TH-THIS IS...
"POYO"...?
PRICKLE
PRICKLE
Z-ZNN!
WAAH!
WHAT'S HAPPENING? AN EARTHQUAKE?
L-LOOK AT THIS!
CREAK
CREAK
CREAK

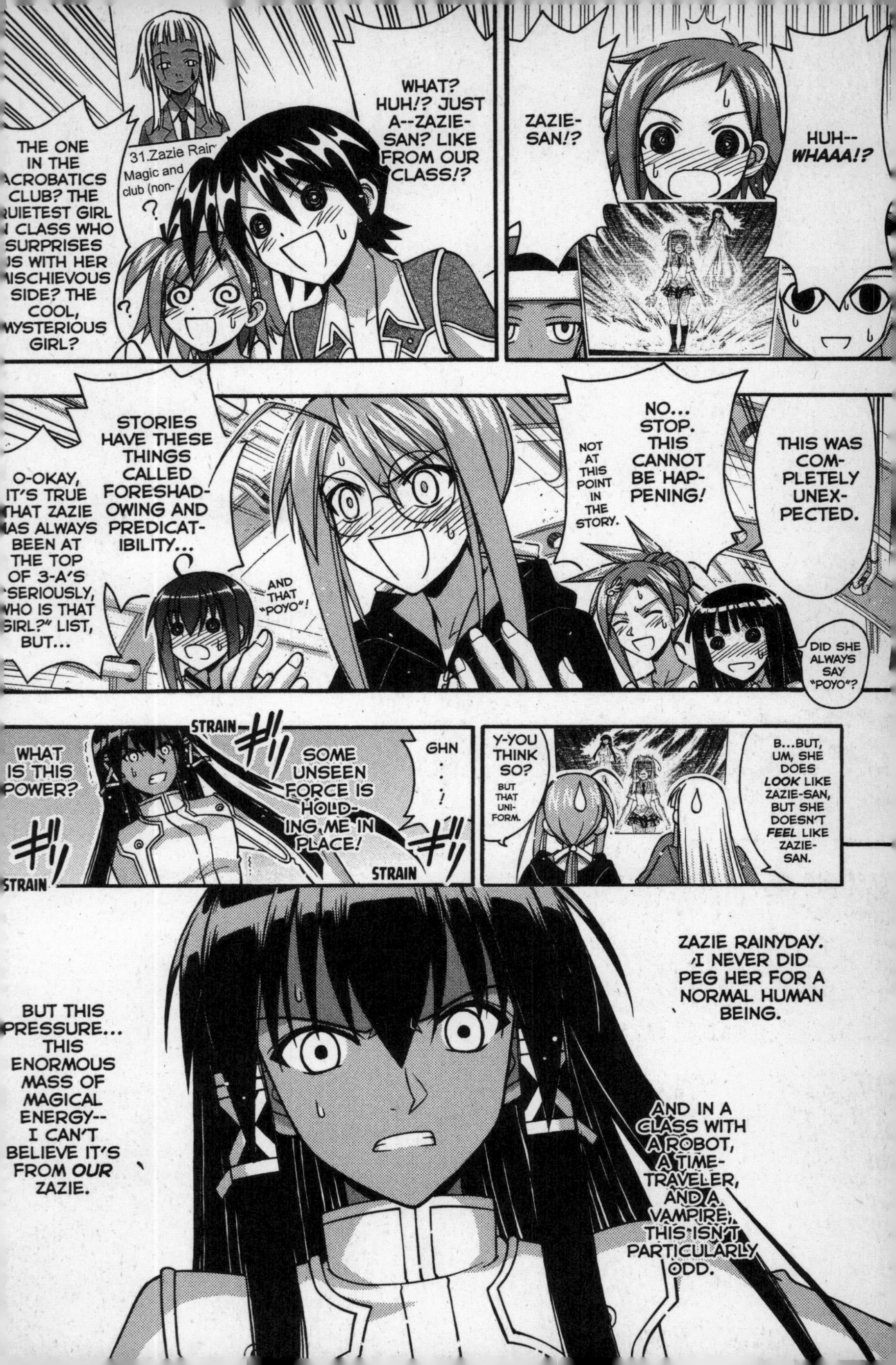
HUH-- WHAAA!?
ZAZIE-SAN!?
WHAT? HUH!? JUST A--ZAZIE-SAN? LIKE FROM OUR CLASS!?
31.Zazie Rain Magic and club (non-
THE ONE IN THE ACROBATICS CLUB? THE QUIETEST GIRL IN CLASS WHO SURPRISES US WITH HER MISCHIEVOUS SIDE? THE COOL, MYSTERIOUS GIRL?
THIS WAS COMPLETELY UNEXPECTED.
NO... STOP. THIS CANNOT BE HAPPENING!
NOT AT THIS POINT IN THE STORY.
STORIES HAVE THESE THINGS CALLED FORESHADOWING AND PREDICATIBILITY...
O-OKAY, IT'S TRUE THAT ZAZIE HAS ALWAYS BEEN AT THE TOP OF 3-A'S "SERIOUSLY, WHO IS THAT GIRL?" LIST, BUT...
AND THAT "POYO"!
DID SHE ALWAYS SAY "POYO"?
B...BUT, UM, SHE DOES LOOK LIKE ZAZIE-SAN, BUT SHE DOESN'T FEEL LIKE ZAZIE-SAN.
Y-YOU THINK SO?
BUT THAT UNIFORM.
GHN...!
SOME UNSEEN FORCE IS HOLDING ME IN PLACE!
STRAIN
STRAIN
WHAT IS THIS POWER?
STRAIN
ZAZIE RAINYDAY. I NEVER DID PEG HER FOR A NORMAL HUMAN BEING.
AND IN A CLASS WITH A ROBOT, A TIME-TRAVELER, AND A VAMPIRE, THIS ISN'T PARTICULARLY ODD.
BUT THIS PRESSURE... THIS ENORMOUS MASS OF MAGICAL ENERGY-- I CAN'T BELIEVE IT'S FROM OUR ZAZIE.

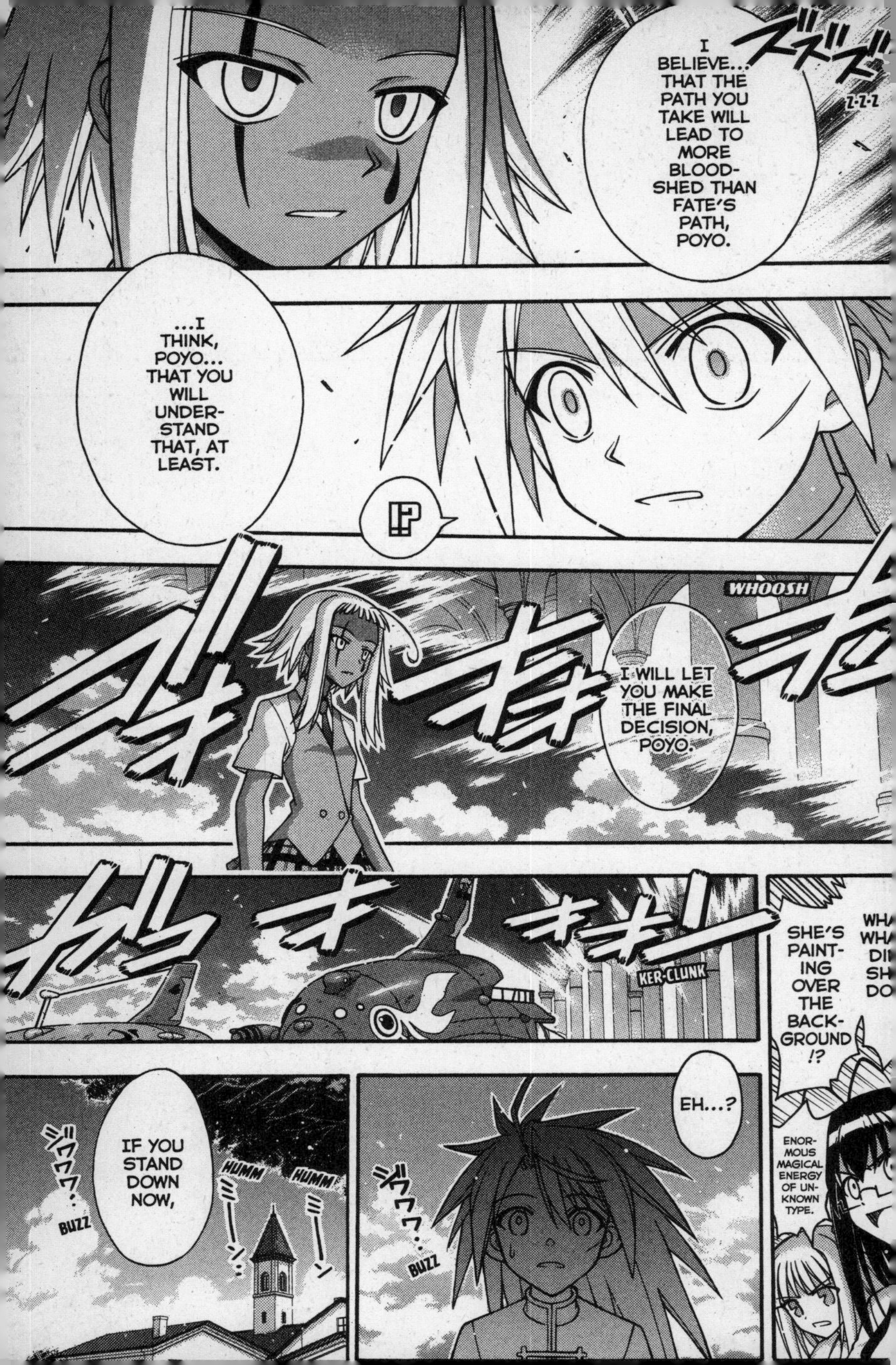

Z-Z-Z
I BELIEVE... THAT THE PATH YOU TAKE WILL LEAD TO MORE BLOOD-SHED THAN FATE'S PATH, POYO.
...I THINK, POYO... THAT YOU WILL UNDER-STAND THAT, AT LEAST.
!?
WHOOSH
I WILL LET YOU MAKE THE FINAL DECISION, POYO.
WHA WHA DI SH DO
SHE'S PAINT-ING OVER THE BACK-GROUND !?
ENOR-MOUS MAGICAL ENERGY OF UN-KNOWN TYPE.
KER-CLUNK
EH...?
BUZZ
IF YOU STAND DOWN NOW,
HUMM
HUMM
BUZZ

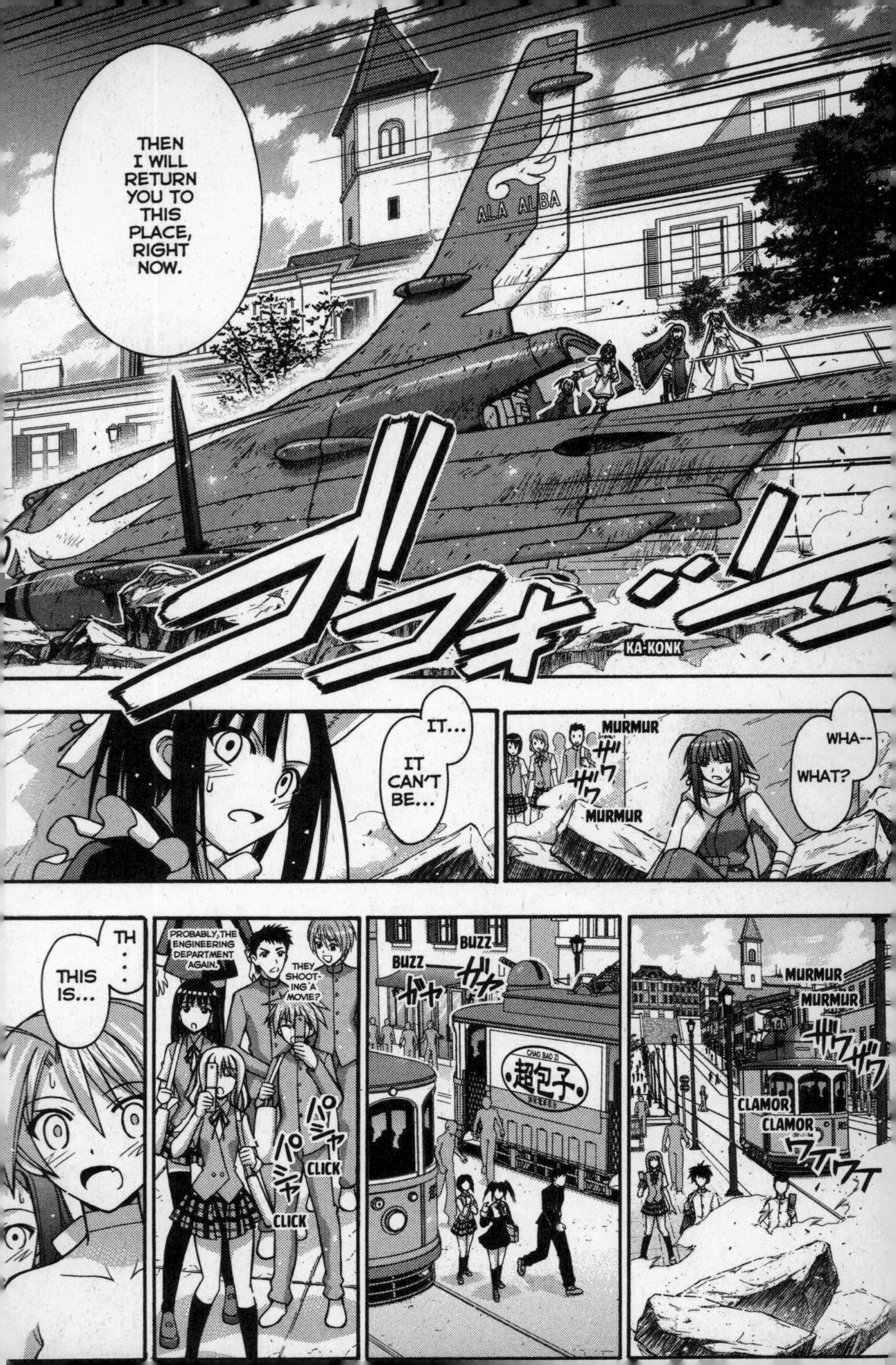
THEN I WILL RETURN YOU TO THIS PLACE, RIGHT NOW.
ALA ALBA
KA-KONK
MURMUR
ザワ
ザワ
MURMUR
WHA-- WHAT?
IT... IT CAN'T BE...
MURMUR
MURMUR
ザワザワ
CLAMOR
CLAMOR
ワイワイ
BUZZ
BUZZ
ガヤ
ガヤ
CHAO BAO ZI
超包子
THEY SHOOTING A MOVIE?
PROBABLY, THE ENGINEERING DEPARTMENT AGAIN.
パシャ
CLICK
パシャ
CLICK
TH... THIS IS...

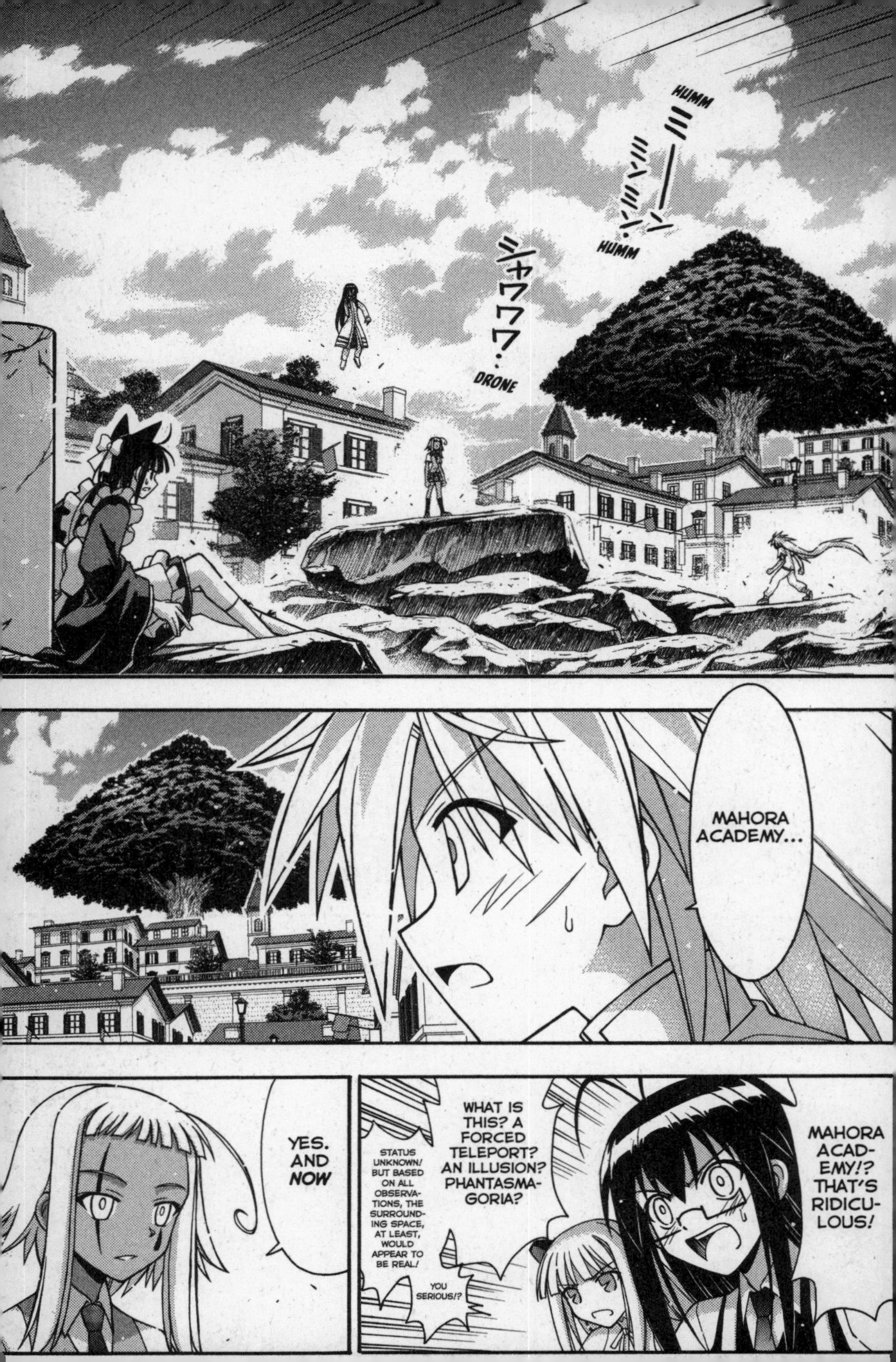
HUMM
ミーーーン
ミンミンミン・
HUMM
シャワワワ・
DRONE
MAHORA ACADEMY...
MAHORA ACADEMY!? THAT'S RIDICULOUS!
WHAT IS THIS? A FORCED TELEPORT? AN ILLUSION? PHANTASMAGORIA?
STATUS UNKNOWN! BUT BASED ON ALL OBSERVATIONS, THE SURROUNDING SPACE, AT LEAST, WOULD APPEAR TO BE REAL!
YOU SERIOUS!?
YES. AND *NOW*

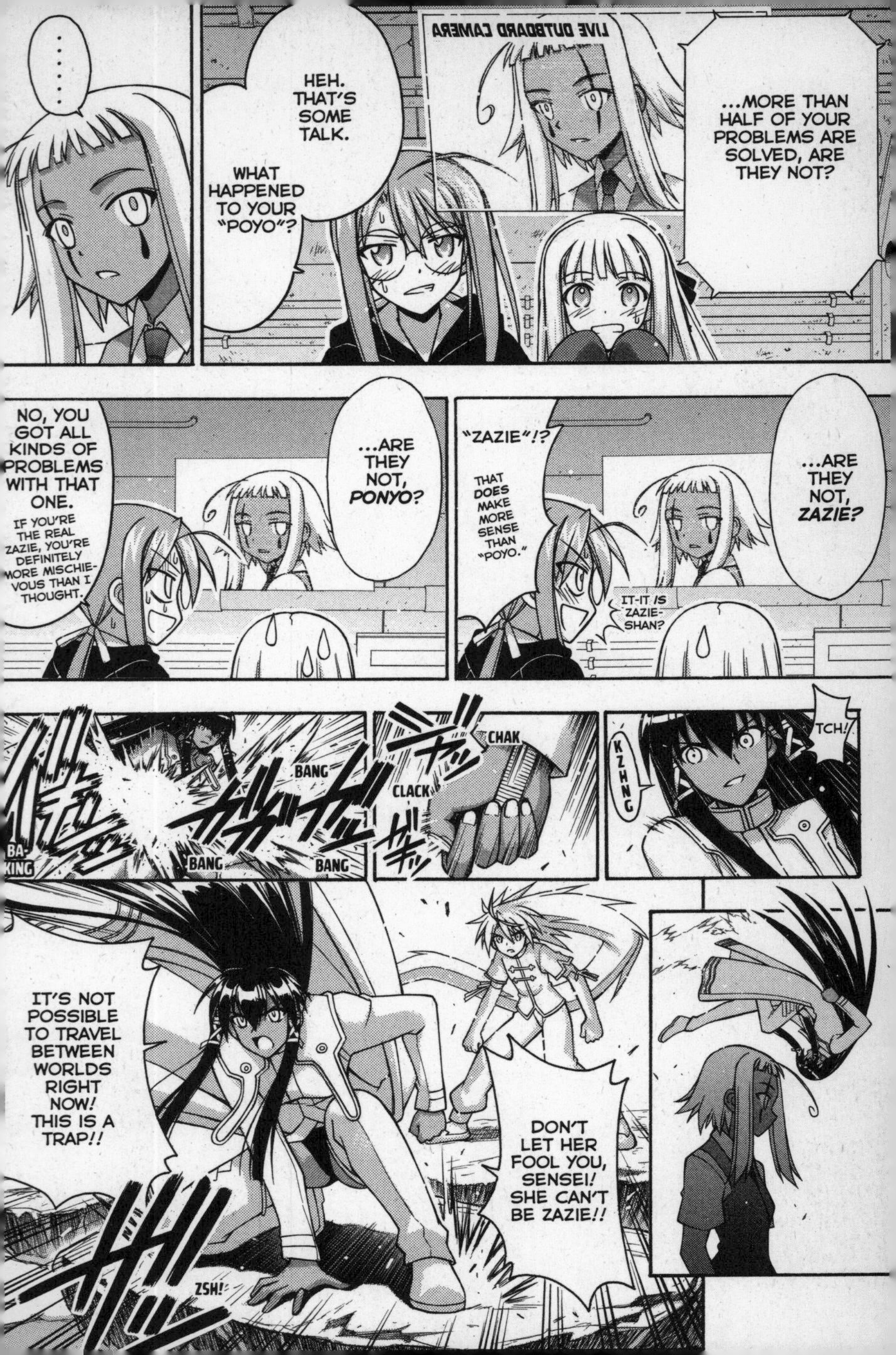

LIVE OUTBOARD CAMERA
...MORE THAN HALF OF YOUR PROBLEMS ARE SOLVED, ARE THEY NOT?
HEH. THAT'S SOME TALK.
WHAT HAPPENED TO YOUR "POYO"?
......
...ARE THEY NOT, ZAZIE?
"ZAZIE"!?
THAT DOES MAKE MORE SENSE THAN "POYO."
IT-IT IS ZAZIE-SHAN?
...ARE THEY NOT, PONYO?
NO, YOU GOT ALL KINDS OF PROBLEMS WITH THAT ONE.
IF YOU'RE THE REAL ZAZIE, YOU'RE DEFINITELY MORE MISCHIEVOUS THAN I THOUGHT.
TCH!
KZHNG
CHAK
CLACK
BANG
BANG
BANG
BA-KING
DON'T LET HER FOOL YOU, SENSEI! SHE CAN'T BE ZAZIE!!
IT'S NOT POSSIBLE TO TRAVEL BETWEEN WORLDS RIGHT NOW! THIS IS A TRAP!!
ZSH!

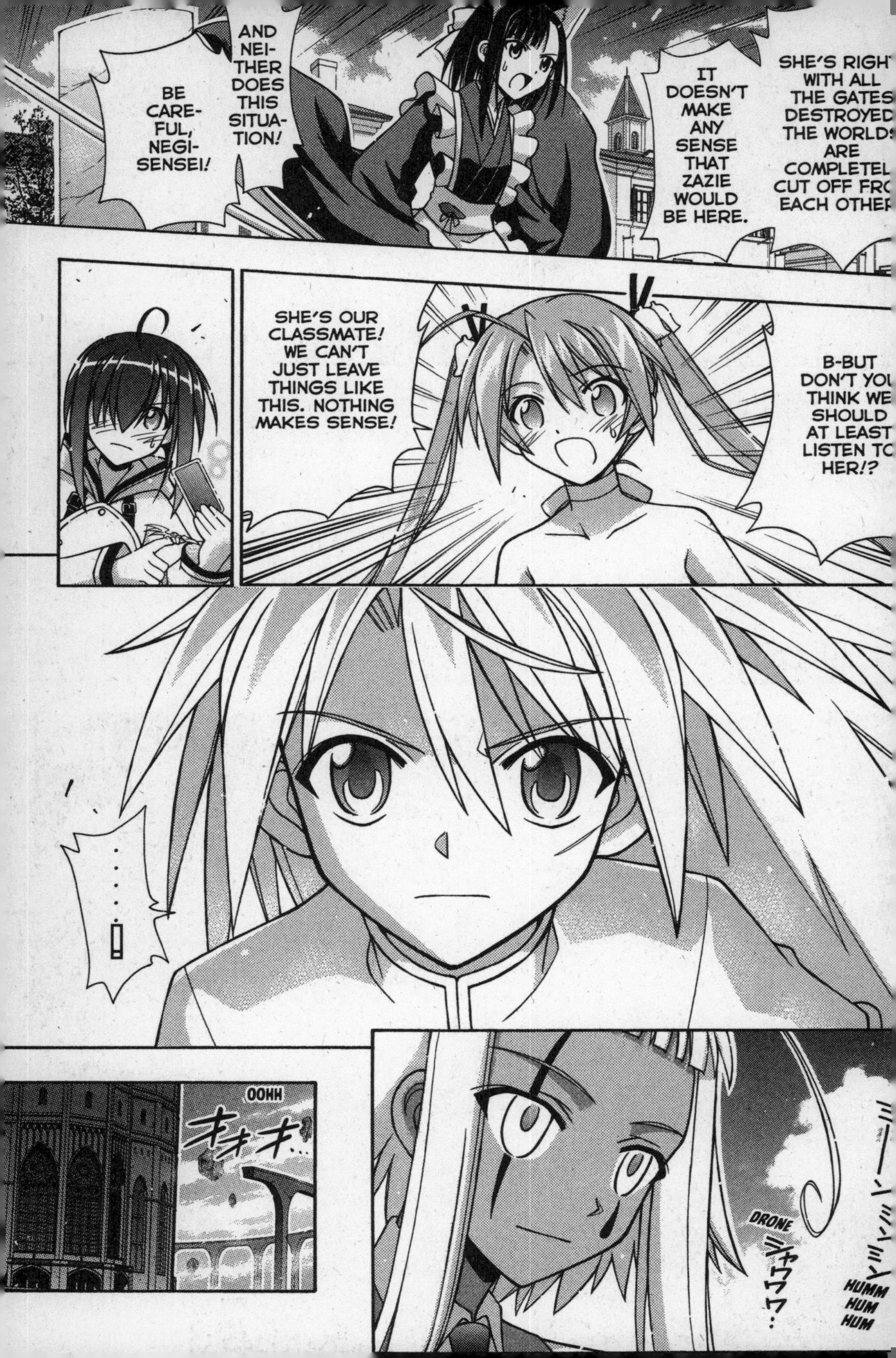
SHE'S RIGHT WITH ALL THE GATES DESTROYED THE WORLDS ARE COMPLETEL CUT OFF FRO EACH OTHER
IT DOESN'T MAKE ANY SENSE THAT ZAZIE WOULD BE HERE.
AND NEITHER DOES THIS SITUATION!
BE CAREFUL, NEGI-SENSEI!
B-BUT DON'T YOU THINK WE SHOULD AT LEAST LISTEN TO HER!?
SHE'S OUR CLASSMATE! WE CAN'T JUST LEAVE THINGS LIKE THIS. NOTHING MAKES SENSE!
......!
ミーンミンミン
HUMM HUM HUM
シャウウウ..
DRONE
オオオ...
OOHH

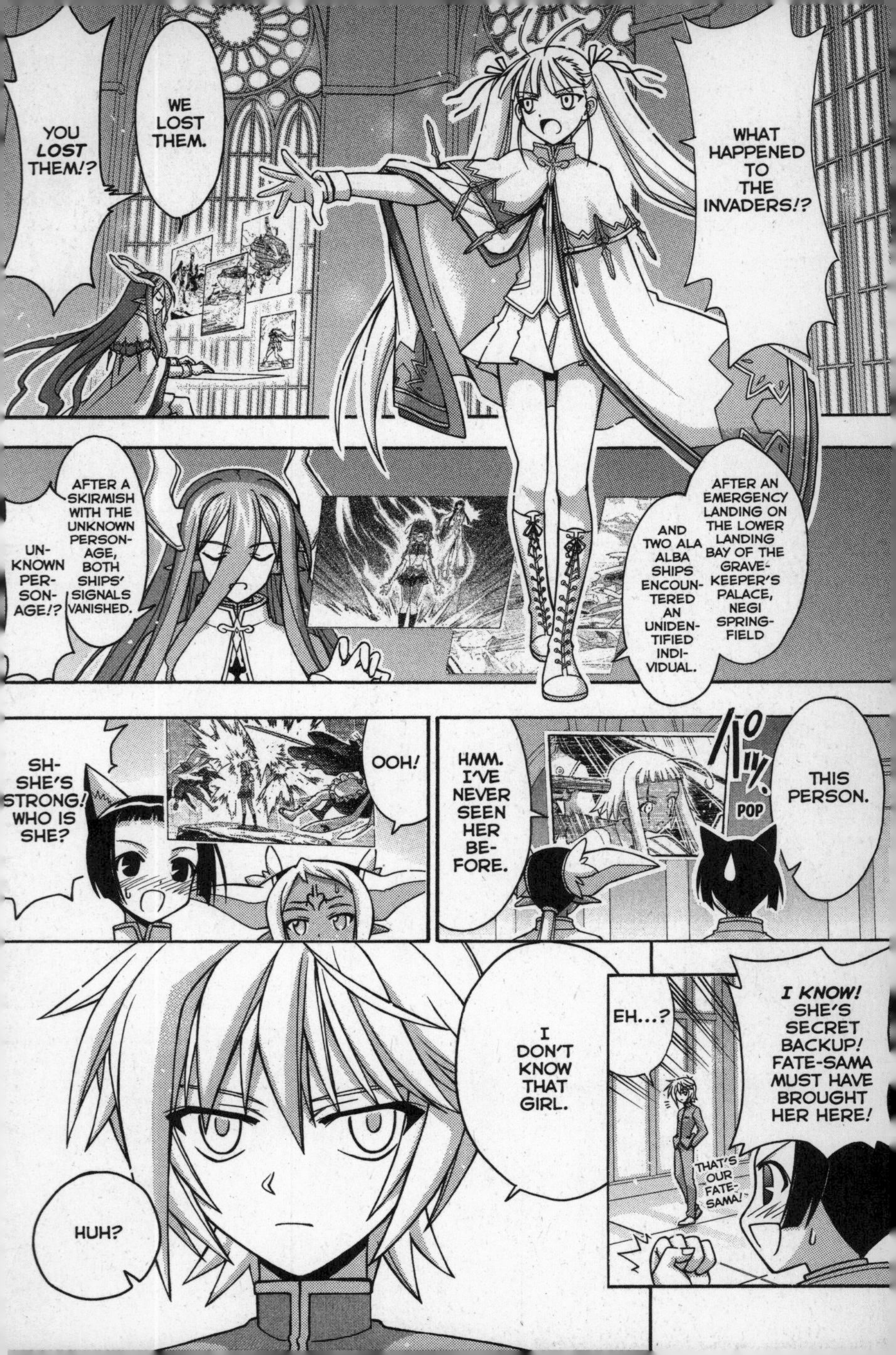
WHAT HAPPENED TO THE INVADERS!?
WE LOST THEM.
YOU *LOST* THEM!?
AFTER AN EMERGENCY LANDING ON THE LOWER LANDING BAY OF THE GRAVEKEEPER'S PALACE, NEGI SPRINGFIELD
AND TWO ALA ALBA SHIPS ENCOUNTERED AN UNIDENTIFIED INDIVIDUAL.
AFTER A SKIRMISH WITH THE UNKNOWN PERSONAGE, BOTH SHIPS' SIGNALS VANISHED.
UNKNOWN PERSONAGE!?
THIS PERSON.
パッ
POP
HMM. I'VE NEVER SEEN HER BEFORE.
OOH!
SH-SHE'S STRONG! WHO IS SHE?
I KNOW! SHE'S SECRET BACKUP! FATE-SAMA MUST HAVE BROUGHT HER HERE!
THAT'S OUR FATE-SAMA!
EH...?
I DON'T KNOW THAT GIRL.
HUH?

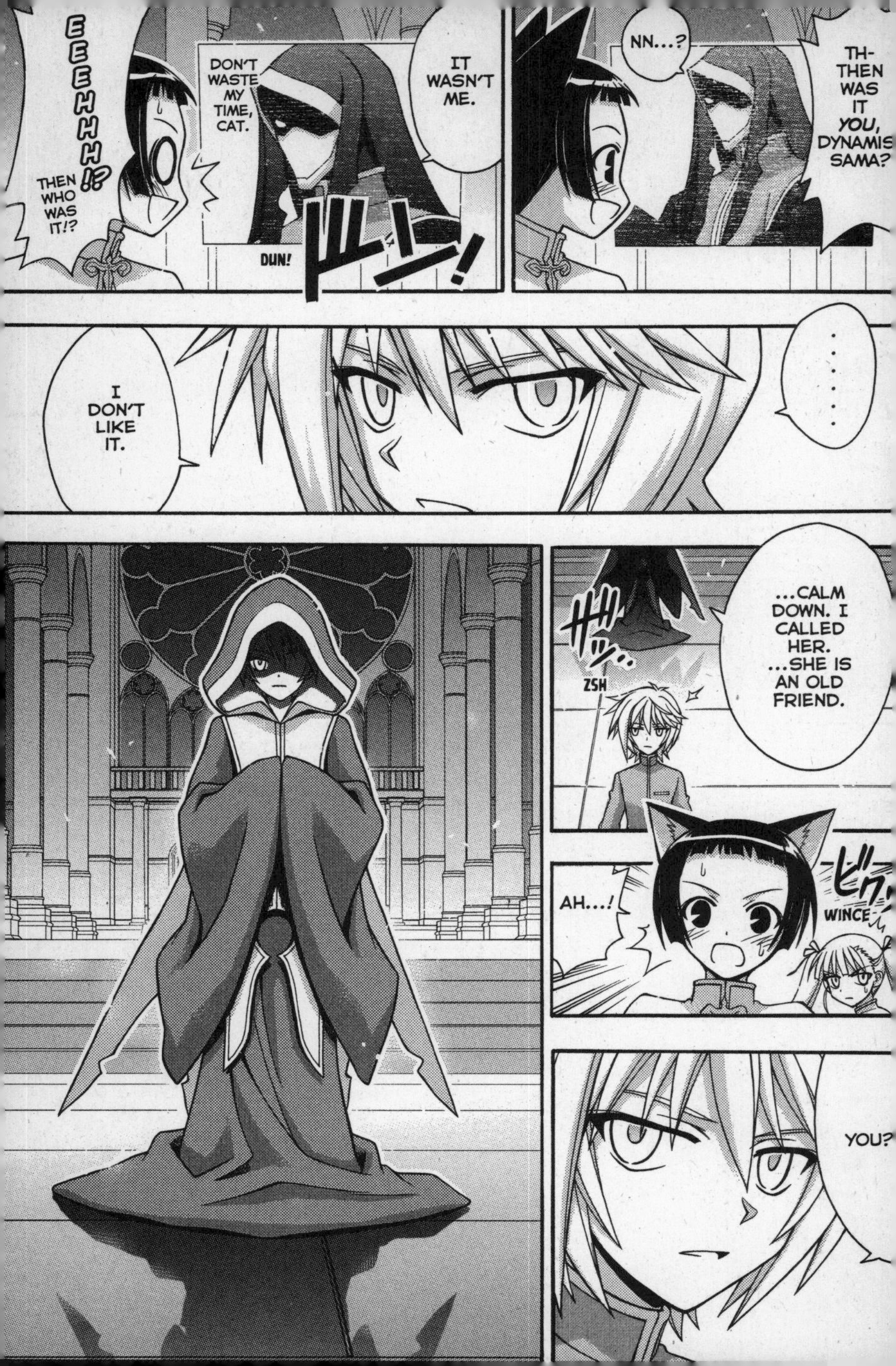
TH-THEN WAS IT YOU, DYNAMIS SAMA?
NN...?
IT WASN'T ME.
DON'T WASTE MY TIME, CAT.
EEEEHHHH!?
THEN WHO WAS IT!?
DUN!
......
I DON'T LIKE IT.
...CALM DOWN. I CALLED HER. ...SHE IS AN OLD FRIEND.
ZSH
WINCE
AH...!
YOU?

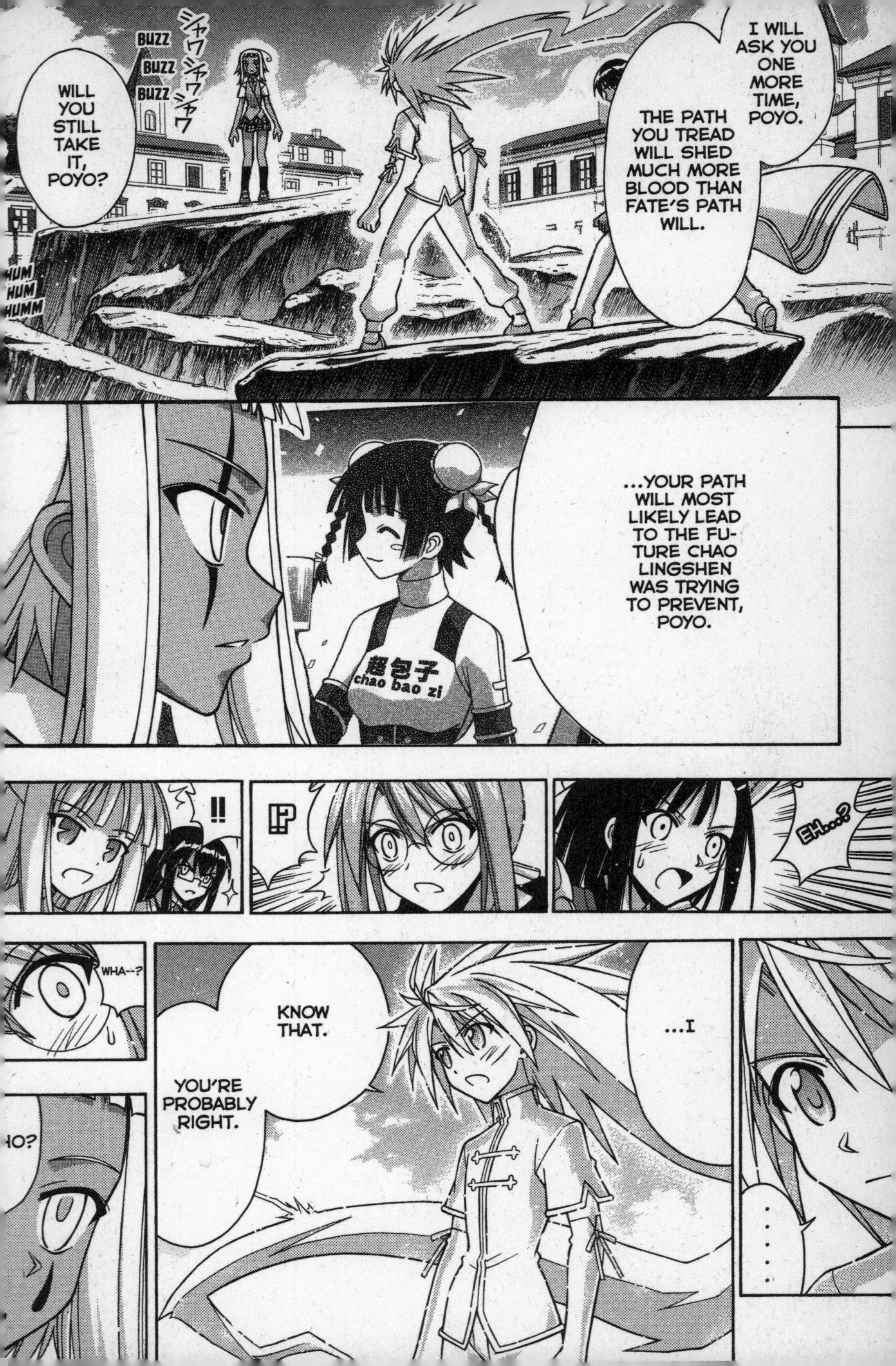
I WILL ASK YOU ONE MORE TIME, POYO.
THE PATH YOU TREAD WILL SHED MUCH MORE BLOOD THAN FATE'S PATH WILL.
シャワシャワシャワ
BUZZ
BUZZ
BUZZ
WILL YOU STILL TAKE IT, POYO?
HUM
HUM
HUMM
...YOUR PATH WILL MOST LIKELY LEAD TO THE FU-TURE CHAO LINGSHEN WAS TRYING TO PREVENT, POYO.
超包子
chao bao zi
EH...?
!?
!!
.....
...I
KNOW THAT.
YOU'RE PROBABLY RIGHT.
WHA--?
HO?

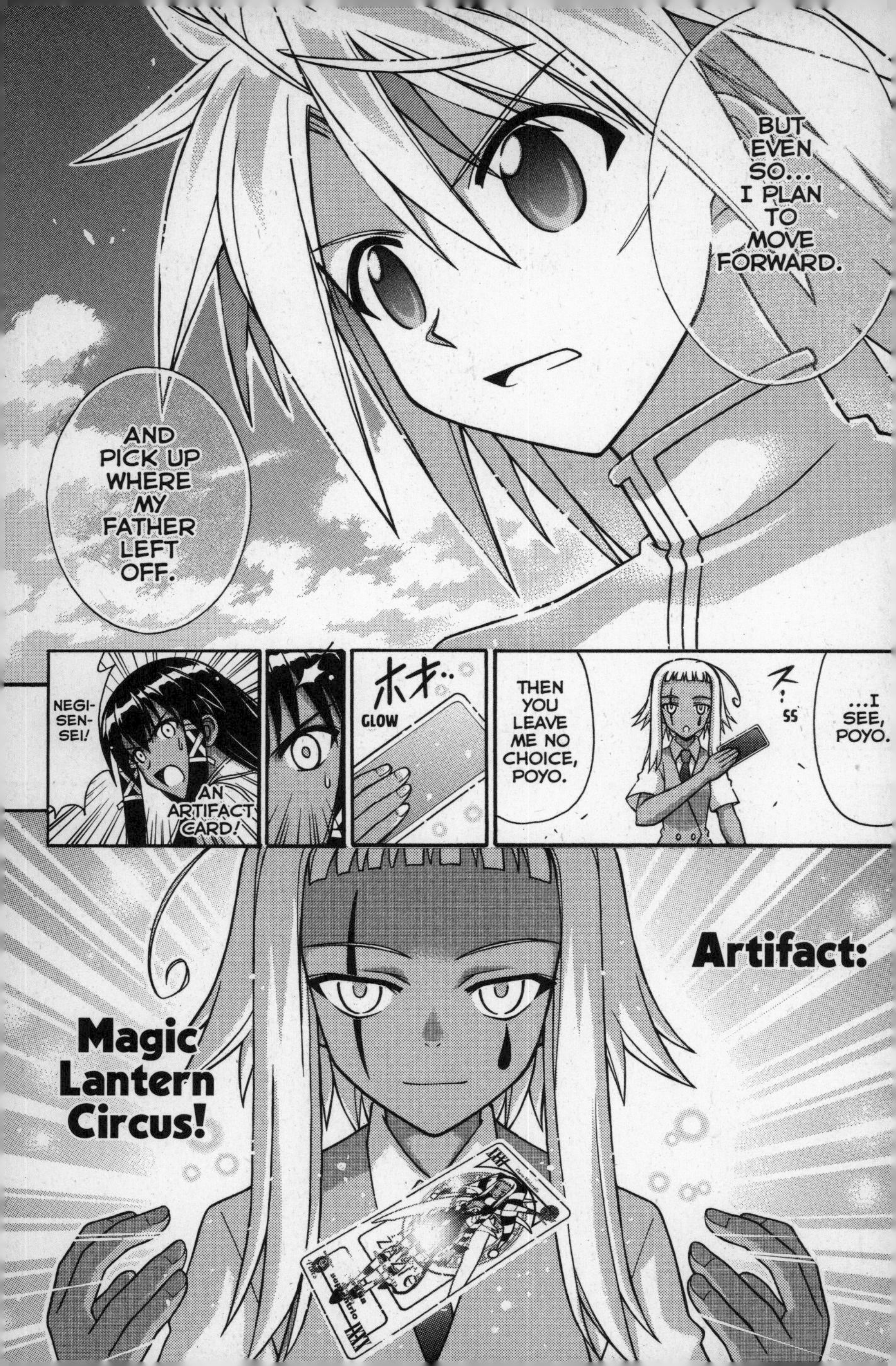
BUT EVEN SO... I PLAN TO MOVE FORWARD.
AND PICK UP WHERE MY FATHER LEFT OFF.
...I SEE, POYO.
ス SS
THEN YOU LEAVE ME NO CHOICE, POYO.
ホオ GLOW
NEGI-SENSEI!
AN ARTIFACT CARD!
Artifact:
Magic Lantern Circus!

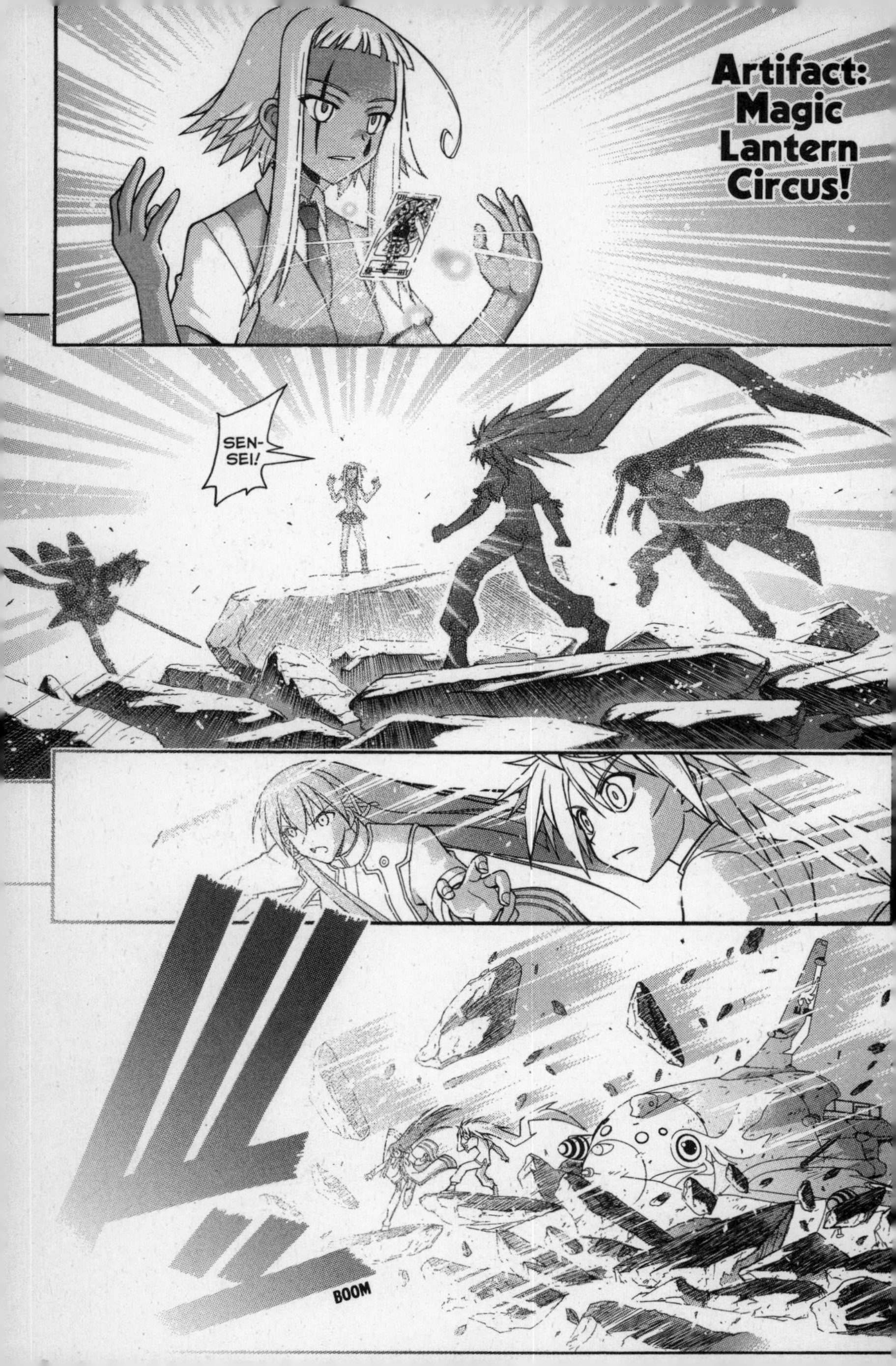
Artifact: Magic Lantern Circus!
SEN-SEI!
BOOM

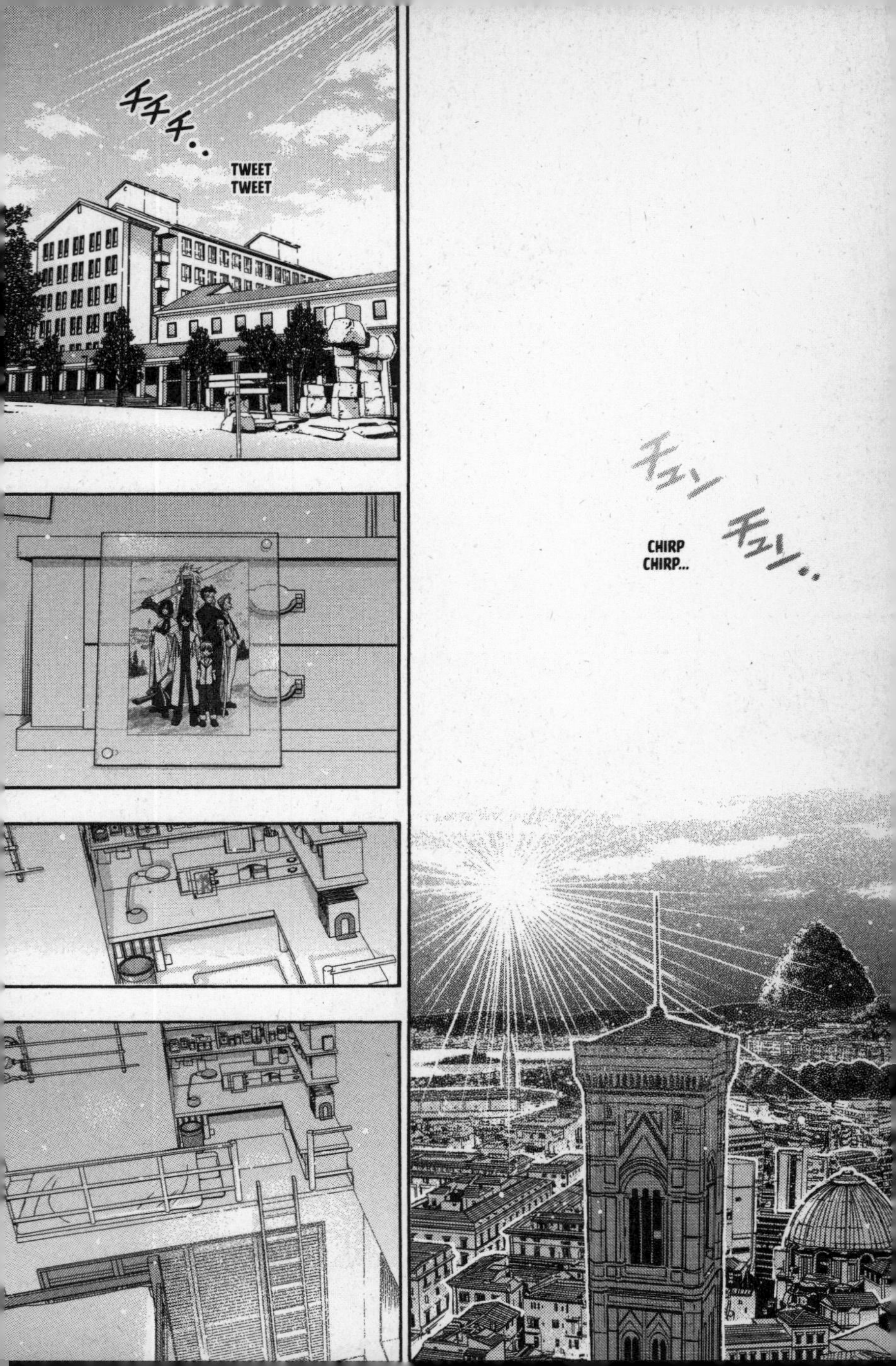
CHIRP
CHIRP...
TWEET
TWEET

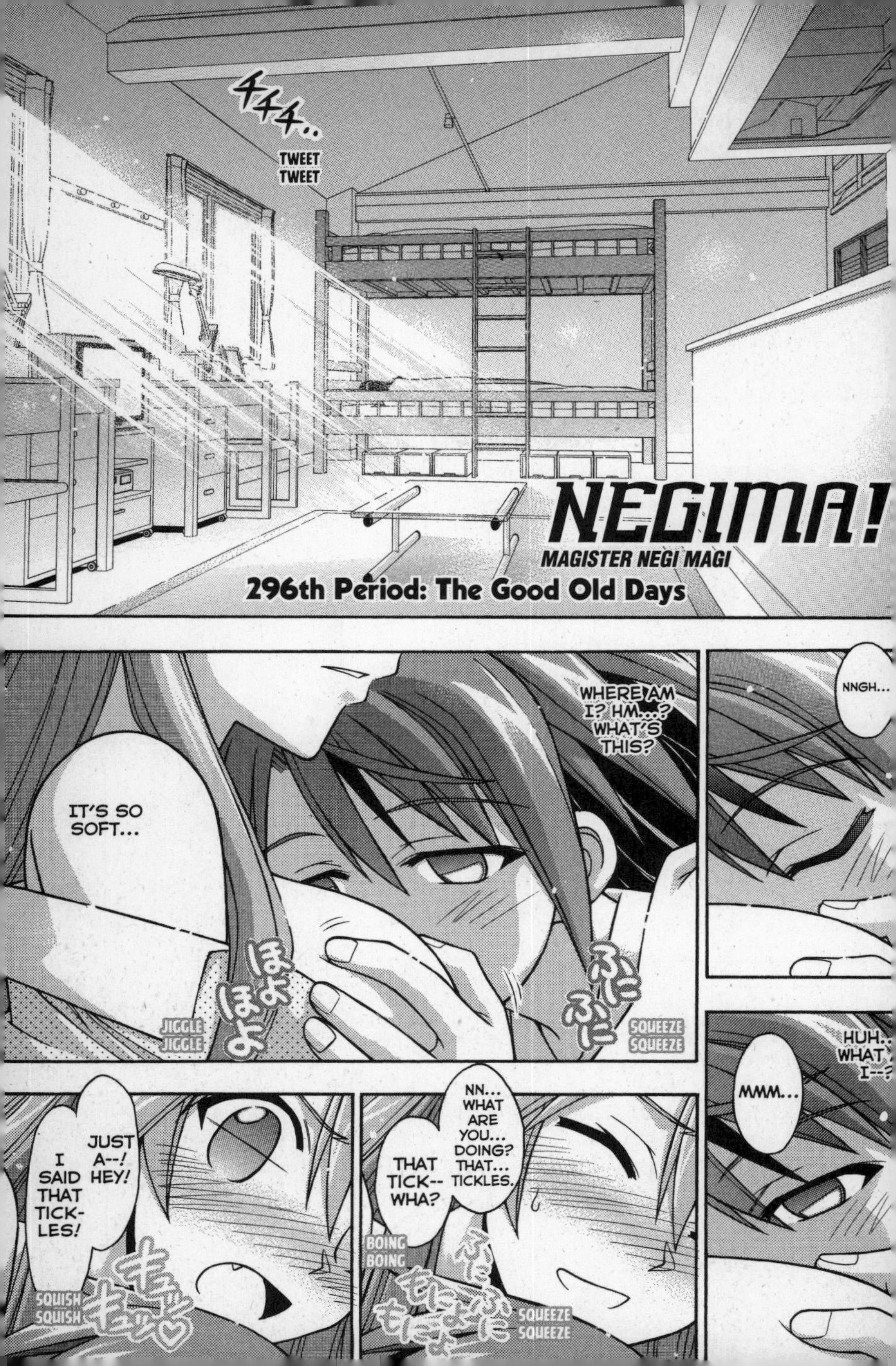
チチチ..
TWEET TWEET
NEGIMA!
MAGISTER NEGI MAGI
296th Period: The Good Old Days
NNGH...
WHERE AM I? HM...? WHAT'S THIS?
IT'S SO SOFT...
ふにふに
SQUEEZE SQUEEZE
ほよほよ
JIGGLE JIGGLE
HUH... WHAT I--?
MMM...
NN... WHAT ARE YOU... DOING? THAT... TICKLES.
THAT TICK-- WHA?
BOING BOING
SQUEEZE SQUEEZE
JUST A--! HEY!
I SAID THAT TICK-LES!
SQUISH SQUISH

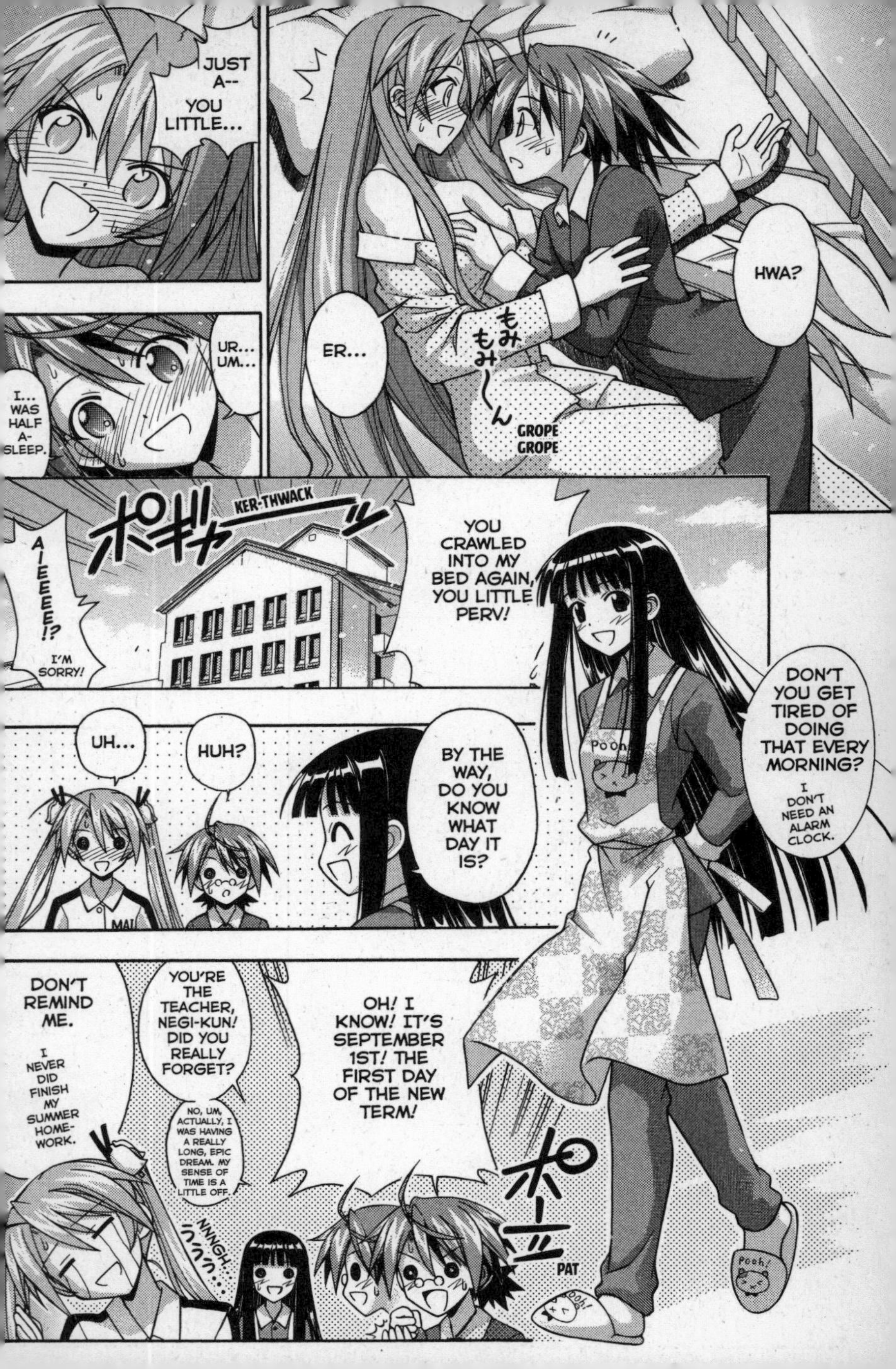
HWA?
ER...
もみもみ〜ん
GROPE GROPE
JUST A--
YOU LITTLE...
UR... UM...
I... WAS HALF A-SLEEP.
ポギャーッ
KER-THWACK
YOU CRAWLED INTO MY BED AGAIN, YOU LITTLE PERV!
AIEEEEE!?
I'M SORRY!
DON'T YOU GET TIRED OF DOING THAT EVERY MORNING?
I DON'T NEED AN ALARM CLOCK.
BY THE WAY, DO YOU KNOW WHAT DAY IT IS?
HUH?
UH...
OH! I KNOW! IT'S SEPTEMBER 1ST! THE FIRST DAY OF THE NEW TERM!
YOU'RE THE TEACHER, NEGI-KUN! DID YOU REALLY FORGET?
NO, UM, ACTUALLY, I WAS HAVING A REALLY LONG, EPIC DREAM. MY SENSE OF TIME IS A LITTLE OFF.
DON'T REMIND ME.
I NEVER DID FINISH MY SUMMER HOME-WORK.
NNNGH うううう...
ポーッ
PAT

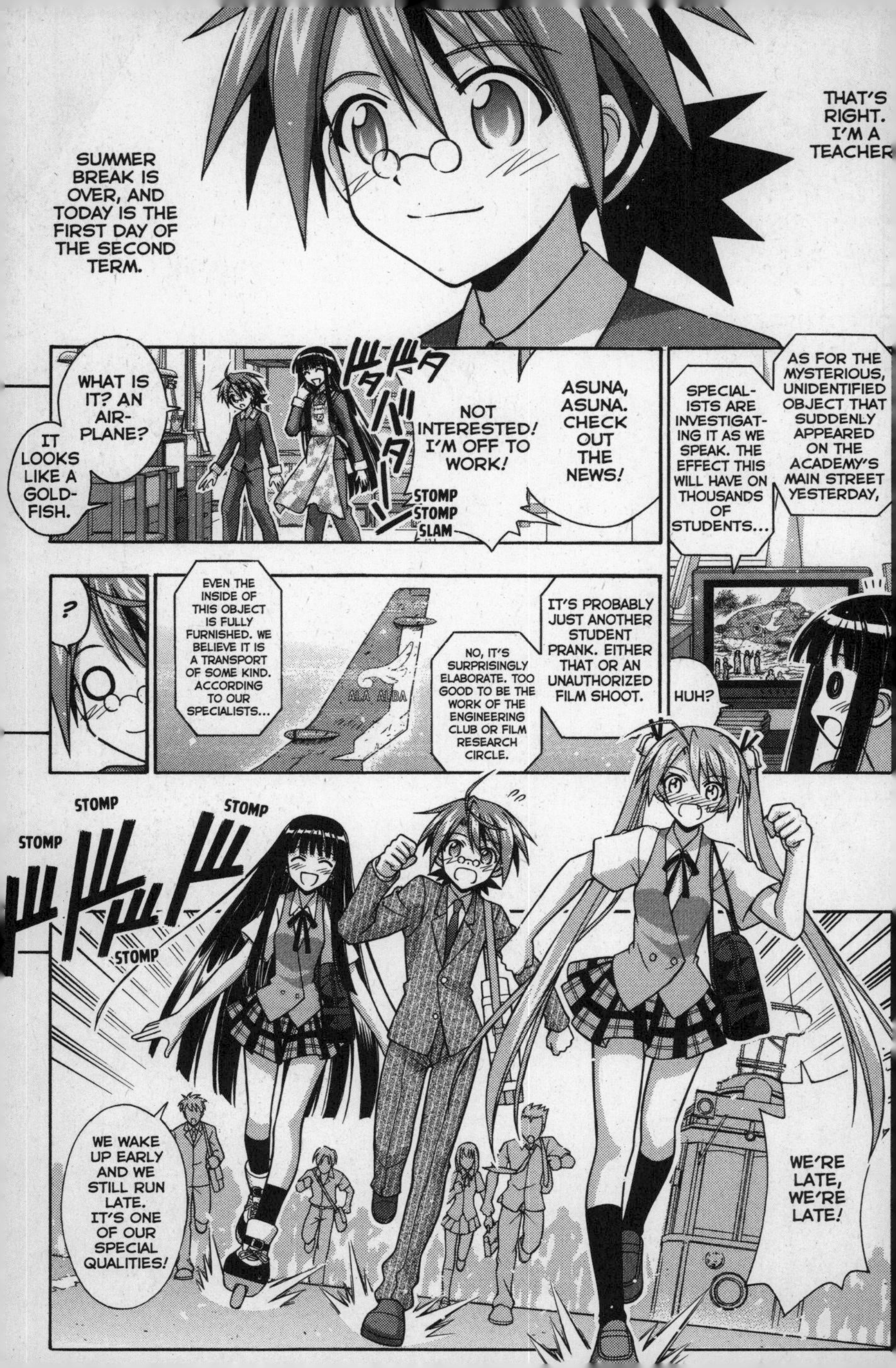
THAT'S RIGHT. I'M A TEACHER
SUMMER BREAK IS OVER, AND TODAY IS THE FIRST DAY OF THE SECOND TERM.
AS FOR THE MYSTERIOUS, UNIDENTIFIED OBJECT THAT SUDDENLY APPEARED ON THE ACADEMY'S MAIN STREET YESTERDAY,
SPECIAL-ISTS ARE INVESTIGAT-ING IT AS WE SPEAK. THE EFFECT THIS WILL HAVE ON THOUSANDS OF STUDENTS...
HUH?
ASUNA, ASUNA. CHECK OUT THE NEWS!
NOT INTERESTED! I'M OFF TO WORK!
STOMP
STOMP
SLAM
WHAT IS IT? AN AIR-PLANE?
IT LOOKS LIKE A GOLD-FISH.
IT'S PROBABLY JUST ANOTHER STUDENT PRANK. EITHER THAT OR AN UNAUTHORIZED FILM SHOOT.
NO, IT'S SURPRISINGLY ELABORATE. TOO GOOD TO BE THE WORK OF THE ENGINEERING CLUB OR FILM RESEARCH CIRCLE.
EVEN THE INSIDE OF THIS OBJECT IS FULLY FURNISHED. WE BELIEVE IT IS A TRANSPORT OF SOME KIND. ACCORDING TO OUR SPECIALISTS...
ALA ALBA
?
WE'RE LATE, WE'RE LATE!
STOMP
STOMP
STOMP
STOMP
WE WAKE UP EARLY AND WE STILL RUN LATE. IT'S ONE OF OUR SPECIAL QUALITIES!

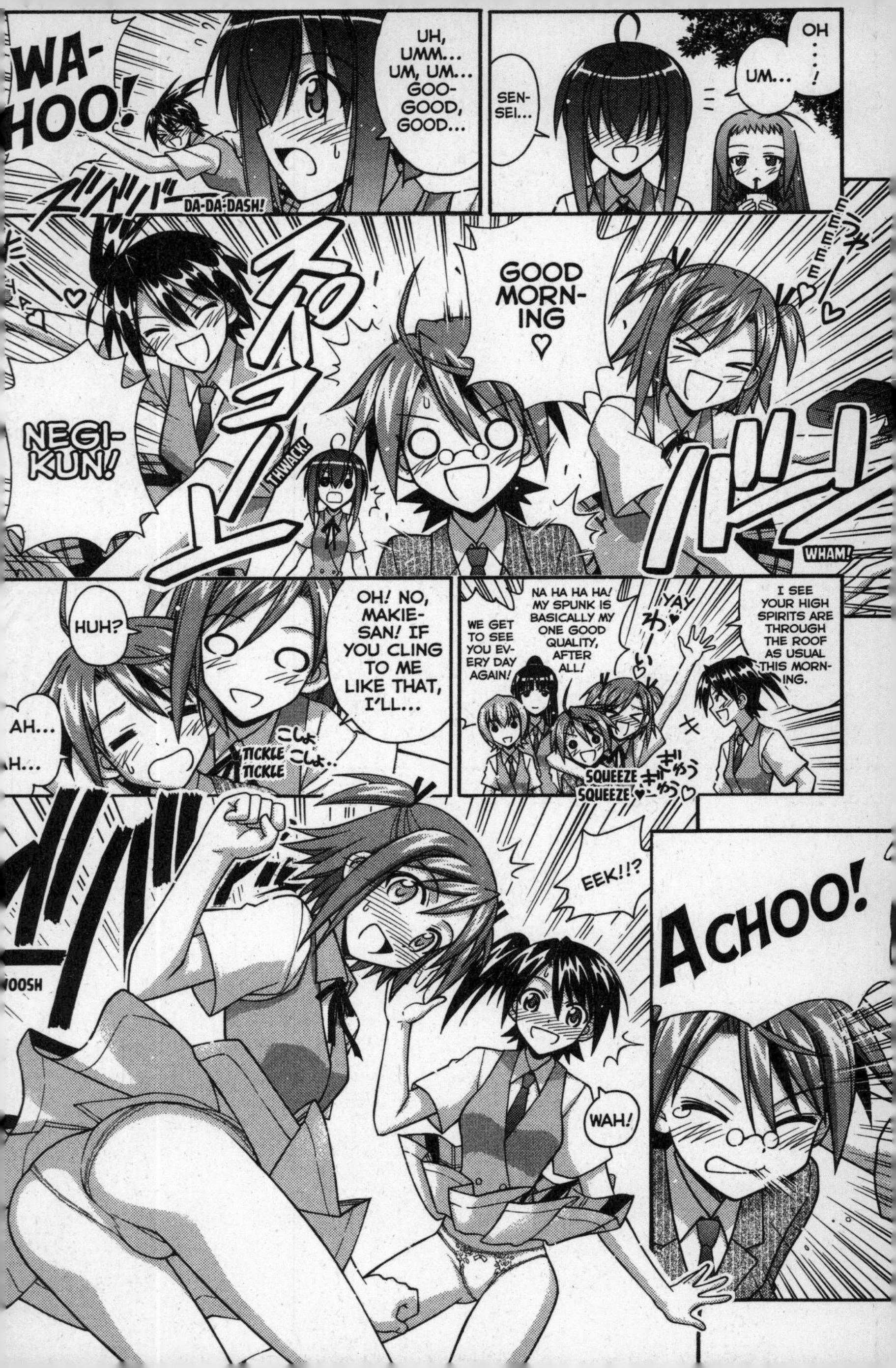
OH...!
UM...
SEN-SEI...
UH, UMM... UM, UM... GOO-GOOD, GOOD...
WA-HOO!
DA-DA-DASH!
EEEEEE
GOOD MORN-ING ♡
WHAM!
THWACK!
NEGI-KUN!
I SEE YOUR HIGH SPIRITS ARE THROUGH THE ROOF AS USUAL THIS MORN-ING.
YAY
NA HA HA HA! MY SPUNK IS BASICALLY MY ONE GOOD QUALITY, AFTER ALL!
WE GET TO SEE YOU EV-ERY DAY AGAIN!
SQUEEZE SQUEEZE
OH! NO, MAKIE-SAN! IF YOU CLING TO ME LIKE THAT, I'LL...
HUH?
AH... H...
TICKLE TICKLE
ACHOO!
EEK!!?
WAH!
WOOSH

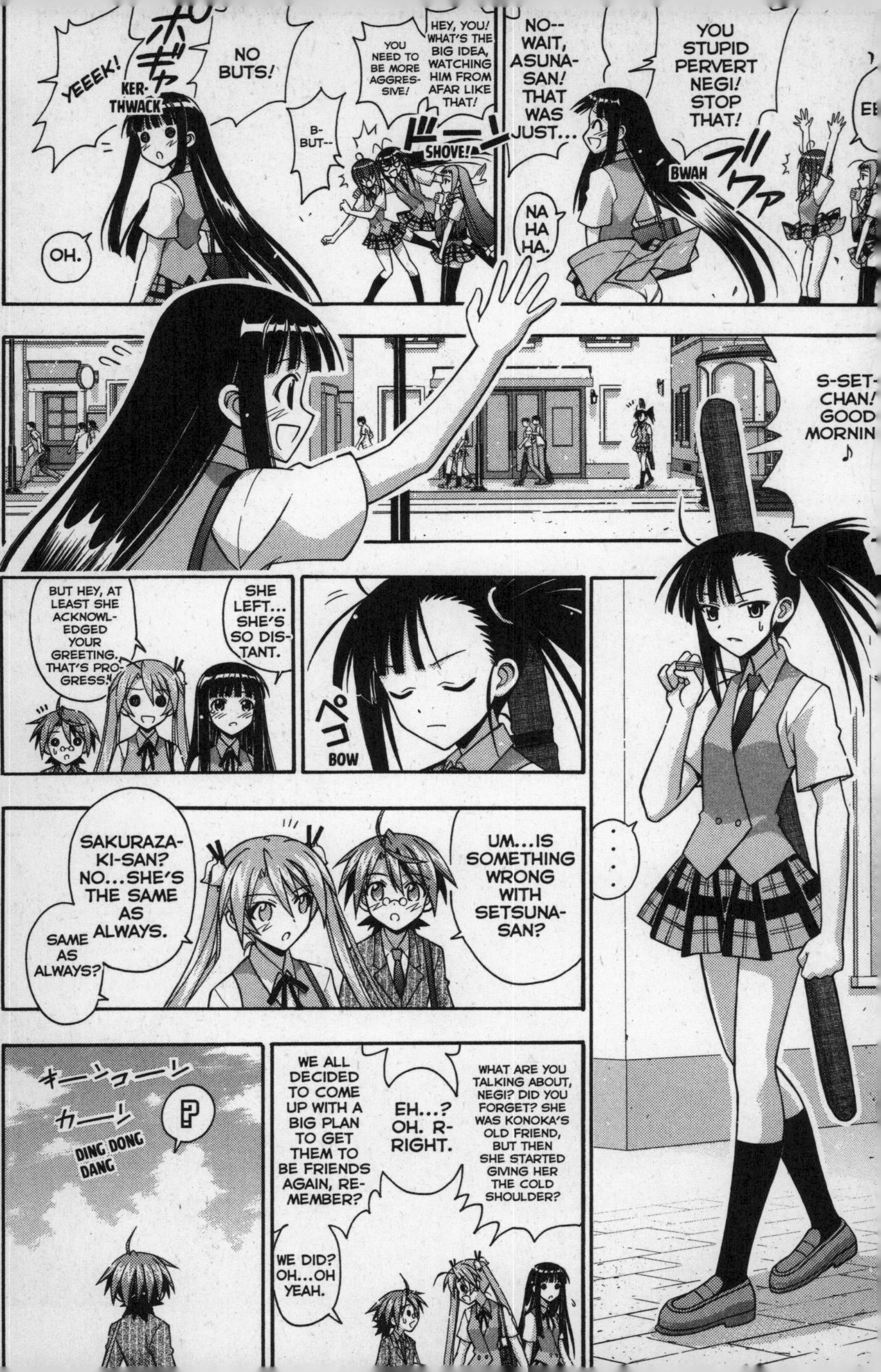
YOU STUPID PERVERT NEGI! STOP THAT!
BWAH
NO-- WAIT, ASUNA-SAN! THAT WAS JUST...
NA HA HA.
HEY, YOU! WHAT'S THE BIG IDEA, WATCHING HIM FROM AFAR LIKE THAT!
YOU NEED TO BE MORE AGGRESSIVE!
B- BUT--
SHOVE!
NO BUTS!
YEEEK!
KER-THWACK
OH.
S-SET-CHAN! GOOD MORNIN ♪
...
BOW
SHE LEFT... SHE'S SO DISTANT.
BUT HEY, AT LEAST SHE ACKNOWLEDGED YOUR GREETING. THAT'S PROGRESS!
UM...IS SOMETHING WRONG WITH SETSUNA-SAN?
SAKURAZAKI-SAN? NO...SHE'S THE SAME AS ALWAYS.
SAME AS ALWAYS?
WHAT ARE YOU TALKING ABOUT, NEGI? DID YOU FORGET? SHE WAS KONOKA'S OLD FRIEND, BUT THEN SHE STARTED GIVING HER THE COLD SHOULDER?
EH...? OH. R-RIGHT.
WE ALL DECIDED TO COME UP WITH A BIG PLAN TO GET THEM TO BE FRIENDS AGAIN, REMEMBER?
WE DID? OH...OH YEAH.
?
DING DONG DANG

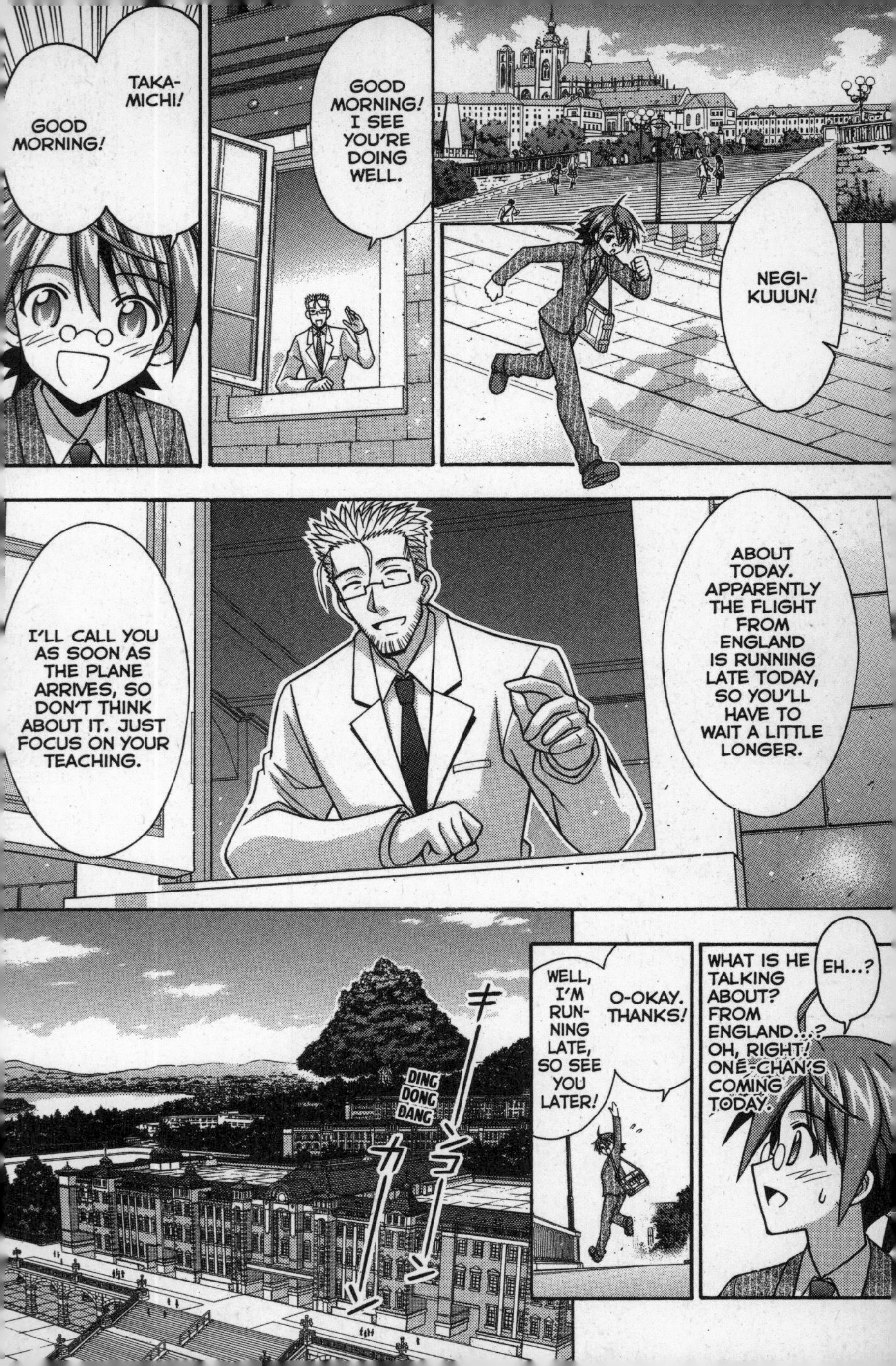
NEGI-KUUUN!
GOOD MORNING! I SEE YOU'RE DOING WELL.
TAKA-MICHI!
GOOD MORNING!
ABOUT TODAY. APPARENTLY THE FLIGHT FROM ENGLAND IS RUNNING LATE TODAY, SO YOU'LL HAVE TO WAIT A LITTLE LONGER.
I'LL CALL YOU AS SOON AS THE PLANE ARRIVES, SO DON'T THINK ABOUT IT. JUST FOCUS ON YOUR TEACHING.
EH...?
WHAT IS HE TALKING ABOUT? FROM ENGLAND...? OH, RIGHT! ONE-CHAN'S COMING TODAY.
O-OKAY. THANKS!
WELL, I'M RUN-NING LATE, SO SEE YOU LATER!
DING DONG DANG

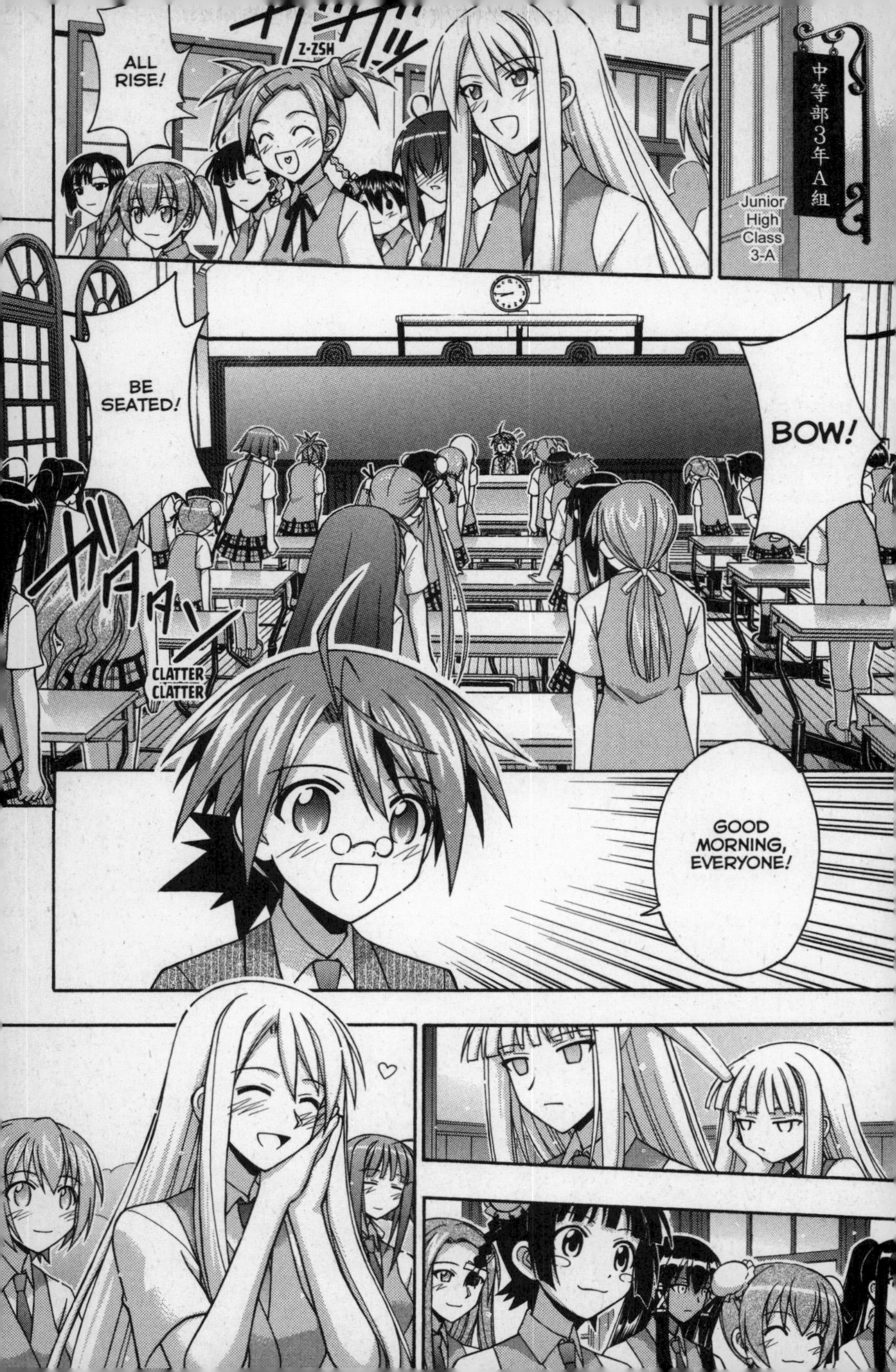
中等部3年A組
Junior High Class 3-A
ALL RISE!
Z-ZSH
BOW!
BE SEATED!
CLATTER CLATTER
GOOD MORNING, EVERYONE!

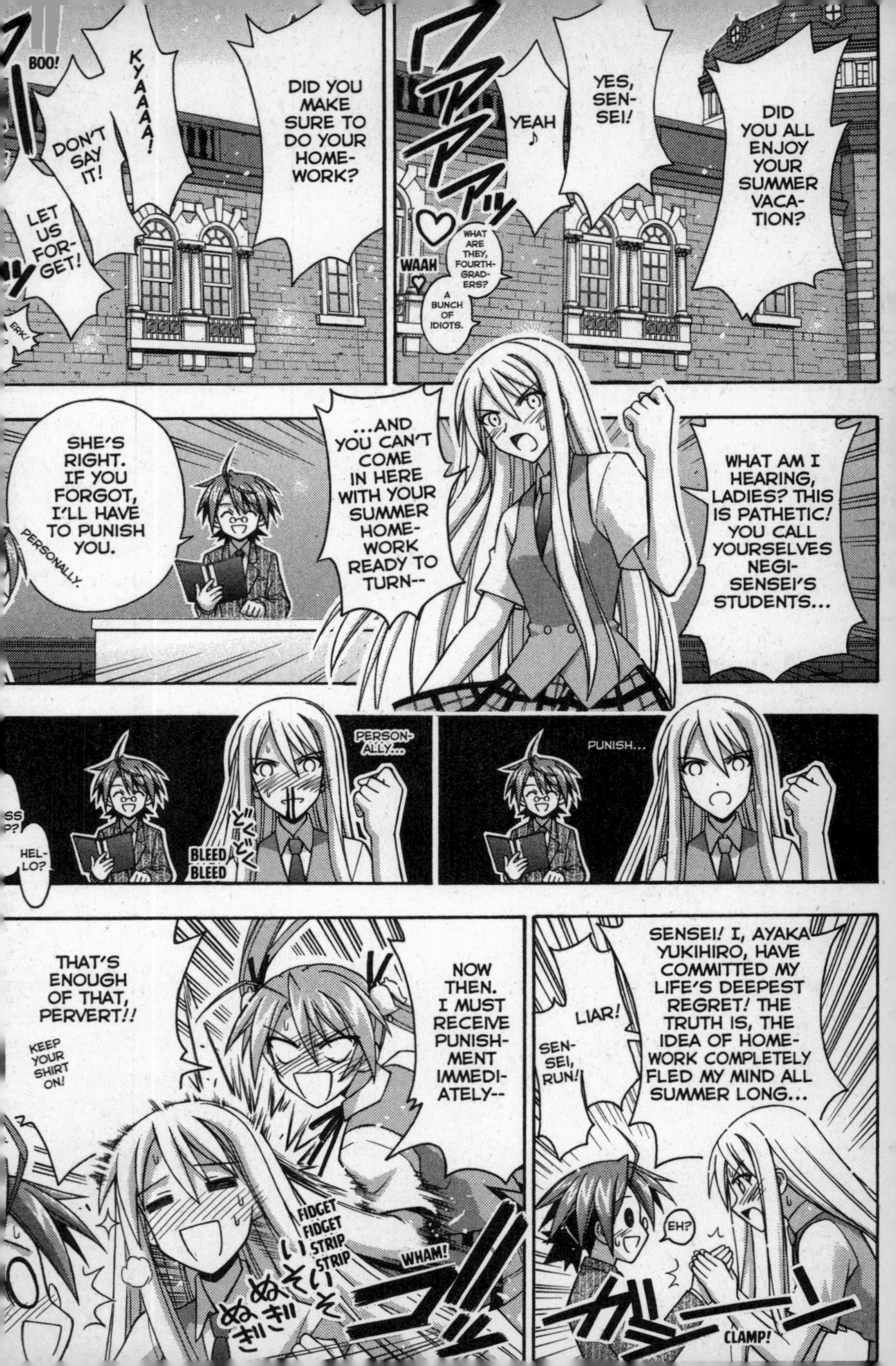
DID YOU ALL ENJOY YOUR SUMMER VACATION?
YES, SENSEI!
YEAH ♪
WHAT ARE THEY, FOURTH-GRADERS?
A BUNCH OF IDIOTS.
WAAH ♡
DID YOU MAKE SURE TO DO YOUR HOMEWORK?
KYAAAA!
DON'T SAY IT!
LET US FORGET!
BOO!
ERK!
WHAT AM I HEARING, LADIES? THIS IS PATHETIC! YOU CALL YOURSELVES NEGI-SENSEI'S STUDENTS...
...AND YOU CAN'T COME IN HERE WITH YOUR SUMMER HOMEWORK READY TO TURN--
SHE'S RIGHT. IF YOU FORGOT, I'LL HAVE TO PUNISH YOU.
PERSONALLY.
PUNISH...
PERSONALLY...
BLEED BLEED
HELLO?
SENSEI! I, AYAKA YUKIHIRO, HAVE COMMITTED MY LIFE'S DEEPEST REGRET! THE TRUTH IS, THE IDEA OF HOMEWORK COMPLETELY FLED MY MIND ALL SUMMER LONG...
LIAR!
SENSEI, RUN!
EH?
CLAMP!
NOW THEN. I MUST RECEIVE PUNISHMENT IMMEDIATELY--
THAT'S ENOUGH OF THAT, PERVERT!!
KEEP YOUR SHIRT ON!
FIDGET FIDGET STRIP STRIP
WHAM!

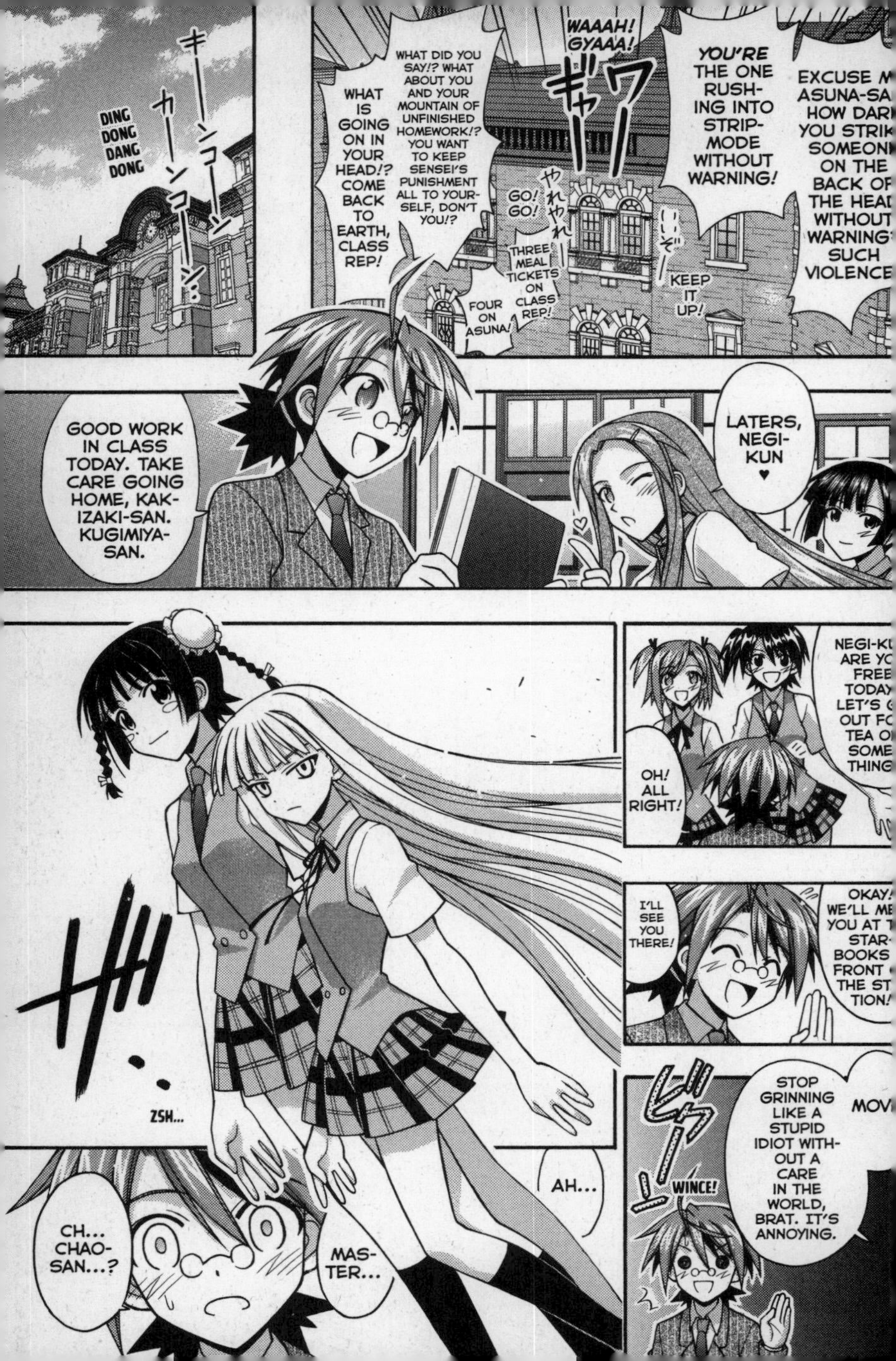
EXCUSE M ASUNA-SA HOW DAR YOU STRIK SOMEON ON THE BACK OF THE HEA WITHOUT WARNING SUCH VIOLENCE
YOU'RE THE ONE RUSHING INTO STRIP-MODE WITHOUT WARNING!
WAAAH! GYAAA!
KEEP IT UP!
GO! GO!
THREE MEAL TICKETS ON CLASS REP!
FOUR ON ASUNA!
WHAT DID YOU SAY!? WHAT ABOUT YOU AND YOUR MOUNTAIN OF UNFINISHED HOMEWORK!? YOU WANT TO KEEP SENSEI'S PUNISHMENT ALL TO YOURSELF, DON'T YOU!?
WHAT IS GOING ON IN YOUR HEAD!? COME BACK TO EARTH, CLASS REP!
DING DONG DANG DONG
LATERS, NEGI-KUN ♥
GOOD WORK IN CLASS TODAY. TAKE CARE GOING HOME, KAKIZAKI-SAN. KUGIMIYA-SAN.
NEGI-KU ARE YO FREE TODAY LET'S OUT FO TEA O SOME THING
OH! ALL RIGHT!
OKAY WE'LL ME YOU AT STAR-BOOKS FRONT THE ST TION!
I'LL SEE YOU THERE!
MOV
STOP GRINNING LIKE A STUPID IDIOT WITHOUT A CARE IN THE WORLD, BRAT. IT'S ANNOYING.
WINCE!
ZSH...
AH...
MASTER...
CH... CHAO-SAN...?

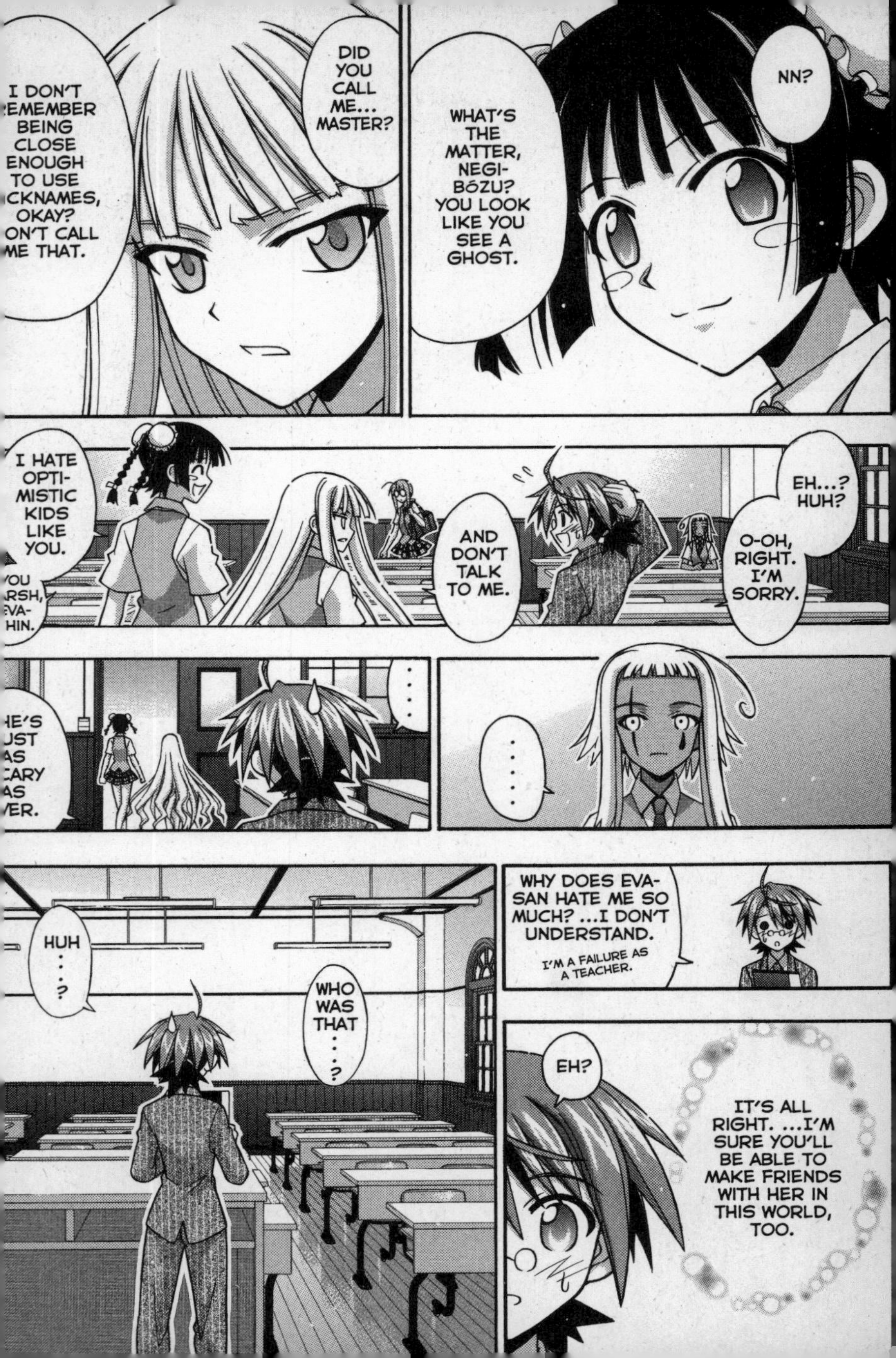
NN?
WHAT'S THE MATTER, NEGI-BŌZU? YOU LOOK LIKE YOU SEE A GHOST.
DID YOU CALL ME... MASTER?
I DON'T EMEMBER BEING CLOSE ENOUGH TO USE CKNAMES, OKAY? ON'T CALL ME THAT.
EH...? HUH?
O-OH, RIGHT. I'M SORRY.
AND DON'T TALK TO ME.
I HATE OPTI-MISTIC KIDS LIKE YOU.
YOU ARSH, EVA-HIN.
. . . .
. . . . . .
HE'S UST AS CARY AS VER.
WHY DOES EVA-SAN HATE ME SO MUCH? ...I DON'T UNDERSTAND.
I'M A FAILURE AS A TEACHER.
EH?
IT'S ALL RIGHT. ...I'M SURE YOU'LL BE ABLE TO MAKE FRIENDS WITH HER IN THIS WORLD, TOO.
HUH . . . ?
WHO WAS THAT . . . ?

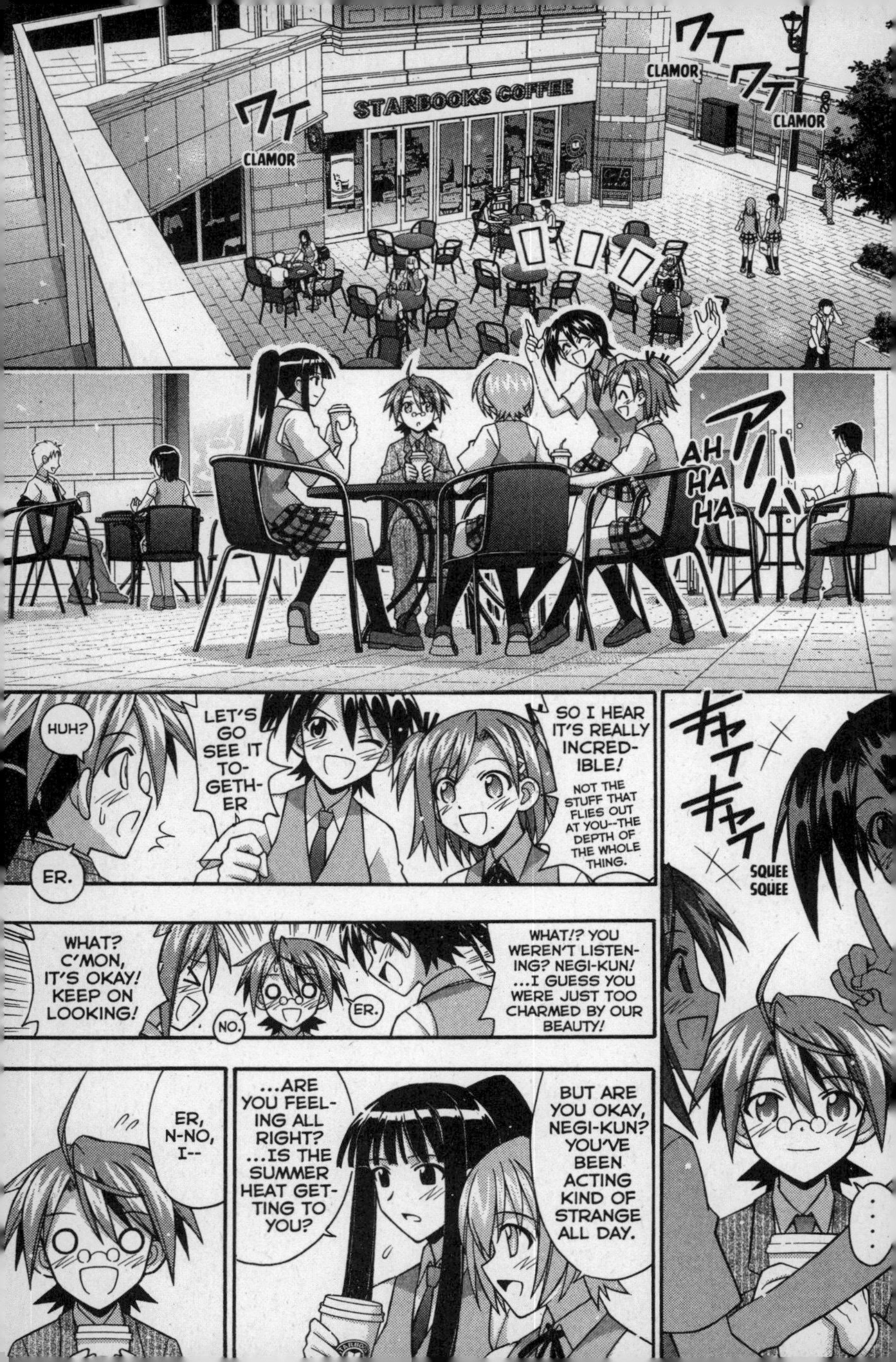
ワイ
CLAMOR
ワイ
CLAMOR
ワイ
CLAMOR
STARBOOKS COFFEE
アハハ
AH HA HA
キャイキャイ
SQUEE SQUEE
...
SO I HEAR IT'S REALLY INCREDIBLE!
NOT THE STUFF THAT FLIES OUT AT YOU--THE DEPTH OF THE WHOLE THING.
LET'S GO SEE IT TOGETHER
HUH?
ER.
WHAT!? YOU WEREN'T LISTENING? NEGI-KUN! ...I GUESS YOU WERE JUST TOO CHARMED BY OUR BEAUTY!
ER.
NO.
WHAT? C'MON, IT'S OKAY! KEEP ON LOOKING!
BUT ARE YOU OKAY, NEGI-KUN? YOU'VE BEEN ACTING KIND OF STRANGE ALL DAY.
...ARE YOU FEELING ALL RIGHT? ...IS THE SUMMER HEAT GETTING TO YOU?
ER, N-NO, I--

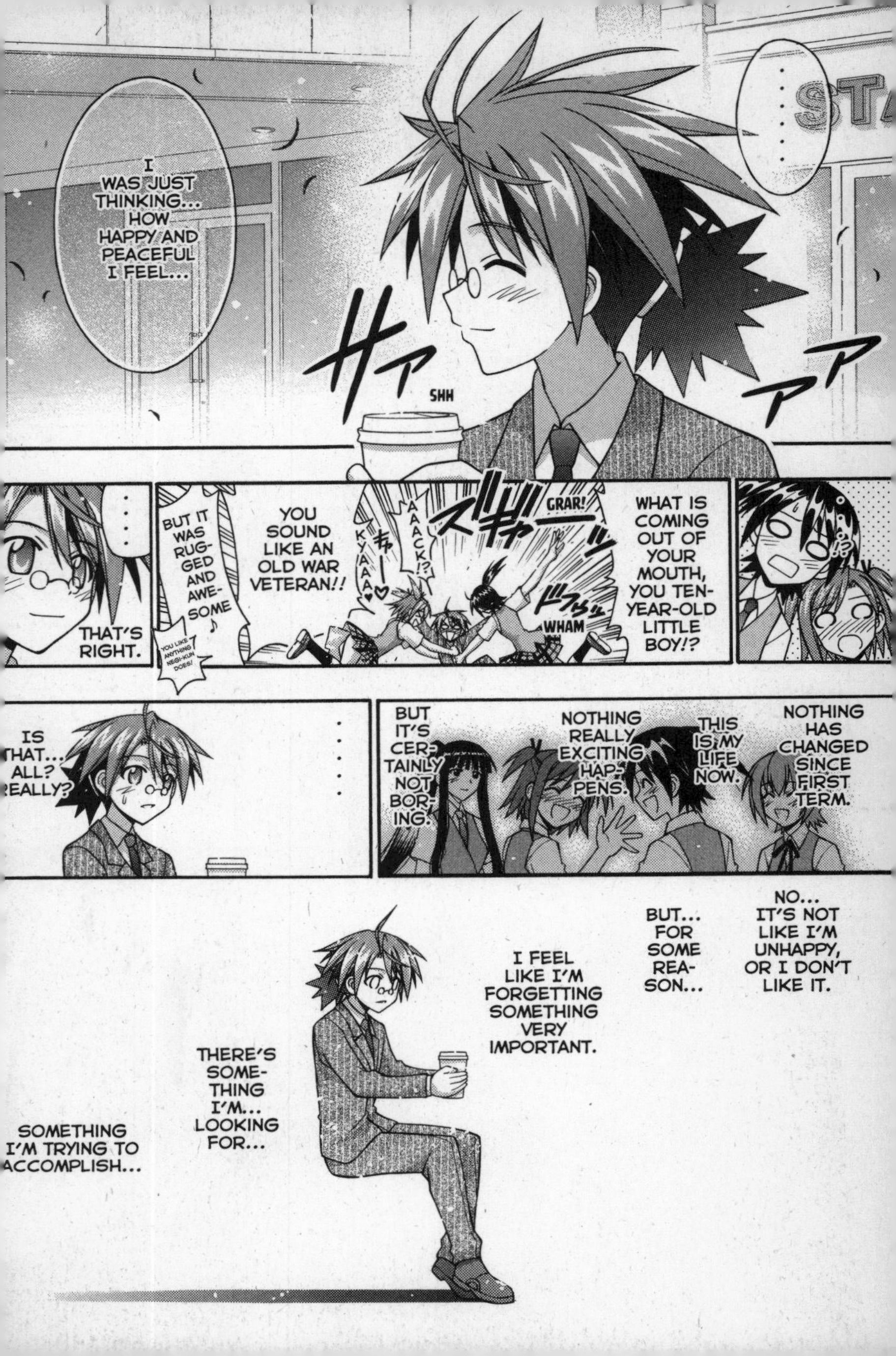
......
I WAS JUST THINKING... HOW HAPPY AND PEACEFUL I FEEL...
SHH
!?
WHAT IS COMING OUT OF YOUR MOUTH, YOU TEN-YEAR-OLD LITTLE BOY!?
GRAR!
WHAM
AAACK!?
KYAAA♥
YOU SOUND LIKE AN OLD WAR VETERAN!!
BUT IT WAS RUGGED AND AWESOME ♪
YOU LIKE ANYTHING NEGI-KUN DOES!
...
THAT'S RIGHT.
NOTHING HAS CHANGED SINCE FIRST TERM.
THIS IS MY LIFE NOW.
NOTHING REALLY EXCITING HAPPENS.
BUT IT'S CERTAINLY NOT BORING.
......
IS THAT... ALL? REALLY?
NO... IT'S NOT LIKE I'M UNHAPPY, OR I DON'T LIKE IT.
BUT... FOR SOME REASON...
I FEEL LIKE I'M FORGETTING SOMETHING VERY IMPORTANT.
THERE'S SOMETHING I'M... LOOKING FOR...
SOMETHING I'M TRYING TO ACCOMPLISH...

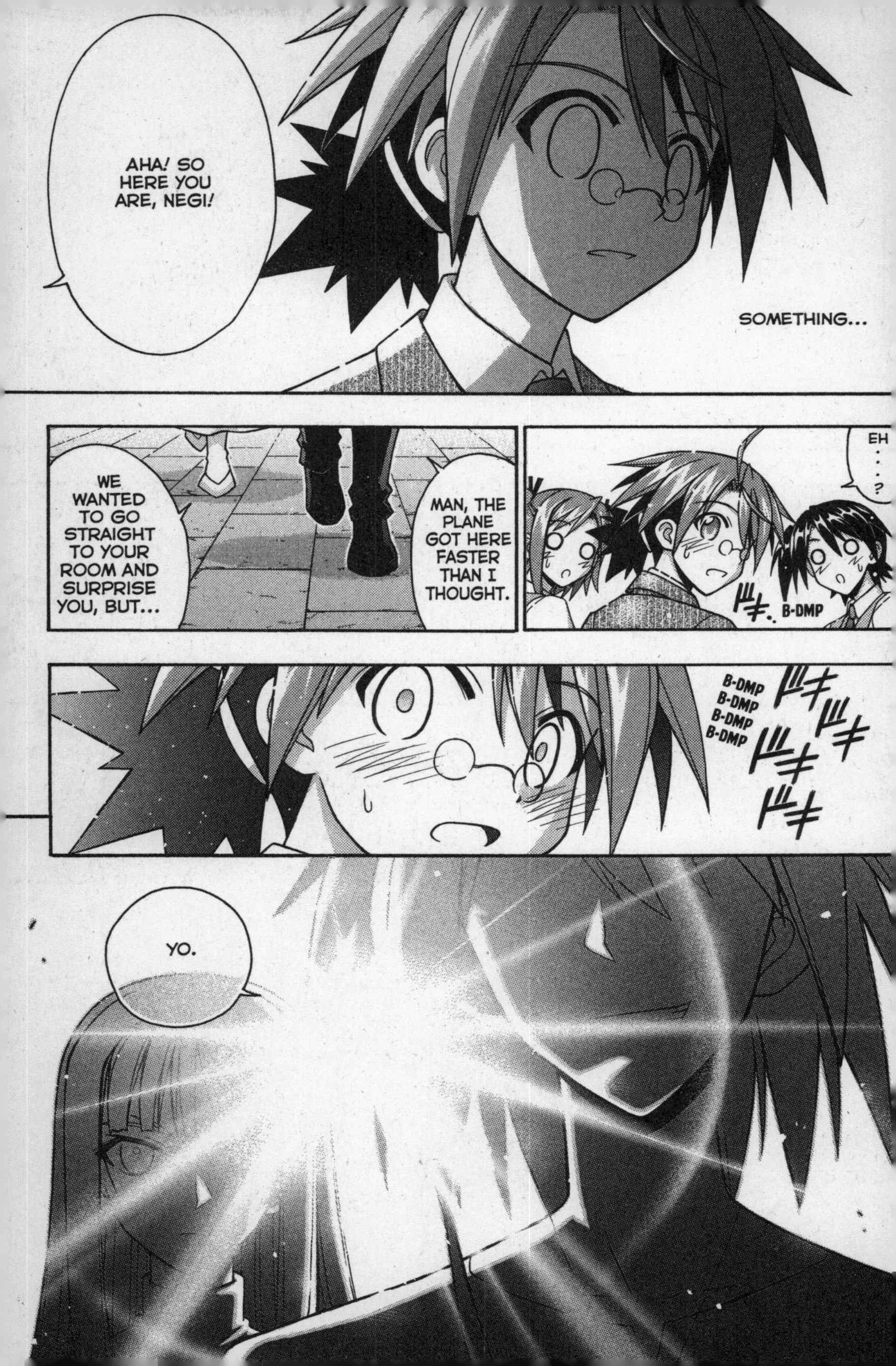
SOMETHING...
AHA! SO HERE YOU ARE, NEGI!
EH . . . ?
B-DMP
MAN, THE PLANE GOT HERE FASTER THAN I THOUGHT.
WE WANTED TO GO STRAIGHT TO YOUR ROOM AND SURPRISE YOU, BUT...
B-DMP B-DMP B-DMP B-DMP
YO.

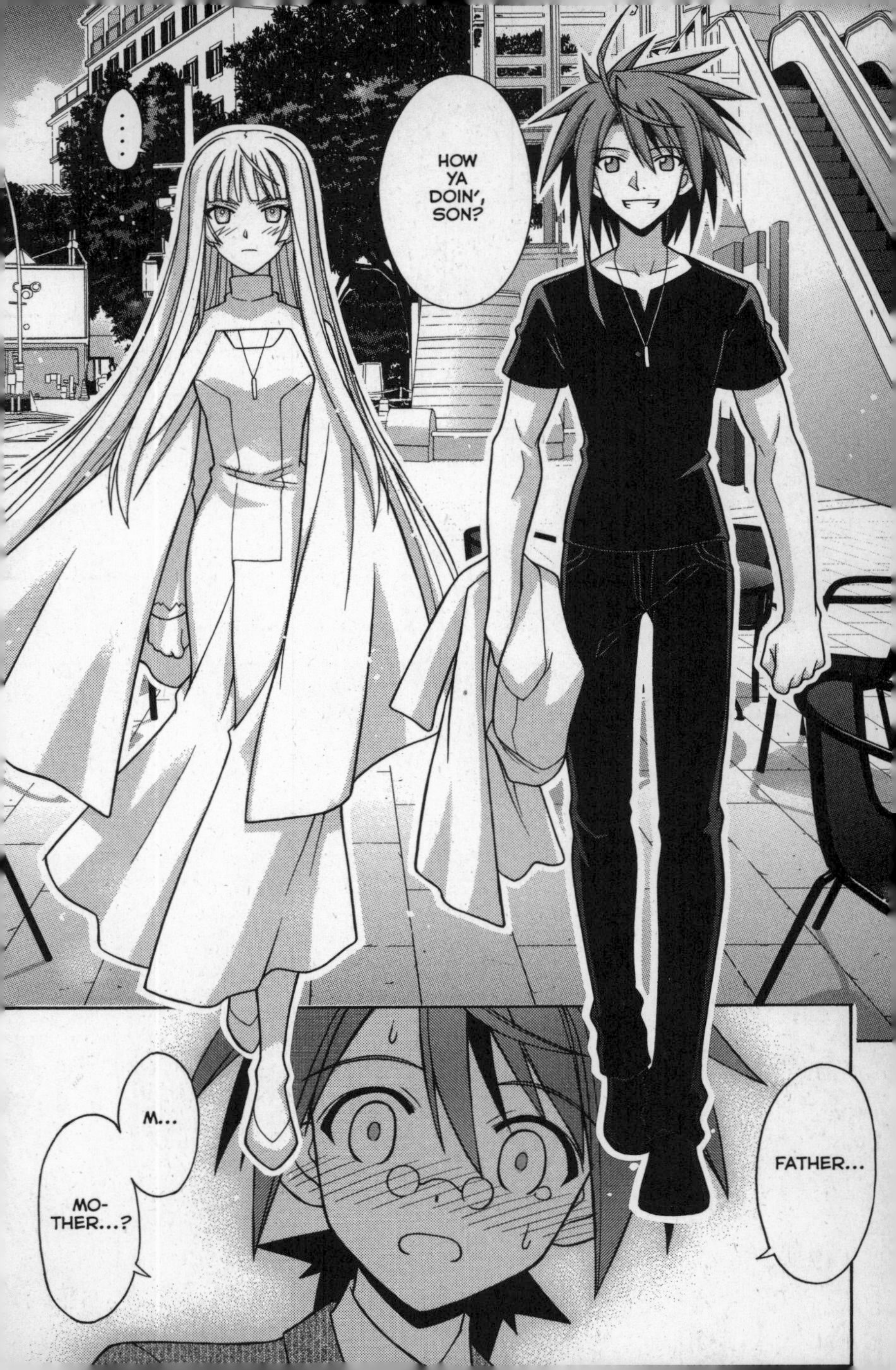
HOW YA DOIN', SON?
...
FATHER...
M... MO-THER...?

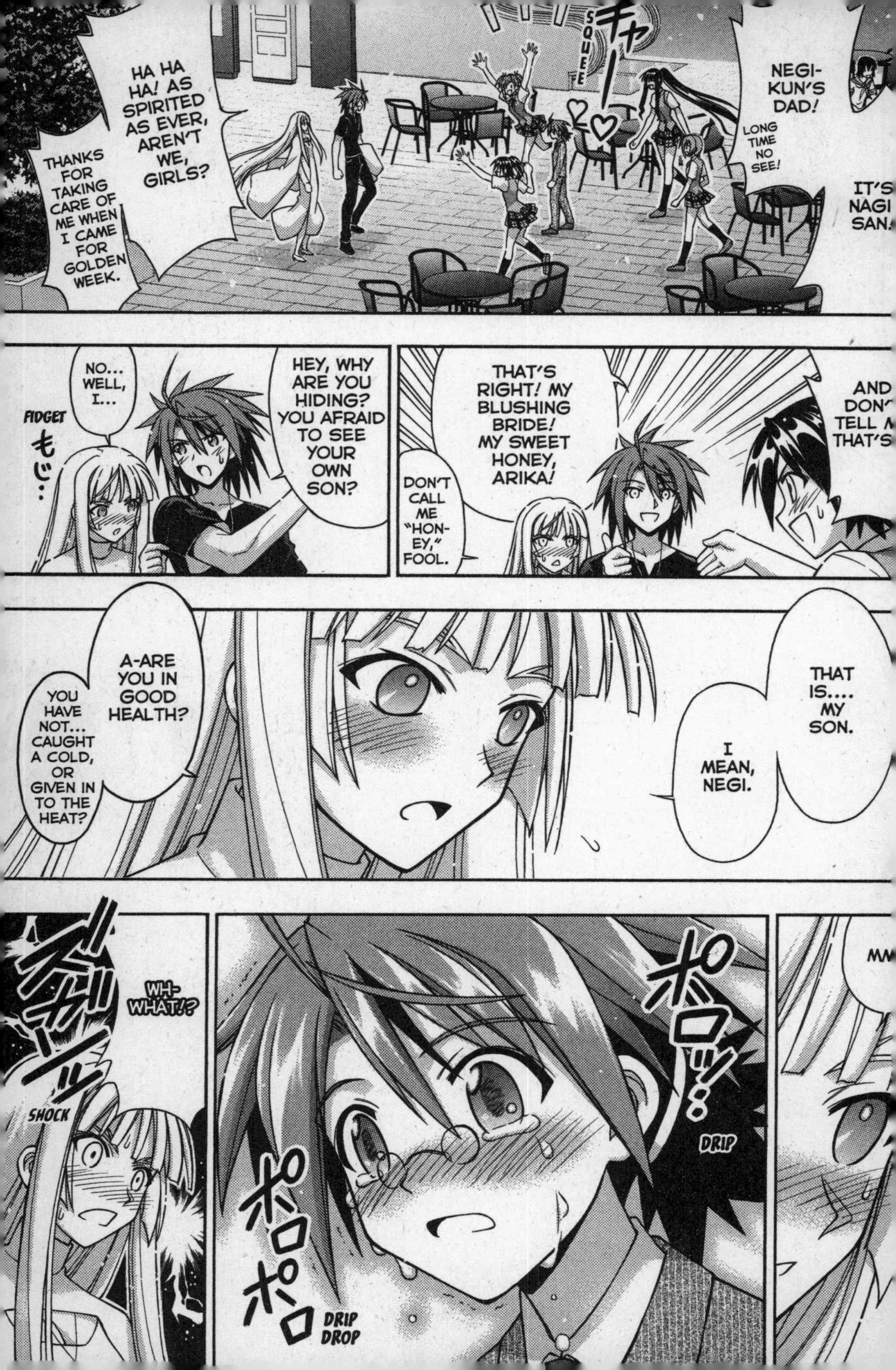
IT'S NAGI SAN
NEGI-KUN'S DAD!
LONG TIME NO SEE!
SQUEE
チャー
HA HA HA! AS SPIRITED AS EVER, AREN'T WE, GIRLS?
THANKS FOR TAKING CARE OF ME WHEN I CAME FOR GOLDEN WEEK.
AND DON'T TELL
THAT'S RIGHT! MY BLUSHING BRIDE! MY SWEET HONEY, ARIKA!
DON'T CALL ME "HONEY," FOOL.
HEY, WHY ARE YOU HIDING? YOU AFRAID TO SEE YOUR OWN SON?
NO... WELL, I...
FIDGET
もじ…
THAT IS.... MY SON.
I MEAN, NEGI.
A-ARE YOU IN GOOD HEALTH?
YOU HAVE NOT... CAUGHT A COLD, OR GIVEN IN TO THE HEAT?
ポロッ!!
DRIP
ポロポロ
DRIP DROP
WH-WHAT!?
SHOCK

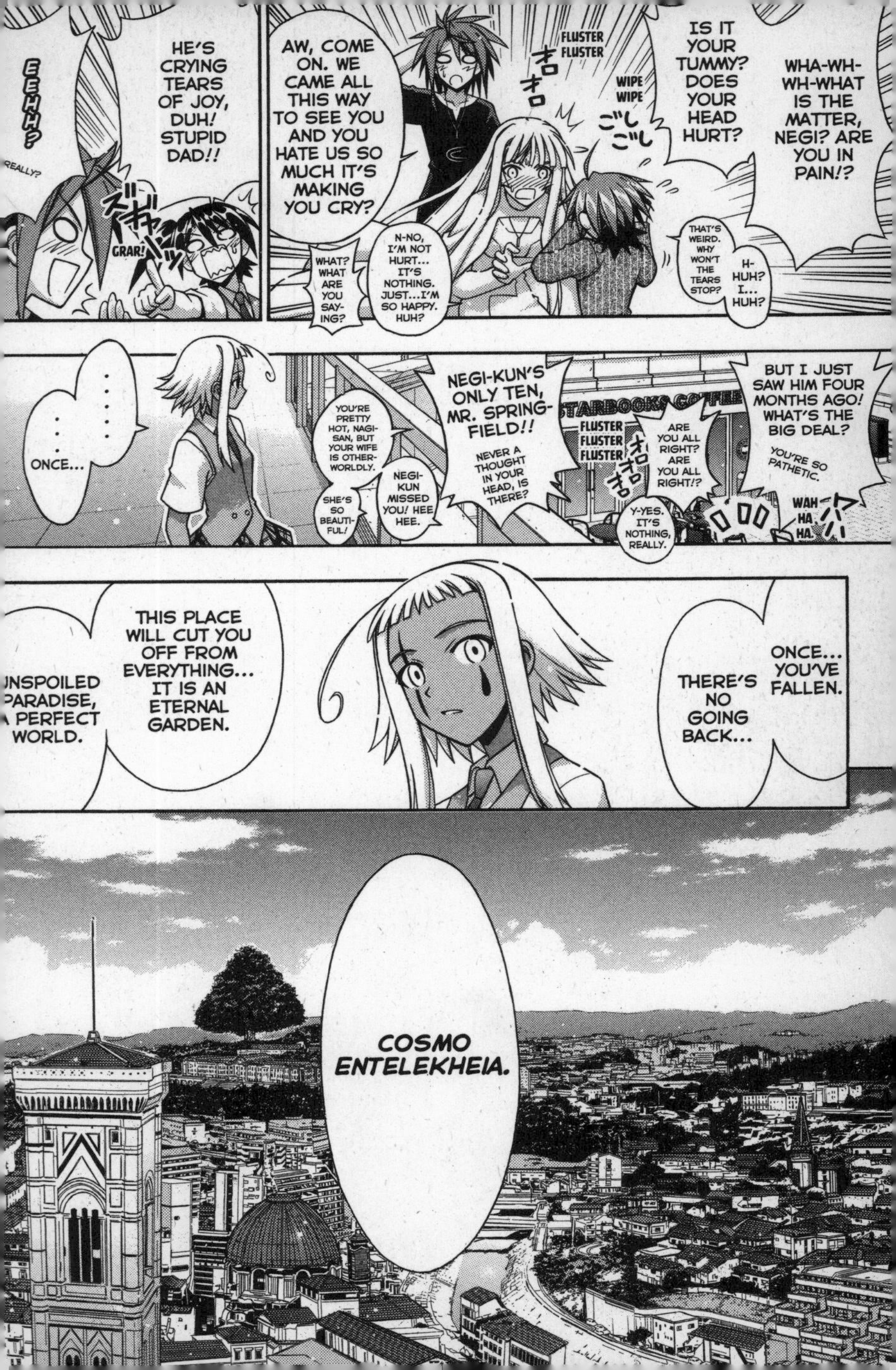
WHA-WH-WH-WHAT IS THE MATTER, NEGI? ARE YOU IN PAIN!?
IS IT YOUR TUMMY? DOES YOUR HEAD HURT?
WIPE WIPE
ごしごし
FLUSTER FLUSTER
オロオロ
AW, COME ON. WE CAME ALL THIS WAY TO SEE YOU AND YOU HATE US SO MUCH IT'S MAKING YOU CRY?
H-HUH? I... HUH?
THAT'S WEIRD. WHY WON'T THE TEARS STOP?
N-NO, I'M NOT HURT... IT'S NOTHING. JUST...I'M SO HAPPY. HUH?
WHAT? WHAT ARE YOU SAYING?
HE'S CRYING TEARS OF JOY, DUH! STUPID DAD!!
GRAR!
EEHHH?
REALLY?
BUT I JUST SAW HIM FOUR MONTHS AGO! WHAT'S THE BIG DEAL?
YOU'RE SO PATHETIC.
WAH HA HA.
ARE YOU ALL RIGHT? ARE YOU ALL RIGHT!?
Y-YES. IT'S NOTHING, REALLY.
FLUSTER FLUSTER FLUSTER
オロオロ
NEGI-KUN'S ONLY TEN, MR. SPRINGFIELD!!
NEVER A THOUGHT IN YOUR HEAD, IS THERE?
YOU'RE PRETTY HOT, NAGI-SAN, BUT YOUR WIFE IS OTHER-WORLDLY.
NEGI-KUN MISSED YOU! HEE HEE.
SHE'S SO BEAUTIFUL!
......
ONCE...
ONCE... YOU'VE FALLEN.
THERE'S NO GOING BACK...
THIS PLACE WILL CUT YOU OFF FROM EVERYTHING... IT IS AN ETERNAL GARDEN.
UNSPOILED PARADISE, A PERFECT WORLD.
COSMO ENTELEKHEIA.

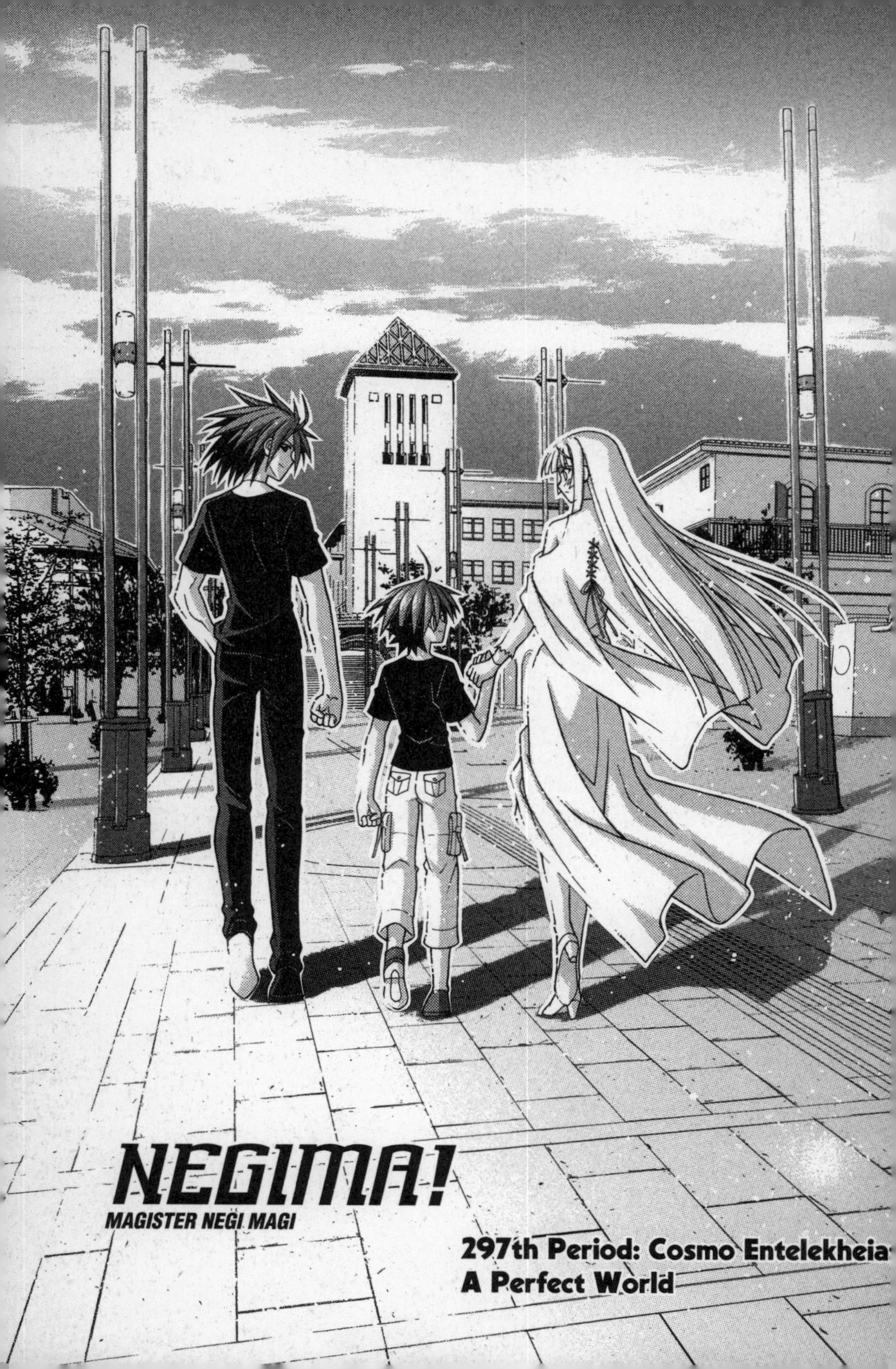
NEGIMA!
MAGISTER NEGI MAGI
297th Period: Cosmo Entelekheia
A Perfect World

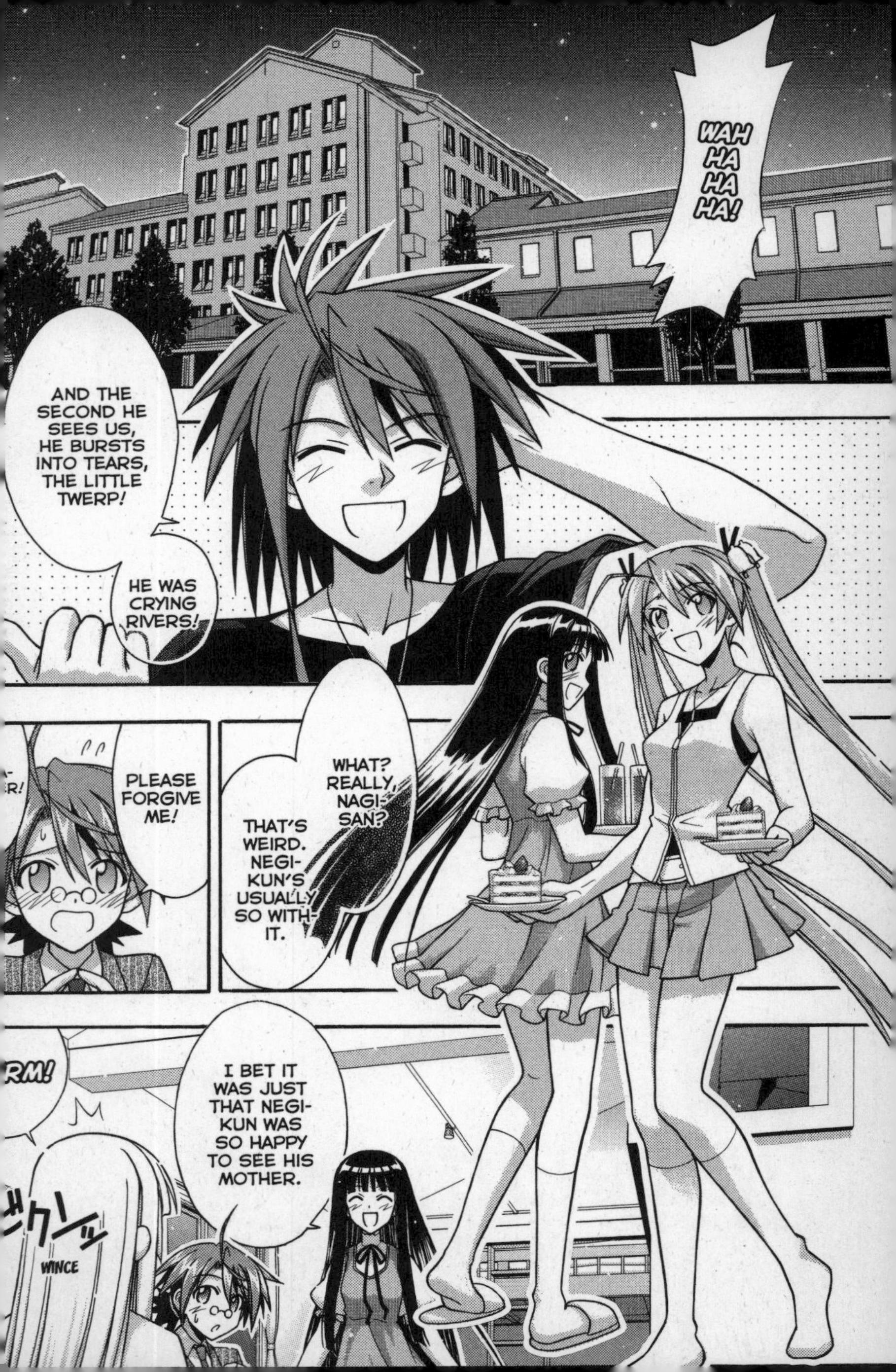
WAH HA HA HA!
AND THE SECOND HE SEES US, HE BURSTS INTO TEARS, THE LITTLE TWERP!
HE WAS CRYING RIVERS!
WHAT? REALLY, NAGI-SAN?
THAT'S WEIRD. NEGI-KUN'S USUALLY SO WITH-IT.
PLEASE FORGIVE ME!
I BET IT WAS JUST THAT NEGI-KUN WAS SO HAPPY TO SEE HIS MOTHER.
WINCE

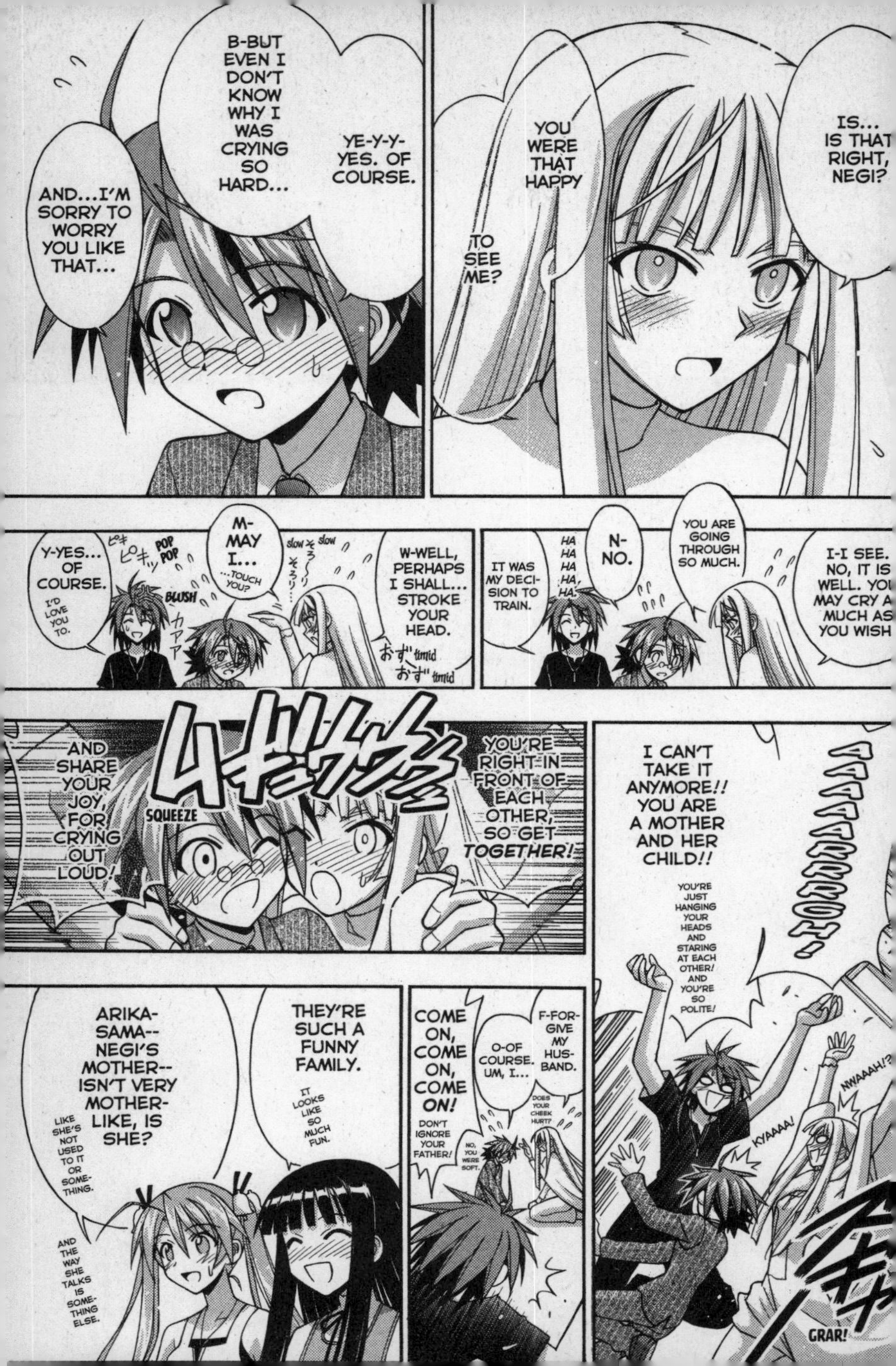
IS... IS THAT RIGHT, NEGI?
YOU WERE THAT HAPPY
TO SEE ME?
YE-Y-Y-YES. OF COURSE.
B-BUT EVEN I DON'T KNOW WHY I WAS CRYING SO HARD...
AND...I'M SORRY TO WORRY YOU LIKE THAT...
I-I SEE. NO, IT IS WELL. YOU MAY CRY AS MUCH AS YOU WISH
YOU ARE GOING THROUGH SO MUCH.
N-NO.
HA HA HA HA, HA.
IT WAS MY DECISION TO TRAIN.
W-WELL, PERHAPS I SHALL... STROKE YOUR HEAD.
slow そろ~ slow そろり...
おず timid おず timid
M-MAY I... ...TOUCH YOU?
BLUSH カァア
POP POP ピキピキッ
Y-YES... OF COURSE.
I'D LOVE YOU TO.
AAAAARRRGH!
I CAN'T TAKE IT ANYMORE!! YOU ARE A MOTHER AND HER CHILD!!
YOU'RE JUST HANGING YOUR HEADS AND STARING AT EACH OTHER! AND YOU'RE SO POLITE!
NWAAAH!?
KYAAAA!
GRAR!
YOU'RE RIGHT IN FRONT OF EACH OTHER, SO GET TOGETHER!
ムギュウウ SQUEEZE
AND SHARE YOUR JOY, FOR CRYING OUT LOUD!
COME ON, COME ON, COME ON!
F-FORGIVE MY HUSBAND.
O-OF COURSE. UM, I...
DON'T IGNORE YOUR FATHER!
DOES YOUR CHEEK HURT?
NO, YOU WERE SOFT.
THEY'RE SUCH A FUNNY FAMILY.
IT LOOKS LIKE SO MUCH FUN.
ARIKA-SAMA--NEGI'S MOTHER--ISN'T VERY MOTHER-LIKE, IS SHE?
LIKE SHE'S NOT USED TO IT OR SOMETHING.
AND THE WAY SHE TALKS IS SOMETHING ELSE.

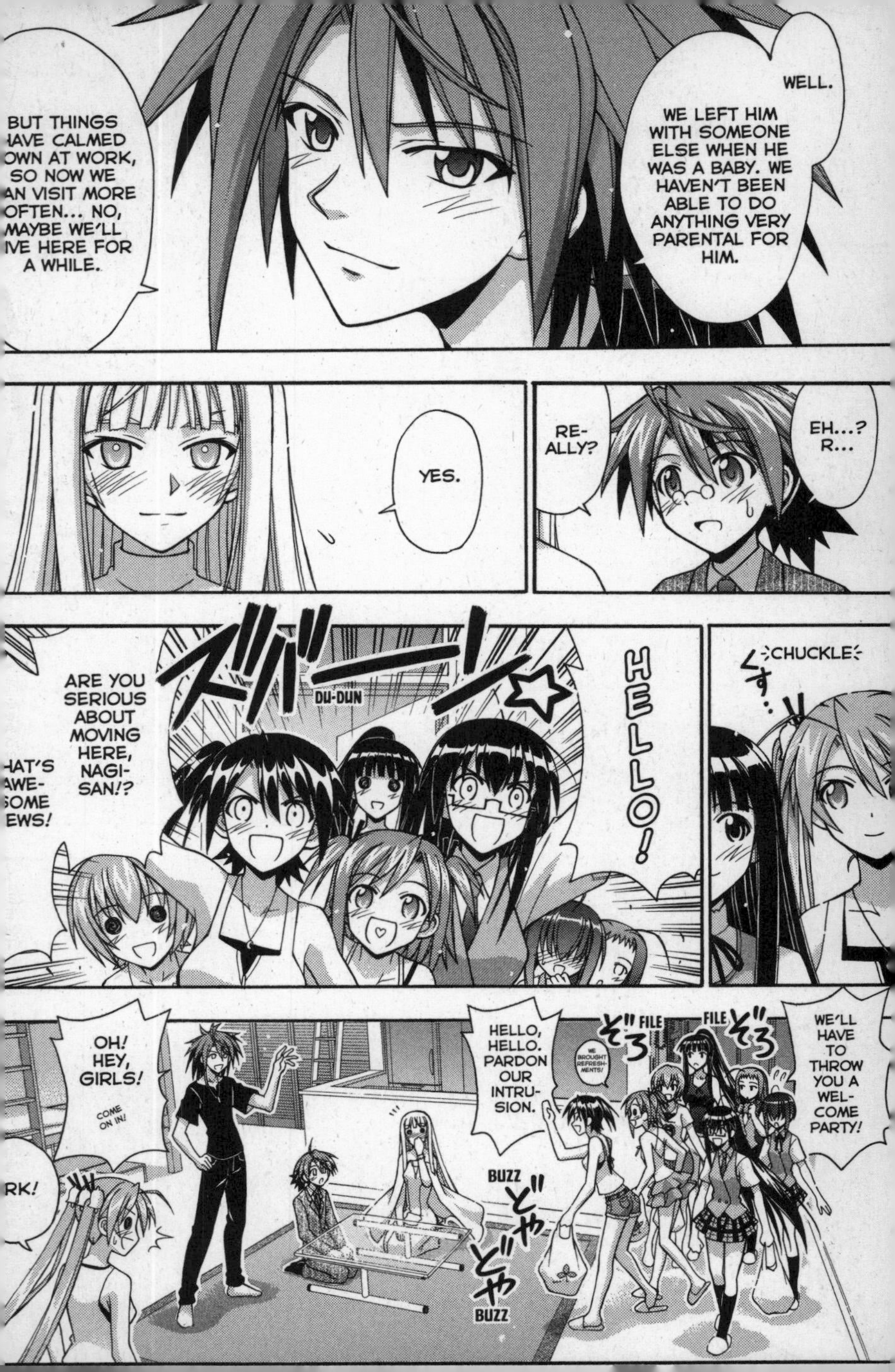
WELL.
WE LEFT HIM WITH SOMEONE ELSE WHEN HE WAS A BABY. WE HAVEN'T BEEN ABLE TO DO ANYTHING VERY PARENTAL FOR HIM.
BUT THINGS IAVE CALMED OWN AT WORK, SO NOW WE AN VISIT MORE OFTEN... NO, MAYBE WE'LL IVE HERE FOR A WHILE.
EH...? R...
RE-ALLY?
YES.
くす…
CHUCKLE
HELLO!
ズバーン!
DU-DUN
ARE YOU SERIOUS ABOUT MOVING HERE, NAGI-SAN!?
HAT'S AWE-SOME EWS!
WE'LL HAVE TO THROW YOU A WEL-COME PARTY!
ぞろ
FILE
ぞろ
FILE
WE BROUGHT REFRESH-MENTS!
HELLO, HELLO. PARDON OUR INTRU-SION.
どや どや
BUZZ
BUZZ
OH! HEY, GIRLS!
COME ON IN!
RK!

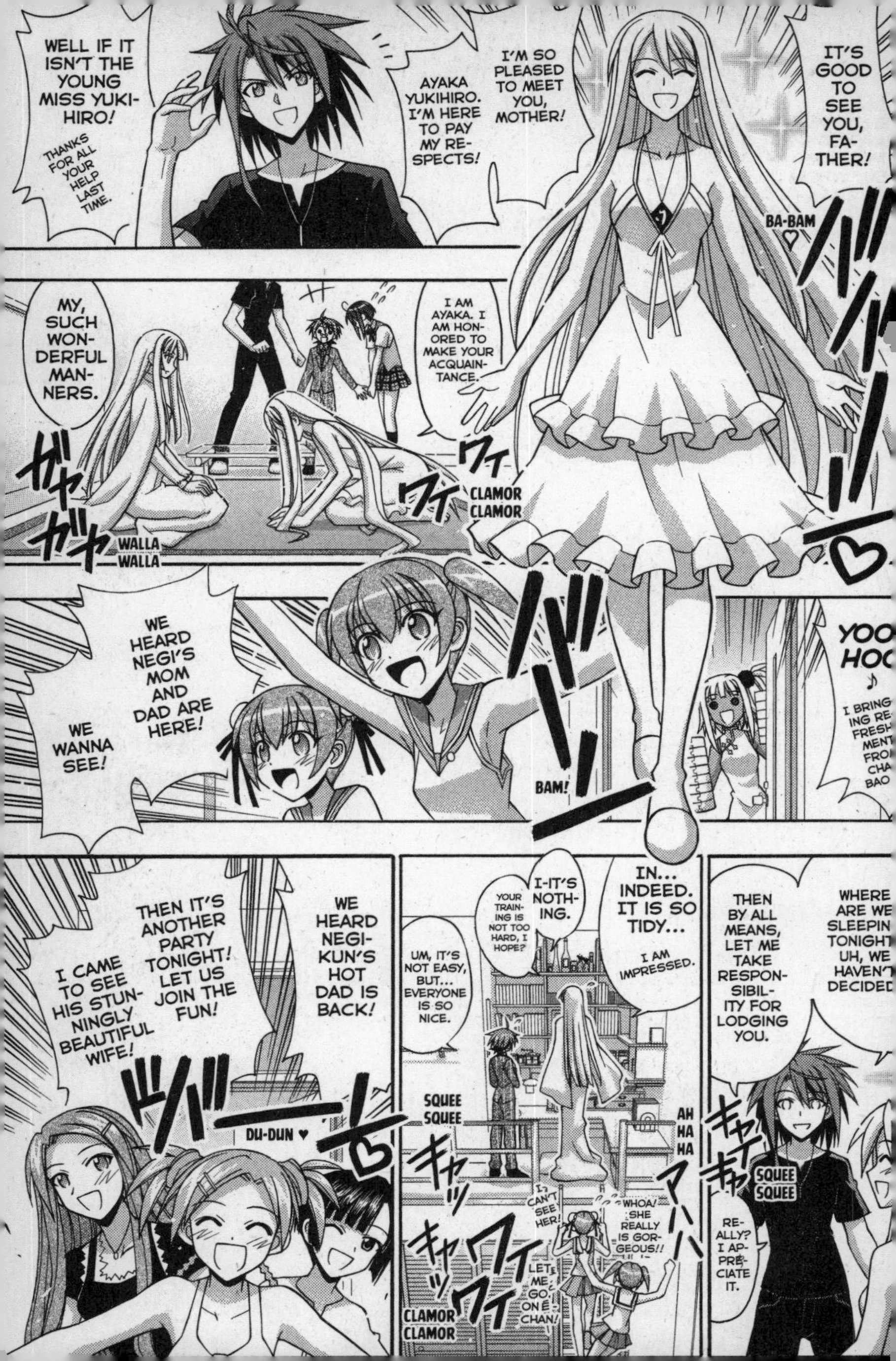
IT'S GOOD TO SEE YOU, FATHER!
I'M SO PLEASED TO MEET YOU, MOTHER!
BA-BAM ♡
AYAKA YUKIHIRO. I'M HERE TO PAY MY RESPECTS!
WELL IF IT ISN'T THE YOUNG MISS YUKIHIRO!
THANKS FOR ALL YOUR HELP LAST TIME.
I AM AYAKA. I AM HONORED TO MAKE YOUR ACQUAINTANCE.
MY, SUCH WONDERFUL MANNERS.
CLAMOR CLAMOR
WALLA WALLA
YOO HOO ♪
I BRINGING REFRESHMENT FRO CHA BAO
WE HEARD NEGI'S MOM AND DAD ARE HERE!
WE WANNA SEE!
BAM!
WHERE ARE WE SLEEPIN TONIGHT
UH, WE HAVEN'T DECIDED
THEN BY ALL MEANS, LET ME TAKE RESPONSIBILITY FOR LODGING YOU.
SQUEE SQUEE
REALLY? I APPRECIATE IT.
IN... INDEED. IT IS SO TIDY...
I AM IMPRESSED.
I-IT'S NOTHING.
YOUR TRAINING IS NOT TOO HARD, I HOPE?
UM, IT'S NOT EASY, BUT... EVERYONE IS SO NICE.
AH HA HA
WHOA! SHE REALLY IS GORGEOUS!!
I CAN'T SEE HER!
LET ME GO, ONE-CHAN!
SQUEE SQUEE
CLAMOR CLAMOR
WE HEARD NEGI-KUN'S HOT DAD IS BACK!
THEN IT'S ANOTHER PARTY TONIGHT! LET US JOIN THE FUN!
I CAME TO SEE HIS STUNNINGLY BEAUTIFUL WIFE!
DU-DUN ♥

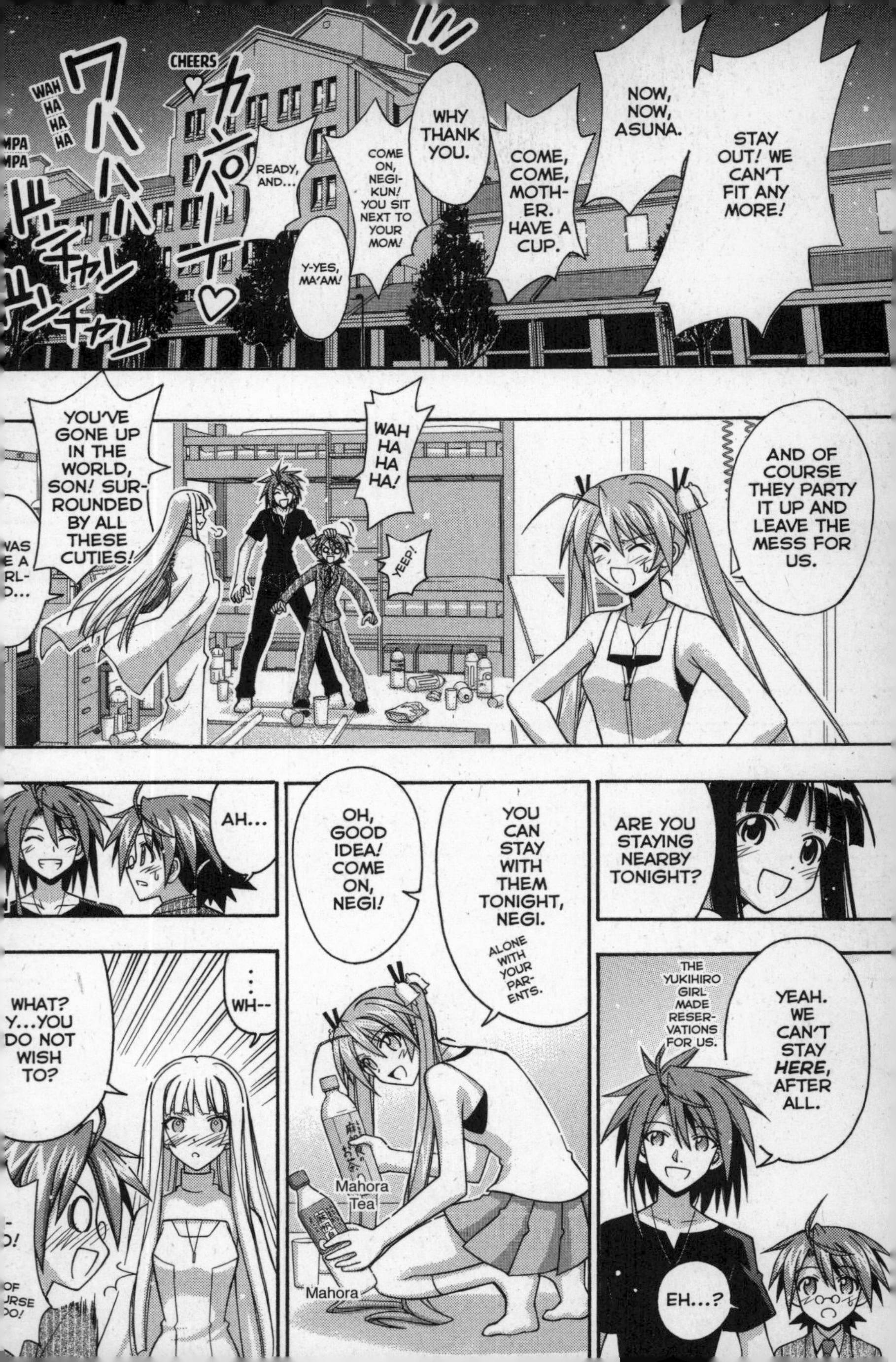
STAY OUT! WE CAN'T FIT ANY MORE!
NOW, NOW, ASUNA.
COME, COME, MOTHER. HAVE A CUP.
WHY THANK YOU.
COME ON, NEGI-KUN! YOU SIT NEXT TO YOUR MOM!
Y-YES, MA'AM!
READY, AND...
CHEERS ♥
WAH HA HA HA
MPA MPA
AND OF COURSE THEY PARTY IT UP AND LEAVE THE MESS FOR US.
WAH HA HA HA!
YEEP!
YOU'VE GONE UP IN THE WORLD, SON! SURROUNDED BY ALL THESE CUTIES!
ARE YOU STAYING NEARBY TONIGHT?
YOU CAN STAY WITH THEM TONIGHT, NEGI.
OH, GOOD IDEA! COME ON, NEGI!
AH...
YEAH. WE CAN'T STAY *HERE*, AFTER ALL.
THE YUKIHIRO GIRL MADE RESERVATIONS FOR US.
EH...?
ALONE WITH YOUR PARENTS.
Mahora Tea
Mahora
...WH--
WHAT? Y...YOU DO NOT WISH TO?

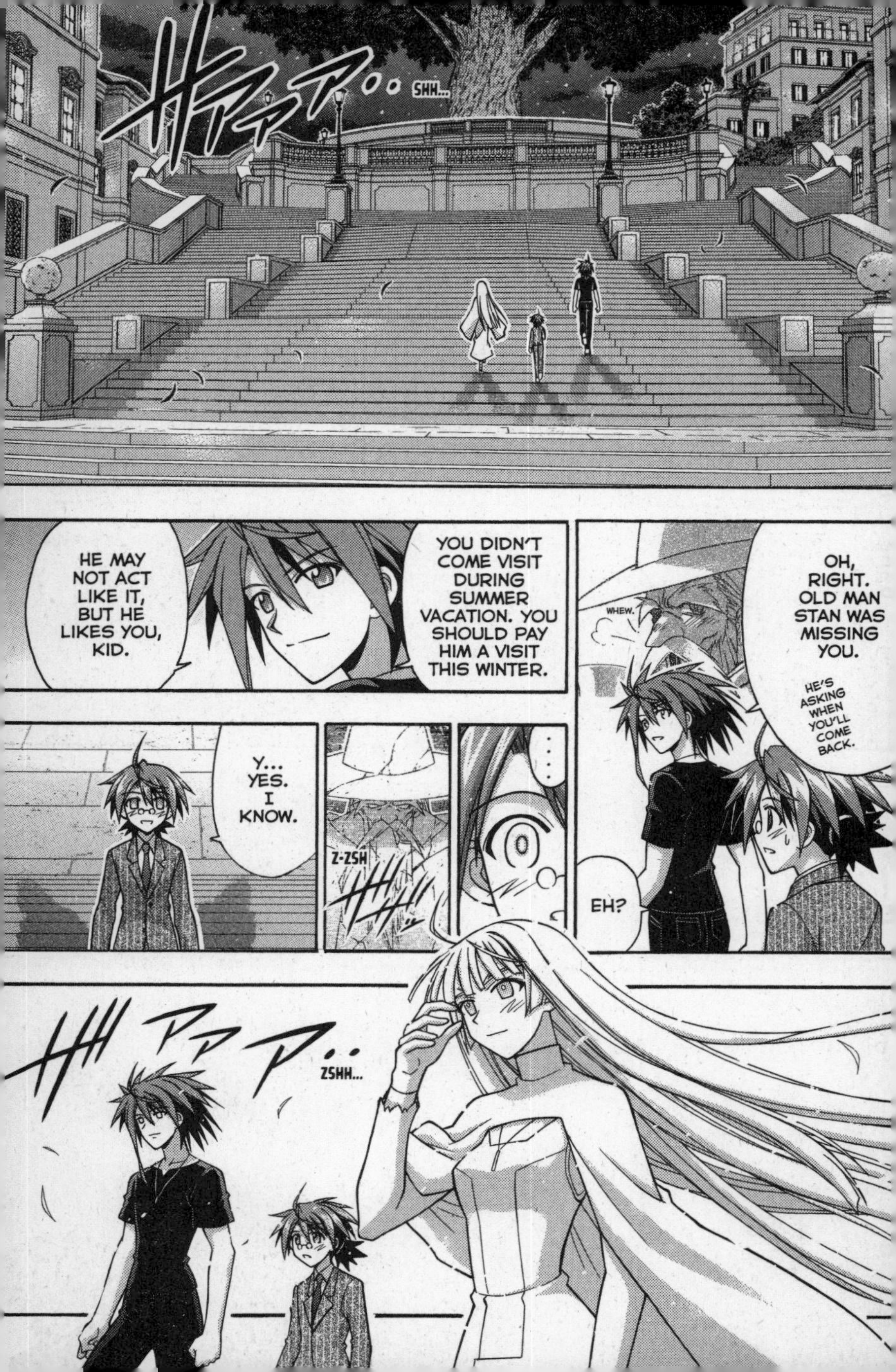
SHH...
OH, RIGHT. OLD MAN STAN WAS MISSING YOU.
WHEW.
HE'S ASKING WHEN YOU'LL COME BACK.
EH?
YOU DIDN'T COME VISIT DURING SUMMER VACATION. YOU SHOULD PAY HIM A VISIT THIS WINTER.
HE MAY NOT ACT LIKE IT, BUT HE LIKES YOU, KID.
....
Z-ZSH
Y... YES. I KNOW.
ZSHH...

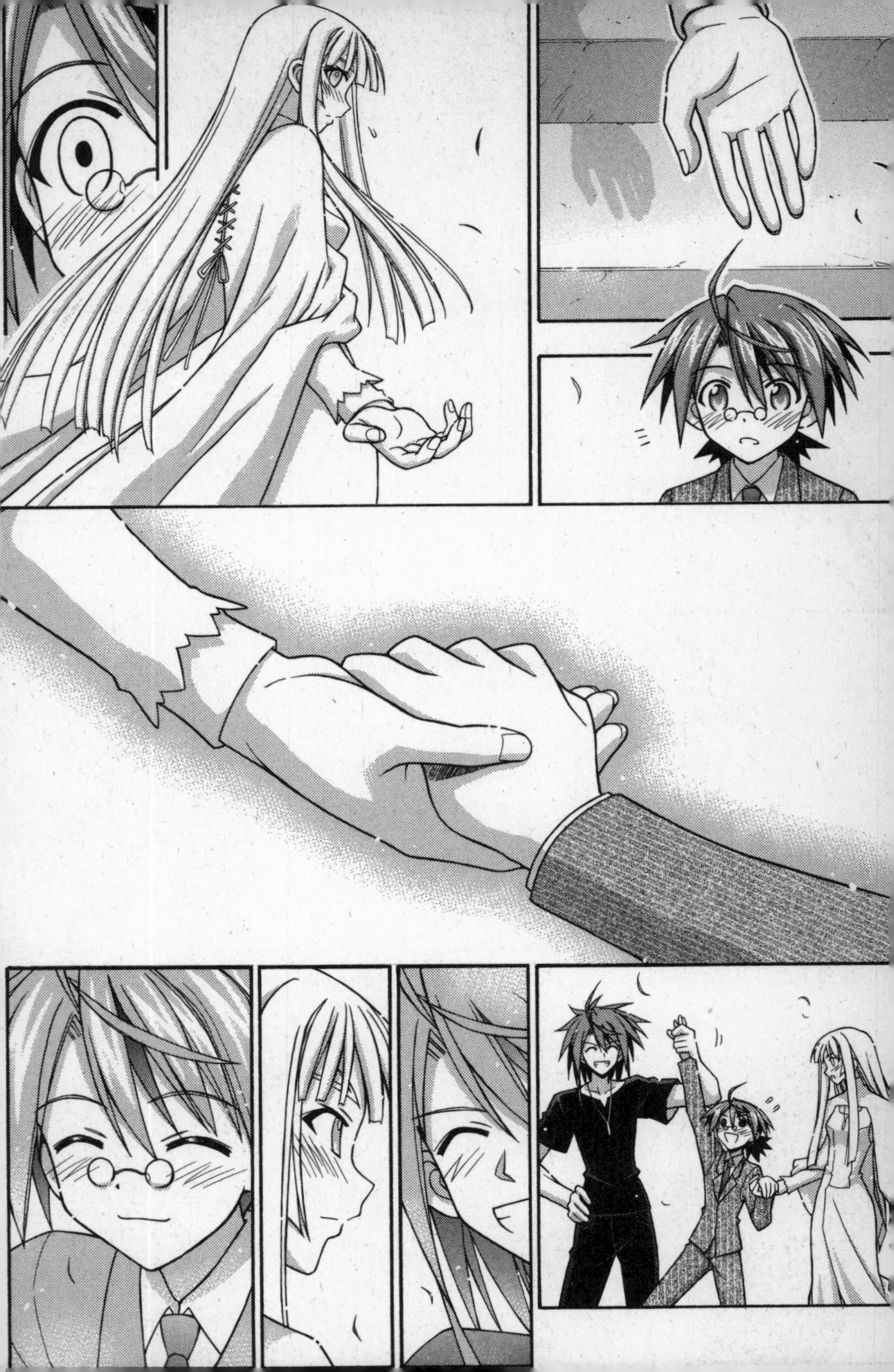

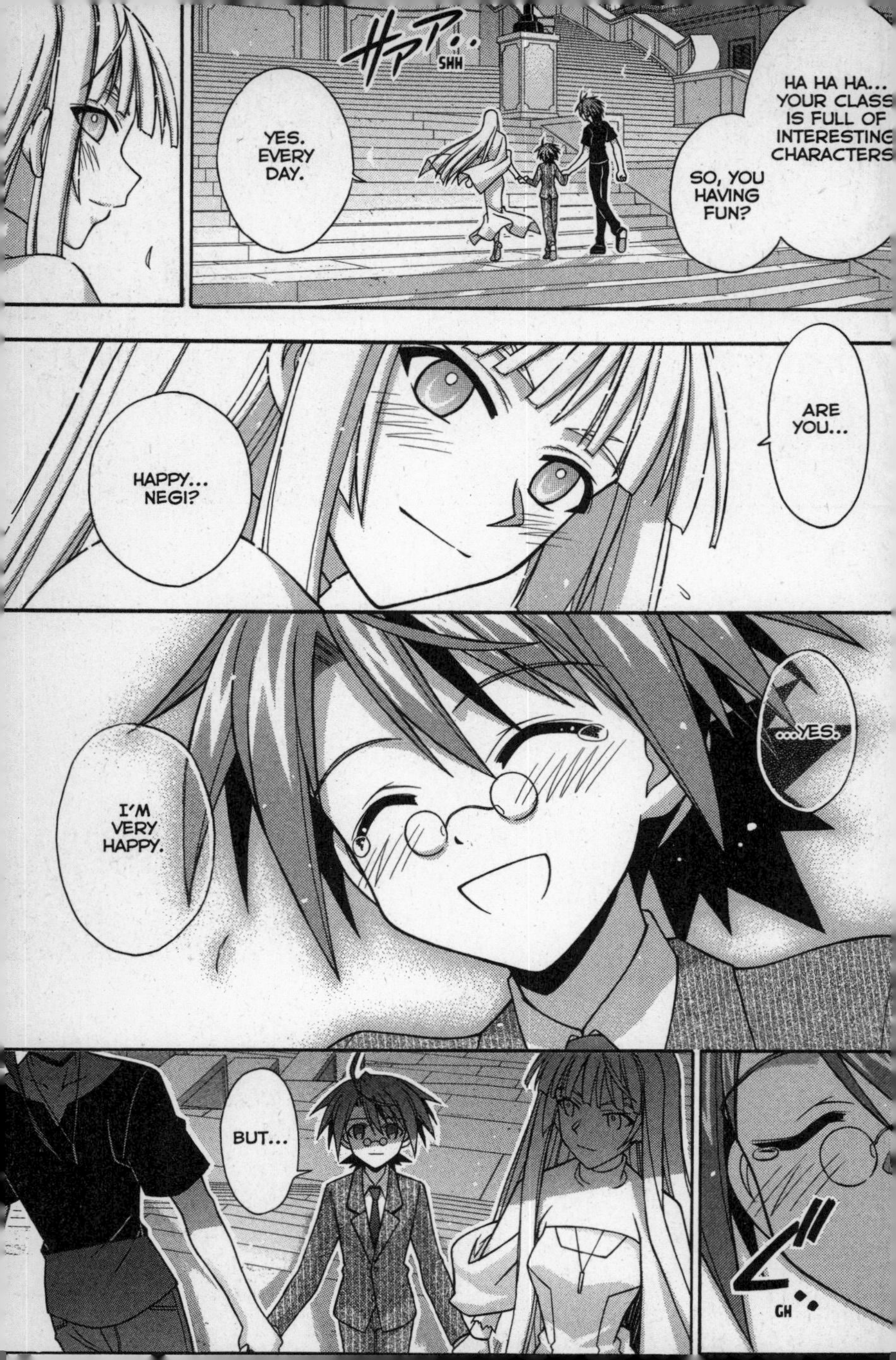
HA HA HA... YOUR CLASS IS FULL OF INTERESTING CHARACTERS
SO, YOU HAVING FUN?
SHH
YES. EVERY DAY.
ARE YOU...
HAPPY... NEGI?
...YES.
I'M VERY HAPPY.
GH
BUT...

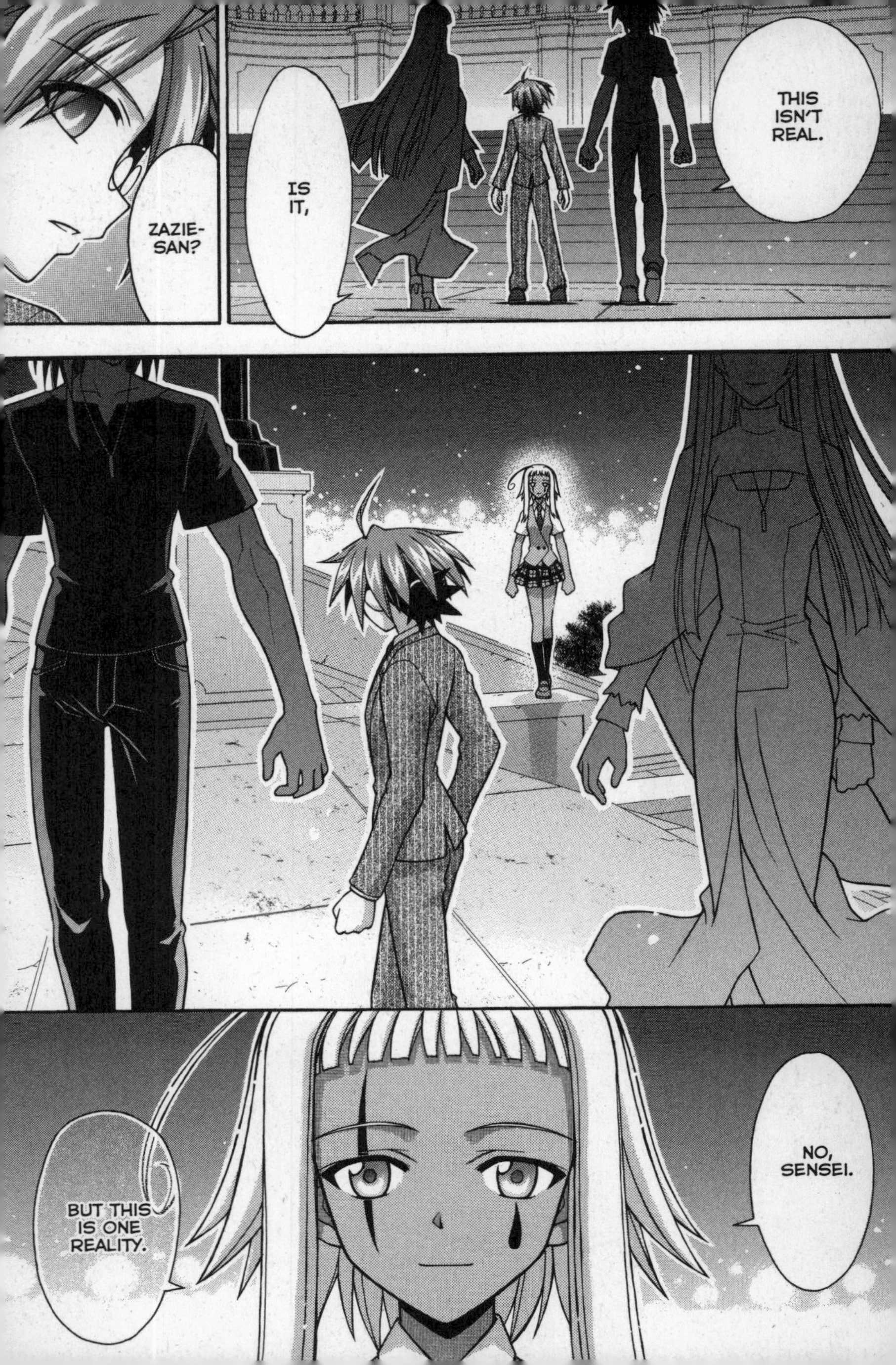
THIS ISN'T REAL.
IS IT,
ZAZIE-SAN?
NO, SENSEI.
BUT THIS IS ONE REALITY.

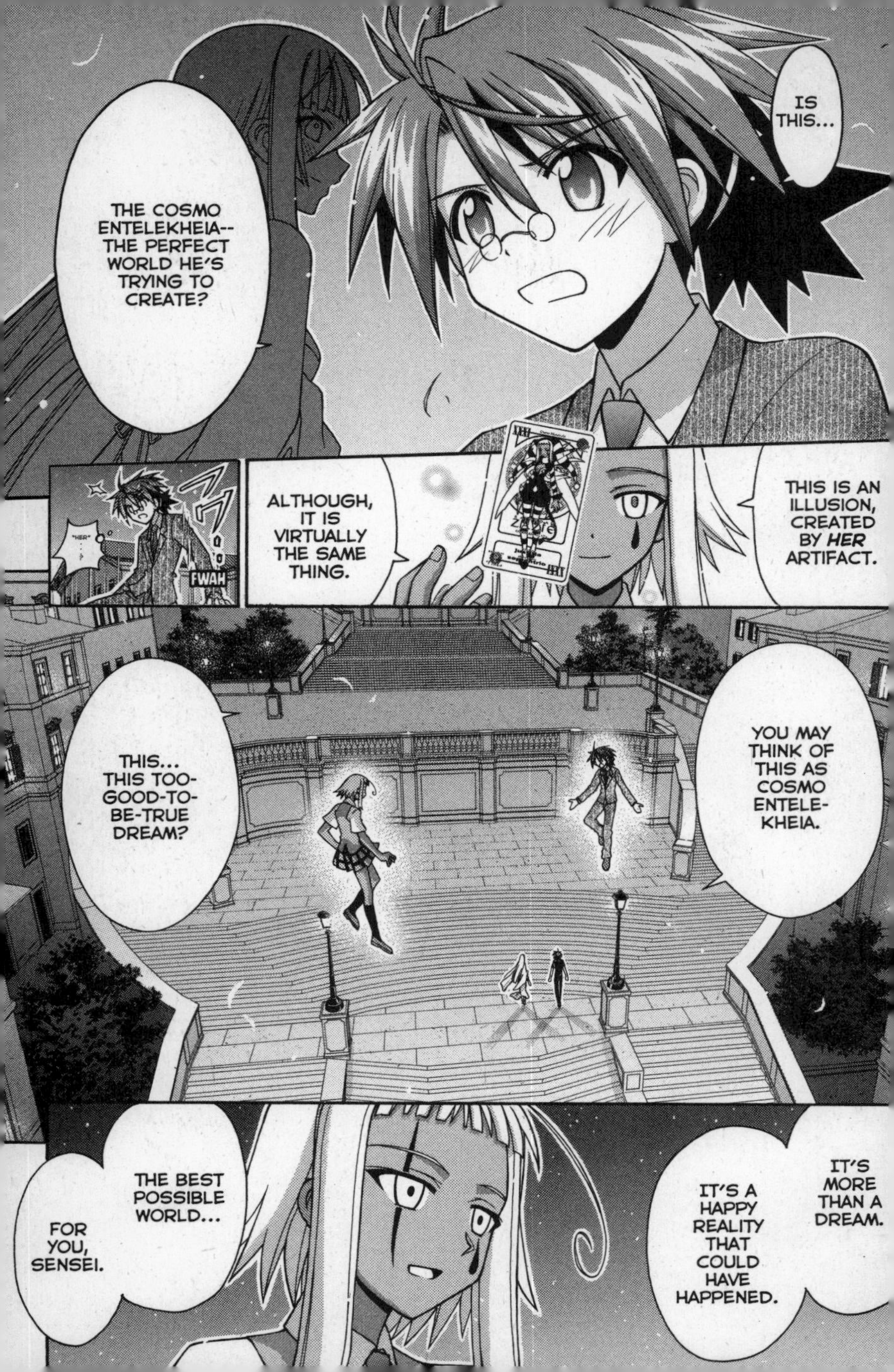
IS THIS...
THE COSMO ENTELEKHEIA-- THE PERFECT WORLD HE'S TRYING TO CREATE?
THIS IS AN ILLUSION, CREATED BY *HER* ARTIFACT.
ALTHOUGH, IT IS VIRTUALLY THE SAME THING.
"HER" ...?
FWAH
YOU MAY THINK OF THIS AS COSMO ENTELEKHEIA.
THIS... THIS TOO-GOOD-TO-BE-TRUE DREAM?
IT'S MORE THAN A DREAM.
IT'S A HAPPY REALITY THAT COULD HAVE HAPPENED.
THE BEST POSSIBLE WORLD...
FOR YOU, SENSEI.

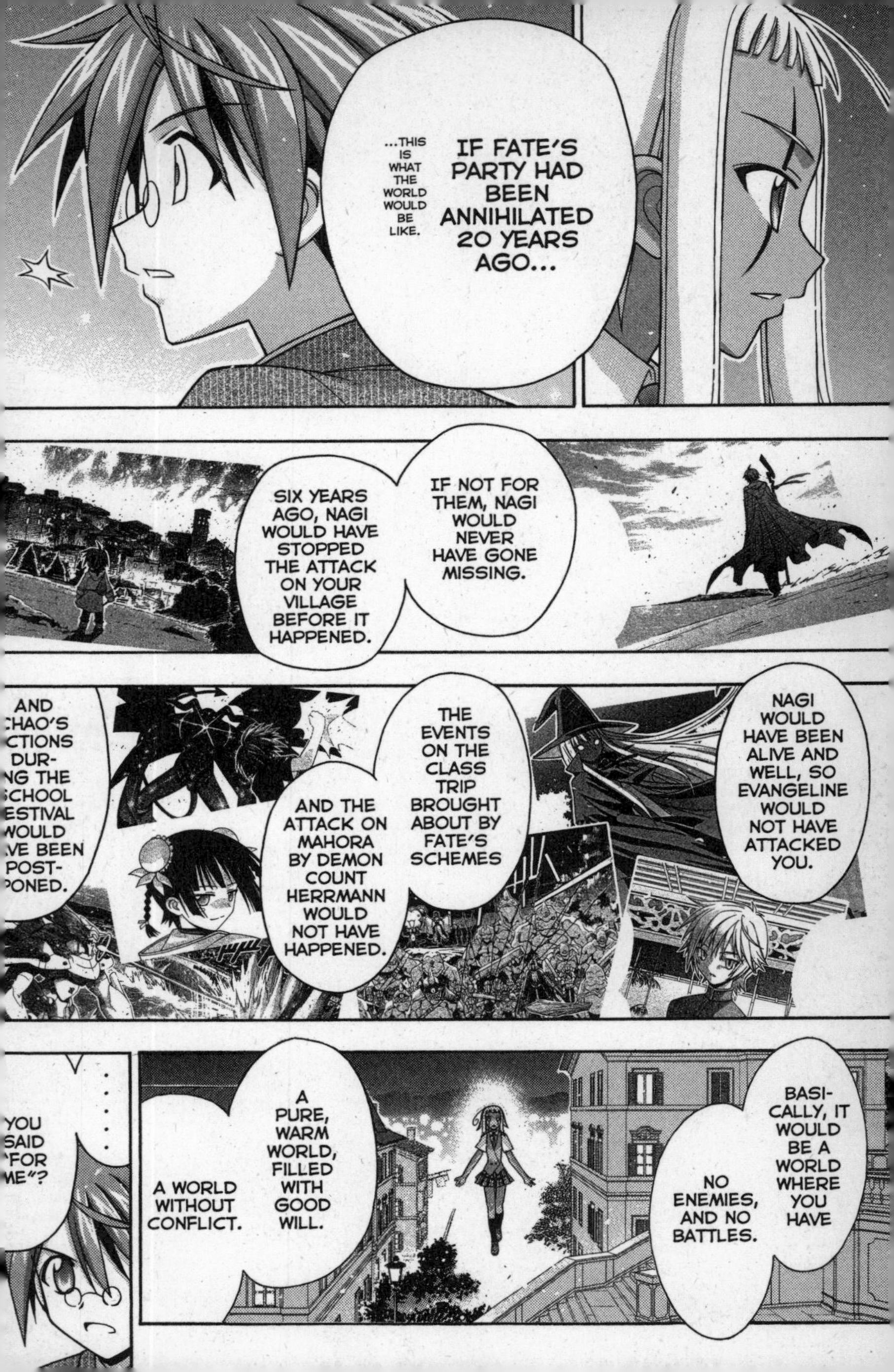
IF FATE'S PARTY HAD BEEN ANNIHILATED 20 YEARS AGO...
...THIS IS WHAT THE WORLD WOULD BE LIKE.
IF NOT FOR THEM, NAGI WOULD NEVER HAVE GONE MISSING.
SIX YEARS AGO, NAGI WOULD HAVE STOPPED THE ATTACK ON YOUR VILLAGE BEFORE IT HAPPENED.
NAGI WOULD HAVE BEEN ALIVE AND WELL, SO EVANGELINE WOULD NOT HAVE ATTACKED YOU.
THE EVENTS ON THE CLASS TRIP BROUGHT ABOUT BY FATE'S SCHEMES
AND THE ATTACK ON MAHORA BY DEMON COUNT HERRMANN WOULD NOT HAVE HAPPENED.
AND CHAO'S CTIONS DUR- NG THE SCHOOL ESTIVAL WOULD VE BEEN POST- PONED.
BASI- CALLY, IT WOULD BE A WORLD WHERE YOU HAVE
NO ENEMIES, AND NO BATTLES.
A PURE, WARM WORLD, FILLED WITH GOOD WILL.
A WORLD WITHOUT CONFLICT.
......
YOU SAID "FOR ME"?

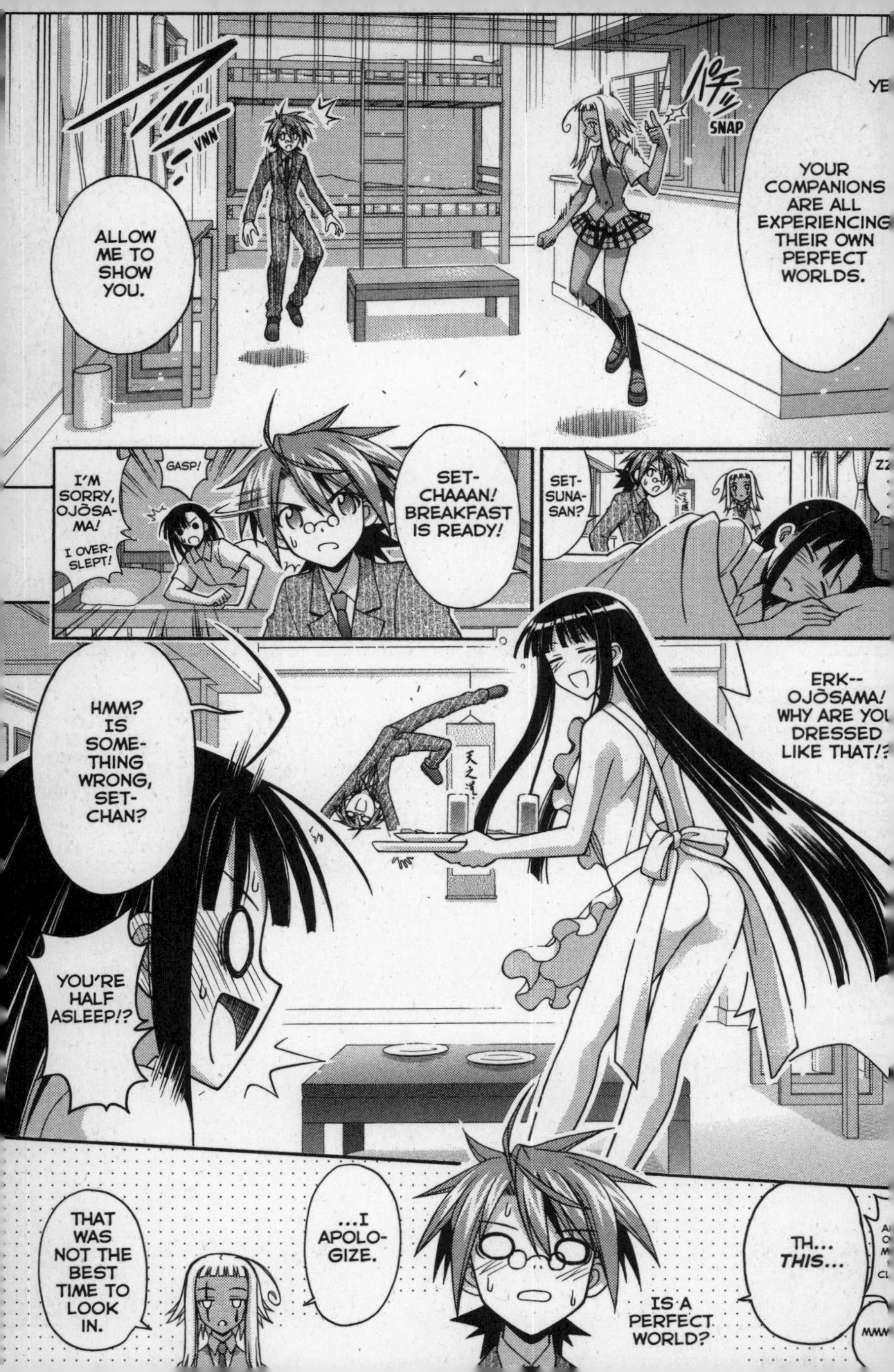
SNAP
YOUR COMPANIONS ARE ALL EXPERIENCING THEIR OWN PERFECT WORLDS.
VNN
ALLOW ME TO SHOW YOU.
SET-SUNA-SAN?
SET-CHAAAN! BREAKFAST IS READY!
GASP!
I'M SORRY, OJŌSAMA!
I OVERSLEPT!
ERK-- OJŌSAMA! WHY ARE YOU DRESSED LIKE THAT!?
HMM? IS SOMETHING WRONG, SET-CHAN?
YOU'RE HALF ASLEEP!?
TH... THIS...
IS A PERFECT WORLD?
...I APOLOGIZE.
THAT WAS NOT THE BEST TIME TO LOOK IN.

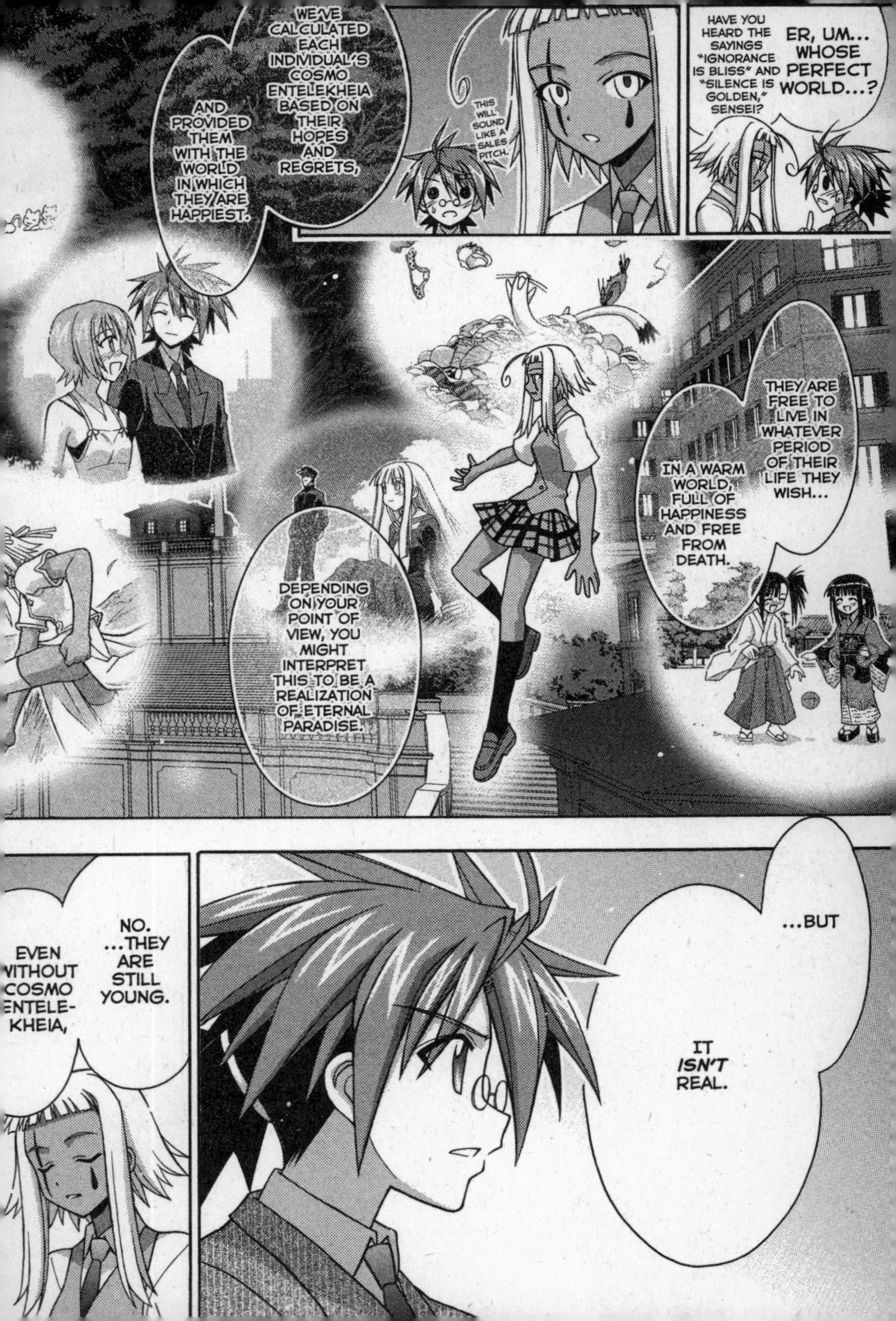
ER, UM... WHOSE PERFECT WORLD...?
HAVE YOU HEARD THE SAYINGS "IGNORANCE IS BLISS" AND "SILENCE IS GOLDEN," SENSEI?
THIS WILL SOUND LIKE A SALES PITCH.
WE'VE CALCULATED EACH INDIVIDUAL'S COSMO ENTELEKHEIA BASED ON THEIR HOPES AND REGRETS,
AND PROVIDED THEM WITH THE WORLD IN WHICH THEY ARE HAPPIEST.
THEY ARE FREE TO LIVE IN WHATEVER PERIOD OF THEIR LIFE THEY WISH...
IN A WARM WORLD, FULL OF HAPPINESS AND FREE FROM DEATH.
DEPENDING ON YOUR POINT OF VIEW, YOU MIGHT INTERPRET THIS TO BE A REALIZATION OF ETERNAL PARADISE.
...BUT
IT *ISN'T* REAL.
NO. ...THEY ARE STILL YOUNG.
EVEN WITHOUT COSMO ENTELE-KHEIA,

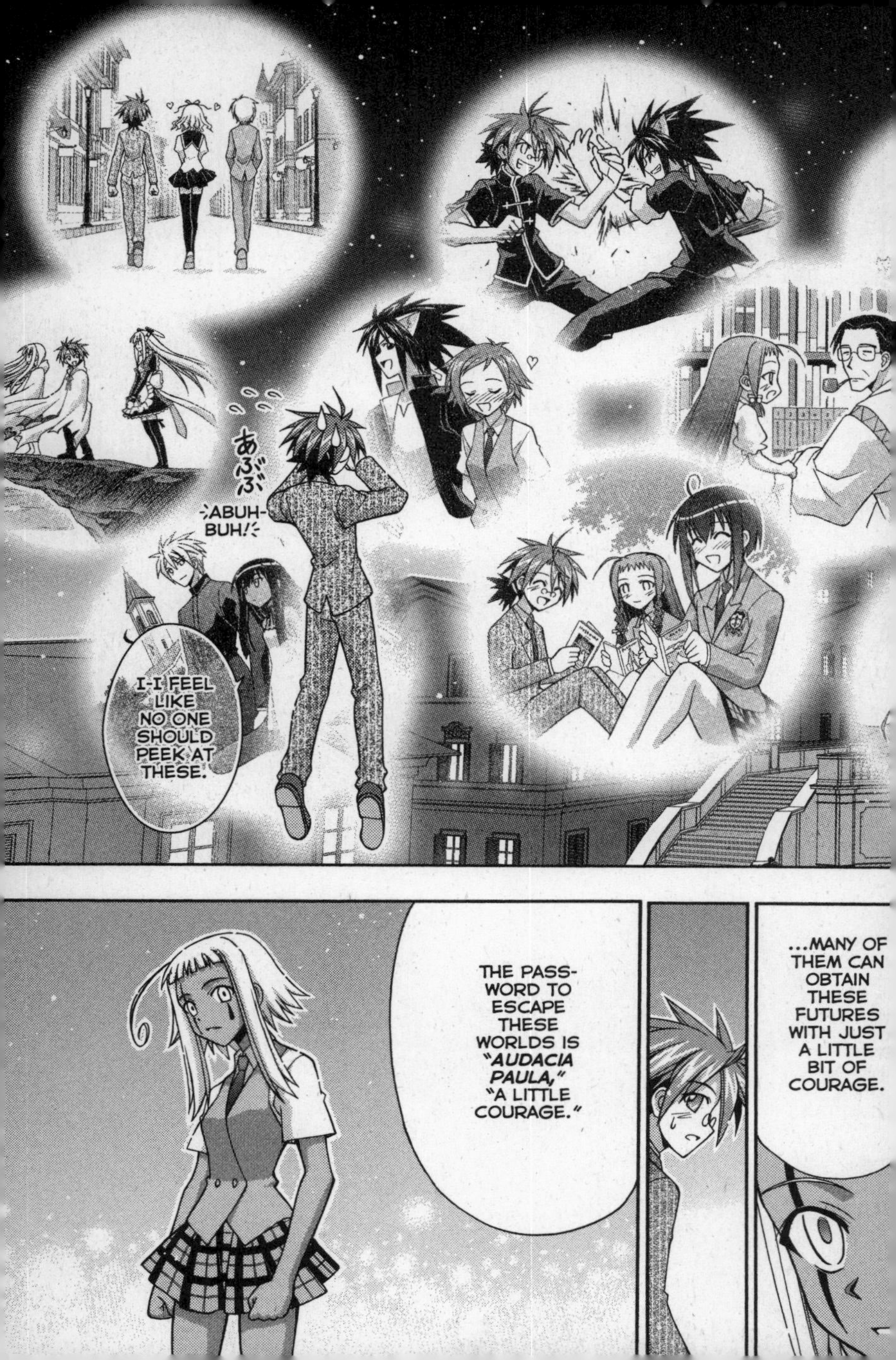
あぶぶ
ABUH-BUH!
I-I FEEL LIKE NO ONE SHOULD PEEK AT THESE.
...MANY OF THEM CAN OBTAIN THESE FUTURES WITH JUST A LITTLE BIT OF COURAGE.
THE PASSWORD TO ESCAPE THESE WORLDS IS *"AUDACIA PAULA,"* "A LITTLE COURAGE."

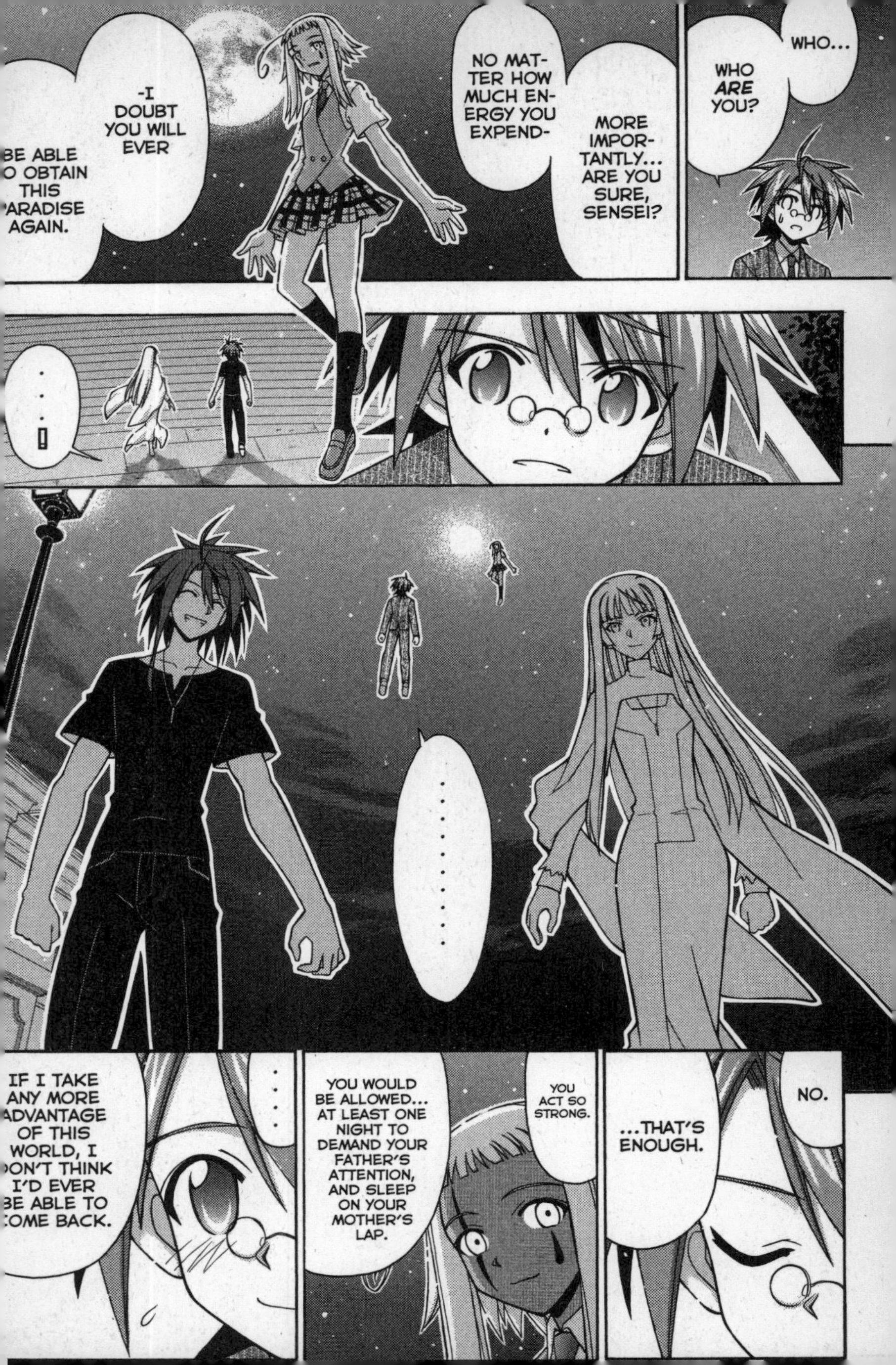
WHO...
WHO ARE YOU?
MORE IMPORTANTLY... ARE YOU SURE, SENSEI?
NO MATTER HOW MUCH ENERGY YOU EXPEND-
-I DOUBT YOU WILL EVER
BE ABLE TO OBTAIN THIS PARADISE AGAIN.
...!
....
NO.
...THAT'S ENOUGH.
YOU ACT SO STRONG.
YOU WOULD BE ALLOWED... AT LEAST ONE NIGHT TO DEMAND YOUR FATHER'S ATTENTION, AND SLEEP ON YOUR MOTHER'S LAP.
....
IF I TAKE ANY MORE ADVANTAGE OF THIS WORLD, I DON'T THINK I'D EVER BE ABLE TO COME BACK.

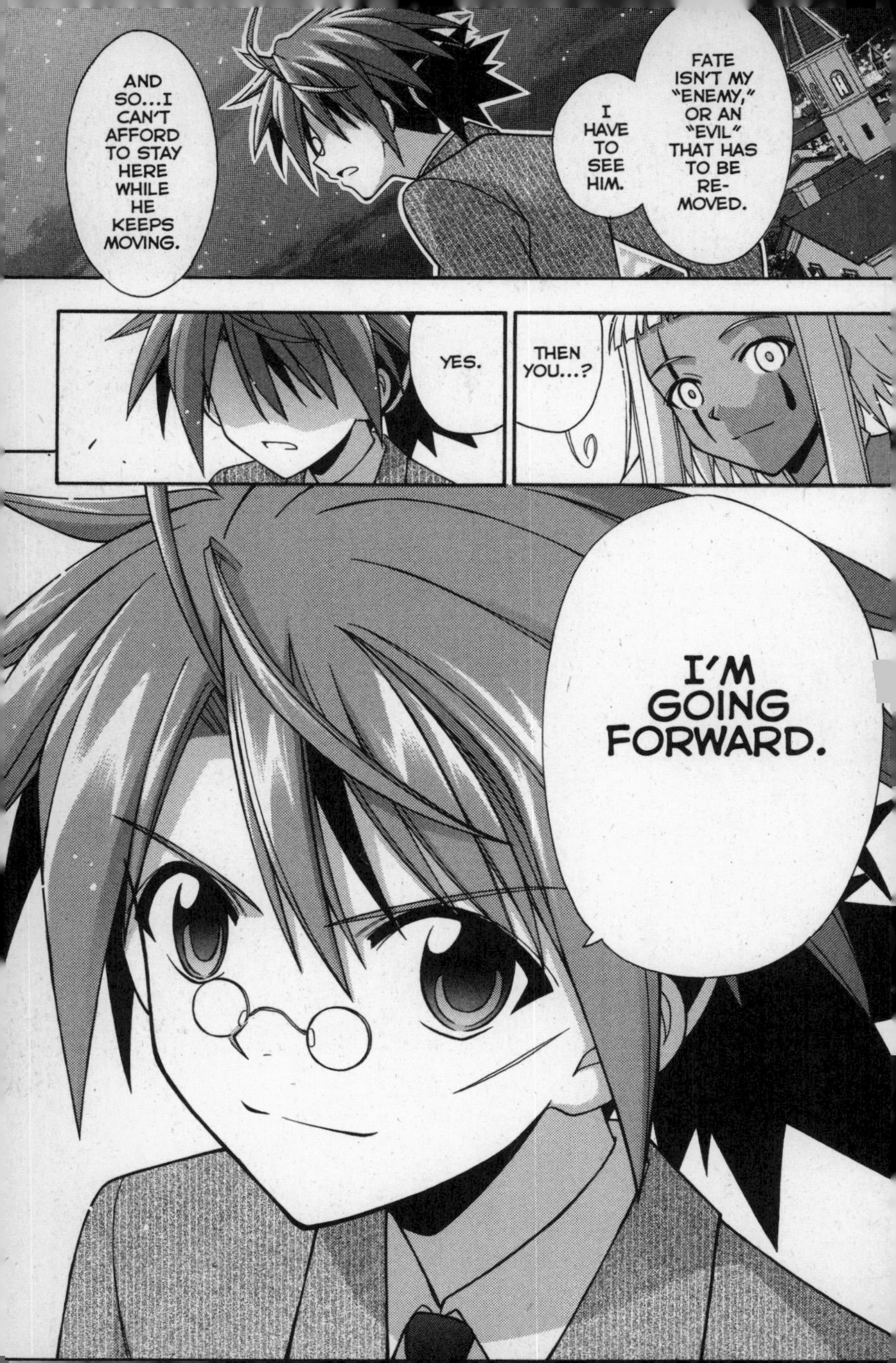
FATE ISN'T MY "ENEMY," OR AN "EVIL" THAT HAS TO BE RE-MOVED.
I HAVE TO SEE HIM.
AND SO...I CAN'T AFFORD TO STAY HERE WHILE HE KEEPS MOVING.
THEN YOU...?
YES.
I'M GOING FORWARD.

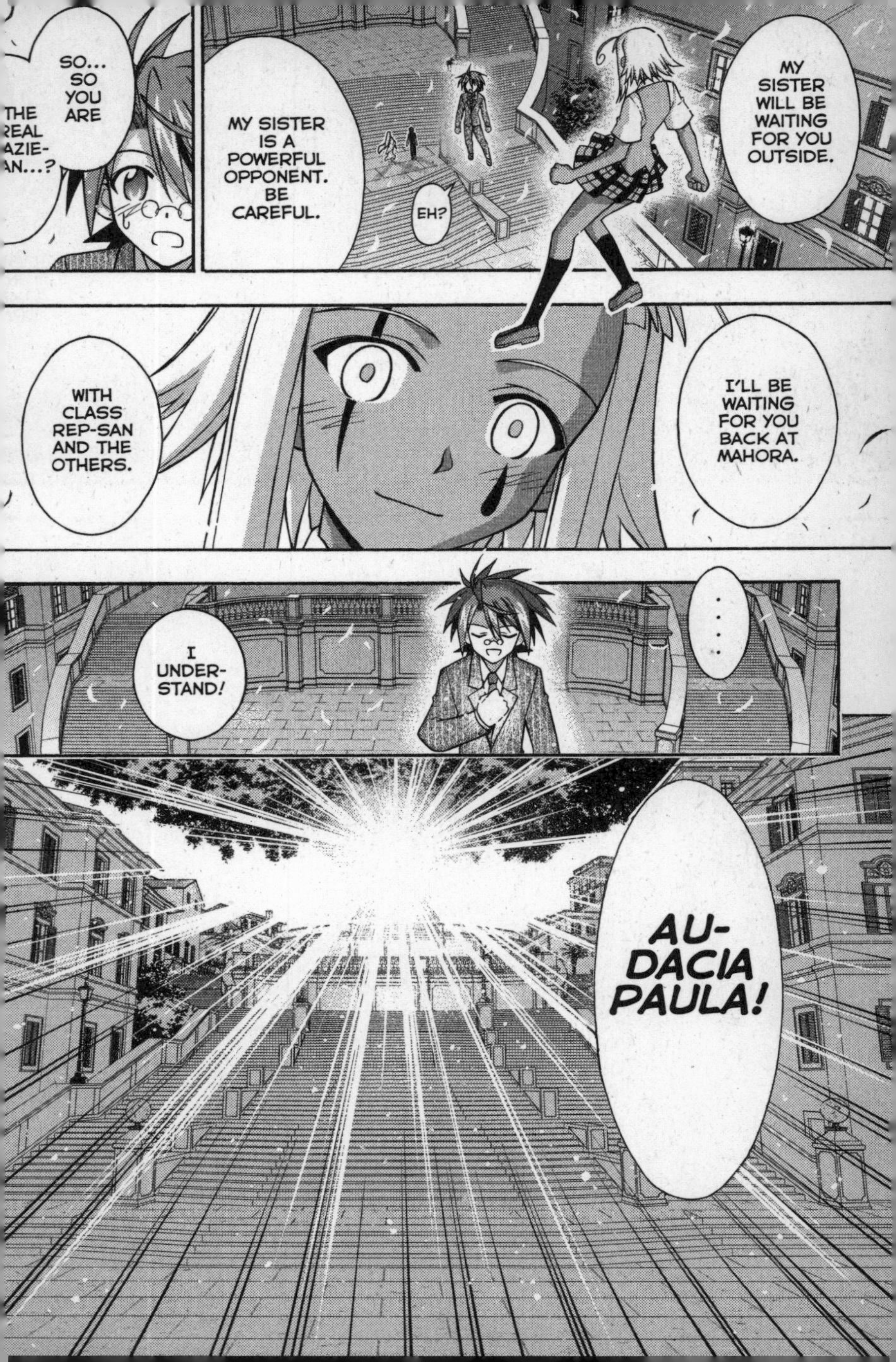
MY SISTER WILL BE WAITING FOR YOU OUTSIDE.
EH?
MY SISTER IS A POWERFUL OPPONENT. BE CAREFUL.
SO... SO YOU ARE THE REAL AZIE- AN...?
I'LL BE WAITING FOR YOU BACK AT MAHORA.
WITH CLASS REP-SAN AND THE OTHERS.
....
I UNDER- STAND!
AU- DACIA PAULA!

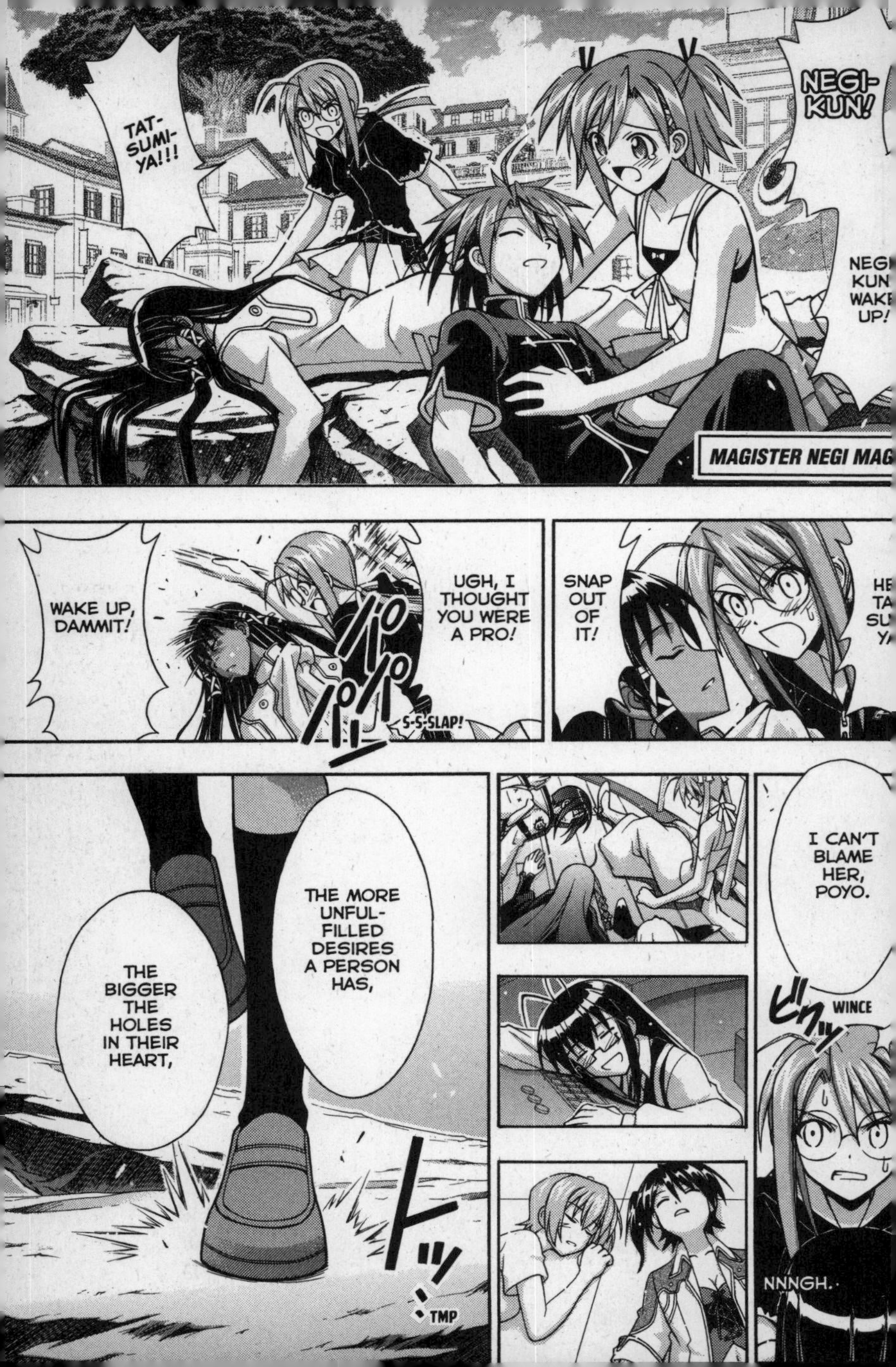
NEGI-KUN!
NEGI KUN WAKE UP!
TAT-SUMI-YA!!!
MAGISTER NEGI MAG
SNAP OUT OF IT!
UGH, I THOUGHT YOU WERE A PRO!
WAKE UP, DAMMIT!
S-S-SLAP!
I CAN'T BLAME HER, POYO.
WINCE
NNNGH.
THE MORE UNFUL-FILLED DESIRES A PERSON HAS,
THE BIGGER THE HOLES IN THEIR HEART,
TMP

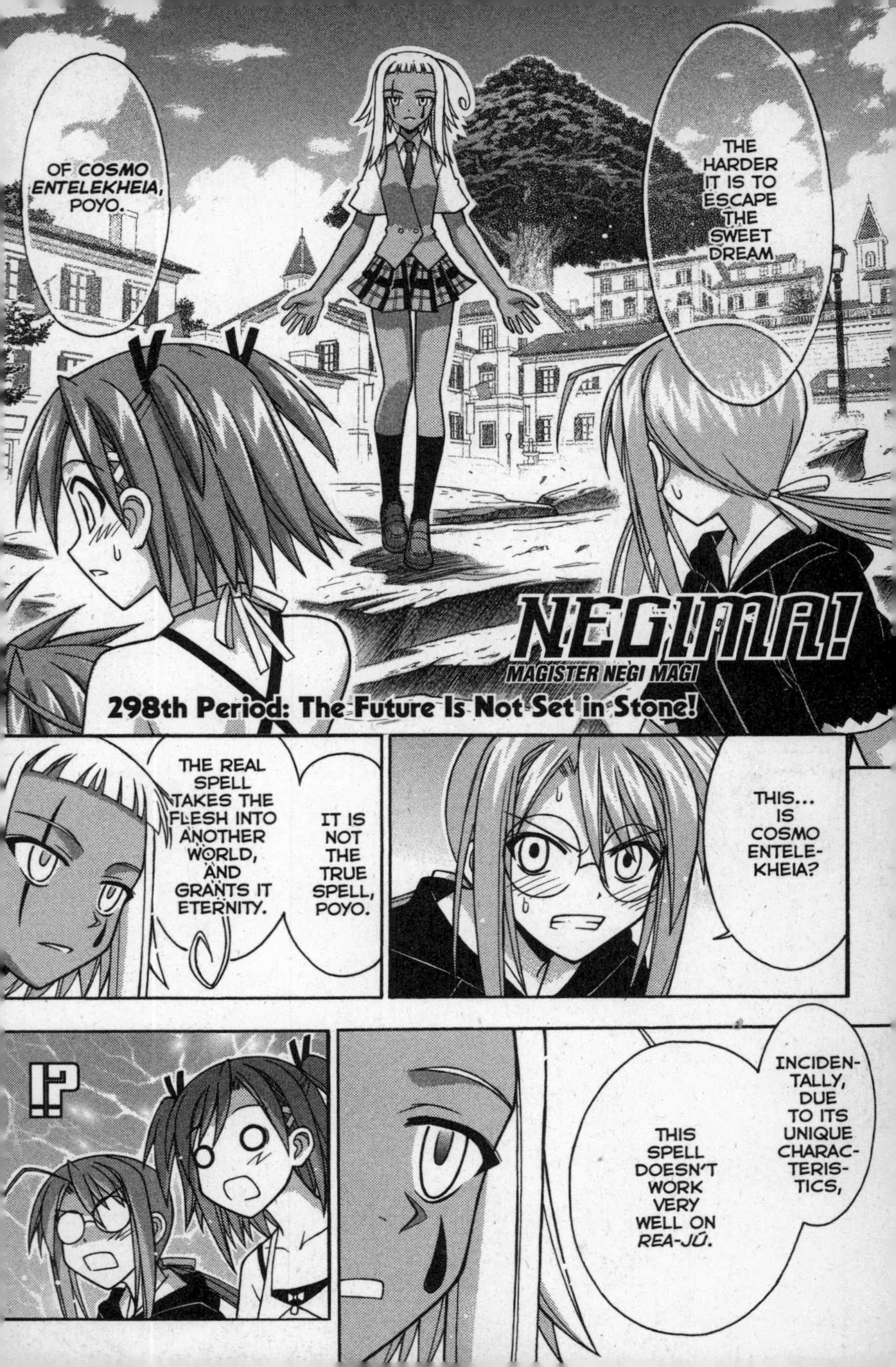
THE HARDER IT IS TO ESCAPE THE SWEET DREAM
OF COSMO ENTELEKHEIA, POYO.
NEGIMA!
MAGISTER NEGI MAGI
298th Period: The Future Is Not Set in Stone!
THIS... IS COSMO ENTELE-KHEIA?
IT IS NOT THE TRUE SPELL, POYO.
THE REAL SPELL TAKES THE FLESH INTO ANOTHER WORLD, AND GRANTS IT ETERNITY.
INCIDEN-TALLY, DUE TO ITS UNIQUE CHARAC-TERIS-TICS,
THIS SPELL DOESN'T WORK VERY WELL ON *REA-JŪ*.
!?

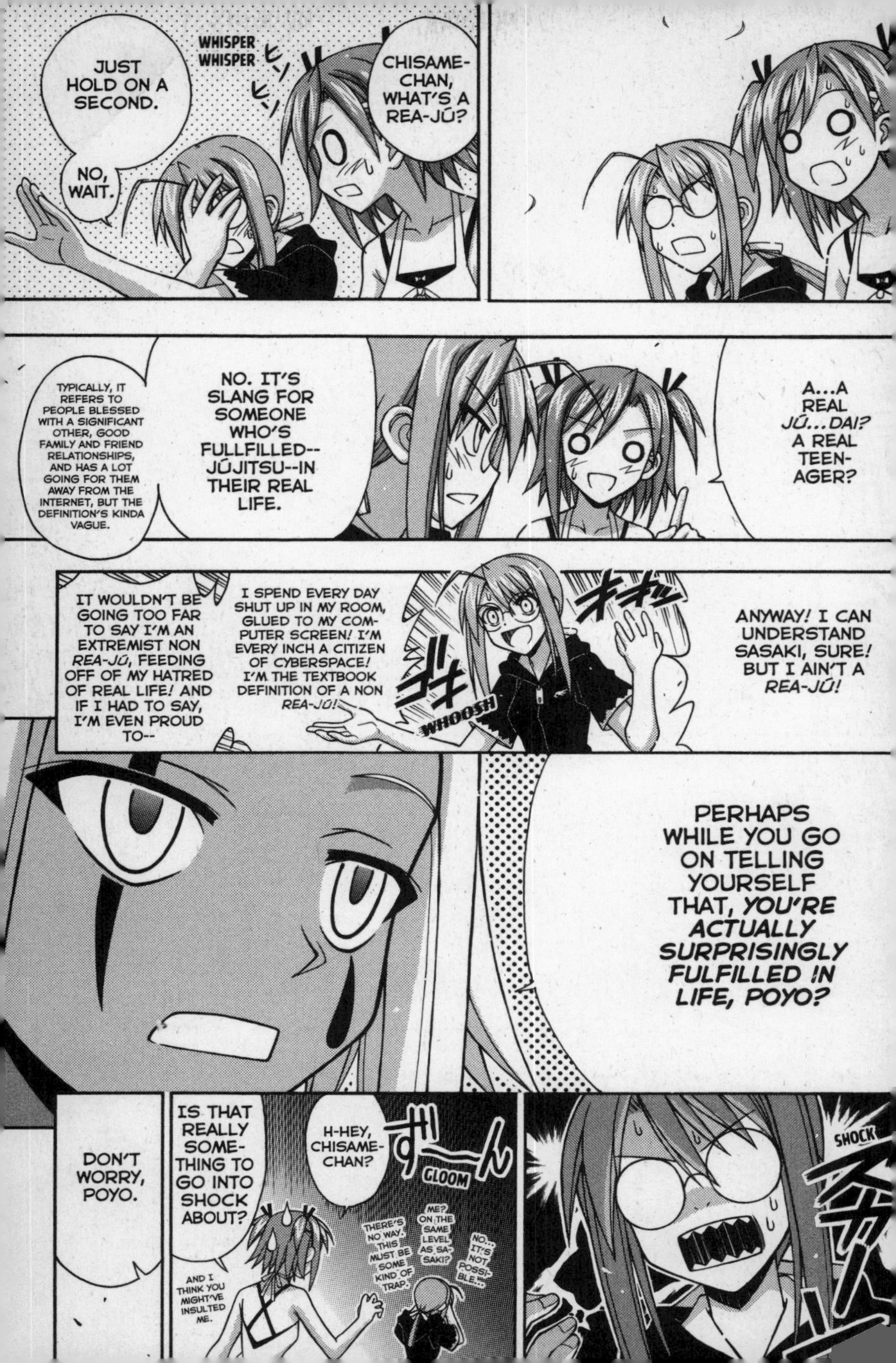
WHISPER WHISPER
CHISAME-CHAN, WHAT'S A REA-JŪ?
JUST HOLD ON A SECOND.
NO, WAIT.
A...A REAL JŪ...DAI? A REAL TEEN-AGER?
NO. IT'S SLANG FOR SOMEONE WHO'S FULLFILLED--JŪJITSU--IN THEIR REAL LIFE.
TYPICALLY, IT REFERS TO PEOPLE BLESSED WITH A SIGNIFICANT OTHER, GOOD FAMILY AND FRIEND RELATIONSHIPS, AND HAS A LOT GOING FOR THEM AWAY FROM THE INTERNET, BUT THE DEFINITION'S KINDA VAGUE.
ANYWAY! I CAN UNDERSTAND SASAKI, SURE! BUT I AIN'T A REA-JŪ!
WHOOSH
I SPEND EVERY DAY SHUT UP IN MY ROOM, GLUED TO MY COMPUTER SCREEN! I'M EVERY INCH A CITIZEN OF CYBERSPACE! I'M THE TEXTBOOK DEFINITION OF A NON REA-JŪ!
IT WOULDN'T BE GOING TOO FAR TO SAY I'M AN EXTREMIST NON REA-JŪ, FEEDING OFF OF MY HATRED OF REAL LIFE! AND IF I HAD TO SAY, I'M EVEN PROUD TO--
PERHAPS WHILE YOU GO ON TELLING YOURSELF THAT, YOU'RE ACTUALLY SURPRISINGLY FULFILLED IN LIFE, POYO?
SHOCK
H-HEY, CHISAME-CHAN?
GLOOM
IS THAT REALLY SOMETHING TO GO INTO SHOCK ABOUT?
NO... IT'S NOT POSSIBLE...
ME? ON THE SAME LEVEL AS SASAKI?
THERE'S NO WAY. THIS MUST BE SOME KIND OF TRAP.
AND I THINK YOU MIGHT'VE INSULTED ME.
DON'T WORRY, POYO.

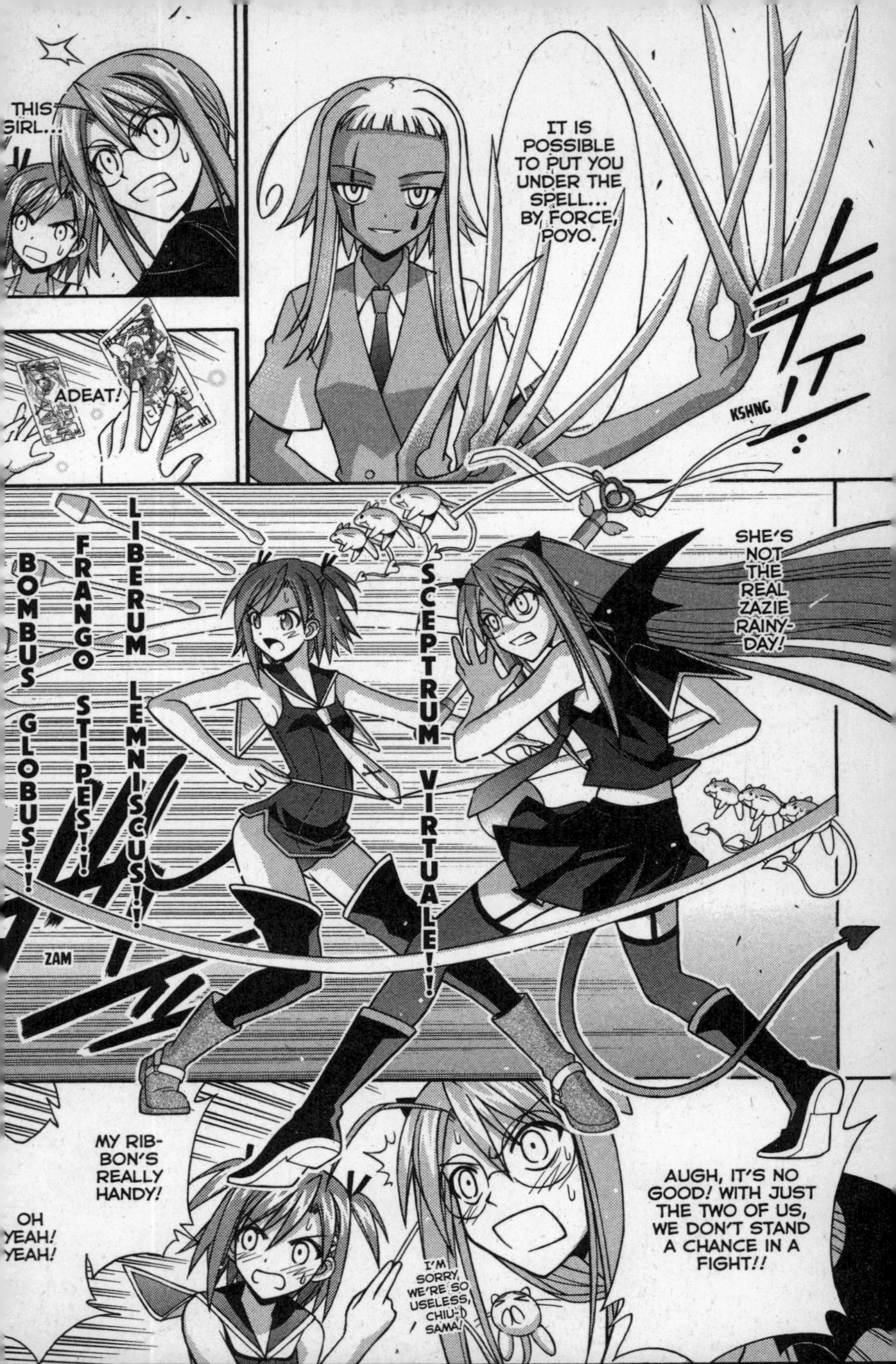
IT IS POSSIBLE TO PUT YOU UNDER THE SPELL... BY FORCE, POYO.
KSHNG
THIS GIRL...
ADEAT!
SHE'S NOT THE REAL ZAZIE RAINY-DAY!
SCEPTRUM VIRTUALE!!
LIBERUM LEMNISCUS!!
FRANGO STIPES!!
BOMBUS GLOBUS!!
ZAM
AUGH, IT'S NO GOOD! WITH JUST THE TWO OF US, WE DON'T STAND A CHANCE IN A FIGHT!!
I'M SORRY, WE'RE SO USELESS, CHIU-SAMA!
MY RIBBON'S REALLY HANDY!
OH YEAH! YEAH!

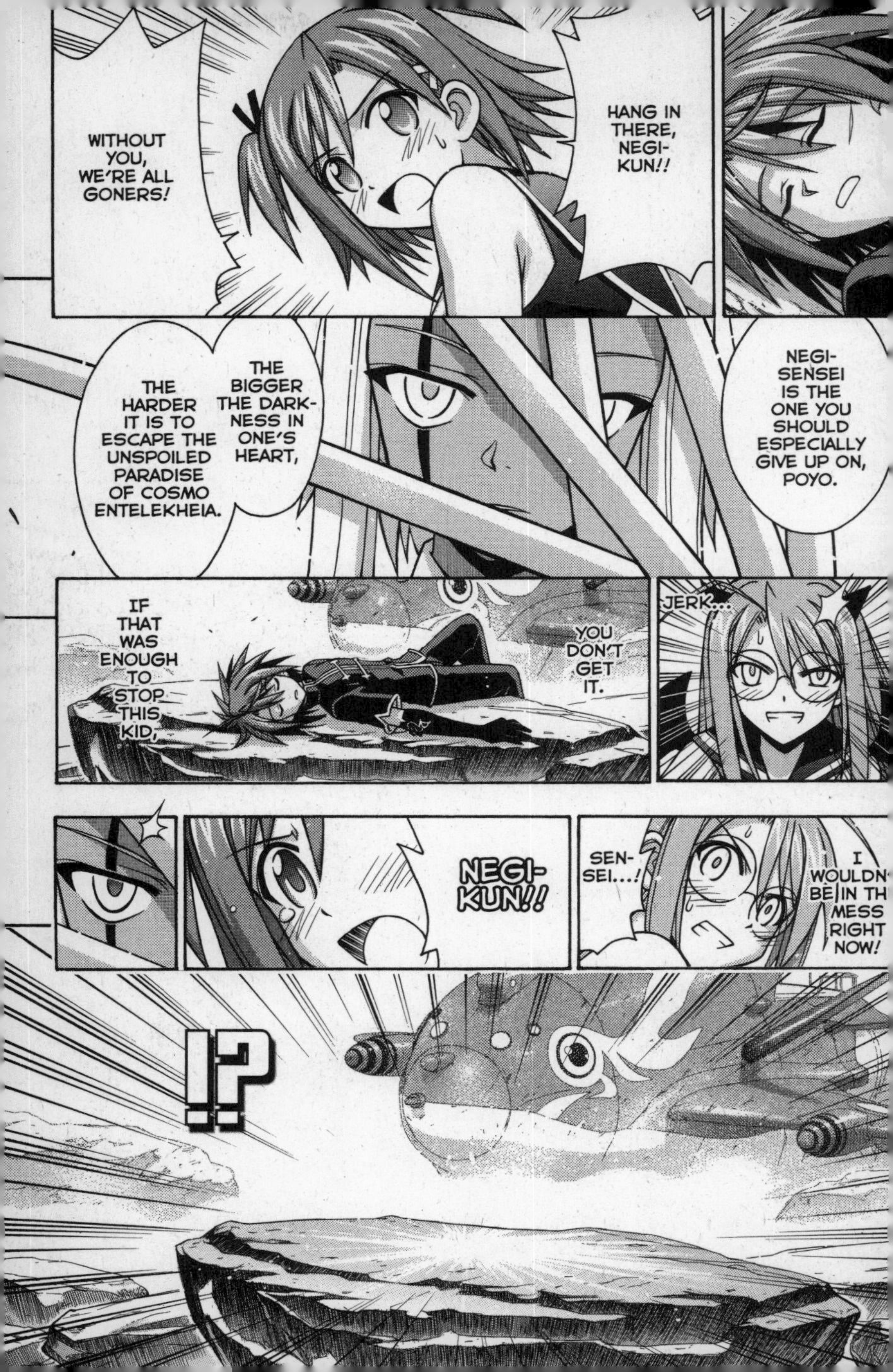
HANG IN THERE, NEGI-KUN!!
WITHOUT YOU, WE'RE ALL GONERS!
NEGI-SENSEI IS THE ONE YOU SHOULD ESPECIALLY GIVE UP ON, POYO.
THE BIGGER THE DARKNESS IN ONE'S HEART,
THE HARDER IT IS TO ESCAPE THE UNSPOILED PARADISE OF COSMO ENTELEKHEIA.
JERK...
YOU DON'T GET IT.
IF THAT WAS ENOUGH TO STOP THIS KID,
I WOULDN BE IN TH MESS RIGHT NOW!
SEN-SEI...!
NEGI-KUN!!
!?

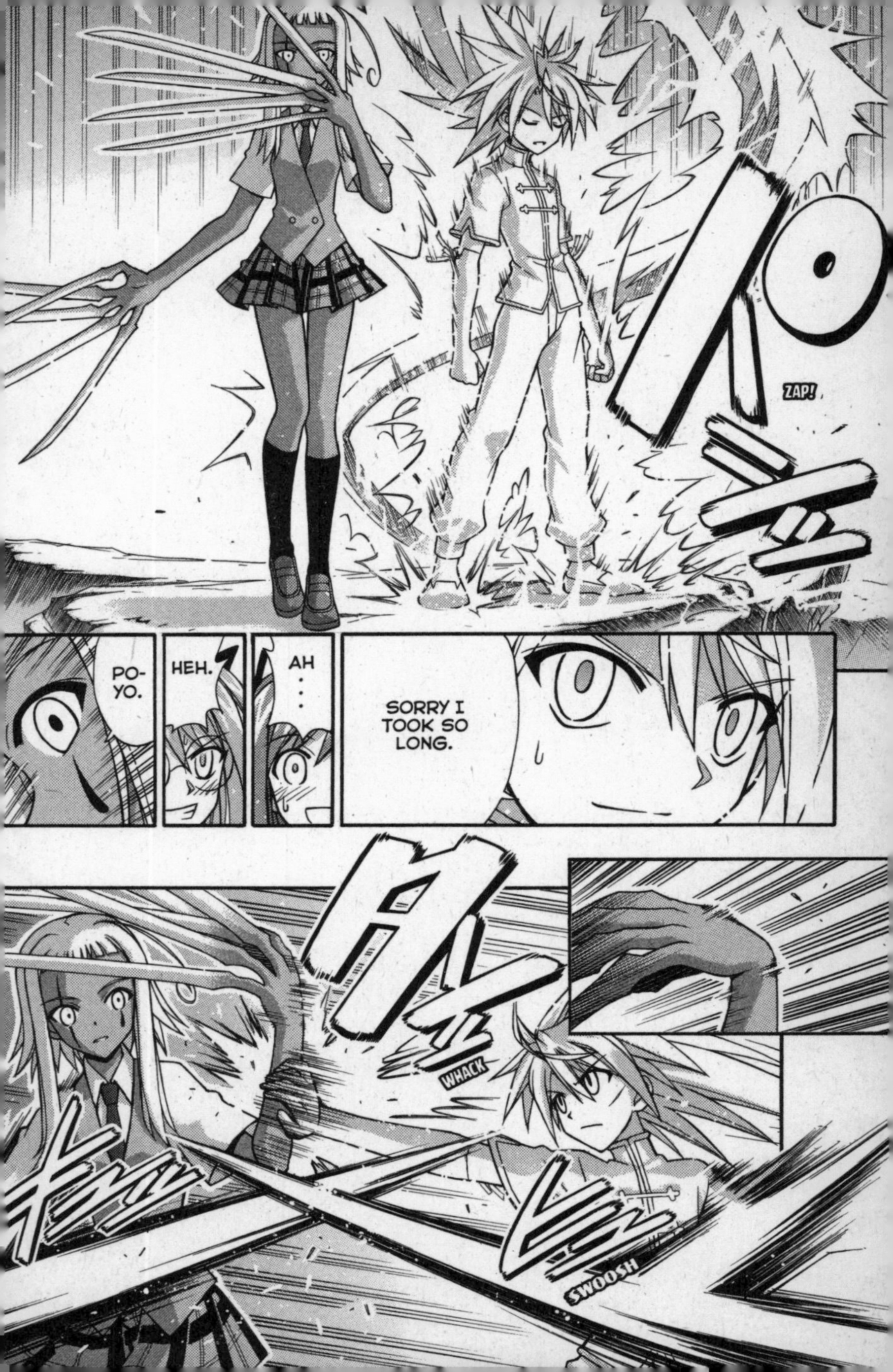
ZAP!
SORRY I TOOK SO LONG.
AH . . .
HEH.
PO-YO.
WHACK
SWOOSH

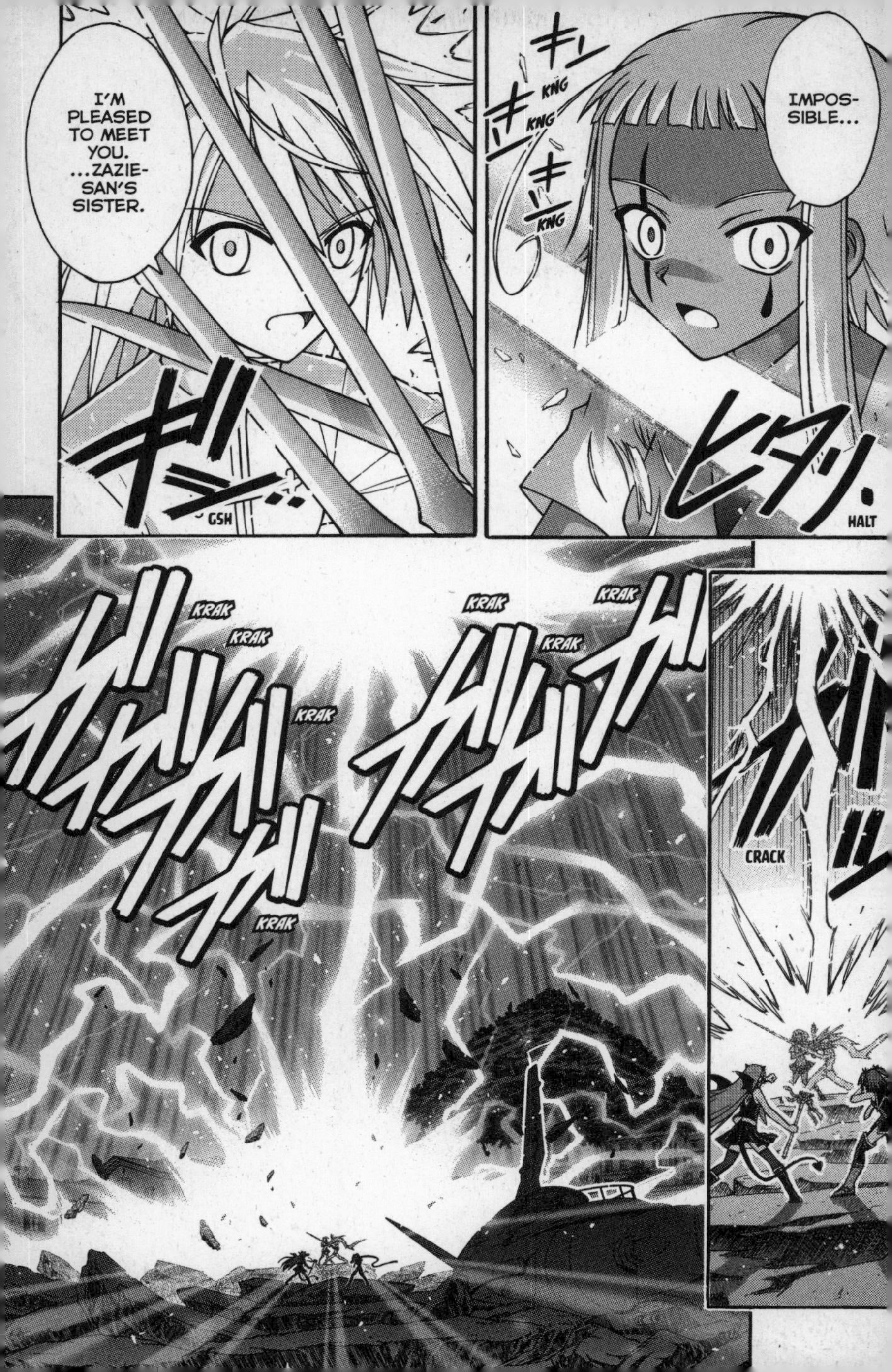

IMPOS-SIBLE...
KNG
KNG
KNG
HALT
I'M PLEASED TO MEET YOU. ...ZAZIE-SAN'S SISTER.
GSH
CRACK
KRAK
KRAK
KRAK
KRAK
KRAK
KRAK

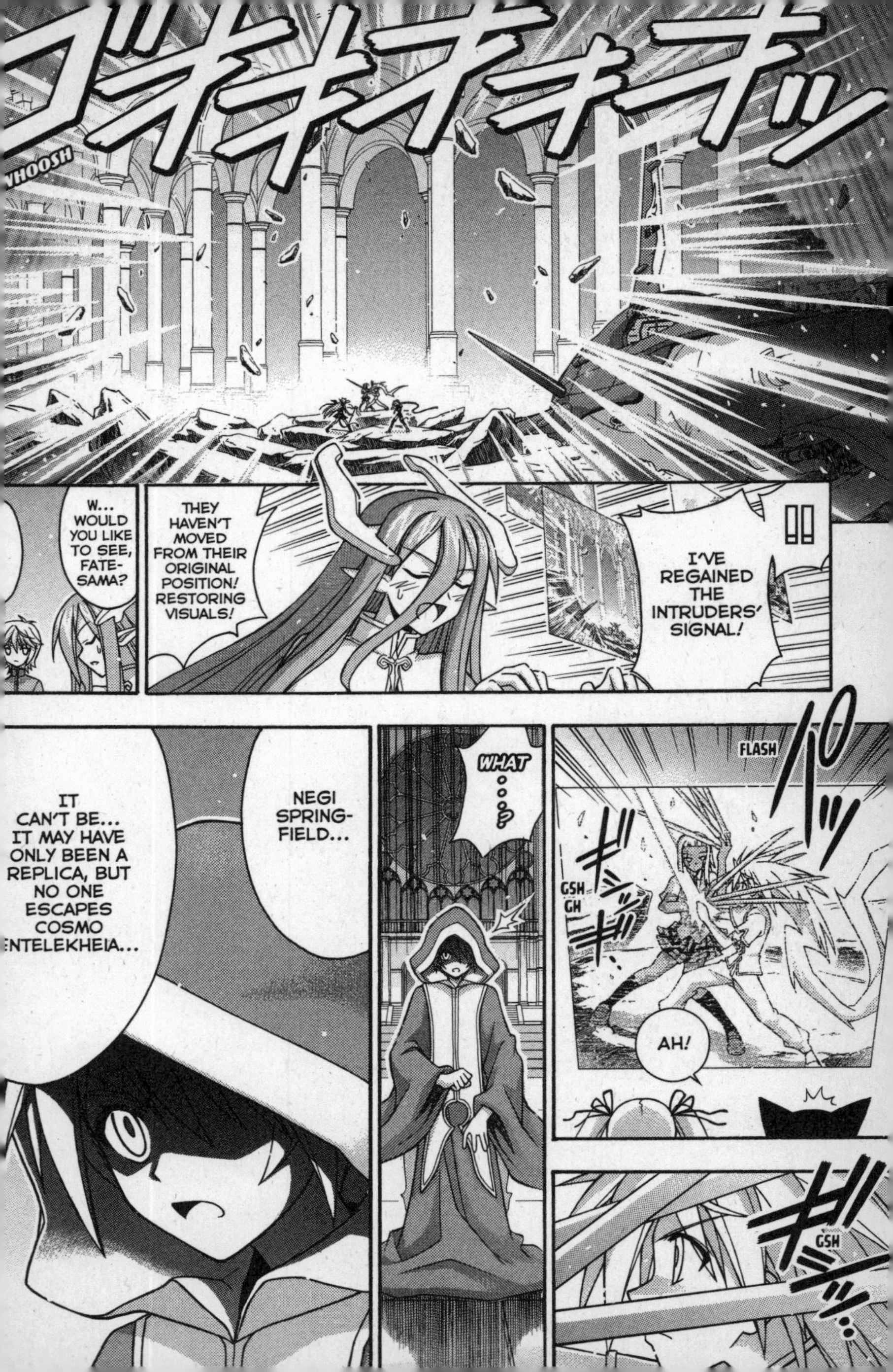
WHOOSH
!!
I'VE REGAINED THE INTRUDERS' SIGNAL!
THEY HAVEN'T MOVED FROM THEIR ORIGINAL POSITION! RESTORING VISUALS!
W... WOULD YOU LIKE TO SEE, FATE-SAMA?
FLASH
GSH GH
AH!
GSH
WHAT...?
NEGI SPRING-FIELD...
IT CAN'T BE... IT MAY HAVE ONLY BEEN A REPLICA, BUT NO ONE ESCAPES COSMO ENTELEKHEIA...

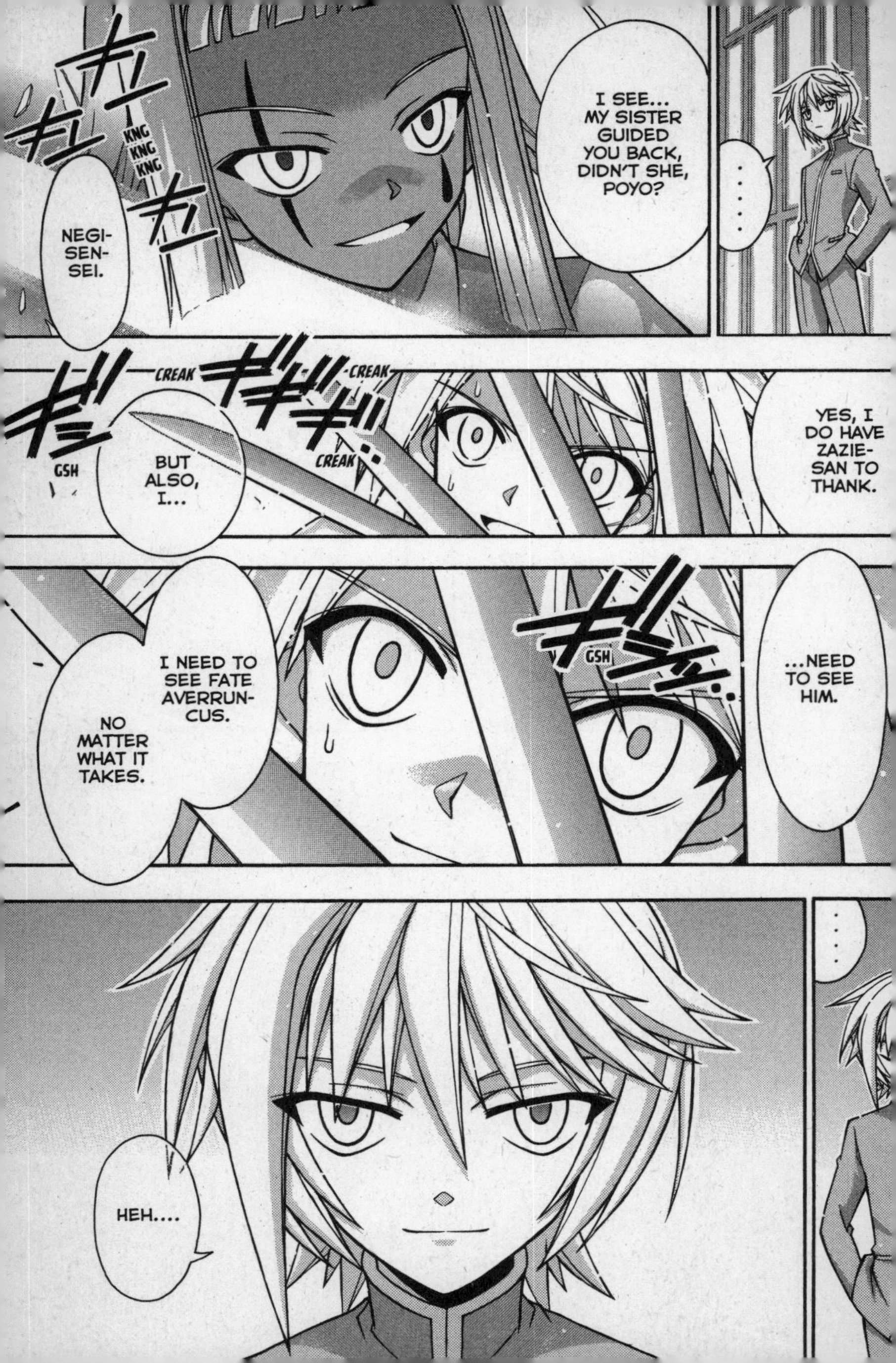
....
I SEE... MY SISTER GUIDED YOU BACK, DIDN'T SHE, POYO?
KNG KNG KNG
NEGI-SENSEI.
YES, I DO HAVE ZAZIE-SAN TO THANK.
CREAK
CREAK
CREAK
BUT ALSO, I...
GSH
...NEED TO SEE HIM.
GSH
I NEED TO SEE FATE AVERRUNCUS.
NO MATTER WHAT IT TAKES.
....
HEH....

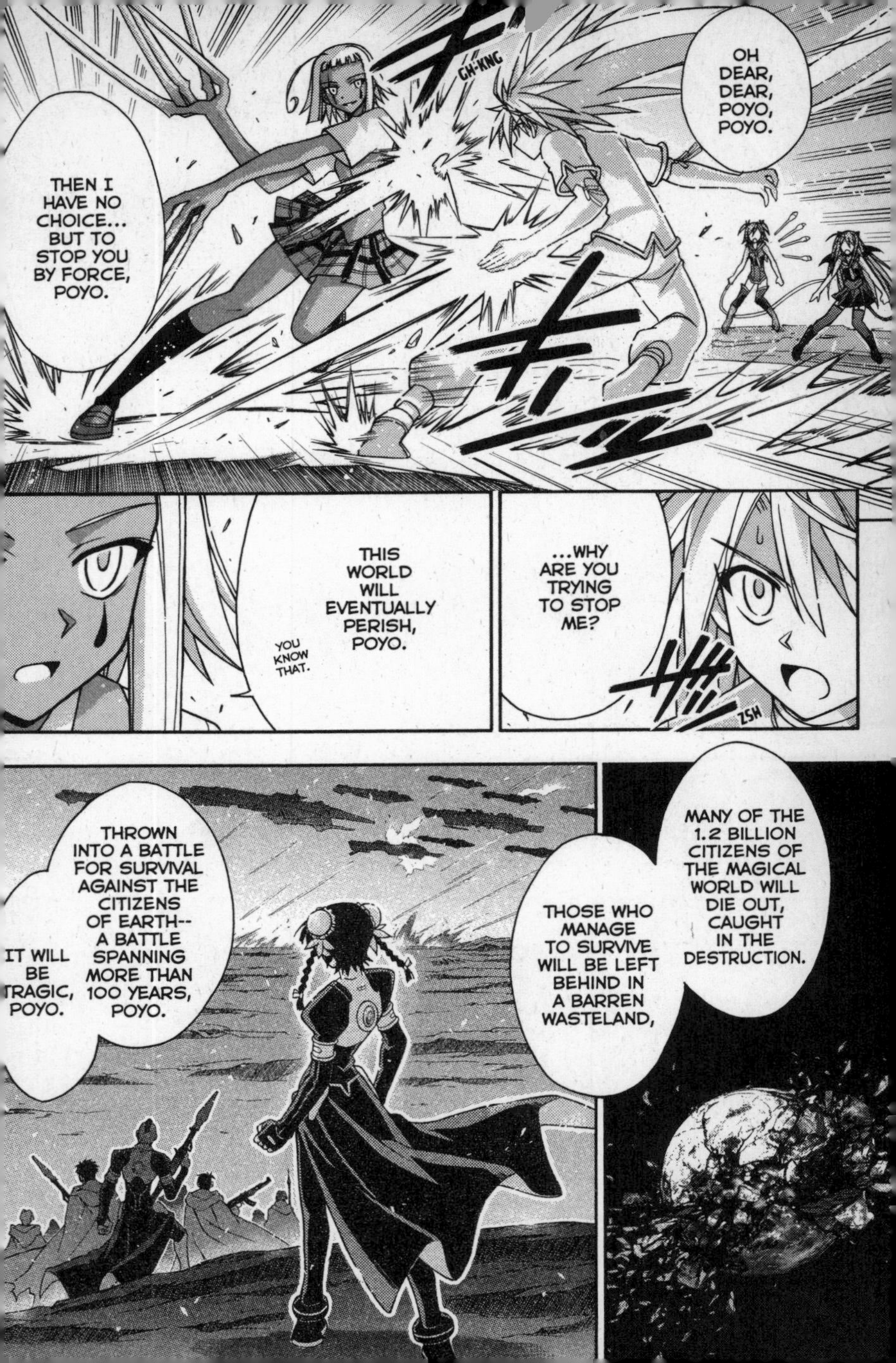
OH DEAR, DEAR, POYO, POYO.
CH-KNG
THEN I HAVE NO CHOICE... BUT TO STOP YOU BY FORCE, POYO.
...WHY ARE YOU TRYING TO STOP ME?
ZSH
THIS WORLD WILL EVENTUALLY PERISH, POYO.
YOU KNOW THAT.
MANY OF THE 1.2 BILLION CITIZENS OF THE MAGICAL WORLD WILL DIE OUT, CAUGHT IN THE DESTRUCTION.
THOSE WHO MANAGE TO SURVIVE WILL BE LEFT BEHIND IN A BARREN WASTELAND,
THROWN INTO A BATTLE FOR SURVIVAL AGAINST THE CITIZENS OF EARTH-- A BATTLE SPANNING MORE THAN 100 YEARS, POYO.
IT WILL BE TRAGIC, POYO.

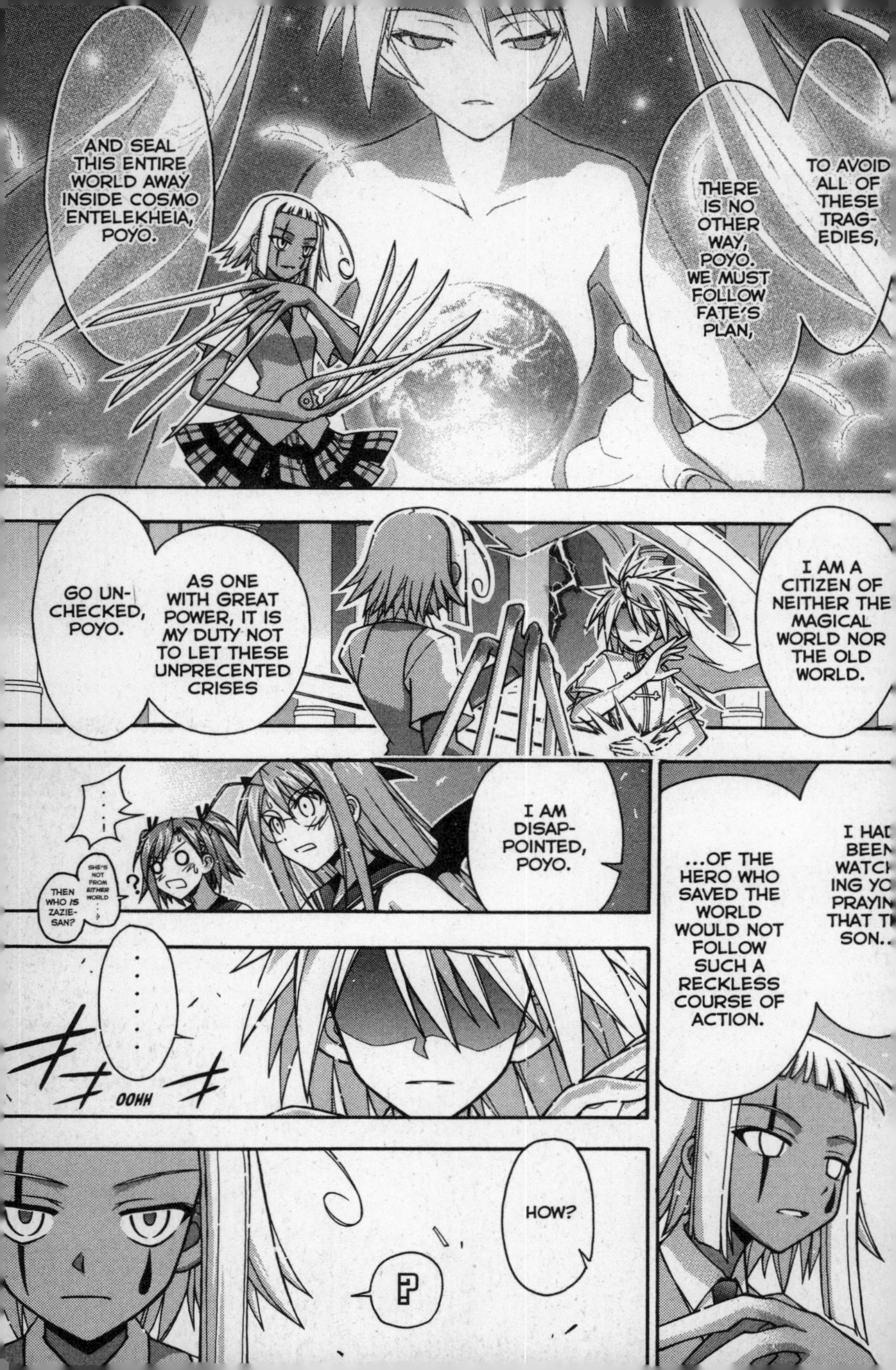
TO AVOID ALL OF THESE TRAG-EDIES,
THERE IS NO OTHER WAY, POYO. WE MUST FOLLOW FATE'S PLAN,
AND SEAL THIS ENTIRE WORLD AWAY INSIDE COSMO ENTELEKHEIA, POYO.
I AM A CITIZEN OF NEITHER THE MAGICAL WORLD NOR THE OLD WORLD.
AS ONE WITH GREAT POWER, IT IS MY DUTY NOT TO LET THESE UNPRECENTED CRISES
GO UN-CHECKED, POYO.
I HAD BEEN WATCH ING YO PRAYIN THAT TI SON..
...OF THE HERO WHO SAVED THE WORLD WOULD NOT FOLLOW SUCH A RECKLESS COURSE OF ACTION.
I AM DISAP-POINTED, POYO.
...!
SHE'S NOT FROM EITHER WORLD...?
THEN WHO IS ZAZIE-SAN?
......
OOHH
HOW?
?

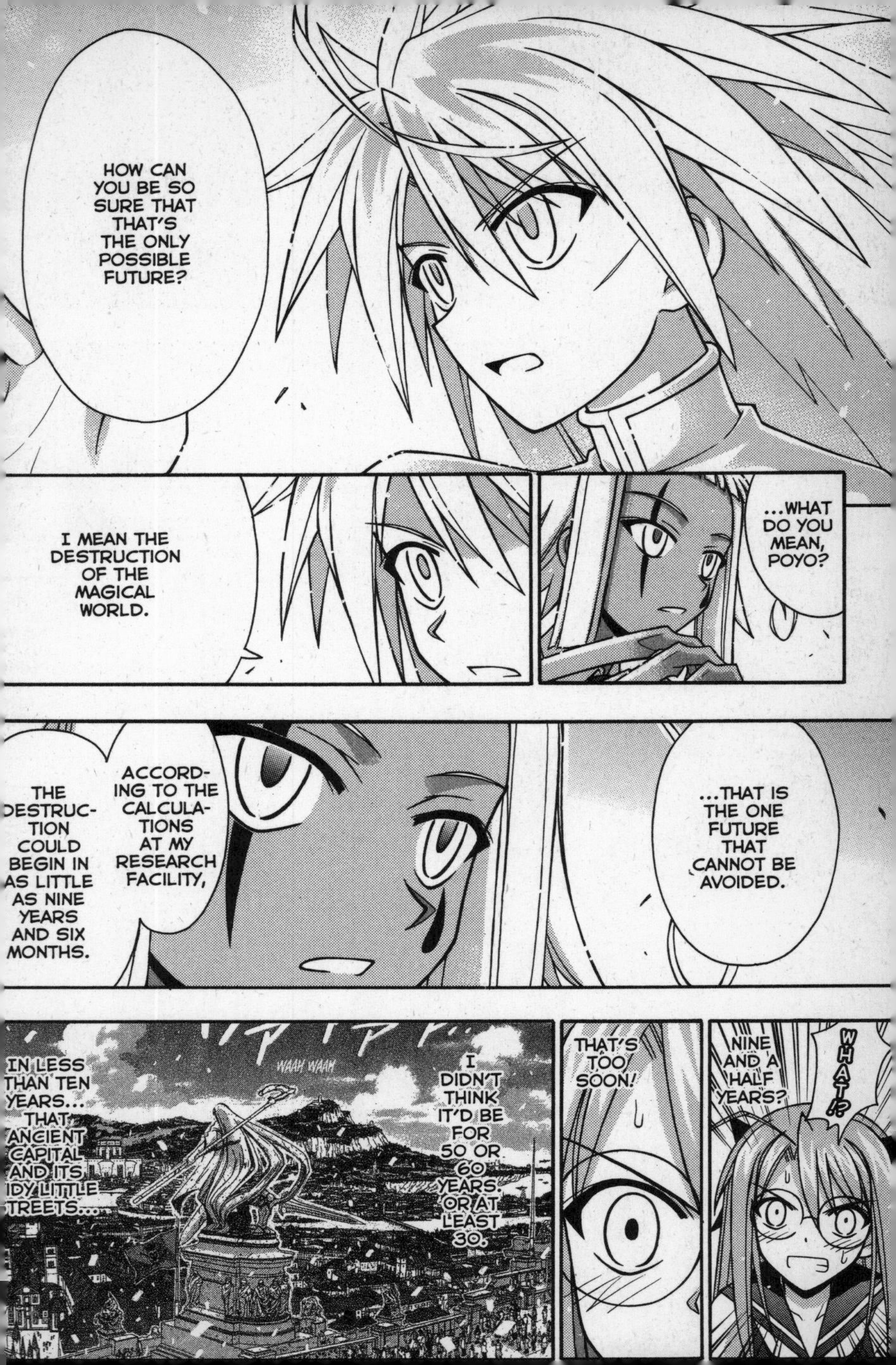
HOW CAN YOU BE SO SURE THAT THAT'S THE ONLY POSSIBLE FUTURE?
...WHAT DO YOU MEAN, POYO?
I MEAN THE DESTRUCTION OF THE MAGICAL WORLD.
...THAT IS THE ONE FUTURE THAT CANNOT BE AVOIDED.
ACCORDING TO THE CALCULATIONS AT MY RESEARCH FACILITY,
THE DESTRUCTION COULD BEGIN IN AS LITTLE AS NINE YEARS AND SIX MONTHS.
WHAT!?
NINE AND A HALF YEARS?
THAT'S TOO SOON!
WAAH WAAH
IN LESS THAN TEN YEARS... THAT ANCIENT CAPITAL AND ITS IDY LITTLE TREETS...
I DIDN'T THINK IT'D BE FOR 50 OR 60 YEARS, OR AT LEAST 30.

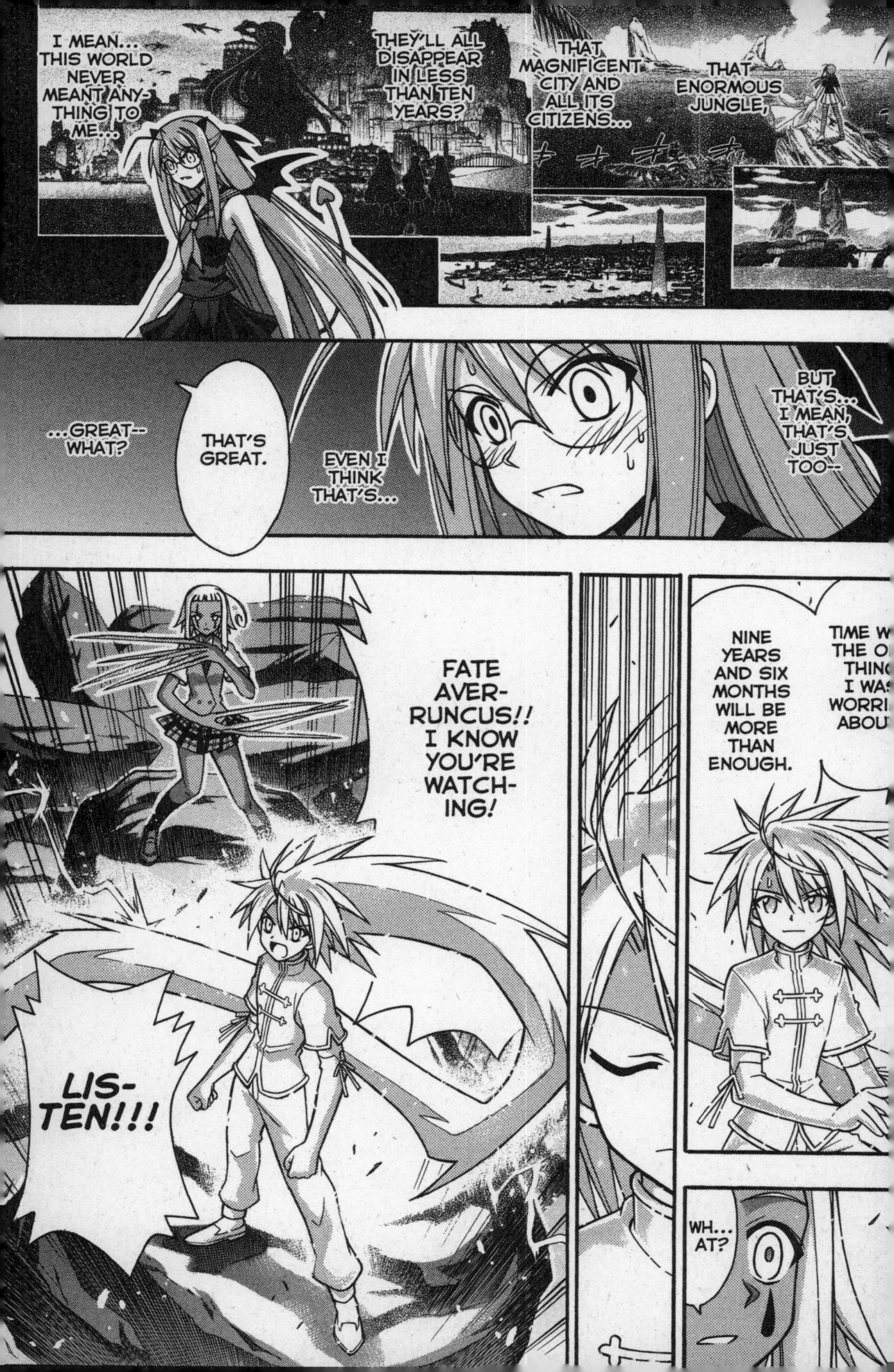
THAT ENORMOUS JUNGLE,
THAT MAGNIFICENT CITY AND ALL ITS CITIZENS...
THEY'LL ALL DISAPPEAR IN LESS THAN TEN YEARS?
I MEAN... THIS WORLD NEVER MEANT ANY-THING TO ME...
BUT THAT'S... I MEAN, THAT'S JUST TOO--
EVEN I THINK THAT'S...
THAT'S GREAT.
...GREAT-- WHAT?
TIME W THE O THING I WAS WORRI ABOU
NINE YEARS AND SIX MONTHS WILL BE MORE THAN ENOUGH.
WH... AT?
FATE AVER-RUNCUS!! I KNOW YOU'RE WATCH-ING!
LIS-TEN!!!

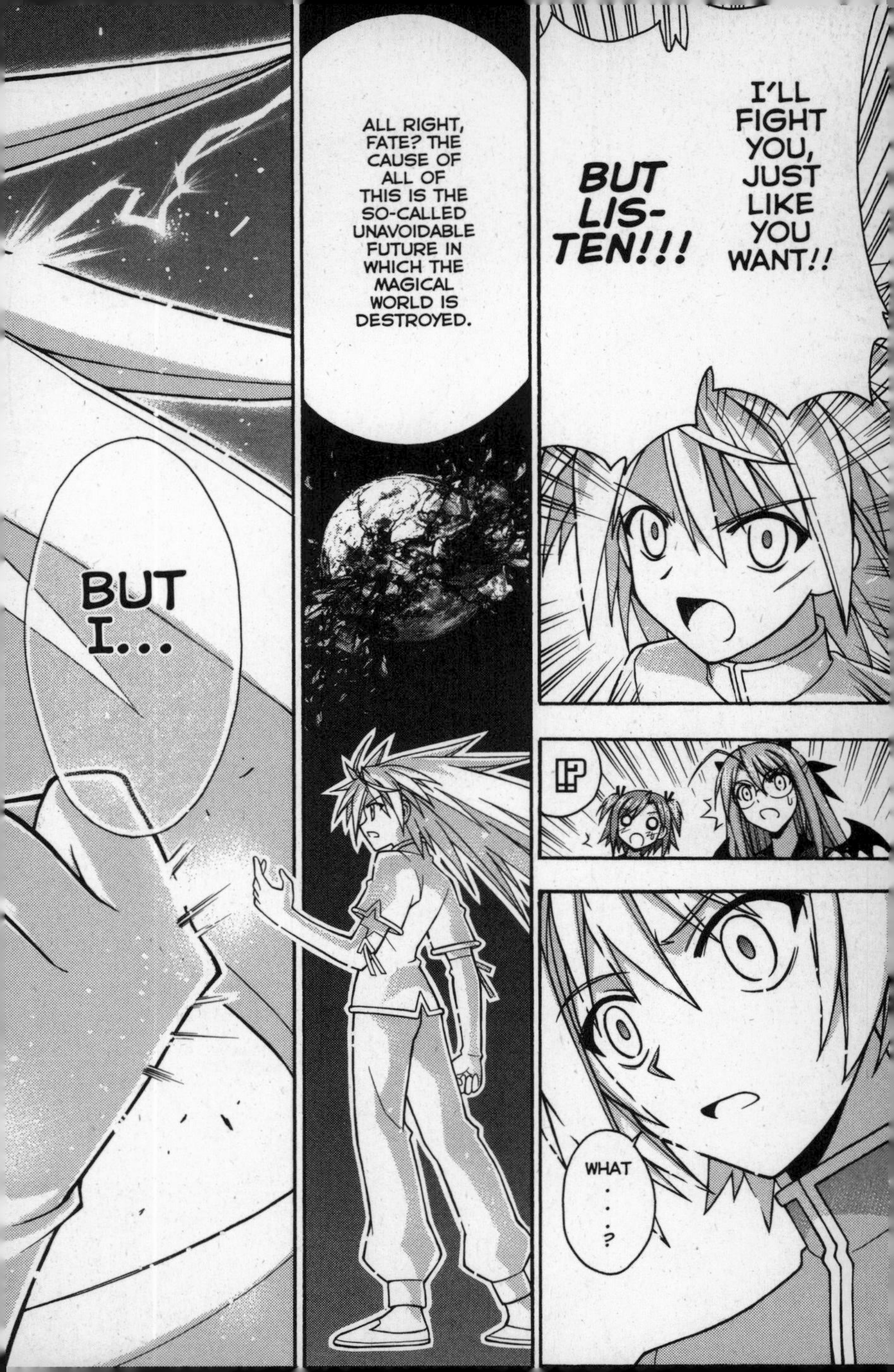
I'LL FIGHT YOU, JUST LIKE YOU WANT!!
BUT LIS-TEN!!!
!?
WHAT...?
ALL RIGHT, FATE? THE CAUSE OF ALL OF THIS IS THE SO-CALLED UNAVOIDABLE FUTURE IN WHICH THE MAGICAL WORLD IS DESTROYED.
BUT I...

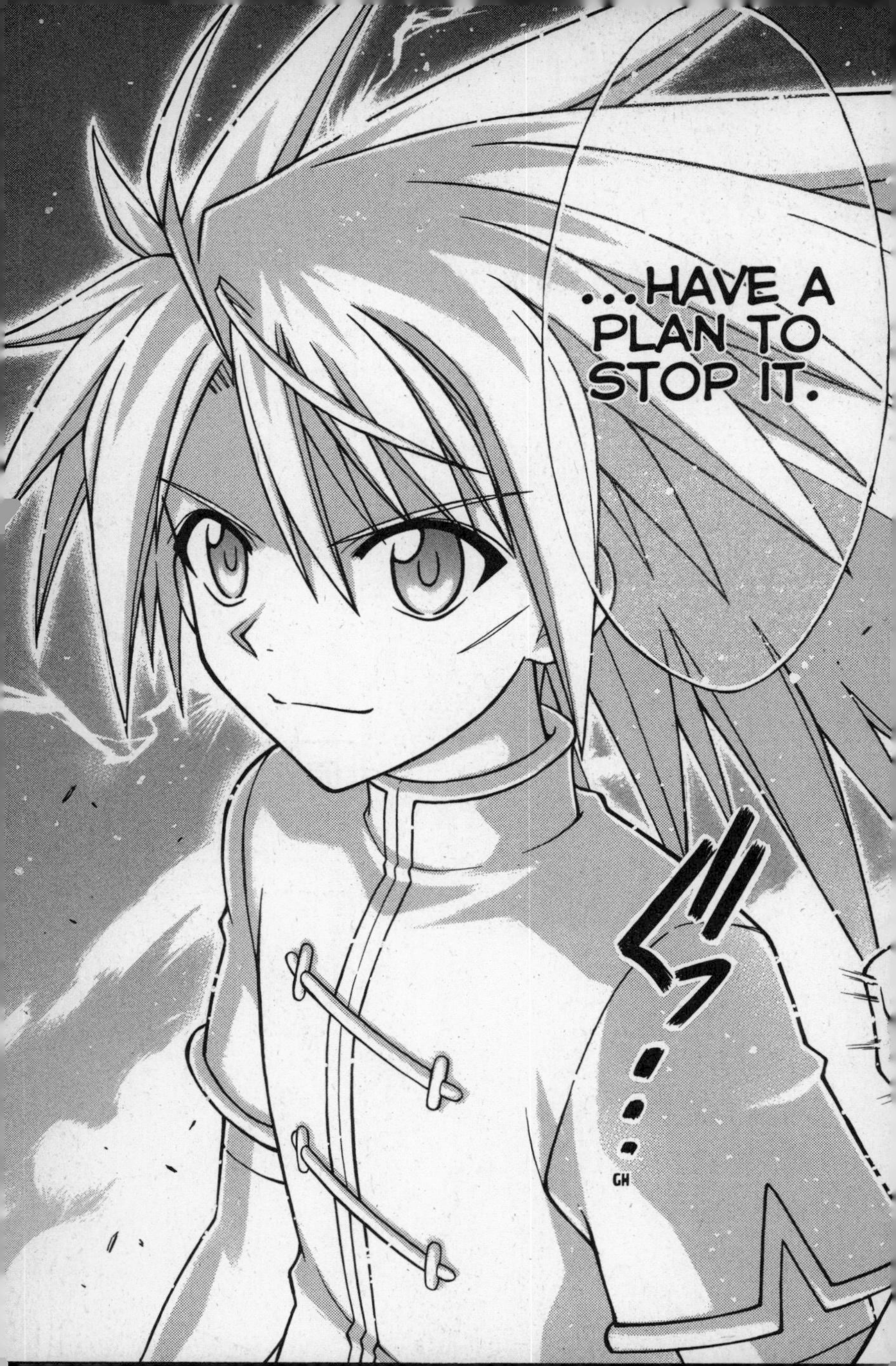
...HAVE A PLAN TO STOP IT.
GH

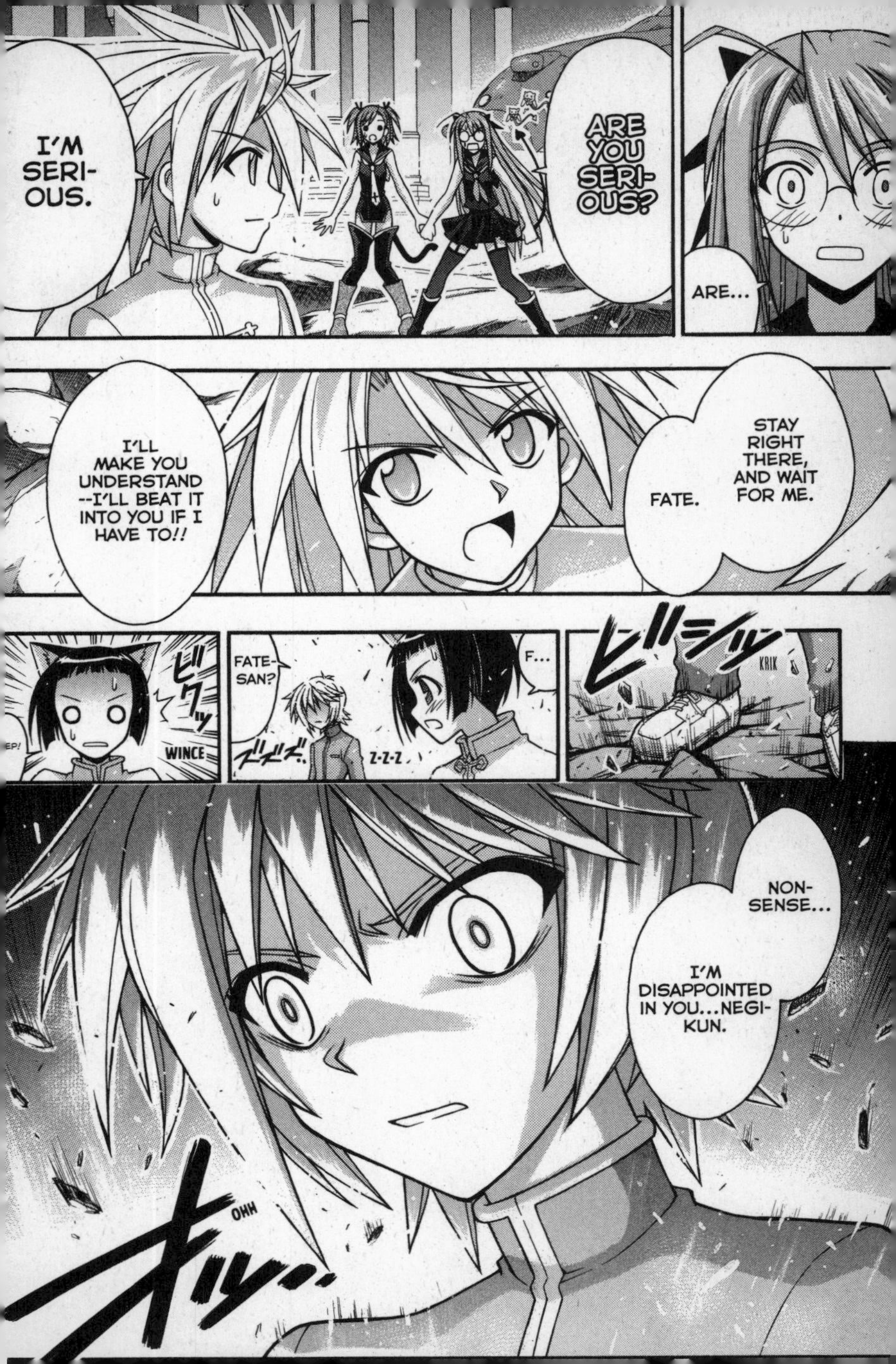
ARE...
ARE YOU SERI-OUS?
I'M SERI-OUS.
FATE. STAY RIGHT THERE, AND WAIT FOR ME.
I'LL MAKE YOU UNDERSTAND --I'LL BEAT IT INTO YOU IF I HAVE TO!!
KRIK
F...
FATE-SAN?
Z-Z-Z
WINCE
EP!
NON-SENSE...
I'M DISAPPOINTED IN YOU...NEGI-KUN.
OHH

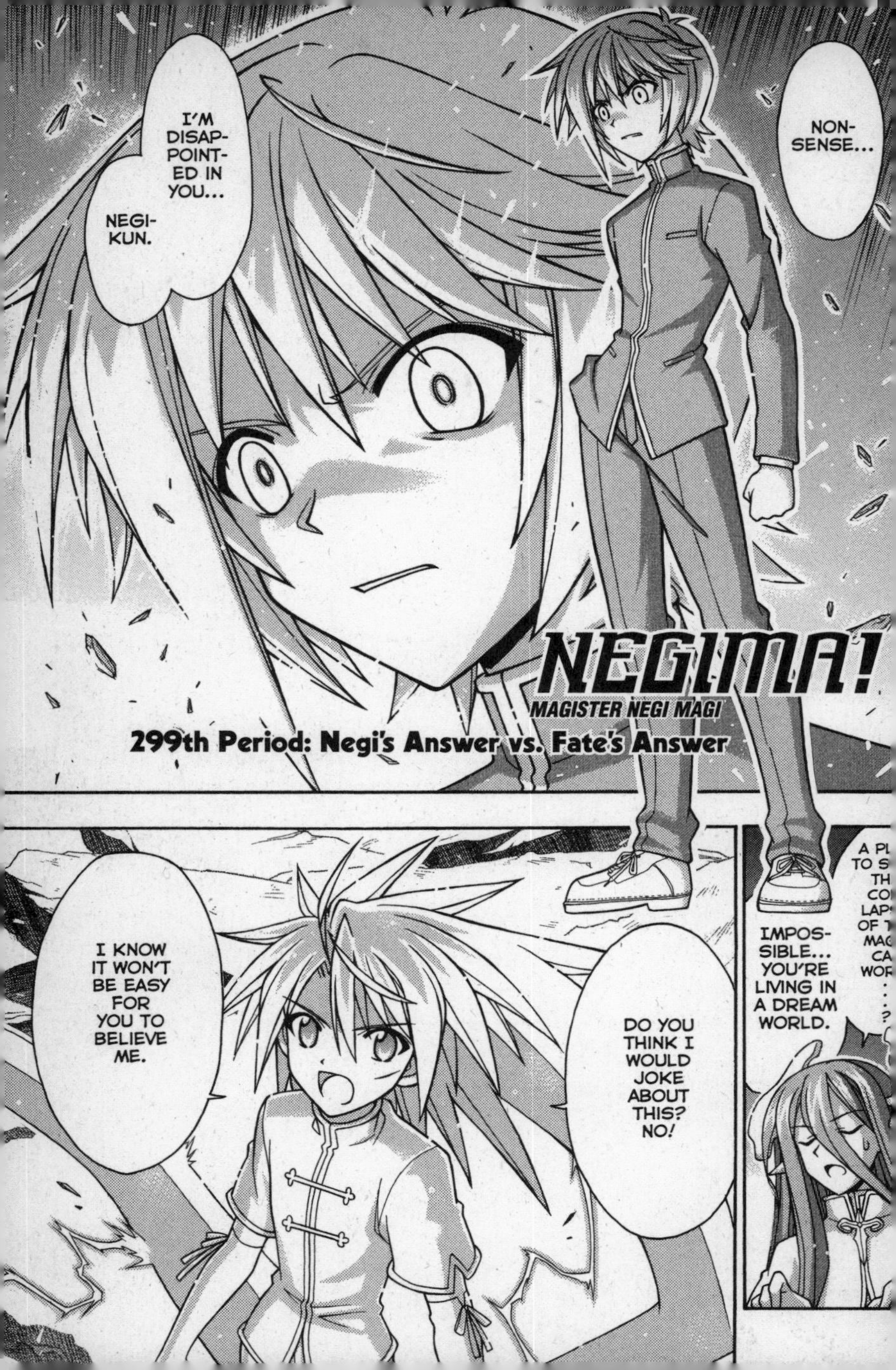
NONSENSE...
I'M DISAPPOINTED IN YOU... NEGI-KUN.
NEGIMA!
MAGISTER NEGI MAGI
299th Period: Negi's Answer vs. Fate's Answer
IMPOSSIBLE... YOU'RE LIVING IN A DREAM WORLD.
DO YOU THINK I WOULD JOKE ABOUT THIS? NO!
I KNOW IT WON'T BE EASY FOR YOU TO BELIEVE ME.

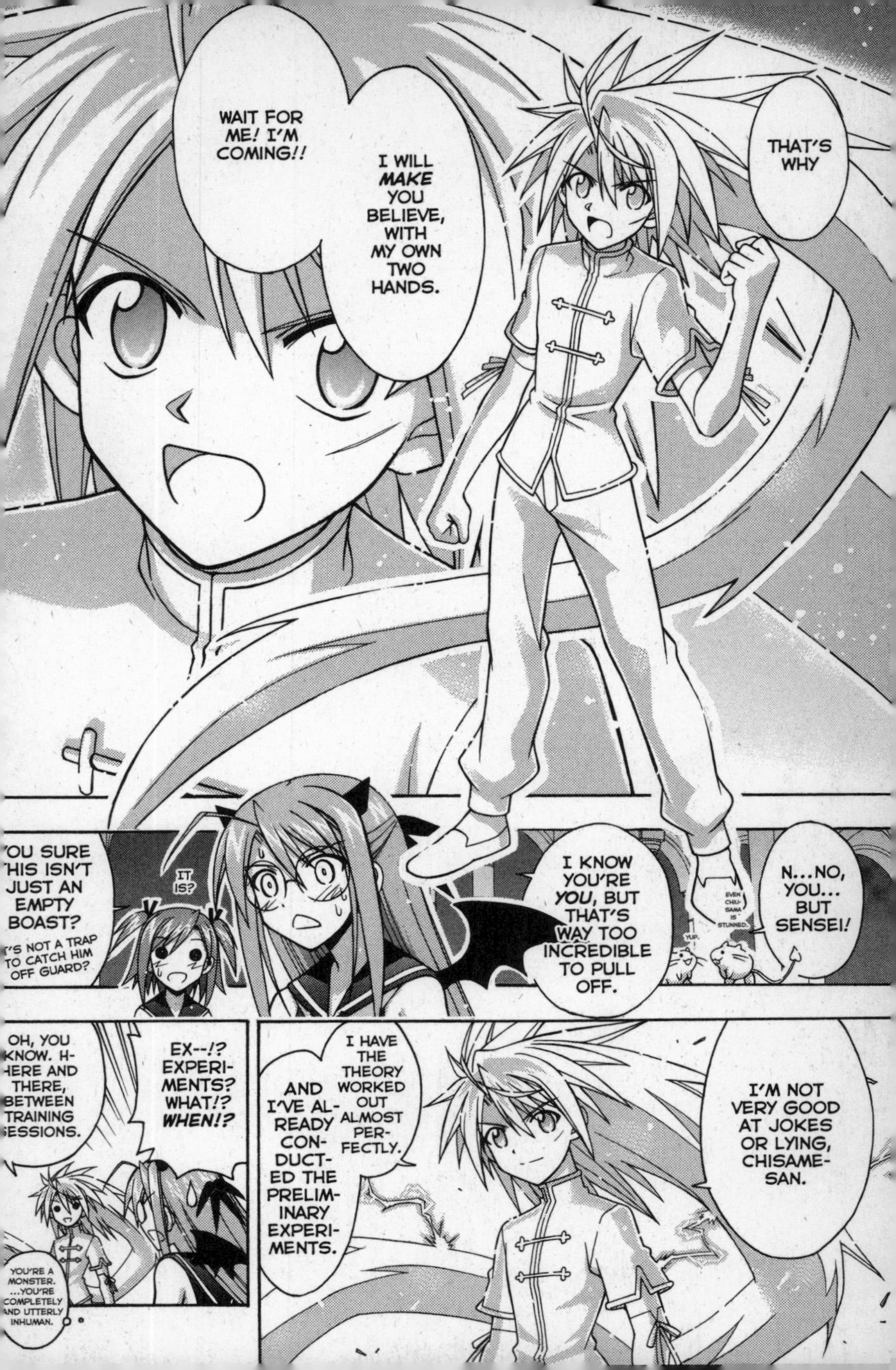
THAT'S WHY
I WILL *MAKE* YOU BELIEVE, WITH MY OWN TWO HANDS.
WAIT FOR ME! I'M COMING!!
N...NO, YOU... BUT SENSEI!
EVEN CHIU-SAMA IS STUNNED.
YUP.
I KNOW YOU'RE *YOU*, BUT THAT'S WAY TOO INCREDIBLE TO PULL OFF.
IT IS?
OU SURE HIS ISN'T JUST AN EMPTY BOAST?
'S NOT A TRAP TO CATCH HIM OFF GUARD?
I'M NOT VERY GOOD AT JOKES OR LYING, CHISAME-SAN.
I HAVE THE THEORY WORKED OUT ALMOST PERFECTLY.
AND I'VE ALREADY CONDUCTED THE PRELIMINARY EXPERIMENTS.
EX--!? EXPERIMENTS? WHAT!? *WHEN!?*
OH, YOU NOW. H-HERE AND THERE, BETWEEN TRAINING ESSIONS.
YOU'RE A MONSTER. ...YOU'RE COMPLETELY AND UTTERLY INHUMAN.

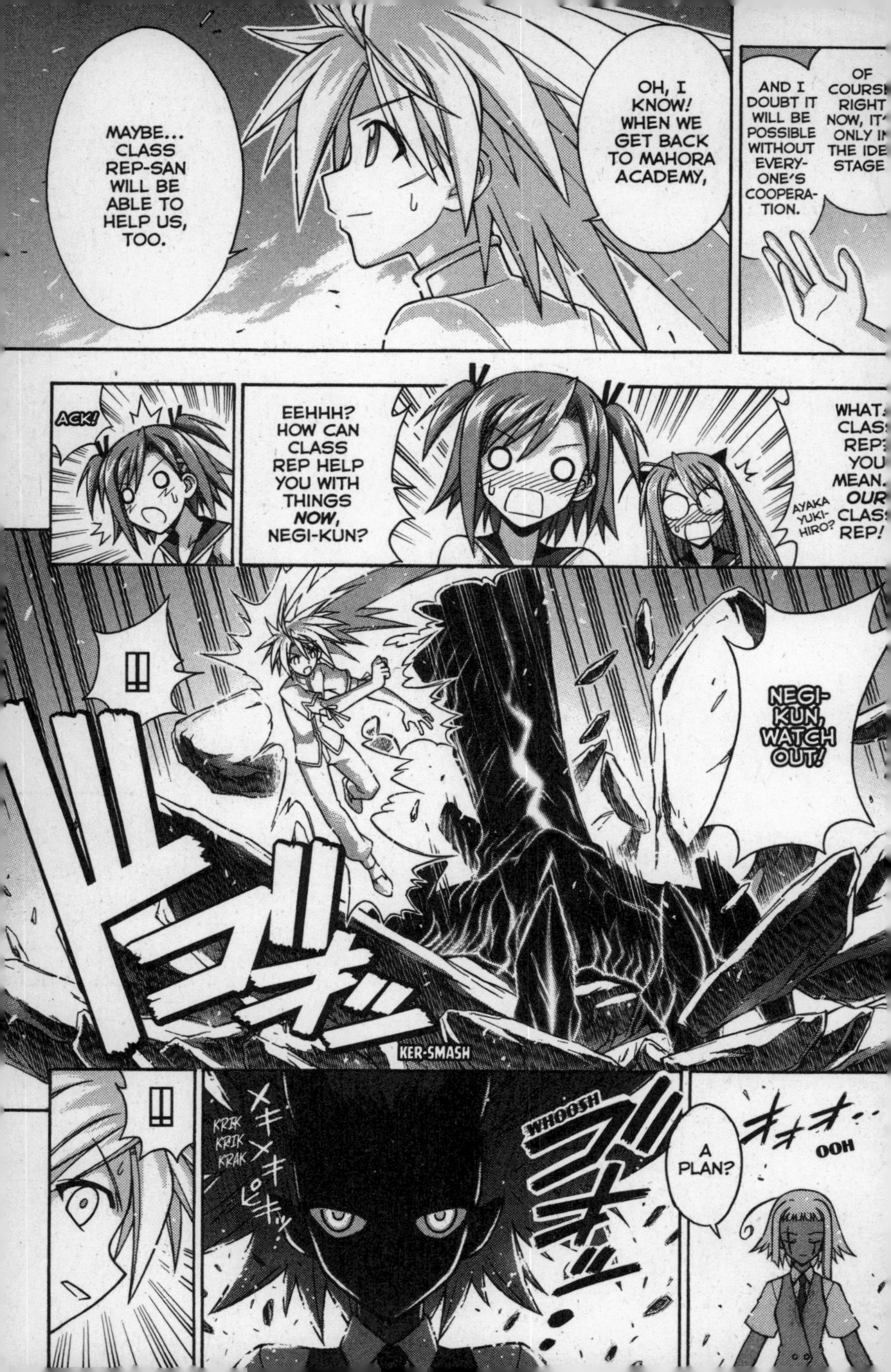
OF COURS RIGHT NOW, IT' ONLY IN THE IDE STAGE
AND I DOUBT IT WILL BE POSSIBLE WITHOUT EVERY-ONE'S COOPERA-TION.
OH, I KNOW! WHEN WE GET BACK TO MAHORA ACADEMY,
MAYBE... CLASS REP-SAN WILL BE ABLE TO HELP US, TOO.
WHAT CLASS REP? YOU MEAN... OUR CLASS REP!
AYAKA YUKI-HIRO?
EEHHH? HOW CAN CLASS REP HELP YOU WITH THINGS NOW, NEGI-KUN?
ACK!
NEGI-KUN, WATCH OUT!
!!
KER-SMASH
オォォ
OOH
A PLAN?
WHOOSH
メキメキピキッ
KRIK KRIK KRAK
!!

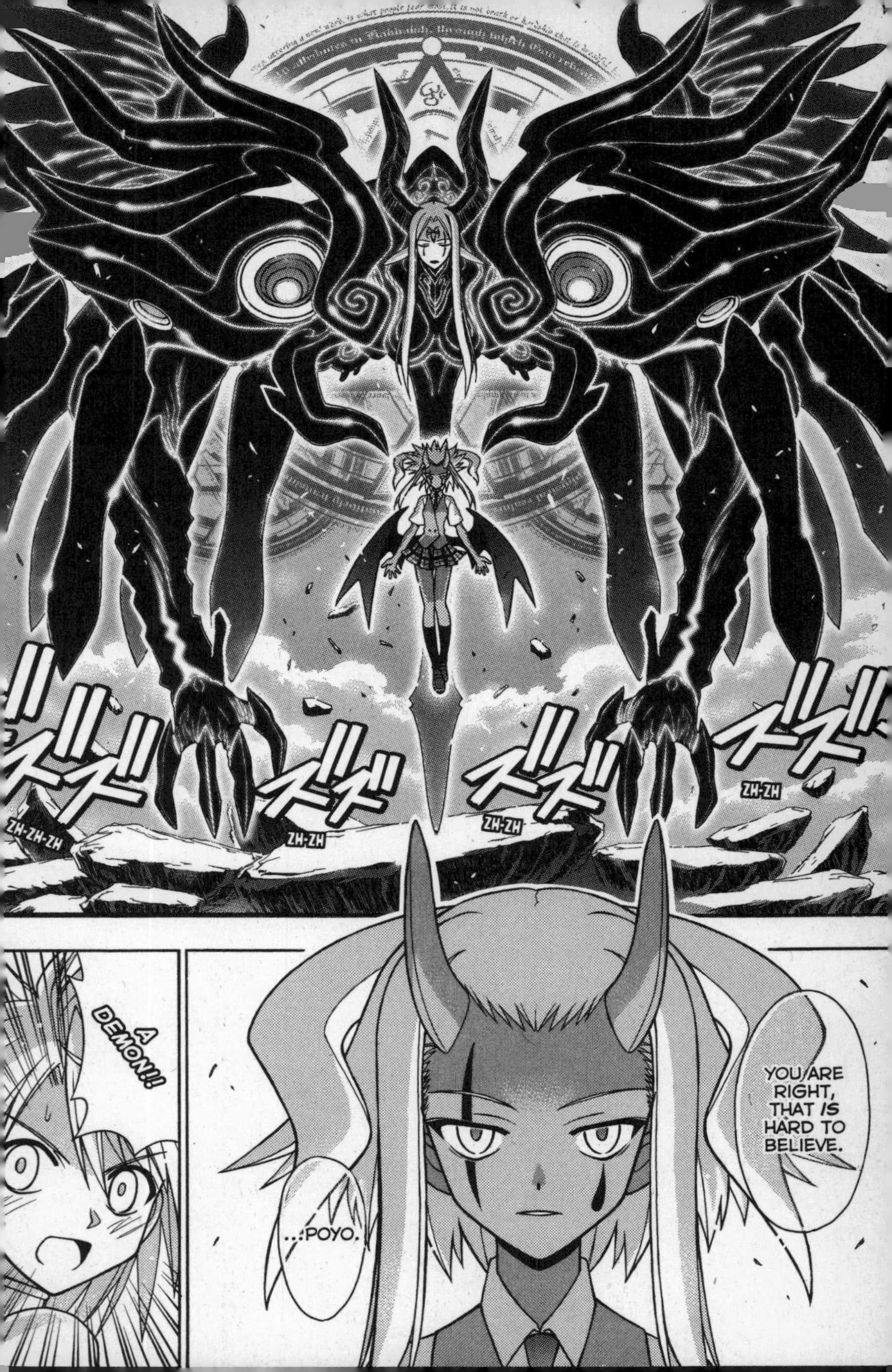
ズズ!!
ZH-ZH
ズズ
ZH-ZH
ズズ
ZH-ZH
ズズ!!
ZH-ZH-ZH
YOU ARE RIGHT, THAT IS HARD TO BELIEVE.
...POYO.
A DEMON!!

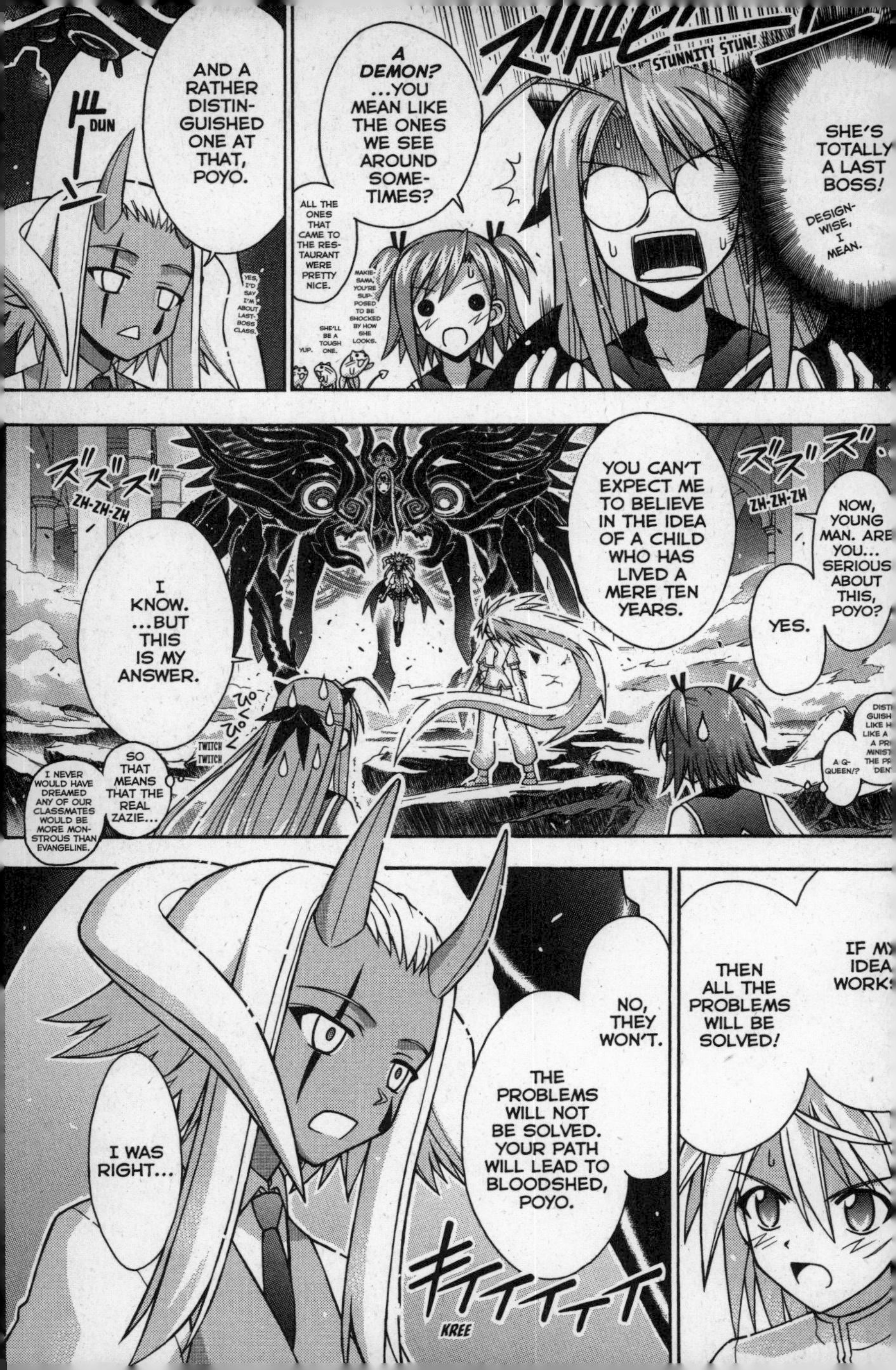
STUNNITY STUN!
SHE'S TOTALLY A LAST BOSS!
DESIGN-WISE, I MEAN.
A DEMON? ...YOU MEAN LIKE THE ONES WE SEE AROUND SOMETIMES?
ALL THE ONES THAT CAME TO THE RESTAURANT WERE PRETTY NICE.
MAKIE-SAMA, YOU'RE SUPPOSED TO BE SHOCKED BY HOW SHE LOOKS.
SHE'LL BE A TOUGH ONE.
YUP.
AND A RATHER DISTINGUISHED ONE AT THAT, POYO.
DUN
YES, I'D SAY I'M ABOUT LAST-BOSS CLASS.
ZH-ZH-ZH
NOW, YOUNG MAN. ARE YOU... SERIOUS ABOUT THIS, POYO?
YES.
YOU CAN'T EXPECT ME TO BELIEVE IN THE IDEA OF A CHILD WHO HAS LIVED A MERE TEN YEARS.
ZH-ZH-ZH
I KNOW. ...BUT THIS IS MY ANSWER.
A Q-QUEEN!?
TWITCH TWITCH
SO THAT MEANS THAT THE REAL ZAZIE...
I NEVER WOULD HAVE DREAMED ANY OF OUR CLASSMATES WOULD BE MORE MONSTROUS THAN EVANGELINE.
IF MY IDEA WORKS
THEN ALL THE PROBLEMS WILL BE SOLVED!
NO, THEY WON'T.
THE PROBLEMS WILL NOT BE SOLVED. YOUR PATH WILL LEAD TO BLOODSHED, POYO.
I WAS RIGHT...
KREE

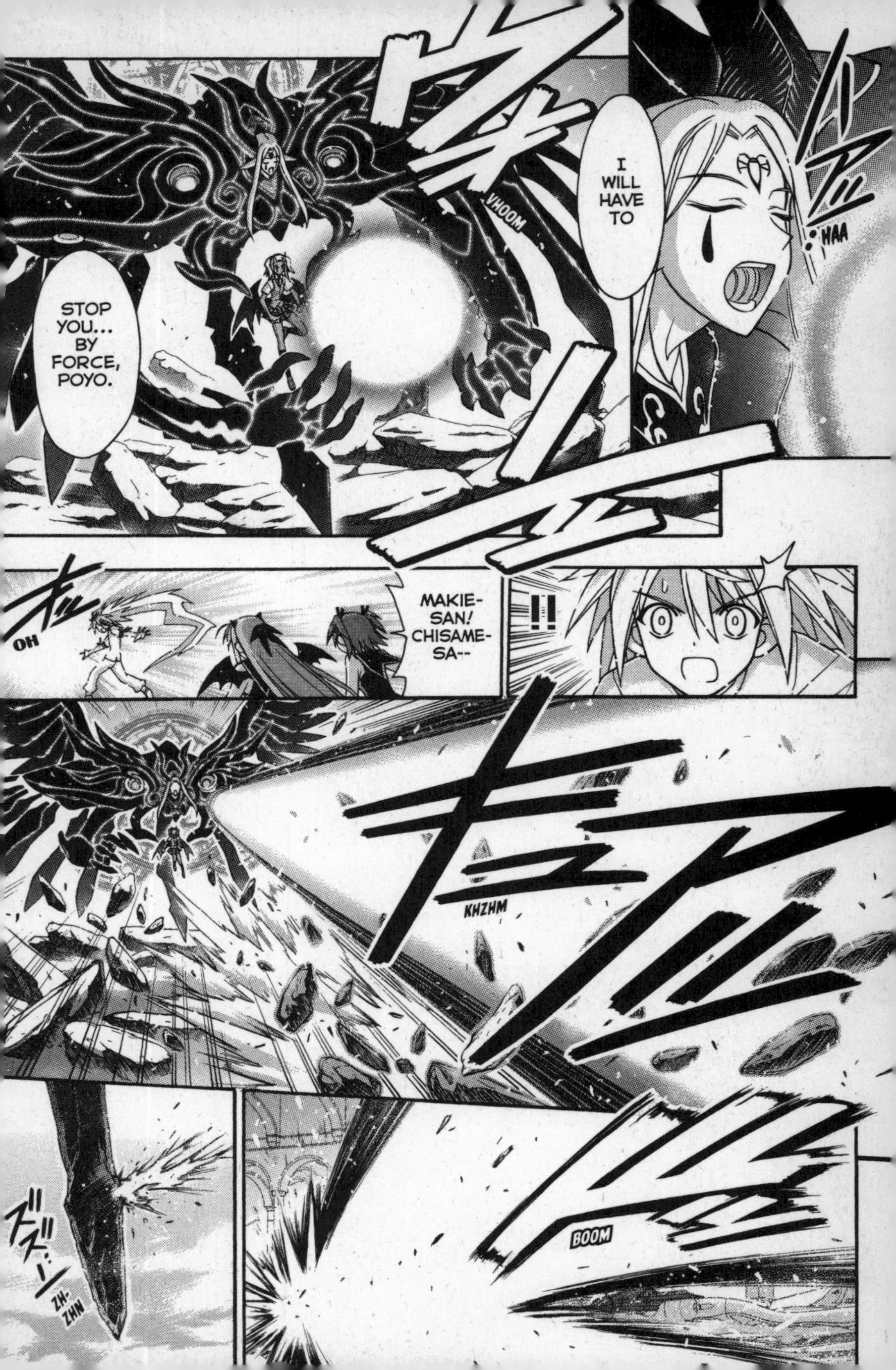
HAA
I WILL HAVE TO
VHOOM
STOP YOU... BY FORCE, POYO.
!!
MAKIE-SAN! CHISAME-SA--
OH
KHZHM
BOOM
ZH-ZHN

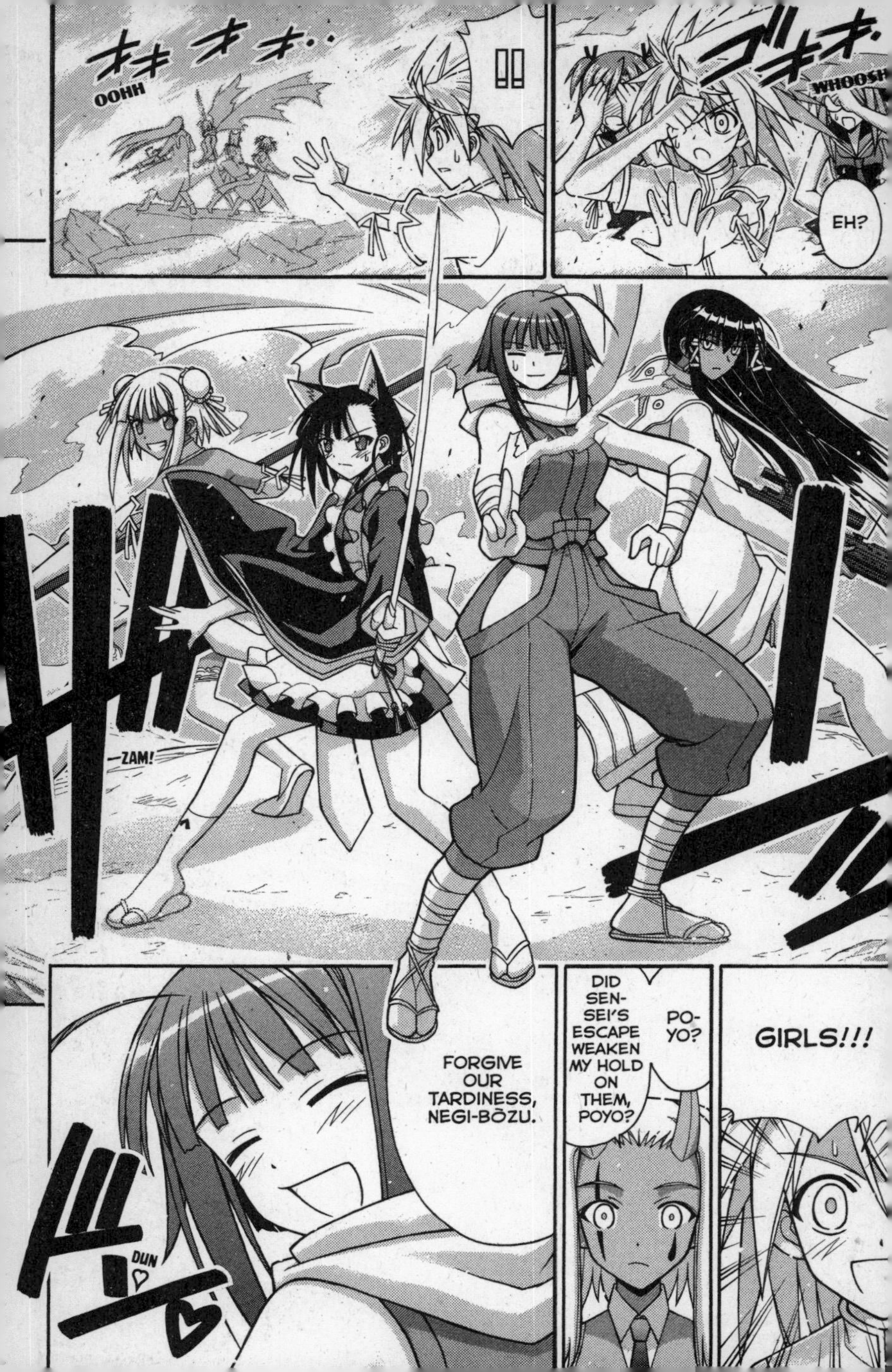
WHOOSH
EH?
OOHH
!!
—ZAM!
GIRLS!!!
PO-YO?
DID SEN-SEI'S ESCAPE WEAKEN MY HOLD ON THEM, POYO?
FORGIVE OUR TARDINESS, NEGI-BŌZU.
DUN

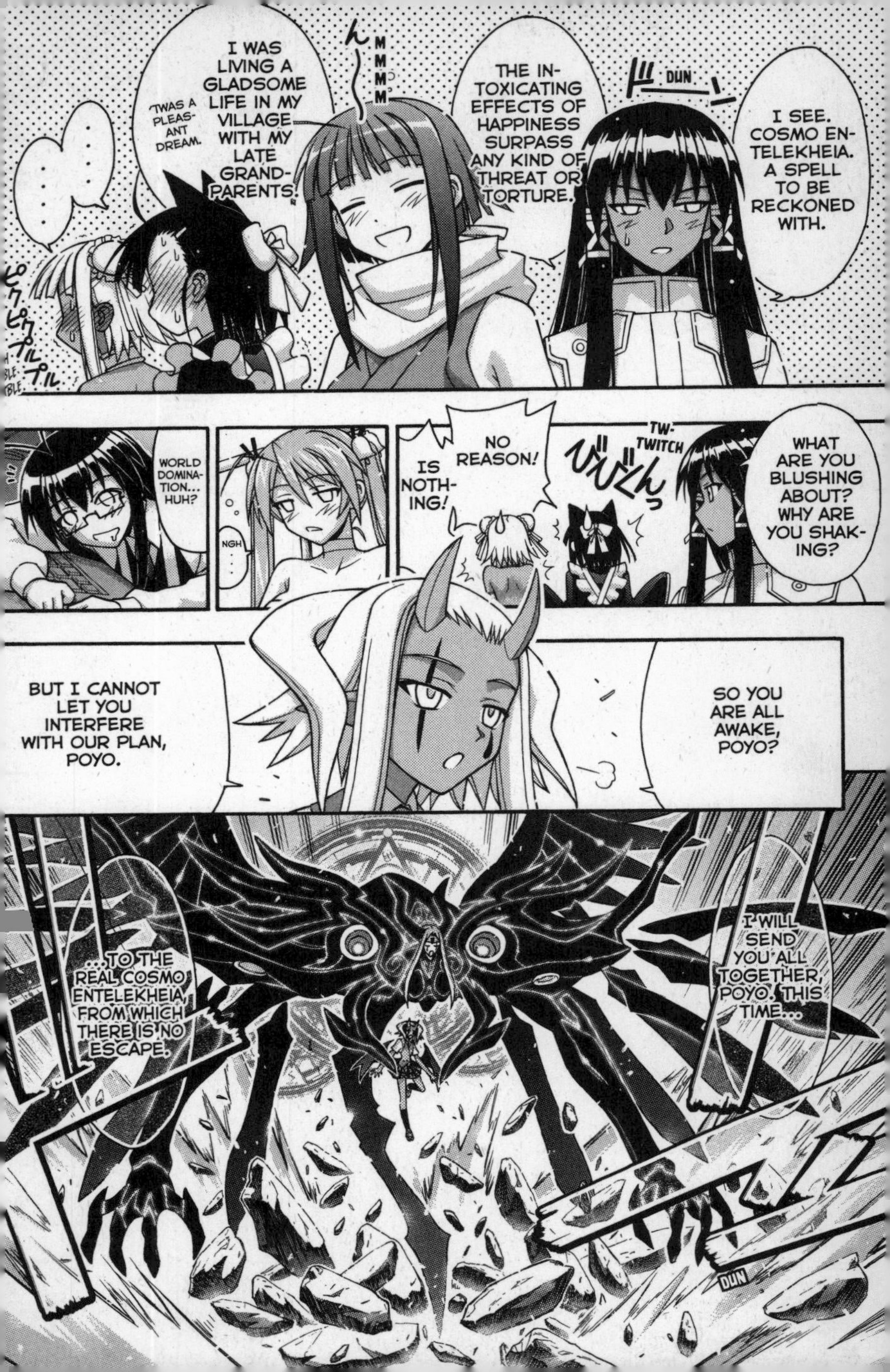
DUN
I SEE. COSMO ENTELEKHEIA. A SPELL TO BE RECKONED WITH.
THE INTOXICATING EFFECTS OF HAPPINESS SURPASS ANY KIND OF THREAT OR TORTURE.
MMMM
I WAS LIVING A GLADSOME LIFE IN MY VILLAGE WITH MY LATE GRANDPARENTS!
'TWAS A PLEASANT DREAM.
......
WHAT ARE YOU BLUSHING ABOUT? WHY ARE YOU SHAKING?
TW-TWITCH
NO REASON!
IS NOTHING!
NGH...
WORLD DOMINATION... HUH?
SO YOU ARE ALL AWAKE, POYO?
BUT I CANNOT LET YOU INTERFERE WITH OUR PLAN, POYO.
I WILL SEND YOU ALL TOGETHER, POYO. THIS TIME...
...TO THE REAL COSMO ENTELEKHEIA, FROM WHICH THERE IS NO ESCAPE.
DUN

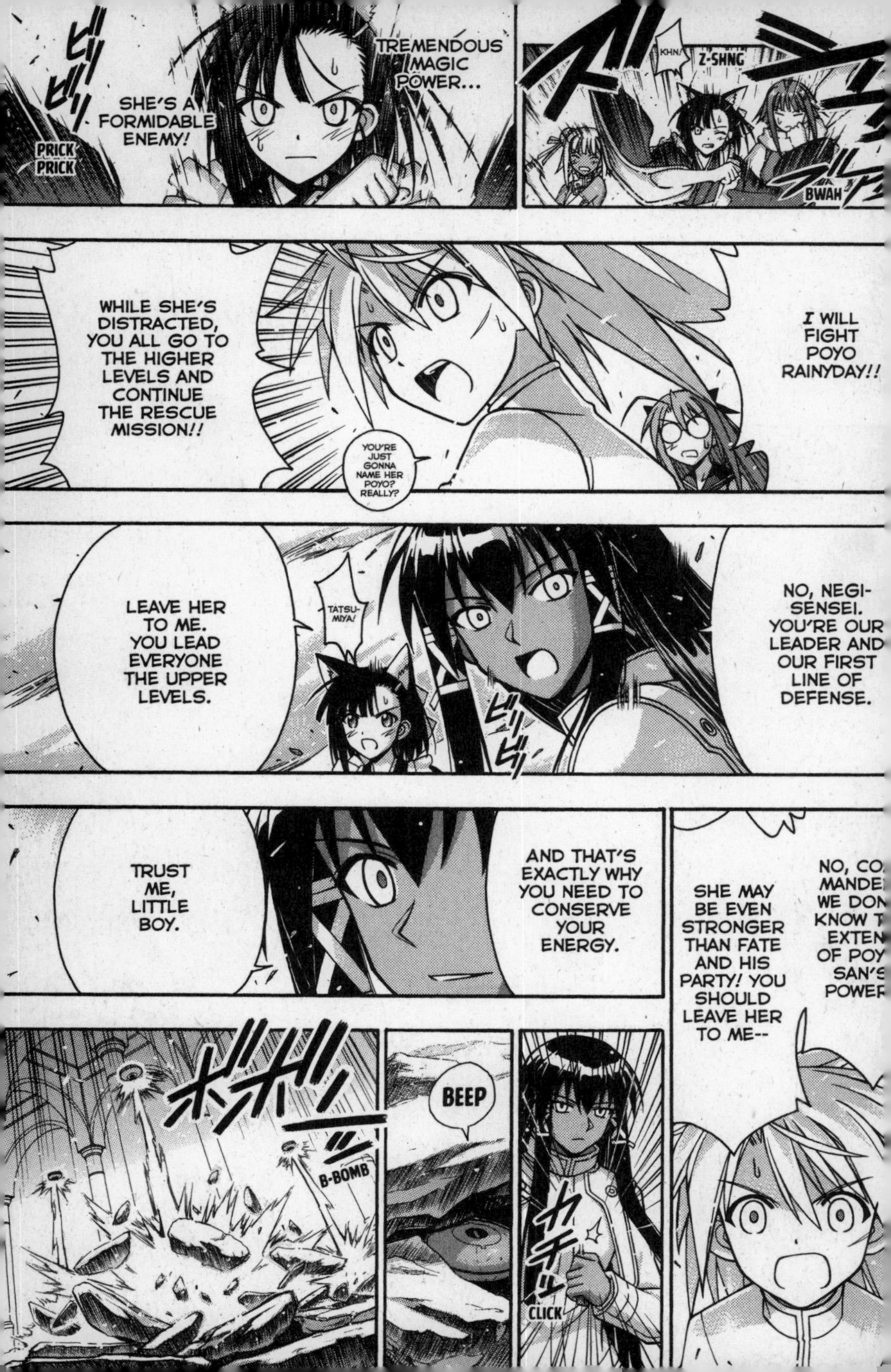
KHN!
Z-SHNG
BWAH
TREMENDOUS MAGIC POWER...
SHE'S A FORMIDABLE ENEMY!
PRICK PRICK
I WILL FIGHT POYO RAINYDAY!!
WHILE SHE'S DISTRACTED, YOU ALL GO TO THE HIGHER LEVELS AND CONTINUE THE RESCUE MISSION!!
YOU'RE JUST GONNA NAME HER POYO? REALLY?
NO, NEGI-SENSEI. YOU'RE OUR LEADER AND OUR FIRST LINE OF DEFENSE.
TATSUMIYA!
LEAVE HER TO ME. YOU LEAD EVERYONE THE UPPER LEVELS.
NO, CO MANDE WE DON KNOW T EXTEN OF POY SAN'S POWER
SHE MAY BE EVEN STRONGER THAN FATE AND HIS PARTY! YOU SHOULD LEAVE HER TO ME--
AND THAT'S EXACTLY WHY YOU NEED TO CONSERVE YOUR ENERGY.
TRUST ME, LITTLE BOY.
CLICK
BEEP
B-BOMB

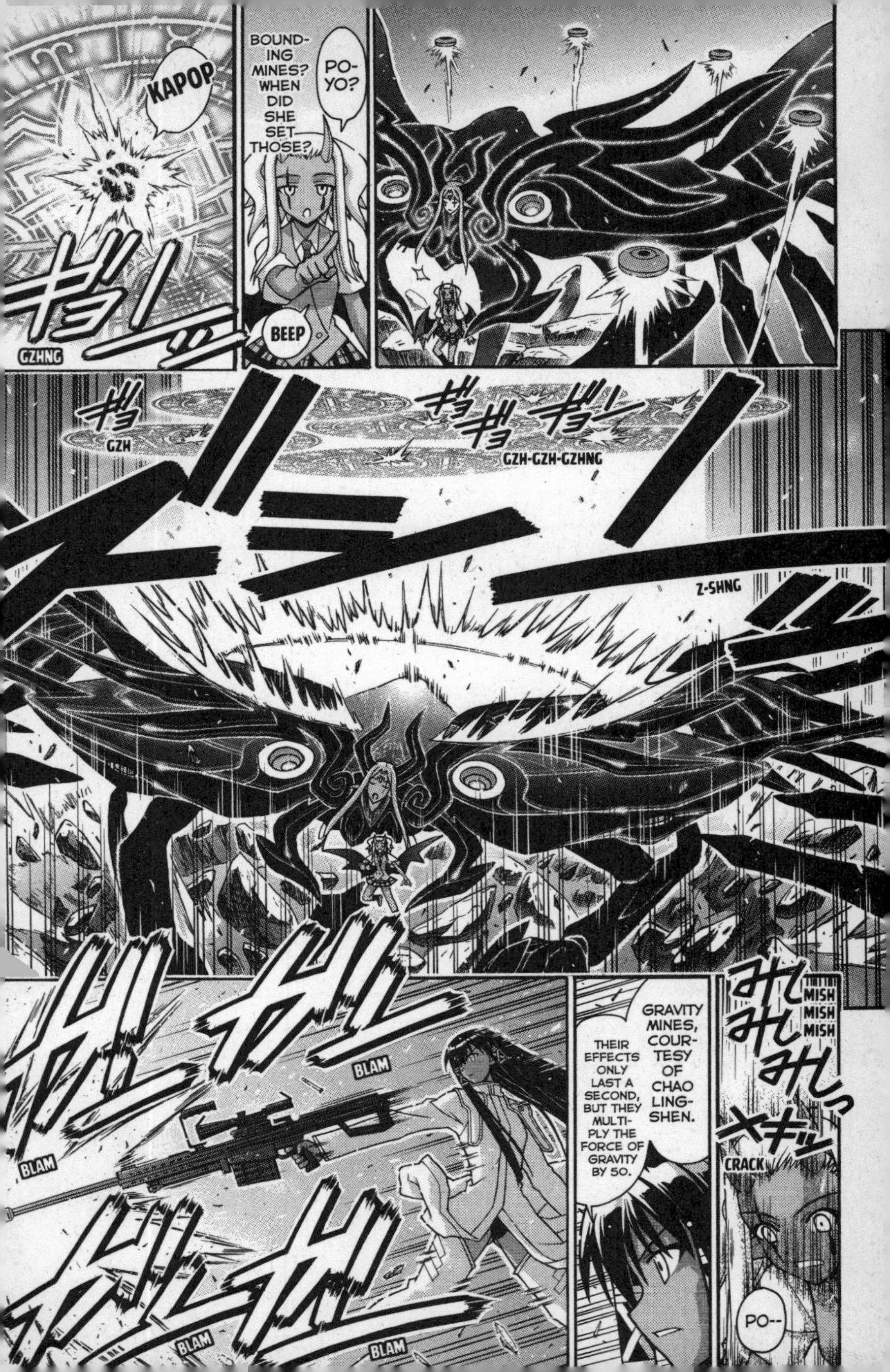
PO-YO?
BOUNDING-ING MINES? WHEN DID SHE SET THOSE?
BEEP
KAPOP
GZHNG
GZH-GZH-GZHNG
GZH
Z-SHNG
MISH MISH MISH
CRACK
PO--
GRAVITY MINES, COUR-TESY OF CHAO LING-SHEN.
THEIR EFFECTS ONLY LAST A SECOND, BUT THEY MULTI-PLY THE FORCE OF GRAVITY BY 50.
BLAM
BLAM
BLAM
BLAM

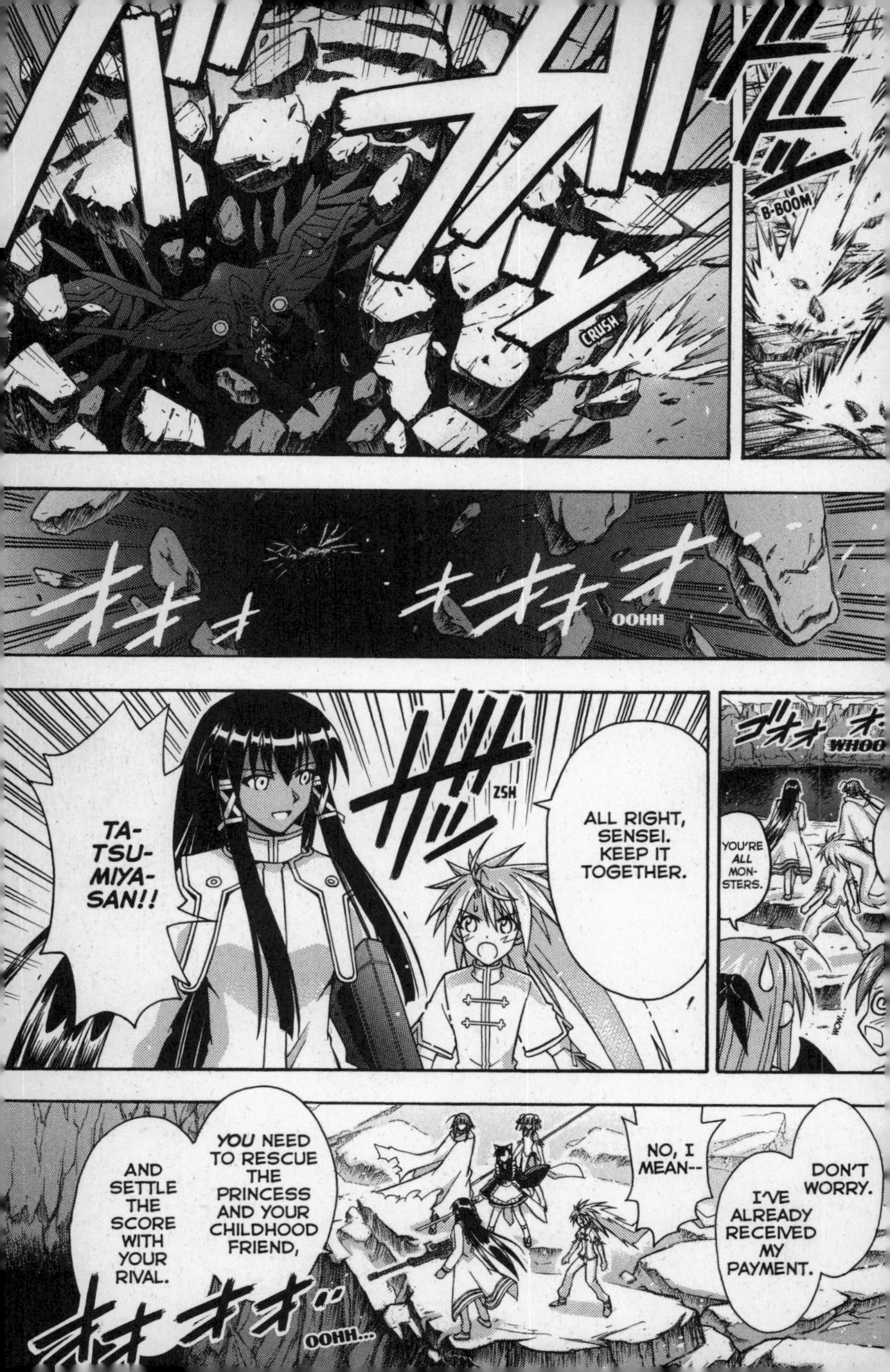
B-BOOM
CRUSH
OOHH
WHOO
YOU'RE *ALL* MONSTERS.
WOW...
ALL RIGHT, SENSEI. KEEP IT TOGETHER.
ZSH
TA-TSU-MIYA-SAN!!
DON'T WORRY. I'VE ALREADY RECEIVED MY PAYMENT.
NO, I MEAN--
YOU NEED TO RESCUE THE PRINCESS AND YOUR CHILDHOOD FRIEND,
AND SETTLE THE SCORE WITH YOUR RIVAL.
OOHH...

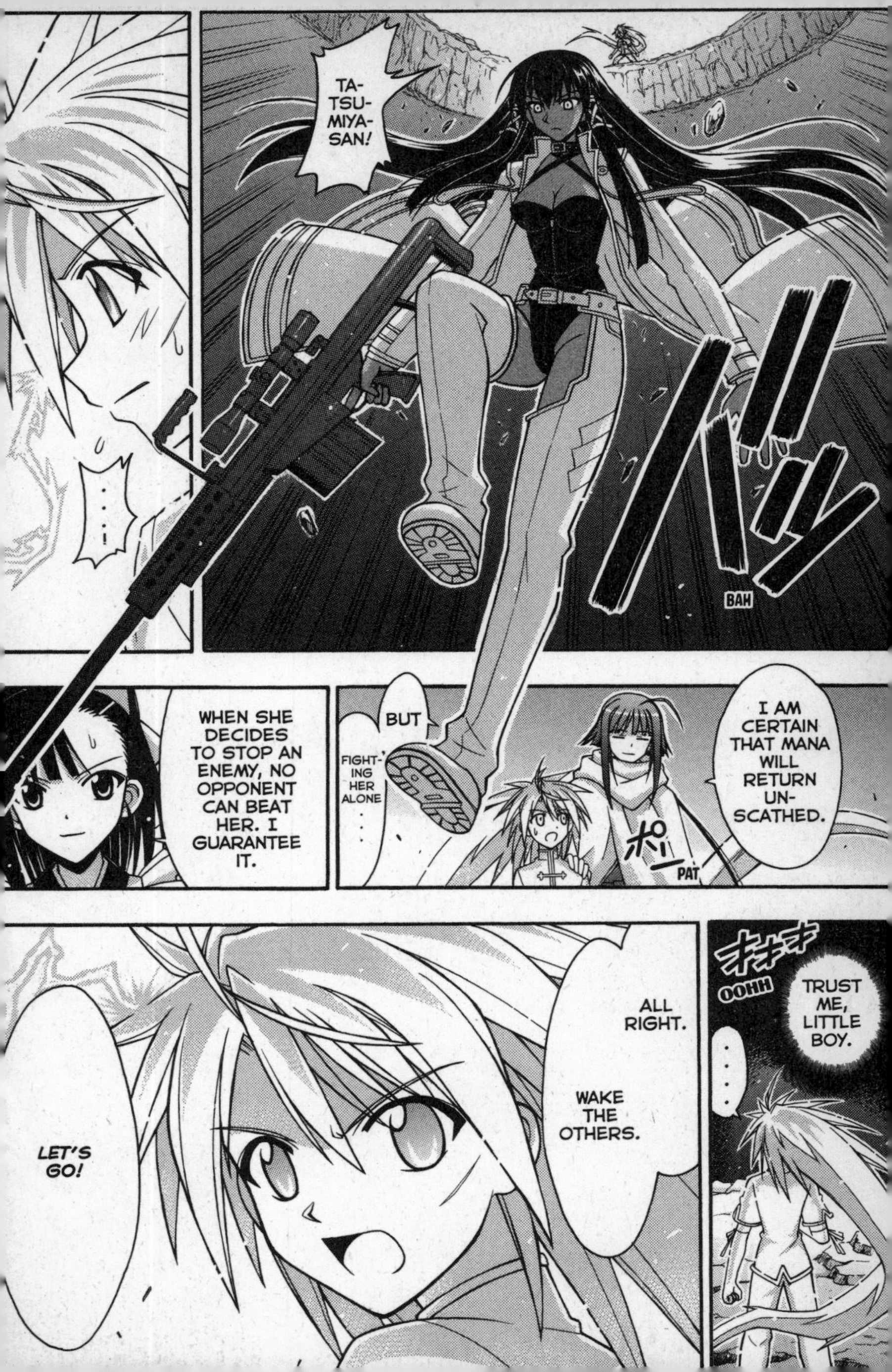
TA-TSU-MIYA-SAN!
BAH
...!
I AM CERTAIN THAT MANA WILL RETURN UN-SCATHED.
PAT
BUT
FIGHTING HER ALONE...
WHEN SHE DECIDES TO STOP AN ENEMY, NO OPPONENT CAN BEAT HER. I GUARANTEE IT.
OOHH
TRUST ME, LITTLE BOY.
...
ALL RIGHT.
WAKE THE OTHERS.
LET'S GO!

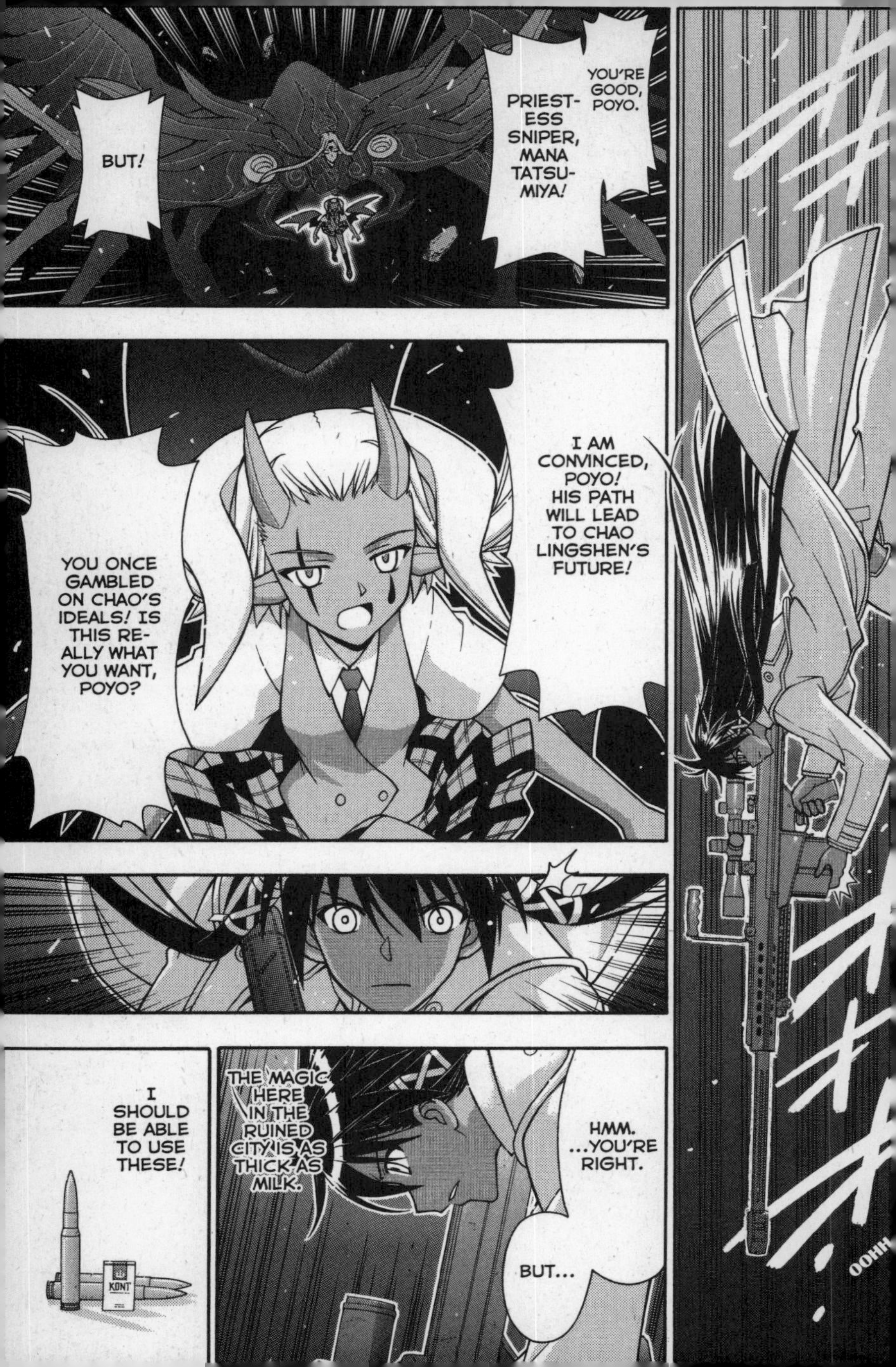

OOHH
YOU'RE GOOD, POYO. PRIEST-ESS SNIPER, MANA TATSU-MIYA!
BUT!
I AM CONVINCED, POYO! HIS PATH WILL LEAD TO CHAO LINGSHEN'S FUTURE!
YOU ONCE GAMBLED ON CHAO'S IDEALS! IS THIS RE-ALLY WHAT YOU WANT, POYO?
HMM. ...YOU'RE RIGHT.
THE MAGIC HERE IN THE RUINED CITY IS AS THICK AS MILK.
BUT...
I SHOULD BE ABLE TO USE THESE!
KONT

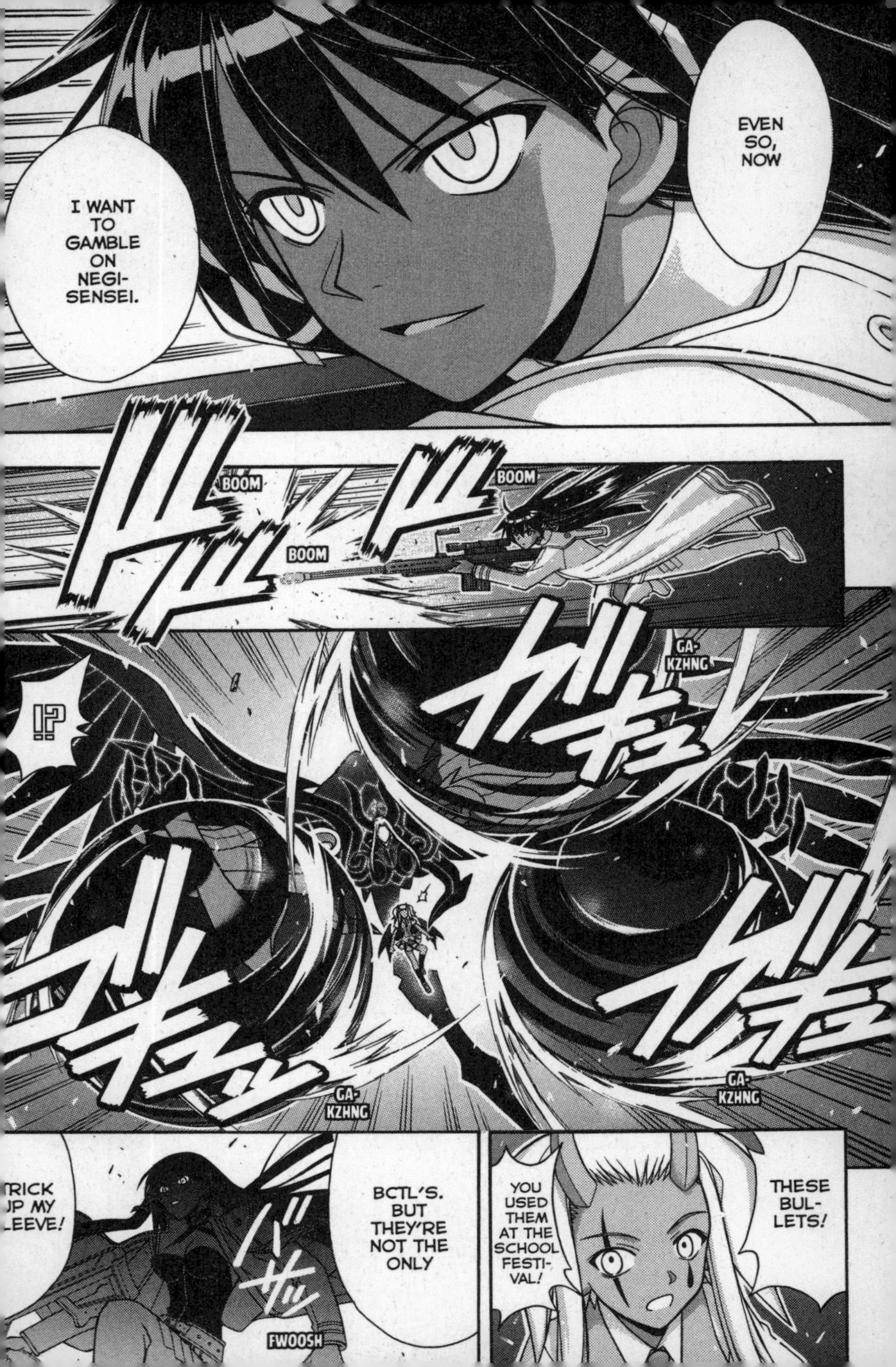
EVEN SO, NOW
I WANT TO GAMBLE ON NEGI-SENSEI.
BOOM
BOOM
BOOM
GA-KZHNG
!?
GA-KZHNG
GA-KZHNG
THESE BULLETS!
YOU USED THEM AT THE SCHOOL FESTIVAL!
BCTL'S. BUT THEY'RE NOT THE ONLY
TRICK UP MY LEEVE!
FWOOSH

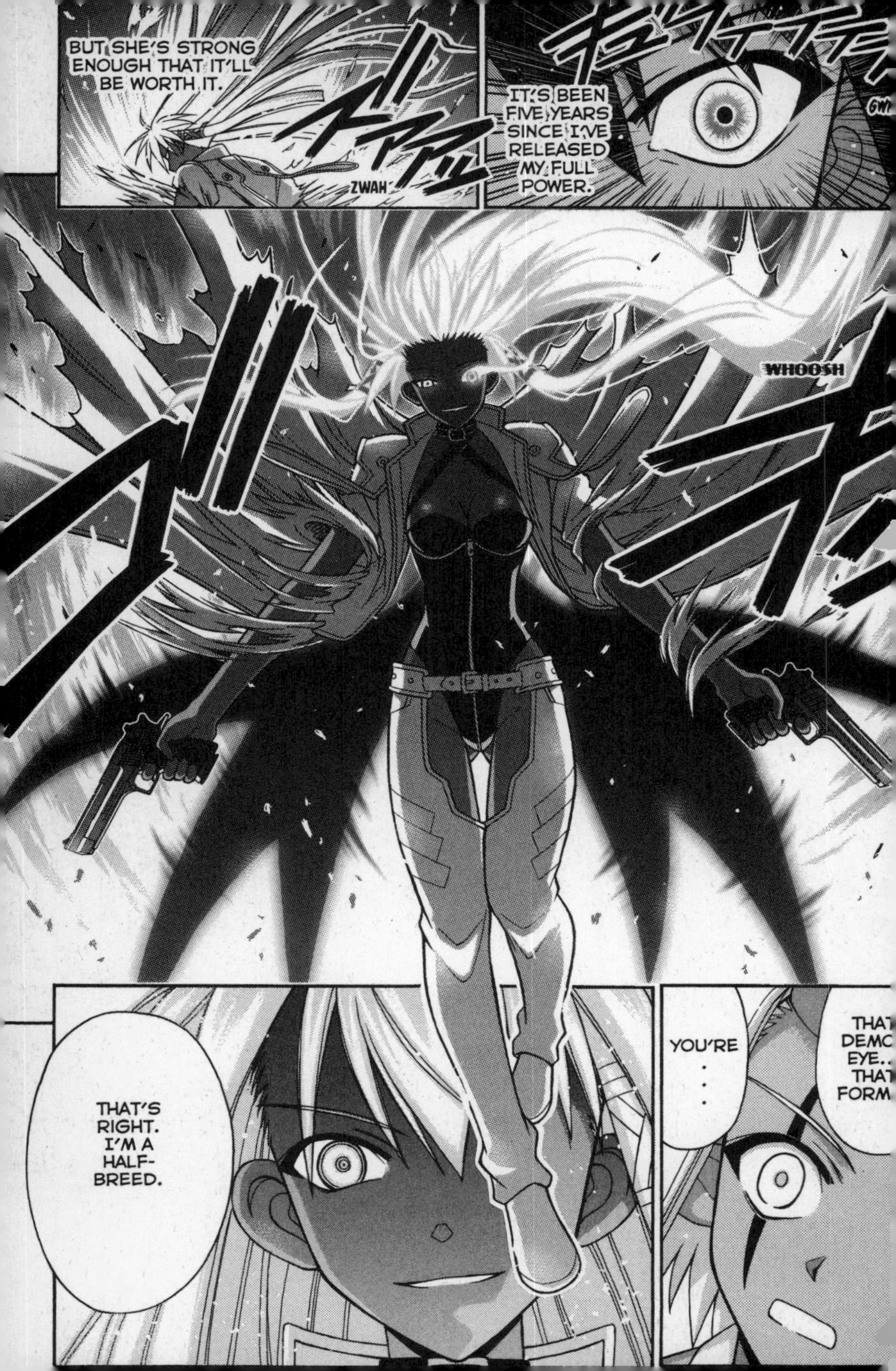
IT'S BEEN FIVE YEARS SINCE I'VE RELEASED MY FULL POWER.
GWI
BUT SHE'S STRONG ENOUGH THAT IT'LL BE WORTH IT.
ZWAH
WHOOSH
THAT DEMO EYE... THAT FORM
YOU'RE . . .
THAT'S RIGHT. I'M A HALF-BREED.

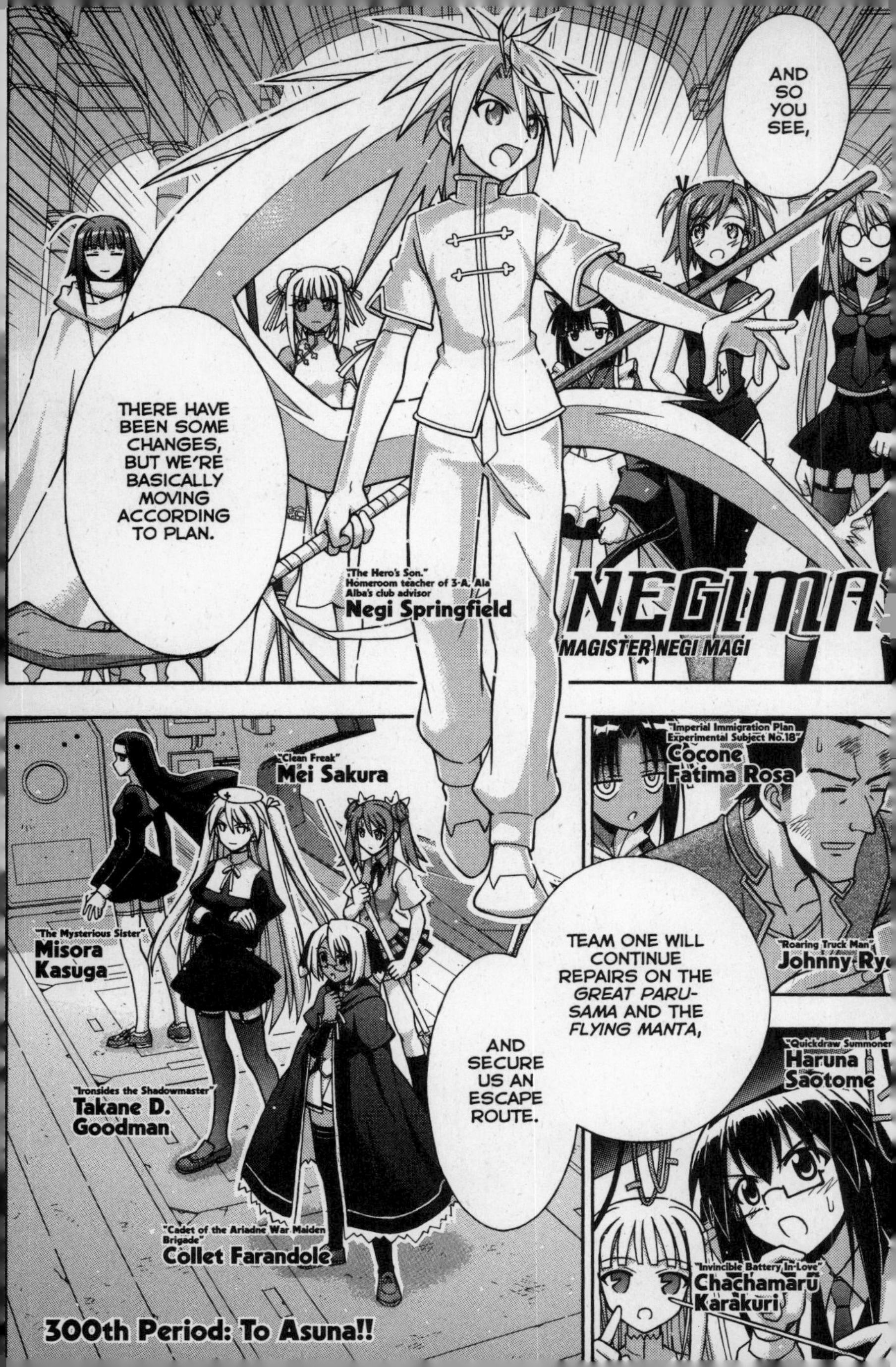
AND SO YOU SEE,
THERE HAVE BEEN SOME CHANGES, BUT WE'RE BASICALLY MOVING ACCORDING TO PLAN.
"The Hero's Son." Homeroom teacher of 3-A, Ala Alba's club advisor
Negi Springfield
NEGIMA
MAGISTER NEGI MAGI
"Imperial Immigration Plan Experimental Subject No.18"
Cocone Fatima Rosa
"Roaring Truck Man"
Johnny Ry
TEAM ONE WILL CONTINUE REPAIRS ON THE GREAT PARU-SAMA AND THE FLYING MANTA,
AND SECURE US AN ESCAPE ROUTE.
"Quickdraw Summoner"
Haruna Saotome
"Invincible Battery In-Love"
Chachamaru Karakuri
"Clean Freak"
Mei Sakura
"The Mysterious Sister"
Misora Kasuga
"Ironsides the Shadowmaster"
Takane D. Goodman
"Cadet of the Ariadne War Maiden Brigade"
Collet Farandole
300th Period: To Asuna!!

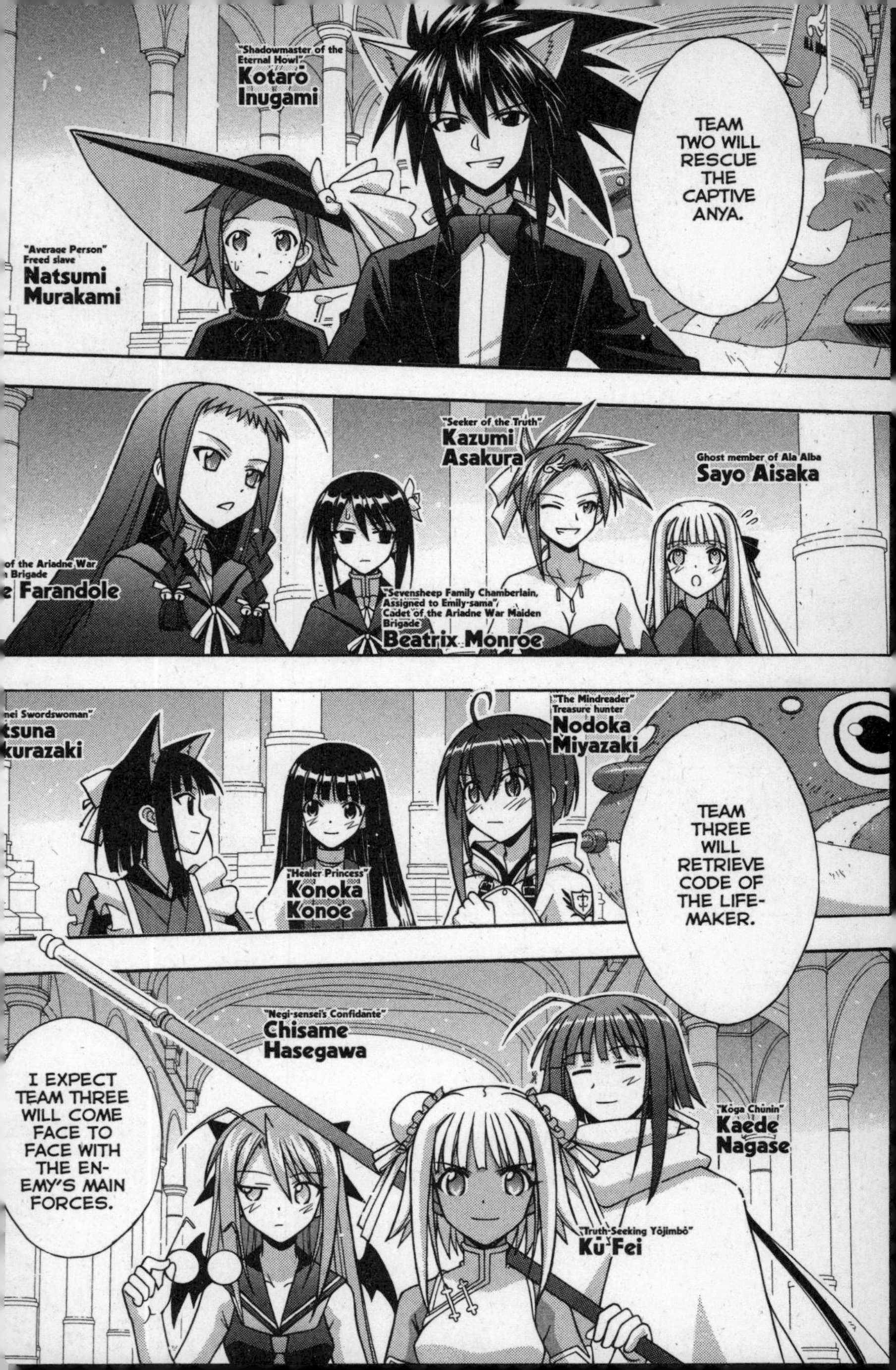

TEAM TWO WILL RESCUE THE CAPTIVE ANYA.
"Shadowmaster of the Eternal Howl"
Kotarō Inugami
"Average Person"
Freed slave
Natsumi Murakami
Ghost member of Ala Alba
Sayo Aisaka
"Seeker of the Truth"
Kazumi Asakura
of the Ariadne War
n Brigade
e Farandole
"Sevensheep Family Chamberlain, Assigned to Emily-sama", Cadet of the Ariadne War Maiden Brigade
Beatrix Monroe
TEAM THREE WILL RETRIEVE CODE OF THE LIFE-MAKER.
"The Mindreader"
Treasure hunter
Nodoka Miyazaki
nei Swordswoman"
tsuna
kurazaki
"Healer Princess"
Konoka Konoe
"Kōga Chūnin"
Kaede Nagase
"Truth-Seeking Yōjimbō"
Kū Fei
"Negi-sensei's Confidante"
Chisame Hasegawa
I EXPECT TEAM THREE WILL COME FACE TO FACE WITH THE EN-EMY'S MAIN FORCES.

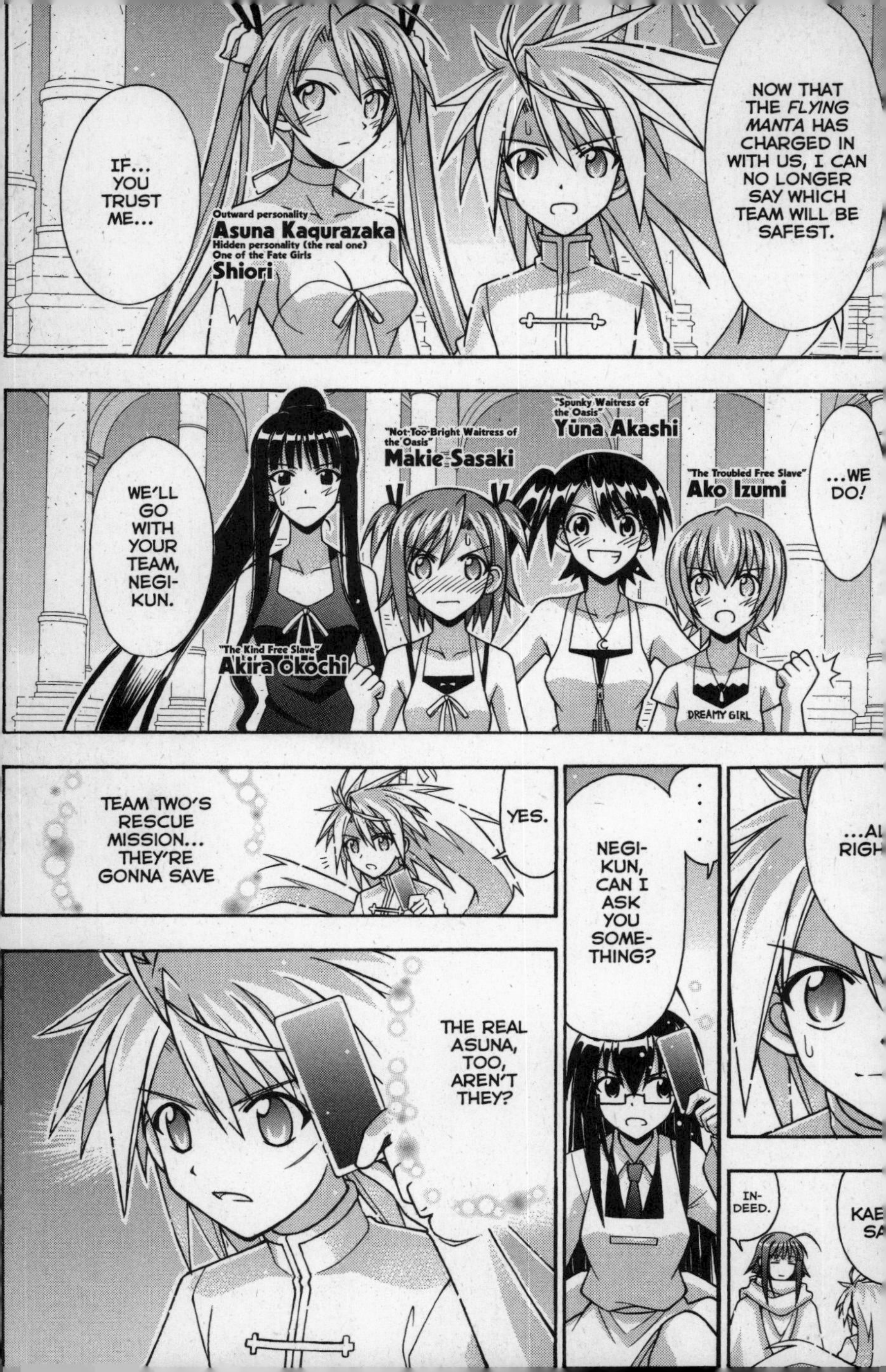
NOW THAT THE *FLYING MANTA* HAS CHARGED IN WITH US, I CAN NO LONGER SAY WHICH TEAM WILL BE SAFEST.
IF... YOU TRUST ME...
Outward personality Asuna Kagurazaka
Hidden personality (the real one) One of the Fate Girls Shiori
...WE DO!
"The Troubled Free Slave" Ako Izumi
"Spunky Waitress of the Oasis" Yūna Akashi
"Not-Too-Bright Waitress of the Oasis" Makie Sasaki
DREAMY GIRL
WE'LL GO WITH YOUR TEAM, NEGI-KUN.
"The Kind Free Slave" Akira Ōkochi
...AL RIGH
KAE SA
IN-DEED.
...
NEGI-KUN, CAN I ASK YOU SOMETHING?
YES.
TEAM TWO'S RESCUE MISSION... THEY'RE GONNA SAVE
THE REAL ASUNA, TOO, AREN'T THEY?

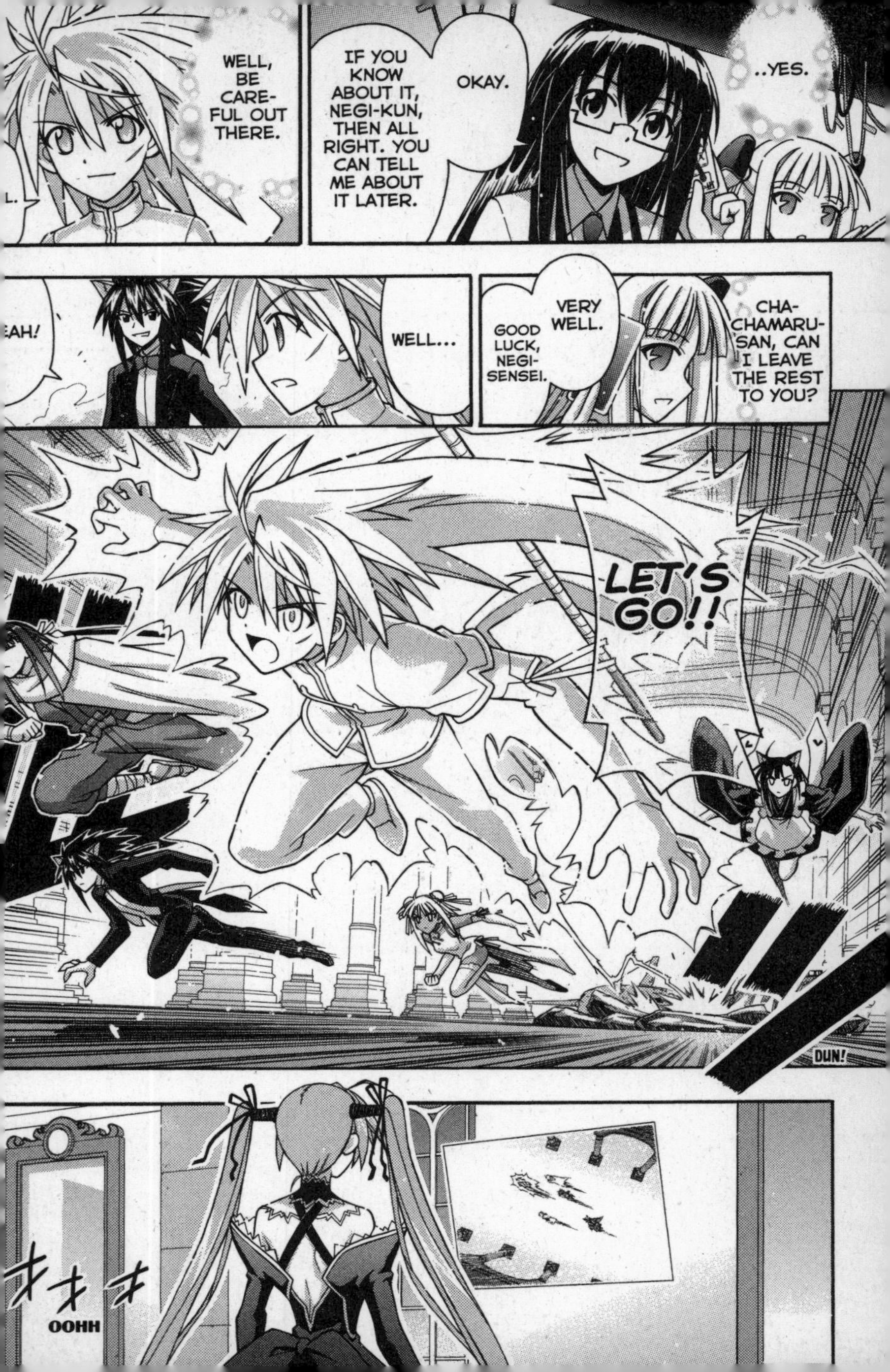
..YES.
OKAY.
IF YOU KNOW ABOUT IT, NEGI-KUN, THEN ALL RIGHT. YOU CAN TELL ME ABOUT IT LATER.
WELL, BE CARE-FUL OUT THERE.
L.
CHA-CHAMARU-SAN, CAN I LEAVE THE REST TO YOU?
VERY WELL.
GOOD LUCK, NEGI-SENSEI.
WELL...
EAH!
LET'S GO!!
DUN!
OOHH

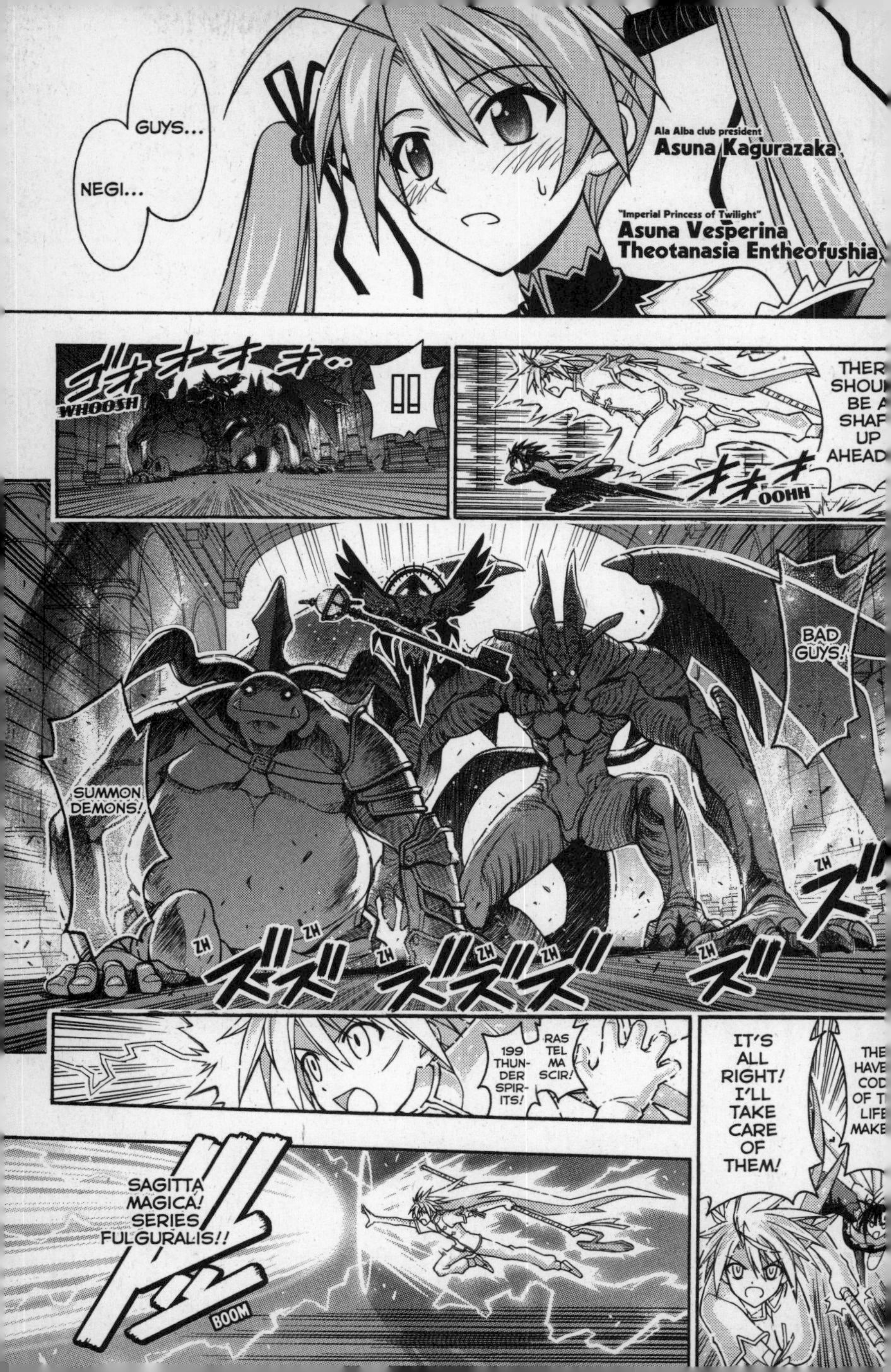

Ala Alba club president
Asuna Kagurazaka
"Imperial Princess of Twilight"
Asuna Vesperina Theotanasia Entheofushia
GUYS...
NEGI...
THER SHOUL BE A SHAF UP AHEAD
OOHH
WHOOSH
!!
BAD GUYS!
SUMMON DEMONS!
ZH
ZH
ZH
ZH
ZH
ZH
ZH
THE HAVE COD OF T LIFE MAKE
IT'S ALL RIGHT! I'LL TAKE CARE OF THEM!
RAS TEL MA SCIR!
199 THUNDER SPIRITS!
SAGITTA MAGICA! SERIES FULGURALIS!!
BOOM

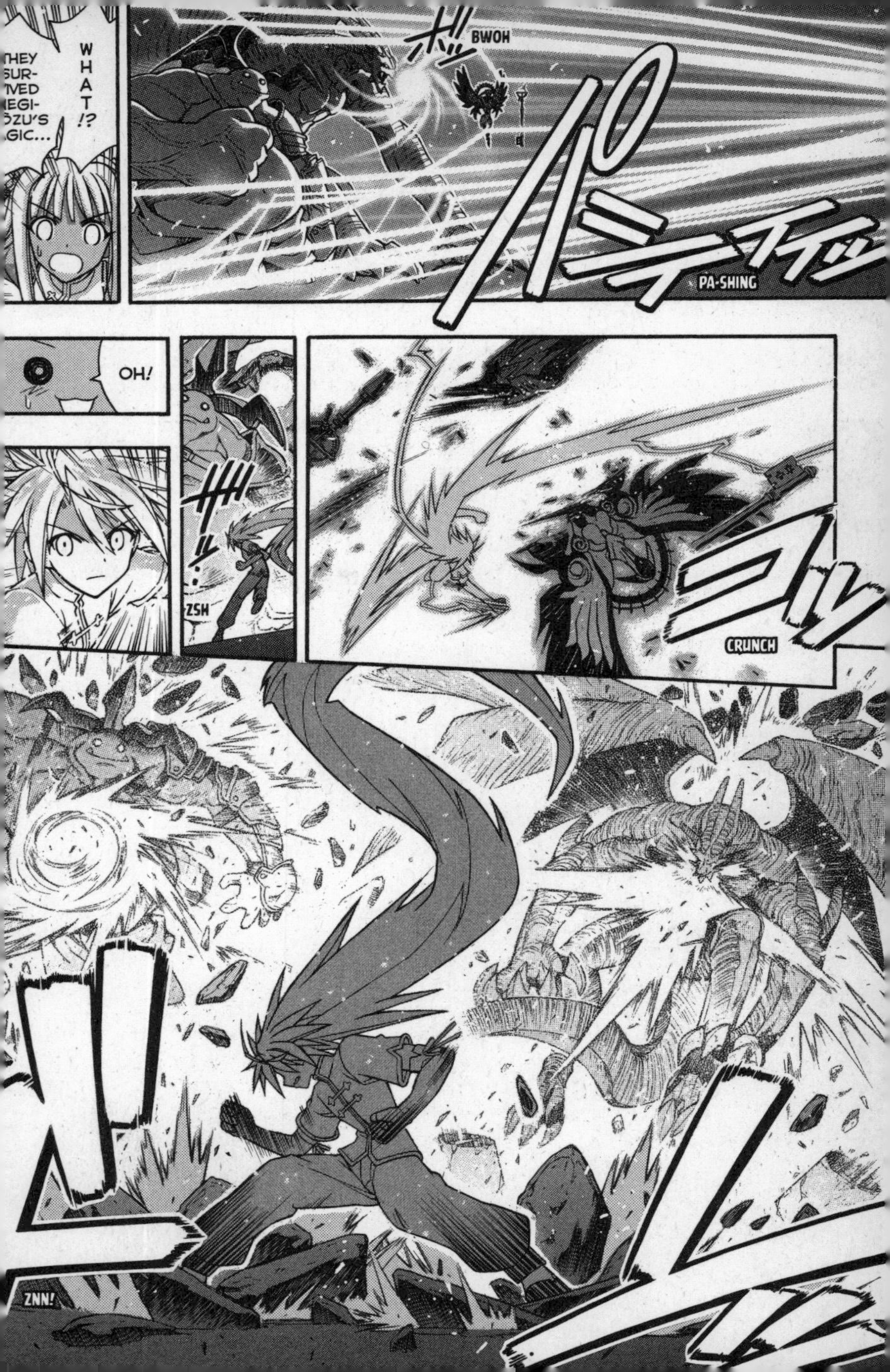
BWOH
PA-SHING
WHAT!?
THEY SUR- IVED EGI- ŌZU'S GIC...
CRUNCH
ZSH
OH!
ZNN!

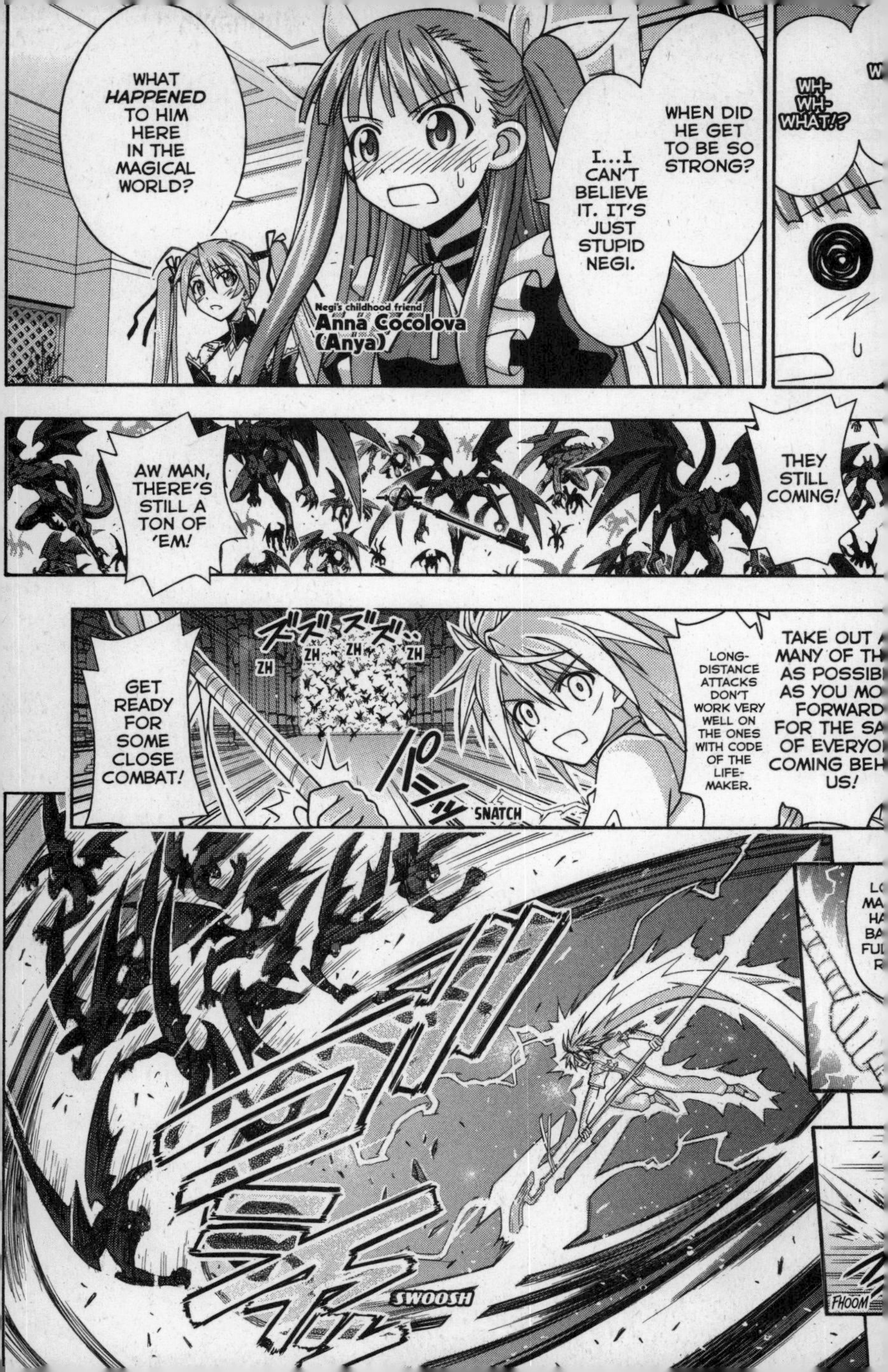
WH-WH-WHAT!?
WHEN DID HE GET TO BE SO STRONG?
I...I CAN'T BELIEVE IT. IT'S JUST STUPID NEGI.
WHAT HAPPENED TO HIM HERE IN THE MAGICAL WORLD?
Negi's childhood friend Anna Cocolova (Anya)
THEY STILL COMING!
AW MAN, THERE'S STILL A TON OF 'EM!
TAKE OUT A MANY OF TH AS POSSIB AS YOU MO FORWARD FOR THE SA OF EVERYO COMING BEH US!
LONG-DISTANCE ATTACKS DON'T WORK VERY WELL ON THE ONES WITH CODE OF THE LIFE-MAKER.
ZH ZH ZH ZH
GET READY FOR SOME CLOSE COMBAT!
SNATCH
FHOOM
SWOOSH

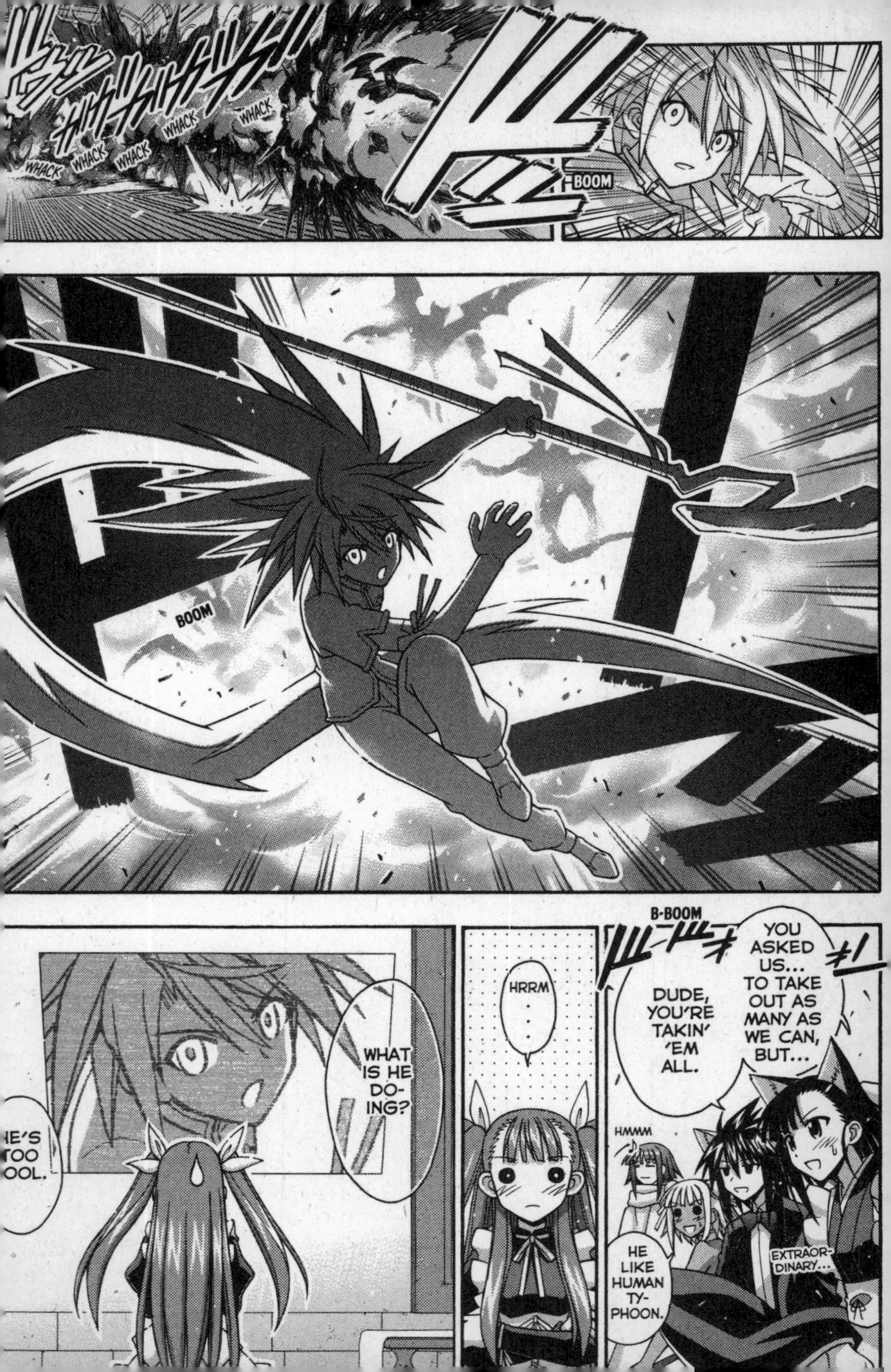
BOOM
WHACK
WHACK
WHACK
WHACK
WHACK
BOOM
B-BOOM
YOU ASKED US... TO TAKE OUT AS MANY AS WE CAN, BUT...
DUDE, YOU'RE TAKIN' 'EM ALL.
HMMM
EXTRAOR-DINARY...
HE LIKE HUMAN TY-PHOON.
HRRM . . .
WHAT IS HE DO-ING?
E'S TOO OOL.

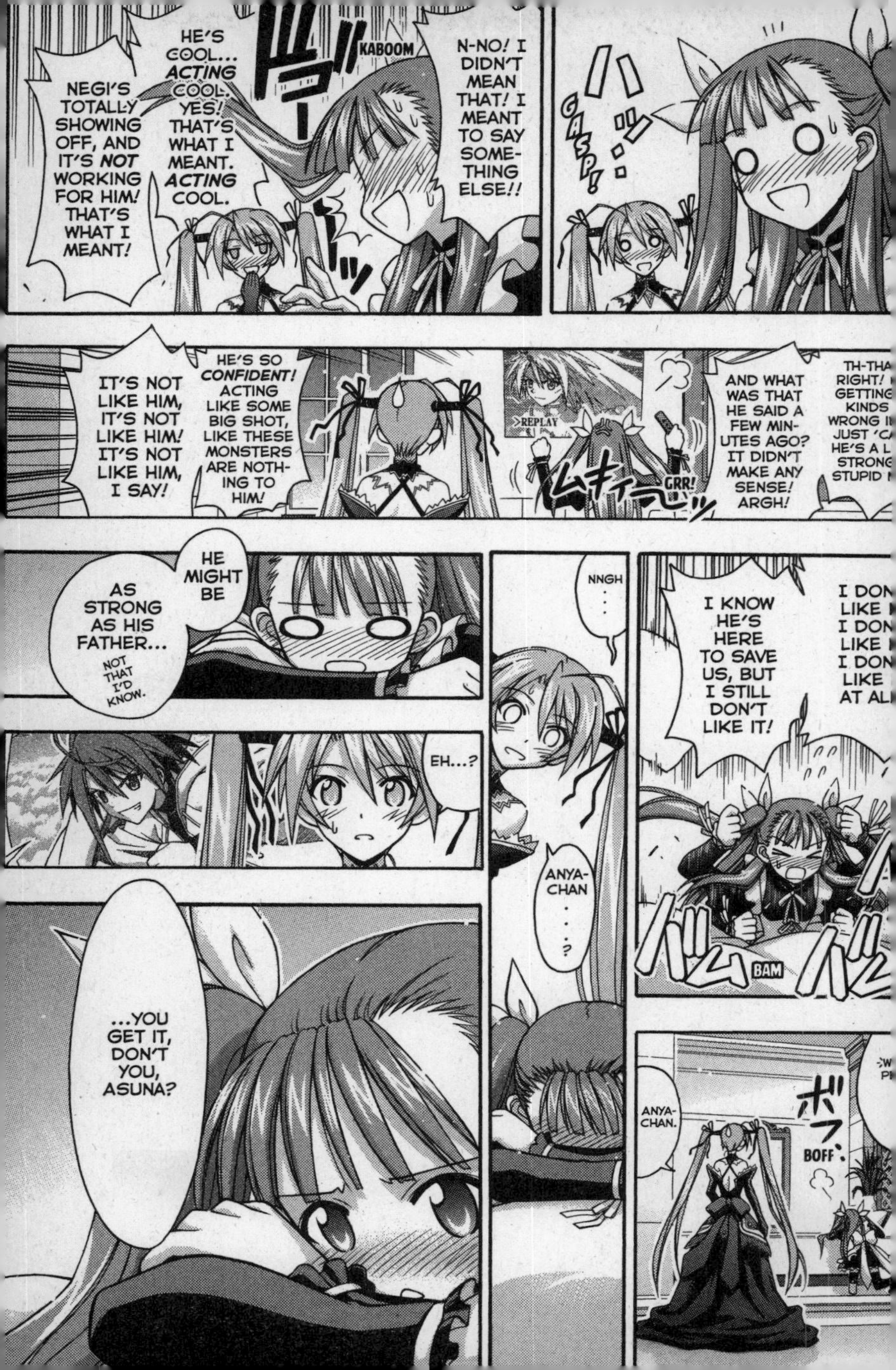

GASP!
N-NO! I DIDN'T MEAN THAT! I MEANT TO SAY SOME-THING ELSE!!
KABOOM
HE'S COOL... ACTING COOL. YES! THAT'S WHAT I MEANT. ACTING COOL.
NEGI'S TOTALLY SHOWING OFF, AND IT'S NOT WORKING FOR HIM! THAT'S WHAT I MEANT!
TH-THA RIGHT! GETTING KINDS WRONG I JUST 'CA HE'S A L STRONG STUPID
AND WHAT WAS THAT HE SAID A FEW MIN-UTES AGO? IT DIDN'T MAKE ANY SENSE! ARGH!
>REPLAY
GRR!
HE'S SO CONFIDENT! ACTING LIKE SOME BIG SHOT, LIKE THESE MONSTERS ARE NOTH-ING TO HIM!
IT'S NOT LIKE HIM, IT'S NOT LIKE HIM! IT'S NOT LIKE HIM, I SAY!
I DON LIKE I DON LIKE I DON LIKE AT AL
I KNOW HE'S HERE TO SAVE US, BUT I STILL DON'T LIKE IT!
BAM
-W PI
ANYA-CHAN.
BOFF
NNGH...
ANYA-CHAN...?
HE MIGHT BE
AS STRONG AS HIS FATHER...
NOT THAT I'D KNOW.
EH...?
...YOU GET IT, DON'T YOU, ASUNA?

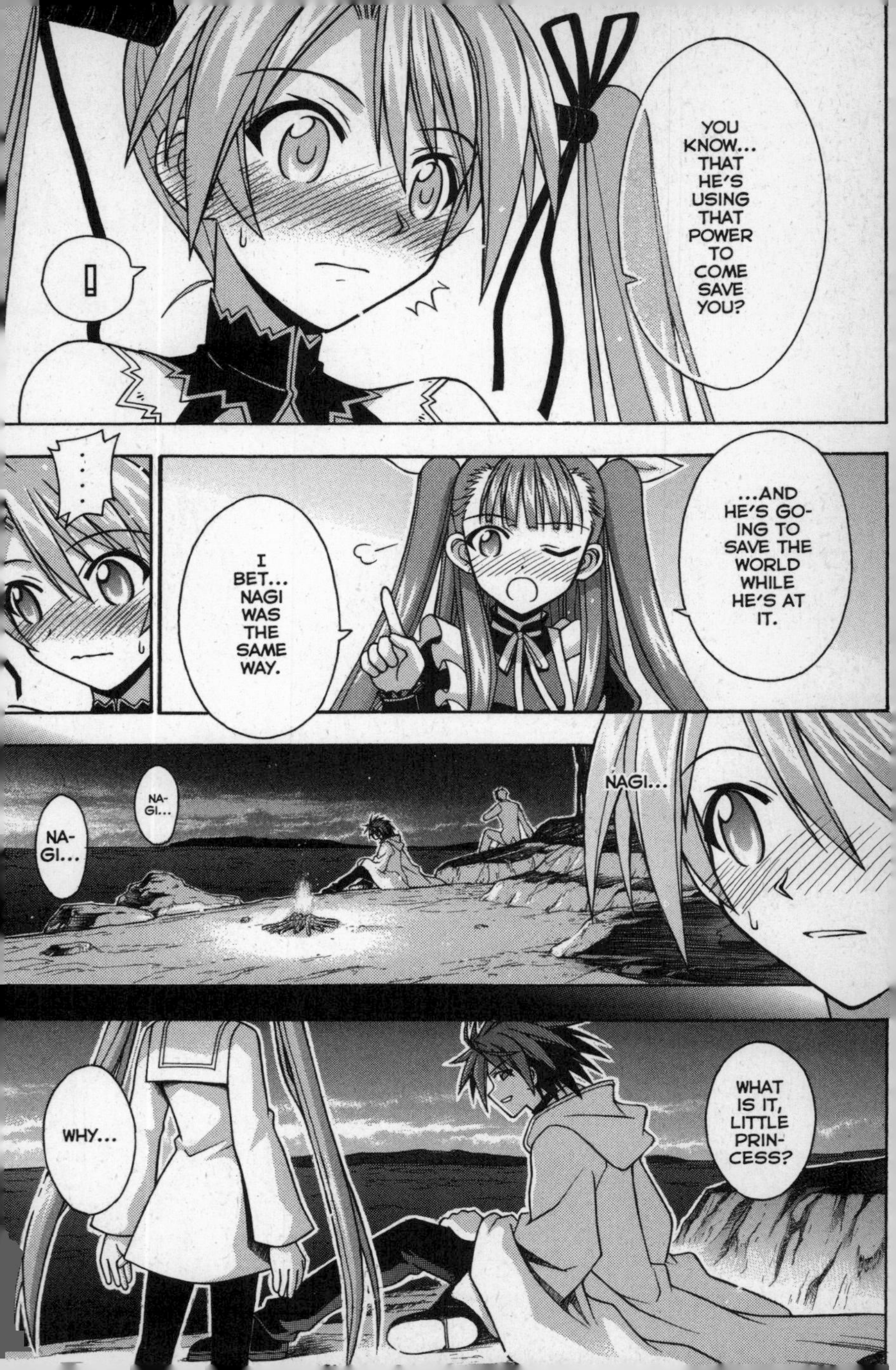
YOU KNOW... THAT HE'S USING THAT POWER TO COME SAVE YOU?
!
...AND HE'S GO-ING TO SAVE THE WORLD WHILE HE'S AT IT.
I BET... NAGI WAS THE SAME WAY.
...
NAGI...
NA-GI...
NA-GI...
WHAT IS IT, LITTLE PRIN-CESS?
WHY...

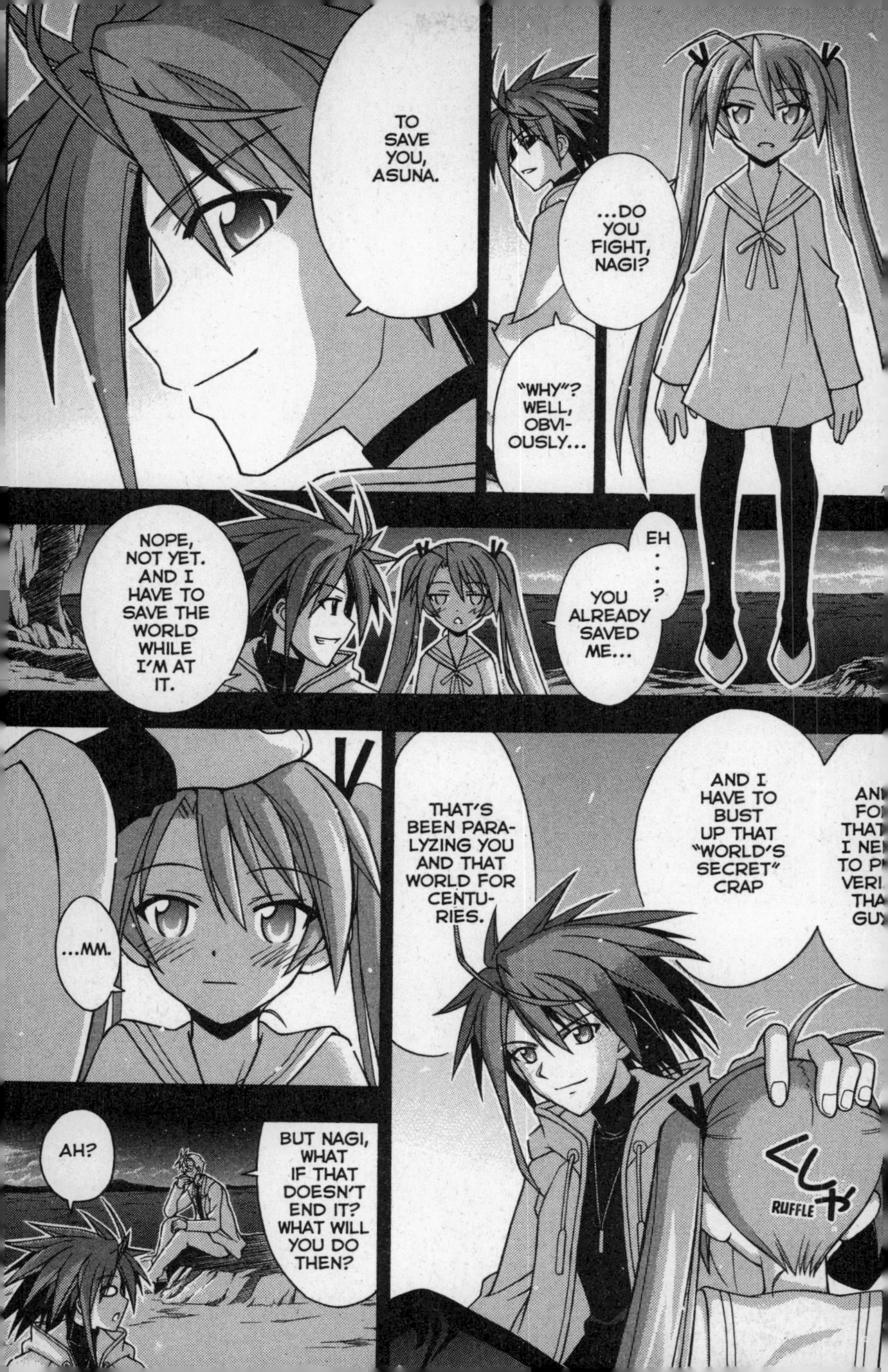
...DO YOU FIGHT, NAGI?
“WHY”? WELL, OBVIOUSLY...
TO SAVE YOU, ASUNA.
EH...? YOU ALREADY SAVED ME...
NOPE, NOT YET. AND I HAVE TO SAVE THE WORLD WHILE I'M AT IT.
AN FO THAT I NE TO P VERI THA GUY
AND I HAVE TO BUST UP THAT “WORLD'S SECRET” CRAP
THAT'S BEEN PARALYZING YOU AND THAT WORLD FOR CENTURIES.
くしゃ
RUFFLE
...MM.
BUT NAGI, WHAT IF THAT DOESN'T END IT? WHAT WILL YOU DO THEN?
AH?

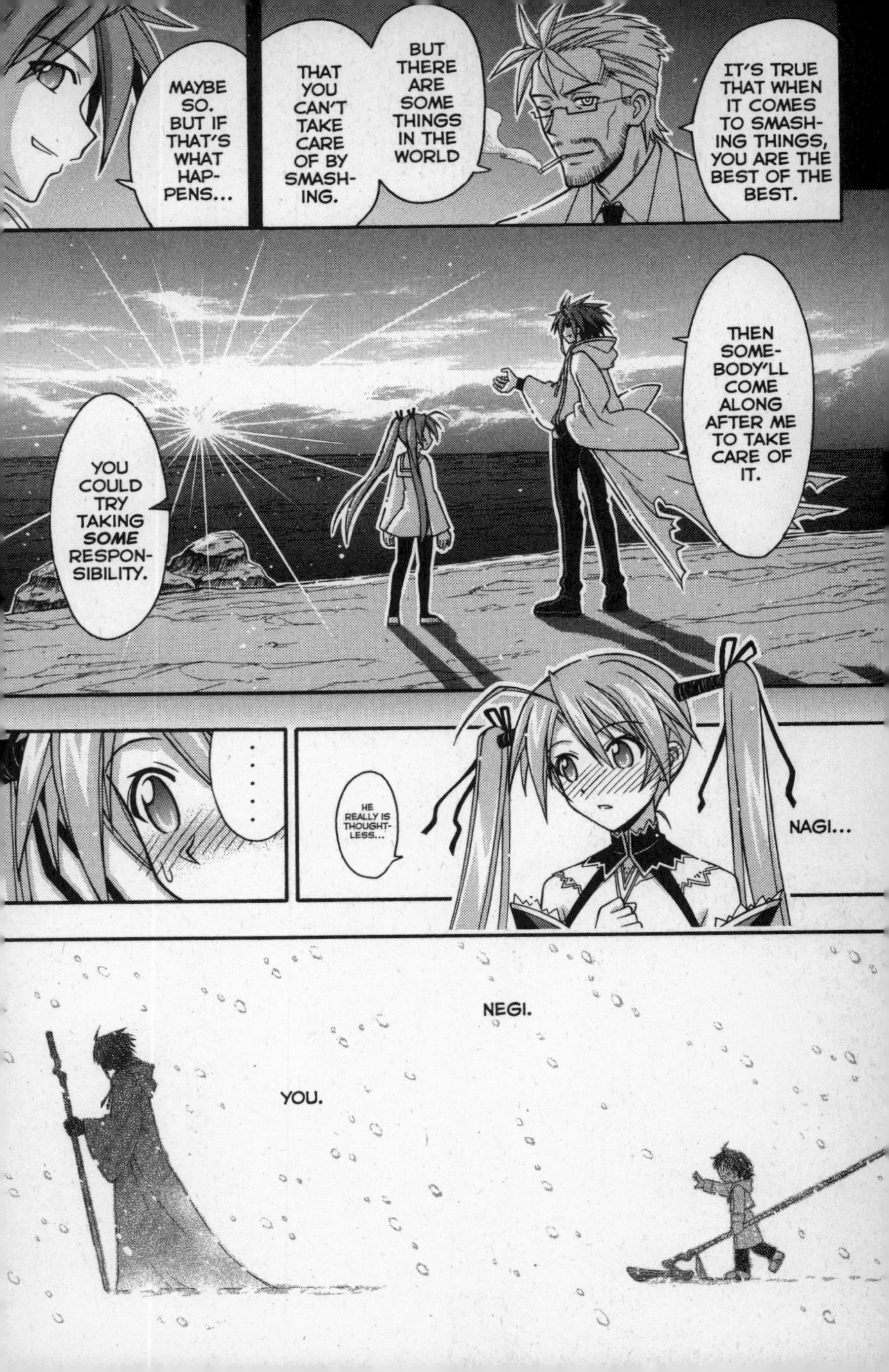
IT'S TRUE THAT WHEN IT COMES TO SMASHING THINGS, YOU ARE THE BEST OF THE BEST.
BUT THERE ARE SOME THINGS IN THE WORLD
THAT YOU CAN'T TAKE CARE OF BY SMASHING.
MAYBE SO. BUT IF THAT'S WHAT HAPPENS...
THEN SOMEBODY'LL COME ALONG AFTER ME TO TAKE CARE OF IT.
YOU COULD TRY TAKING *SOME* RESPONSIBILITY.
NAGI...
HE REALLY IS THOUGHTLESS...
......
NEGI.
YOU.

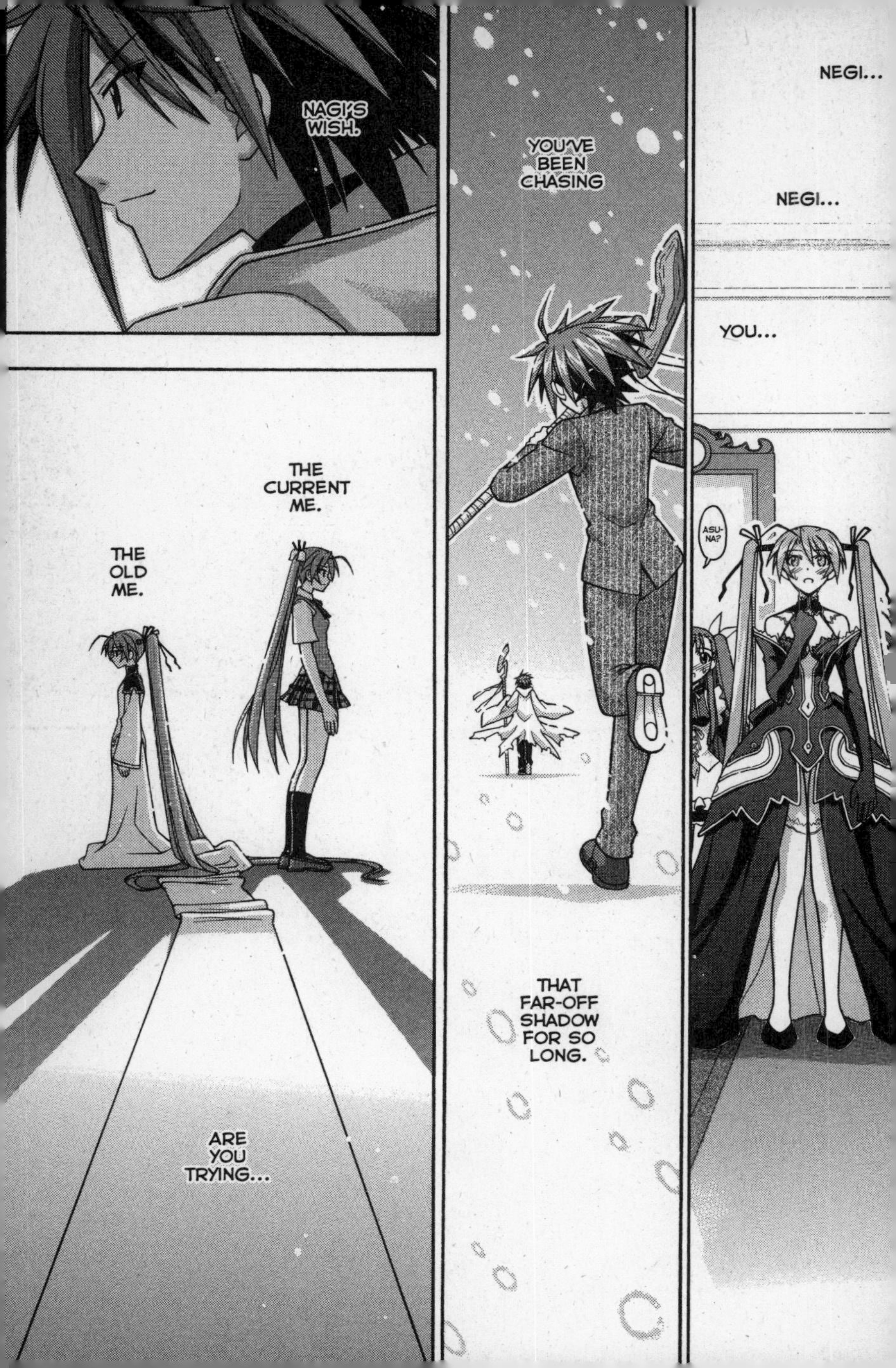
NEGI...
NEGI...
YOU...
ASU-NA?
YOU'VE BEEN CHASING
THAT FAR-OFF SHADOW FOR SO LONG.
NAGI'S WISH.
THE CURRENT ME.
THE OLD ME.
ARE YOU TRYING...

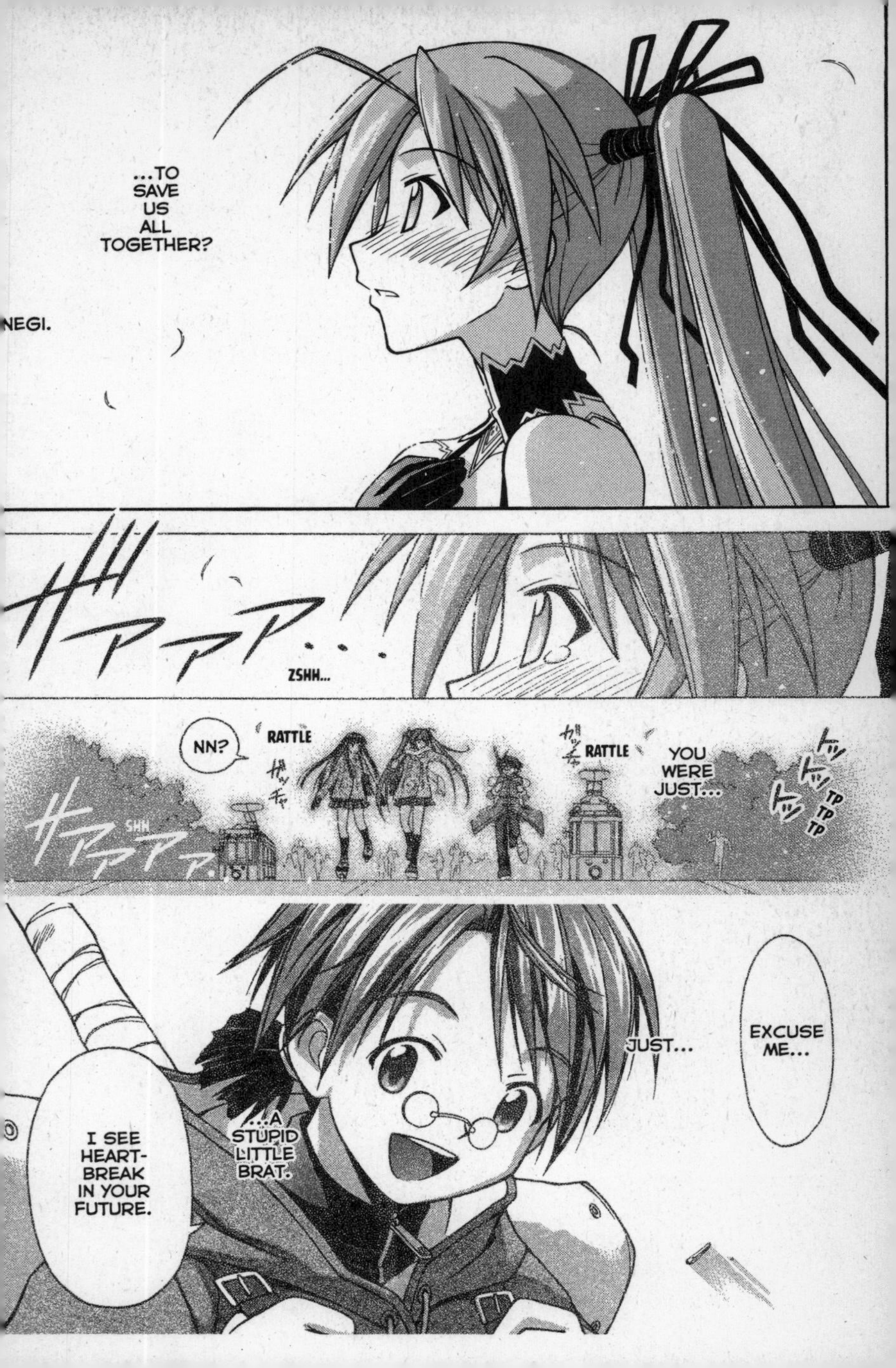

...TO SAVE US ALL TOGETHER?
NEGI.
ザァァア...
ZSHH...
TP TP TP
YOU WERE JUST...
RATTLE
NN?
RATTLE
サァァァァ
SHH
EXCUSE ME...
JUST...
...A STUPID LITTLE BRAT.
I SEE HEART-BREAK IN YOUR FUTURE.

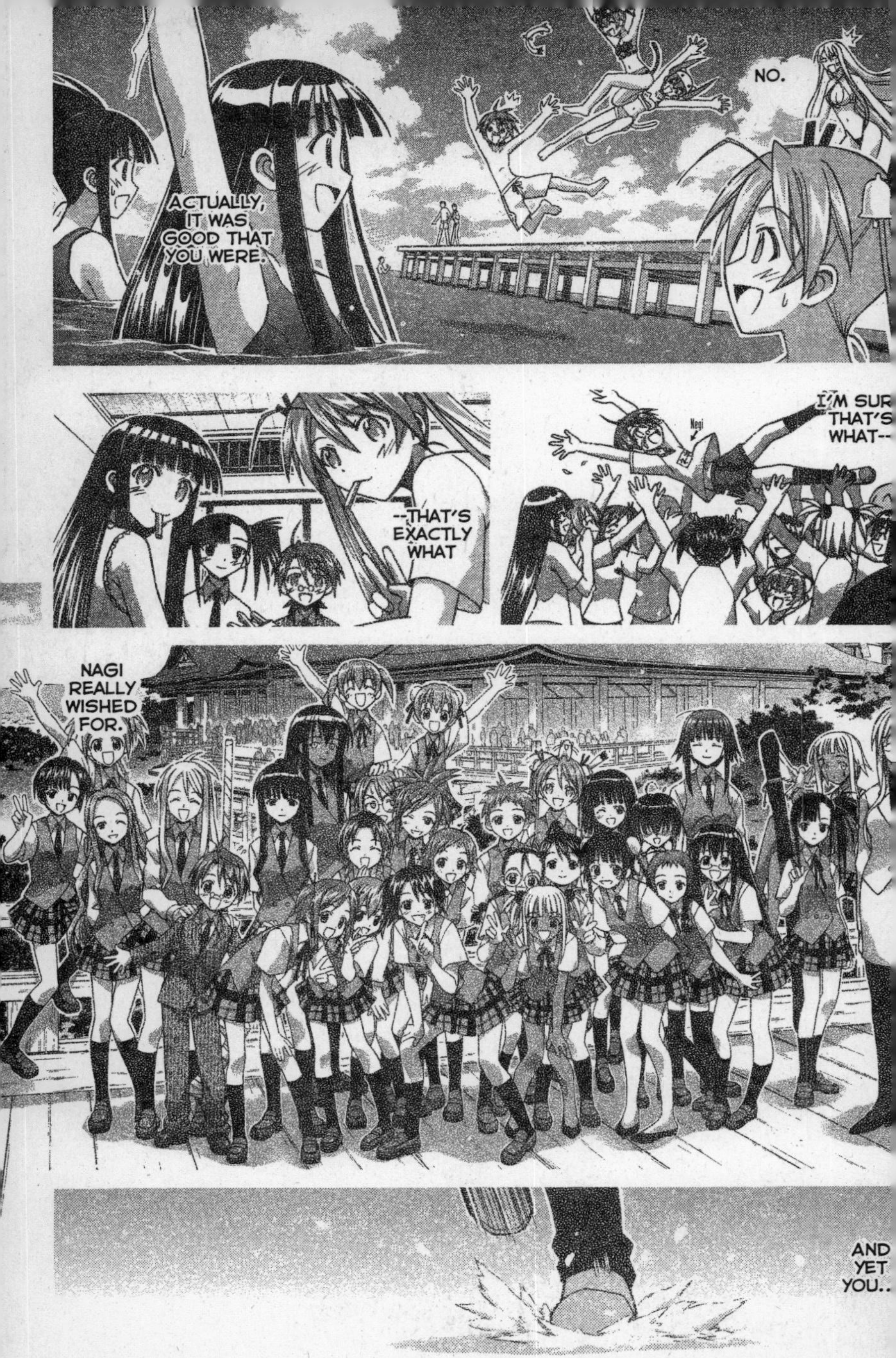
NO.
ACTUALLY, IT WAS GOOD THAT YOU WERE.
I'M SUR THAT'S WHAT--
Negi
--THAT'S EXACTLY WHAT
NAGI REALLY WISHED FOR.
AND YET YOU...

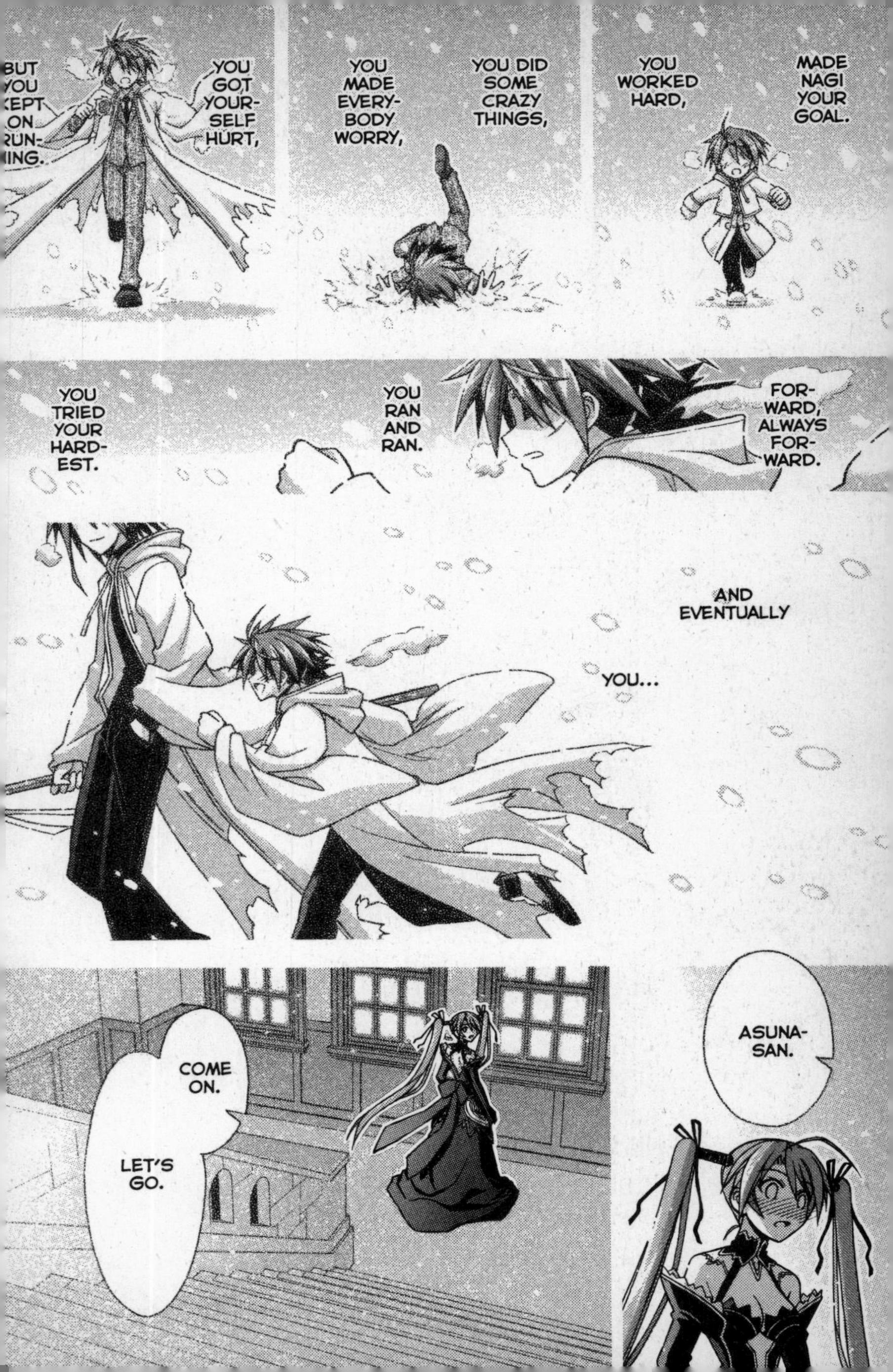
MADE NAGI YOUR GOAL.
YOU WORKED HARD,
YOU DID SOME CRAZY THINGS,
YOU MADE EVERY-BODY WORRY,
YOU GOT YOUR-SELF HURT,
BUT YOU KEPT ON RUN-NING.
FOR-WARD, ALWAYS FOR-WARD.
YOU RAN AND RAN.
YOU TRIED YOUR HARD-EST.
AND EVENTUALLY
YOU...
ASUNA-SAN.
COME ON.
LET'S GO.

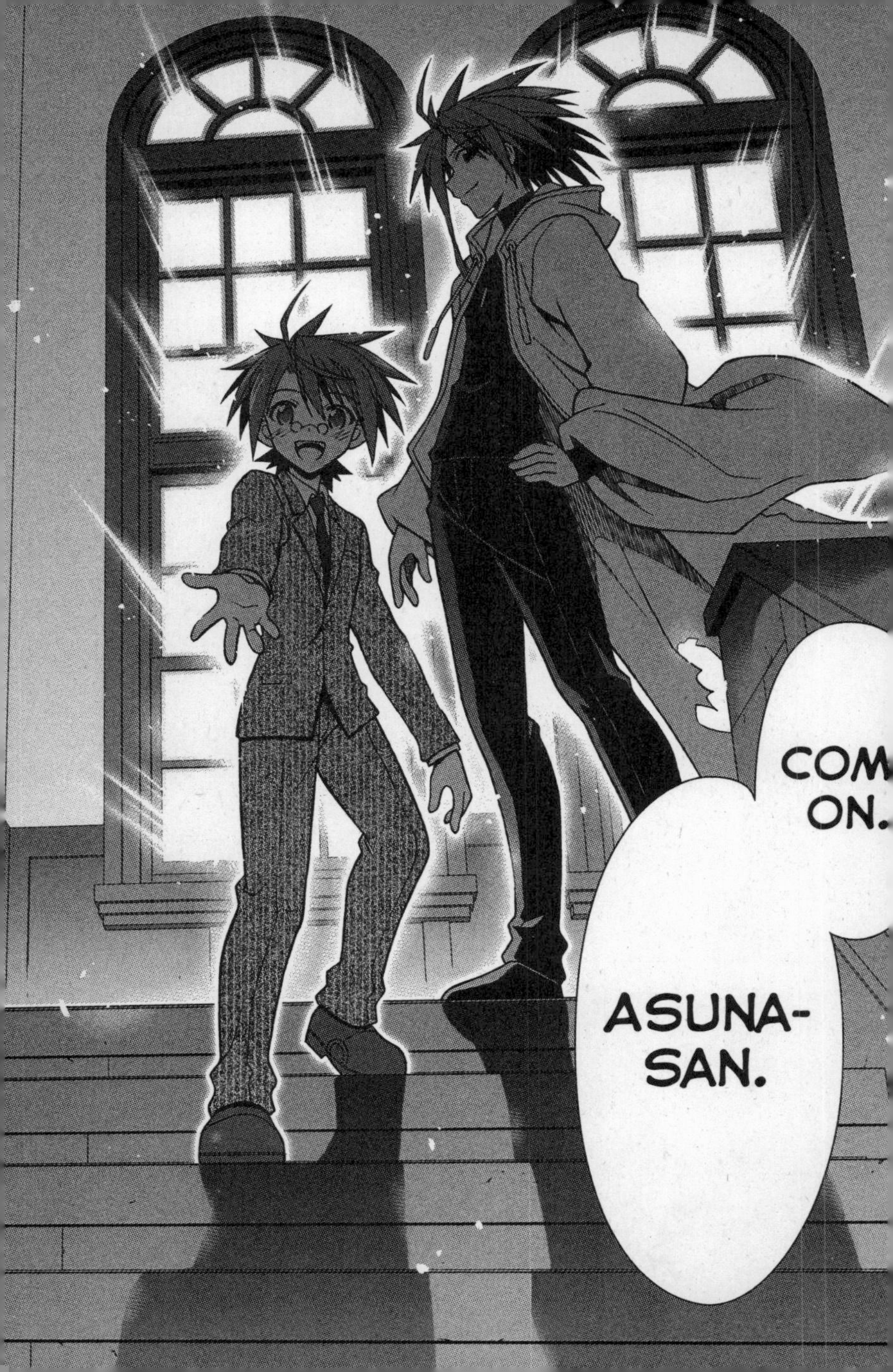
COM
ON.
ASUNA-
SAN.

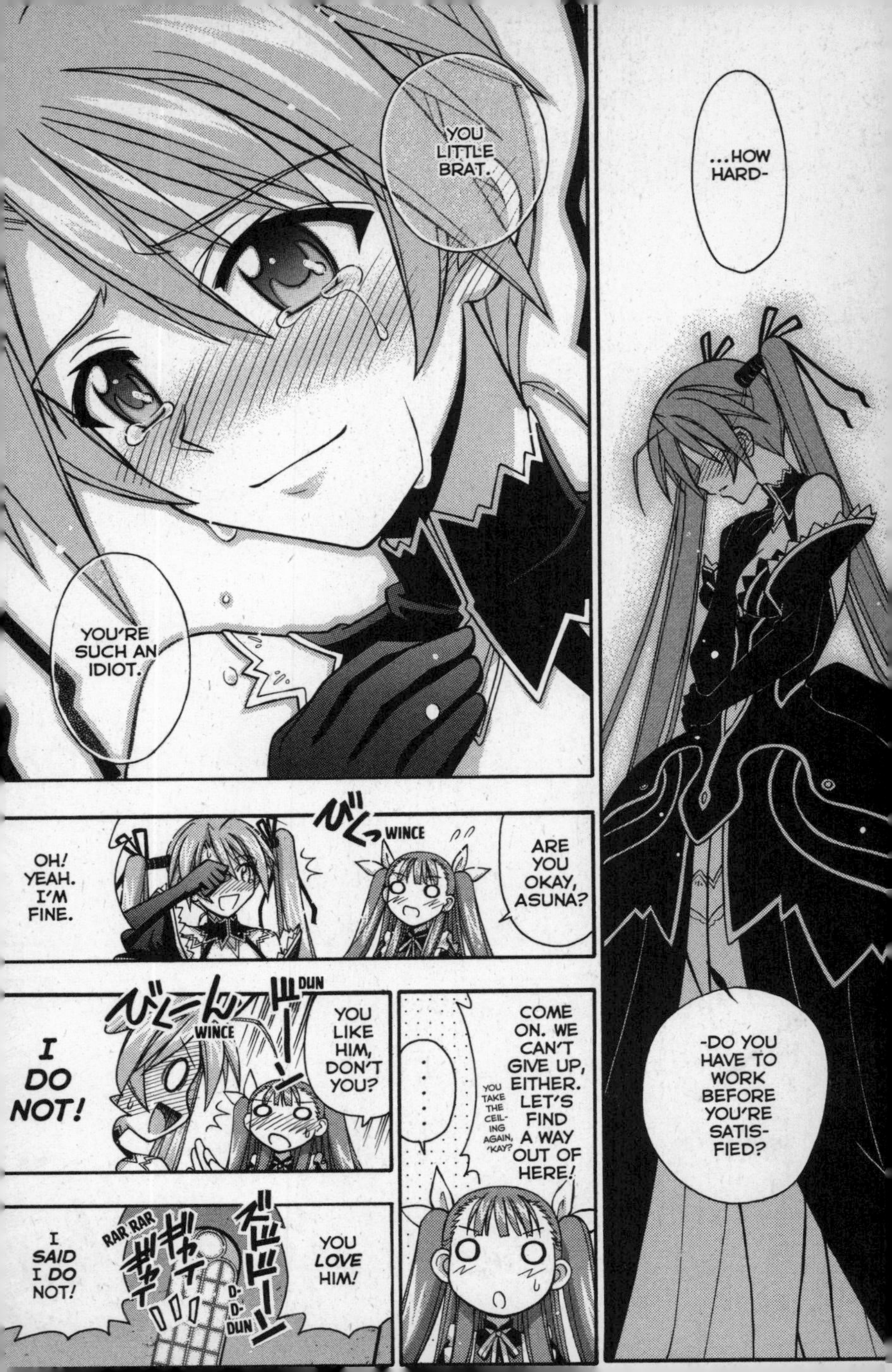
...HOW HARD-
-DO YOU HAVE TO WORK BEFORE YOU'RE SATISFIED?
YOU LITTLE BRAT.
YOU'RE SUCH AN IDIOT.
びくっ WINCE
ARE YOU OKAY, ASUNA?
OH! YEAH. I'M FINE.
ドーン DUN
YOU LIKE HIM, DON'T YOU?
びくーん WINCE
I DO NOT!
YOU LOVE HIM!
ズドドドーン D-D-DUN
ギャイギャイ RAR RAR
I SAID I DO NOT!
...
COME ON. WE CAN'T GIVE UP, EITHER. LET'S FIND A WAY OUT OF HERE!
YOU TAKE THE CEIL-ING AGAIN, 'KAY?

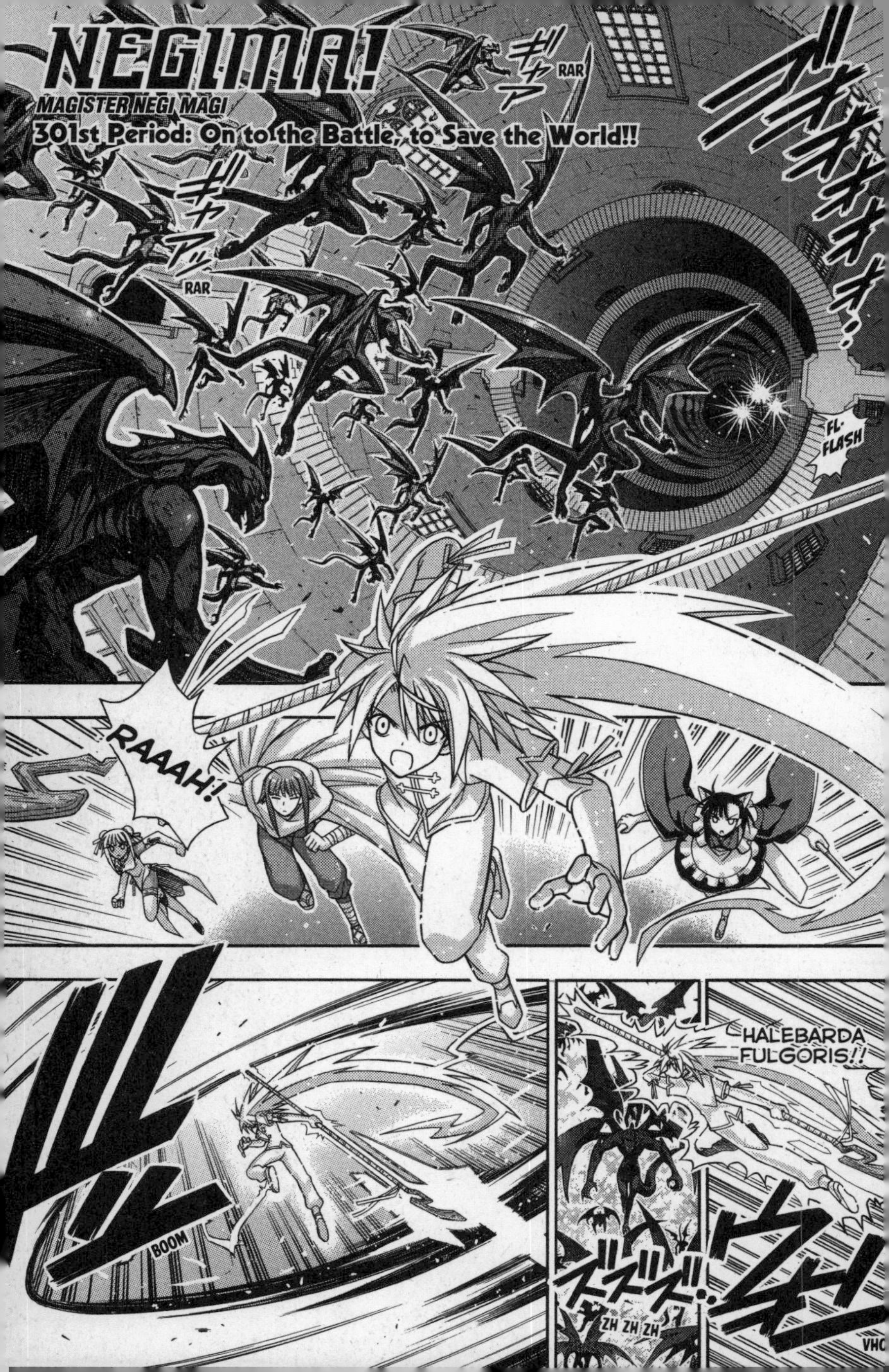
NEGIMA!
MAGISTER NEGI MAGI
301st Period: On to the Battle, to Save the World!!
ギャア
RAR
FL-FLASH
ギャアッ
RAR
RAAAH!
HALEBARDA FULGORIS!!
VHO
ズズズ
ZH ZH ZH
BOOM

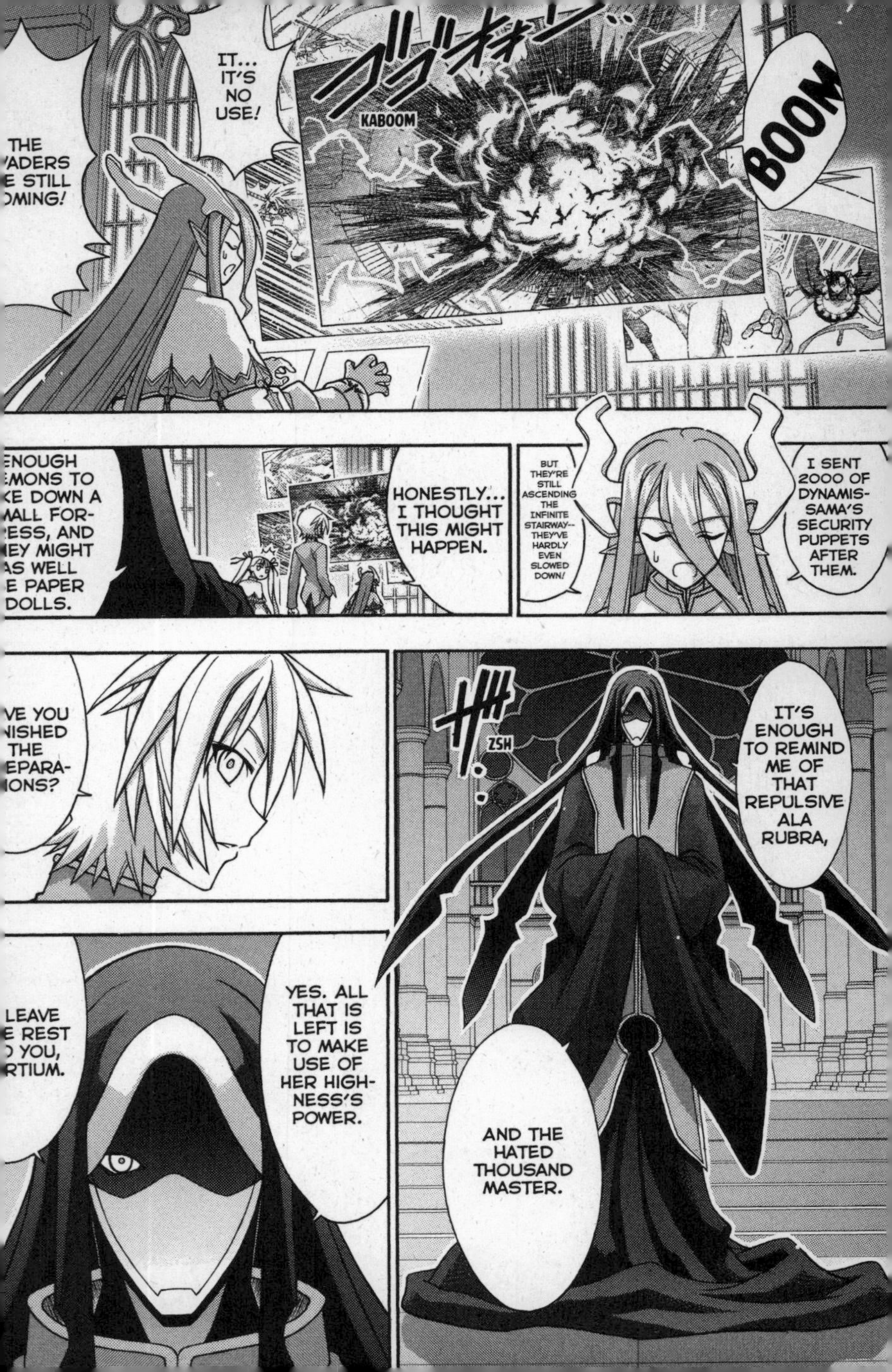
KABOOM
BOOM
IT... IT'S NO USE!
THE VADERS E STILL OMING!
I SENT 2000 OF DYNAMIS-SAMA'S SECURITY PUPPETS AFTER THEM.
BUT THEY'RE STILL ASCENDING THE INFINITE STAIRWAY-- THEY'VE HARDLY EVEN SLOWED DOWN!
HONESTLY... I THOUGHT THIS MIGHT HAPPEN.
ENOUGH EMONS TO KE DOWN A MALL FOR-RESS, AND HEY MIGHT AS WELL E PAPER DOLLS.
ZSH
IT'S ENOUGH TO REMIND ME OF THAT REPULSIVE ALA RUBRA,
AND THE HATED THOUSAND MASTER.
VE YOU NISHED THE EPARA-IONS?
YES. ALL THAT IS LEFT IS TO MAKE USE OF HER HIGH-NESS'S POWER.
LEAVE E REST O YOU, RTIUM.

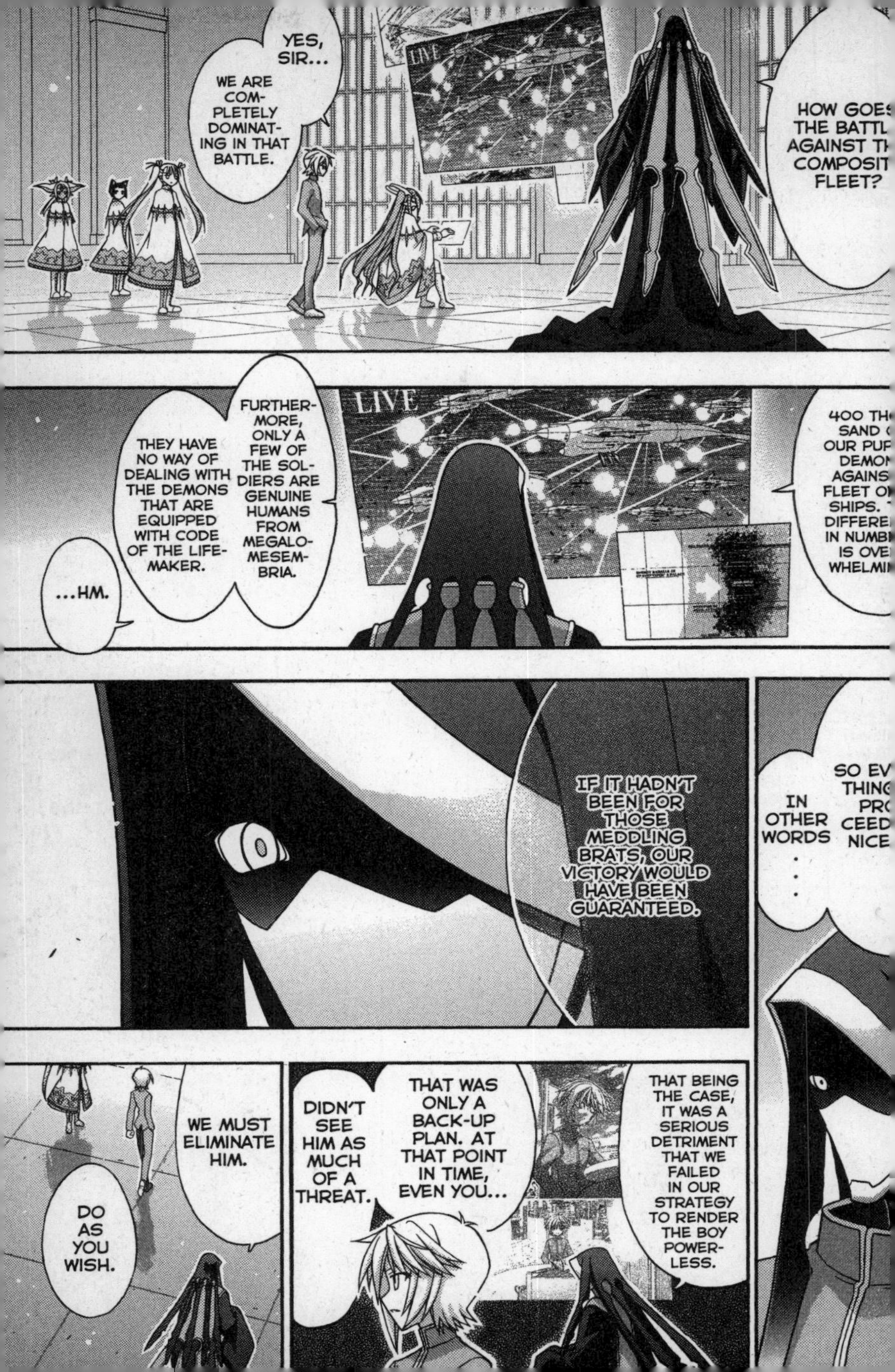

HOW GOES THE BATTL AGAINST TH COMPOSIT FLEET?
YES, SIR...
WE ARE COMPLETELY DOMINATING IN THAT BATTLE.
400 TH SAND O OUR PUP DEMON AGAINS FLEET OF SHIPS. T DIFFERE IN NUMB IS OVER WHELMI
FURTHERMORE, ONLY A FEW OF THE SOLDIERS ARE GENUINE HUMANS FROM MEGALOMESEMBRIA.
THEY HAVE NO WAY OF DEALING WITH THE DEMONS THAT ARE EQUIPPED WITH CODE OF THE LIFE-MAKER.
...HM.
SO EV THING PR CEED NICE
IN OTHER WORDS...
IF IT HADN'T BEEN FOR THOSE MEDDLING BRATS, OUR VICTORY WOULD HAVE BEEN GUARANTEED.
THAT BEING THE CASE, IT WAS A SERIOUS DETRIMENT THAT WE FAILED IN OUR STRATEGY TO RENDER THE BOY POWERLESS.
THAT WAS ONLY A BACK-UP PLAN. AT THAT POINT IN TIME, EVEN YOU...
DIDN'T SEE HIM AS MUCH OF A THREAT.
WE MUST ELIMINATE HIM.
DO AS YOU WISH.

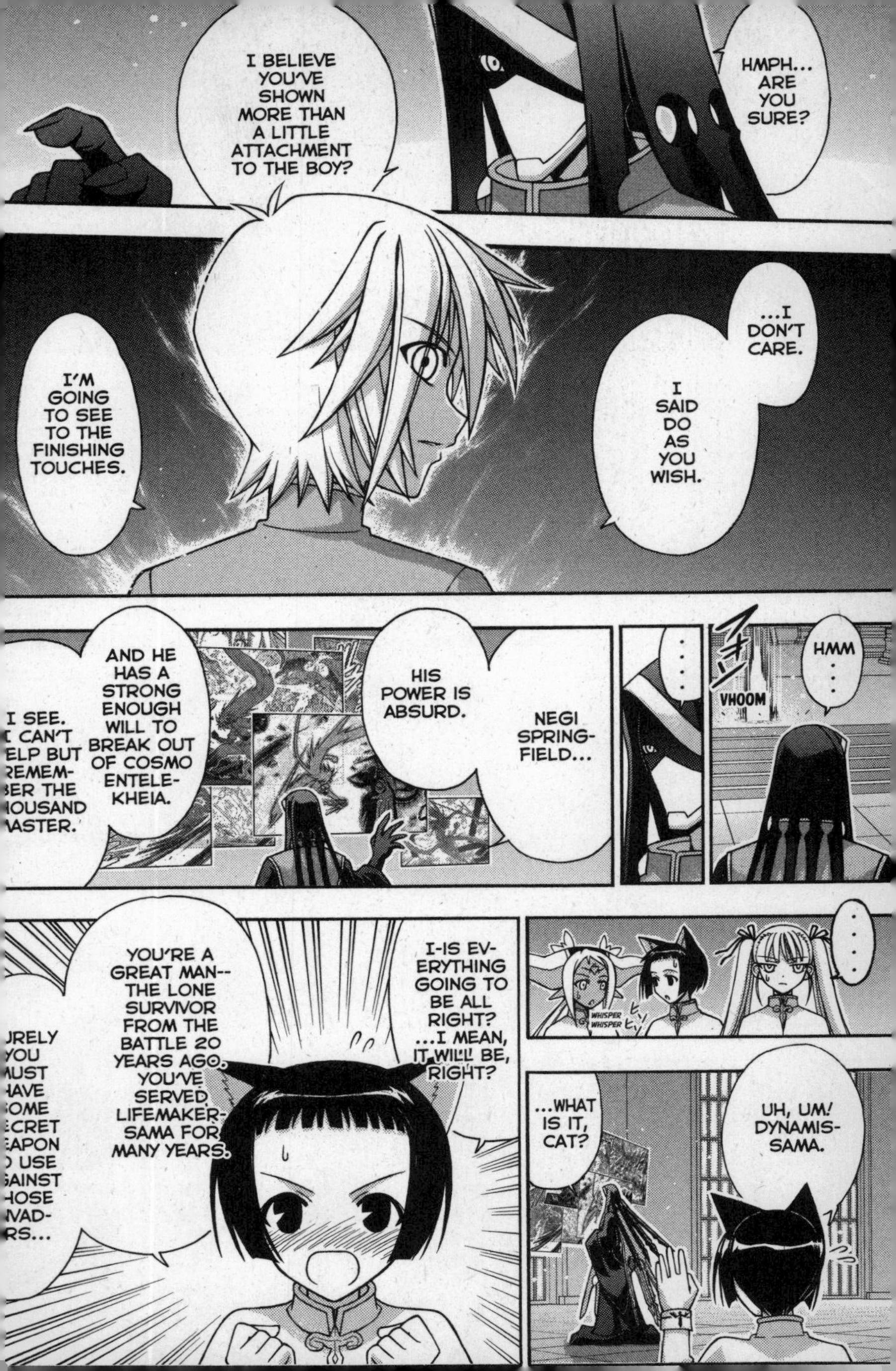
HMPH... ARE YOU SURE?
I BELIEVE YOU'VE SHOWN MORE THAN A LITTLE ATTACHMENT TO THE BOY?
...I DON'T CARE.
I SAID DO AS YOU WISH.
I'M GOING TO SEE TO THE FINISHING TOUCHES.
HMM...
VHOOM
...
NEGI SPRINGFIELD...
HIS POWER IS ABSURD.
AND HE HAS A STRONG ENOUGH WILL TO BREAK OUT OF COSMO ENTELEKHEIA.
I SEE. CAN'T ELP BUT REMEMBER THE HOUSAND ASTER.
...
WHISPER WHISPER
UH, UM! DYNAMIS-SAMA.
...WHAT IS IT, CAT?
I-IS EVERYTHING GOING TO BE ALL RIGHT? ...I MEAN, IT WILL BE, RIGHT?
YOU'RE A GREAT MAN-- THE LONE SURVIVOR FROM THE BATTLE 20 YEARS AGO. YOU'VE SERVED LIFEMAKER-SAMA FOR MANY YEARS.
URELY YOU MUST HAVE OME ECRET EAPON O USE GAINST HOSE NVADERS...

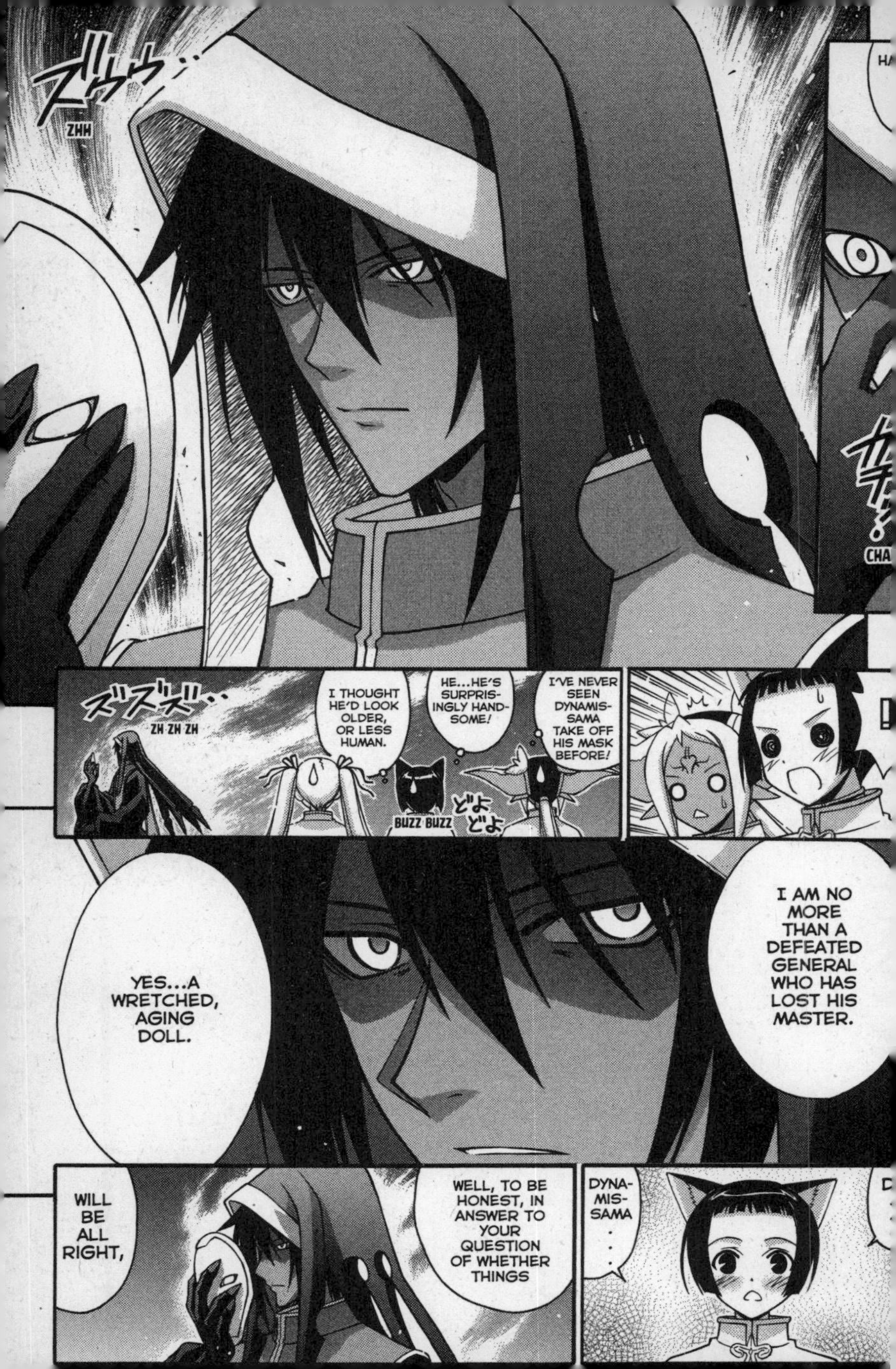

ZHH
!
ZH ZH ZH
I'VE NEVER SEEN DYNAMIS-SAMA TAKE OFF HIS MASK BEFORE!
HE...HE'S SURPRIS-INGLY HAND-SOME!
I THOUGHT HE'D LOOK OLDER, OR LESS HUMAN.
BUZZ BUZZ
I AM NO MORE THAN A DEFEATED GENERAL WHO HAS LOST HIS MASTER.
YES...A WRETCHED, AGING DOLL.
DYNA-MIS-SAMA . . .
WELL, TO BE HONEST, IN ANSWER TO YOUR QUESTION OF WHETHER THINGS
WILL BE ALL RIGHT,

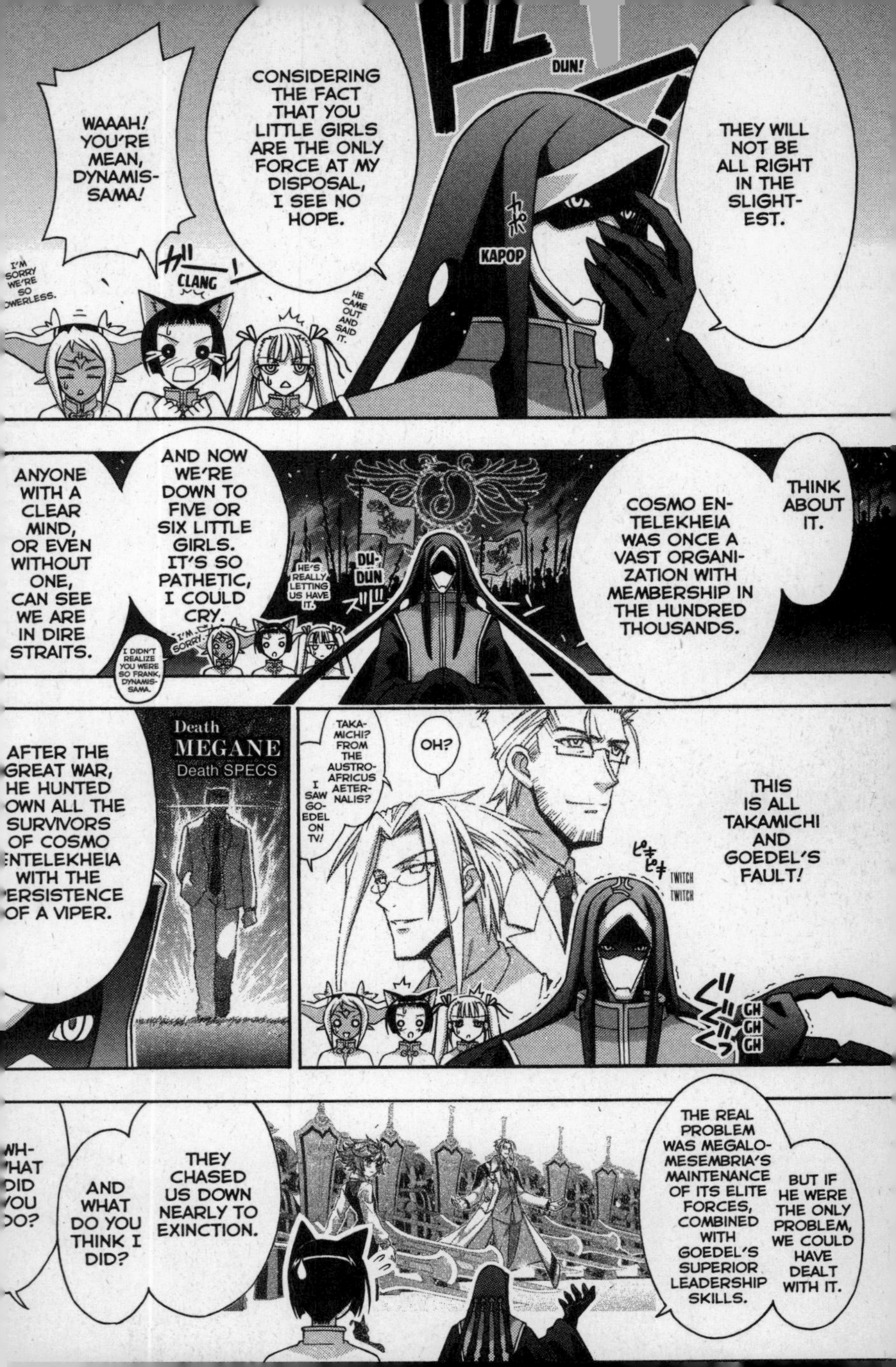
DUN!
THEY WILL NOT BE ALL RIGHT IN THE SLIGHTEST.
KAPOP
CONSIDERING THE FACT THAT YOU LITTLE GIRLS ARE THE ONLY FORCE AT MY DISPOSAL, I SEE NO HOPE.
WAAAH! YOU'RE MEAN, DYNAMIS-SAMA!
CLANG
HE CAME OUT AND SAID IT.
I'M SORRY WE'RE SO OWERLESS.
THINK ABOUT IT.
COSMO EN-TELEKHEIA WAS ONCE A VAST ORGANI-ZATION WITH MEMBERSHIP IN THE HUNDRED THOUSANDS.
DU-DUN
HE'S REALLY LETTING US HAVE IT.
AND NOW WE'RE DOWN TO FIVE OR SIX LITTLE GIRLS. IT'S SO PATHETIC, I COULD CRY.
ANYONE WITH A CLEAR MIND, OR EVEN WITHOUT ONE, CAN SEE WE ARE IN DIRE STRAITS.
I'M SORRY.
I DIDN'T REALIZE YOU WERE SO FRANK, DYNAMIS-SAMA.
THIS IS ALL TAKAMICHI AND GOEDEL'S FAULT!
OH?
TAKA-MICHI? FROM THE AUSTRO-AFRICUS AETER-NALIS?
I SAW GO-EDEL ON TV!
TWITCH TWITCH
GH GH GH
Death MEGANE Death SPECS
AFTER THE GREAT WAR, HE HUNTED OWN ALL THE SURVIVORS OF COSMO NTELEKHEIA WITH THE ERSISTENCE OF A VIPER.
BUT IF HE WERE THE ONLY PROBLEM, WE COULD HAVE DEALT WITH IT.
THE REAL PROBLEM WAS MEGALO-MESEMBRIA'S MAINTENANCE OF ITS ELITE FORCES, COMBINED WITH GOEDEL'S SUPERIOR LEADERSHIP SKILLS.
THEY CHASED US DOWN NEARLY TO EXINCTION.
AND WHAT DO YOU THINK I DID?
WH- HAT DID OU OO?

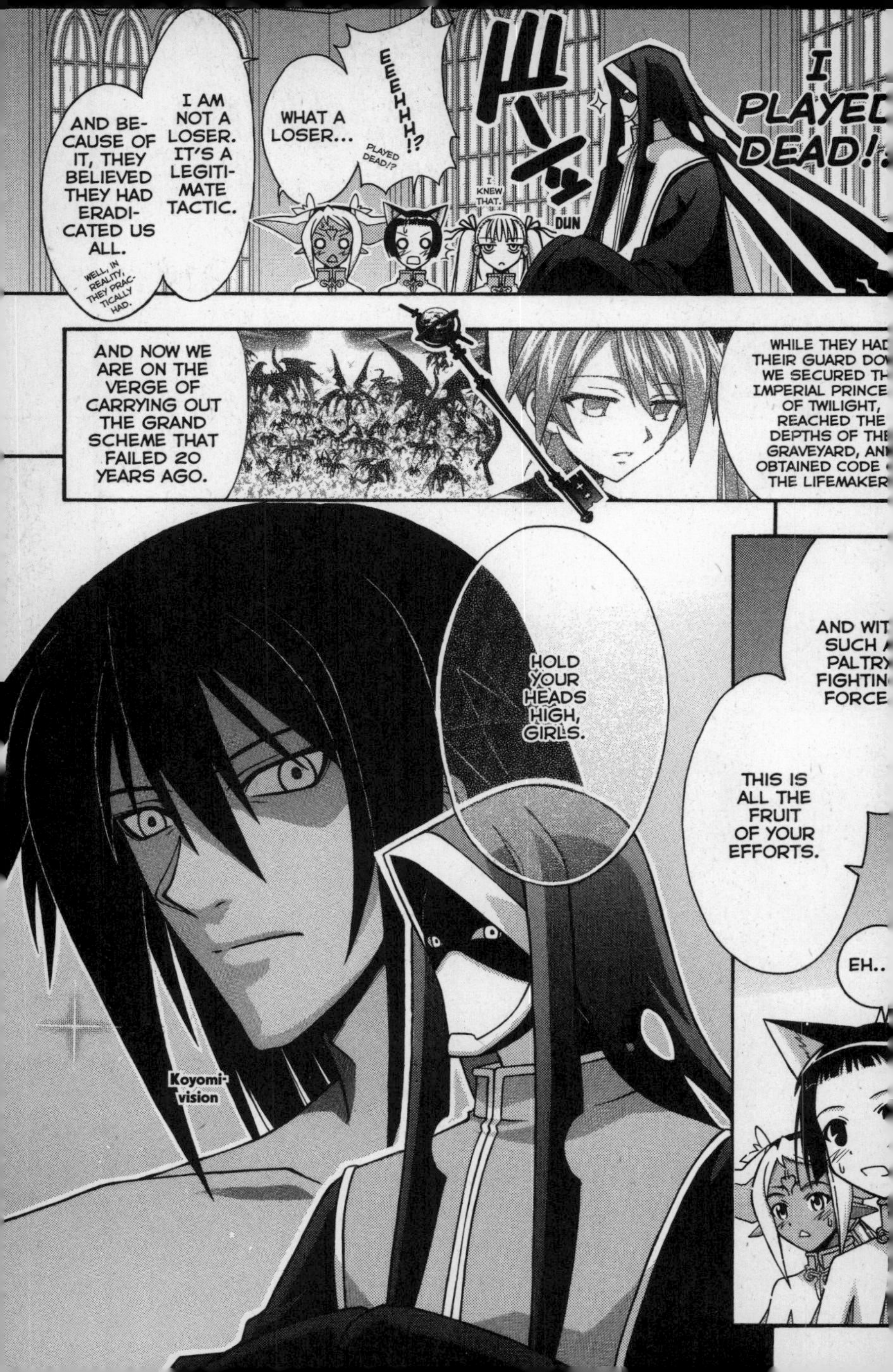
I PLAYED DEAD!!
DUN
I KNEW THAT.
EEEHHH!?
PLAYED DEAD!?
WHAT A LOSER...
I AM NOT A LOSER. IT'S A LEGITIMATE TACTIC.
AND BECAUSE OF IT, THEY BELIEVED THEY HAD ERADICATED US ALL.
WELL, IN REALITY, THEY PRACTICALLY HAD.
WHILE THEY HAD THEIR GUARD DOW WE SECURED TH IMPERIAL PRINCE OF TWILIGHT, REACHED THE DEPTHS OF THE GRAVEYARD, AN OBTAINED CODE THE LIFEMAKER
AND NOW WE ARE ON THE VERGE OF CARRYING OUT THE GRAND SCHEME THAT FAILED 20 YEARS AGO.
AND WIT SUCH PALTRY FIGHTING FORCE
THIS IS ALL THE FRUIT OF YOUR EFFORTS.
EH..
HOLD YOUR HEADS HIGH, GIRLS.
Koyomi-vision

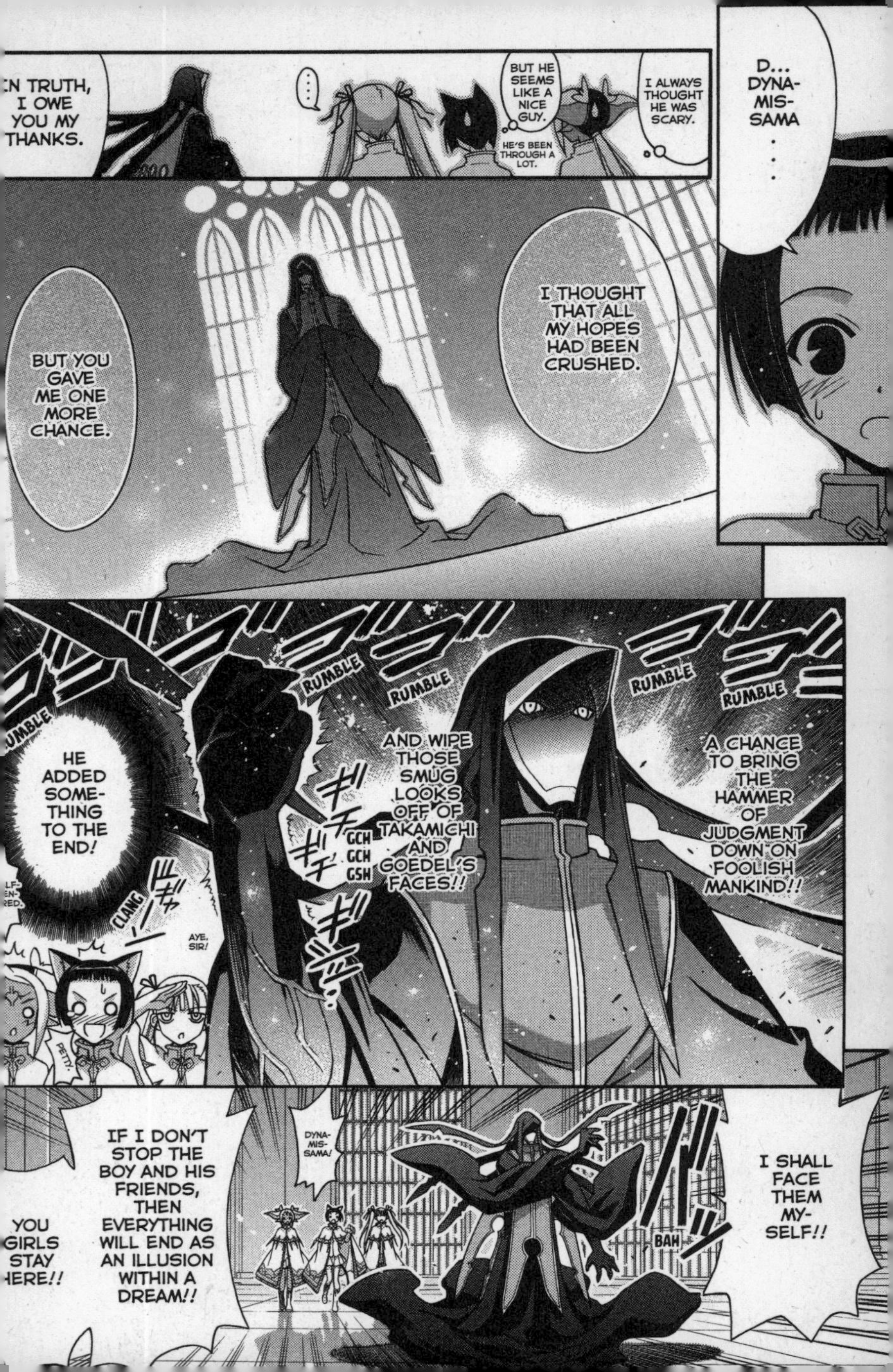
D... DYNA-MIS-SAMA . . .
I ALWAYS THOUGHT HE WAS SCARY.
BUT HE SEEMS LIKE A NICE GUY.
HE'S BEEN THROUGH A LOT.
. . . .
IN TRUTH, I OWE YOU MY THANKS.
I THOUGHT THAT ALL MY HOPES HAD BEEN CRUSHED.
BUT YOU GAVE ME ONE MORE CHANCE.
RUMBLE
RUMBLE
RUMBLE
RUMBLE
RUMBLE
A CHANCE TO BRING THE HAMMER OF JUDGMENT DOWN ON FOOLISH MANKIND!!
AND WIPE THOSE SMUG LOOKS OFF OF TAKAMICHI AND GOEDEL'S FACES!!
GCH GCH GSH
HE ADDED SOME-THING TO THE END!
CLANG
AYE, SIR!
PETTY.
I SHALL FACE THEM MY-SELF!!
BAH
DYNA-MIS-SAMA!
IF I DON'T STOP THE BOY AND HIS FRIENDS, THEN EVERYTHING WILL END AS AN ILLUSION WITHIN A DREAM!!
YOU GIRLS STAY HERE!!

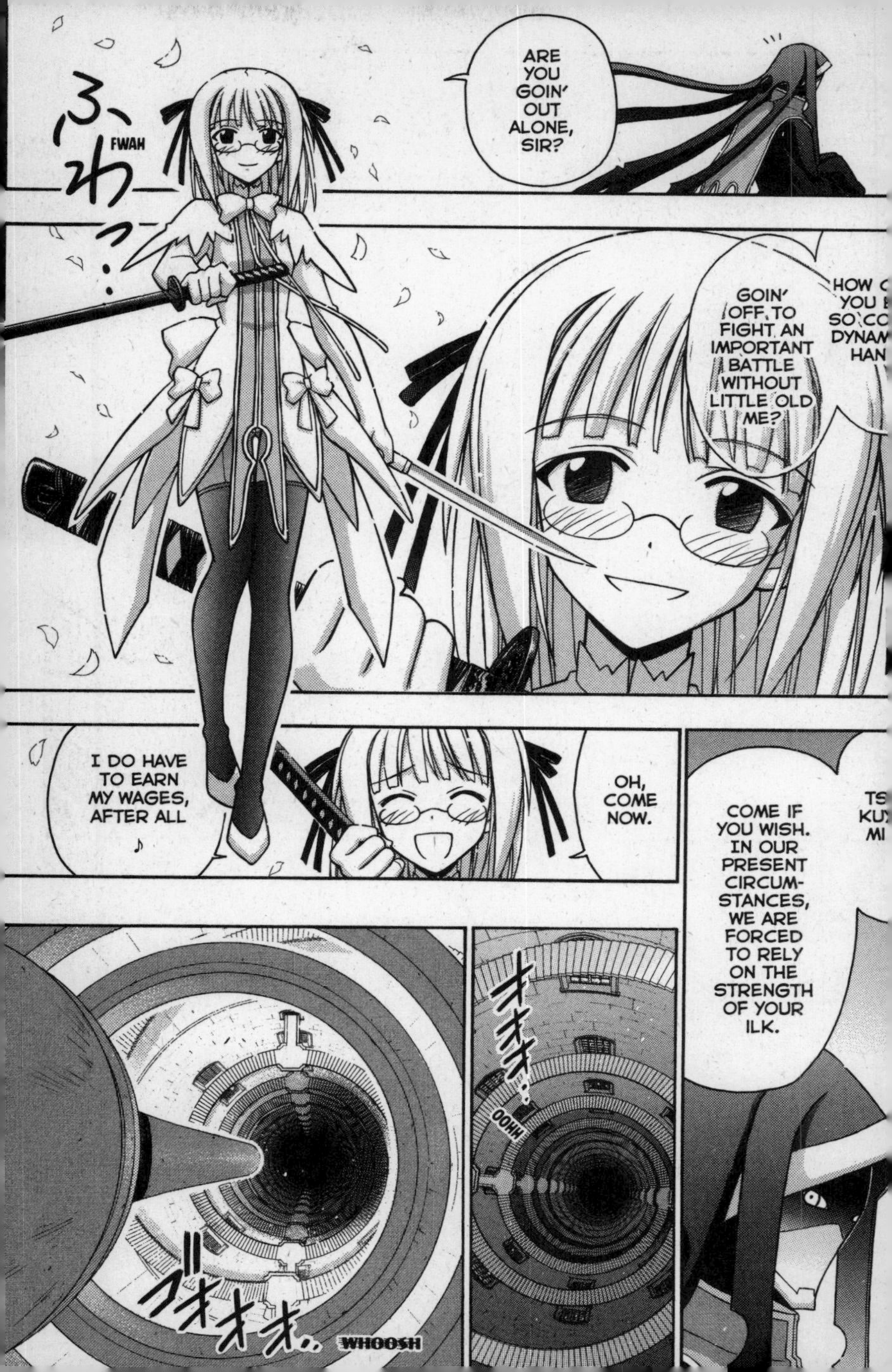

ARE YOU GOIN' OUT ALONE, SIR?
GOIN' OFF TO FIGHT AN IMPORTANT BATTLE WITHOUT LITTLE OLD ME?
ふわっ
FWAH
COME IF YOU WISH. IN OUR PRESENT CIRCUM-STANCES, WE ARE FORCED TO RELY ON THE STRENGTH OF YOUR ILK.
OH, COME NOW.
I DO HAVE TO EARN MY WAGES, AFTER ALL ♪
オオオ
OOHH
ゴオオオ
WHOOSH

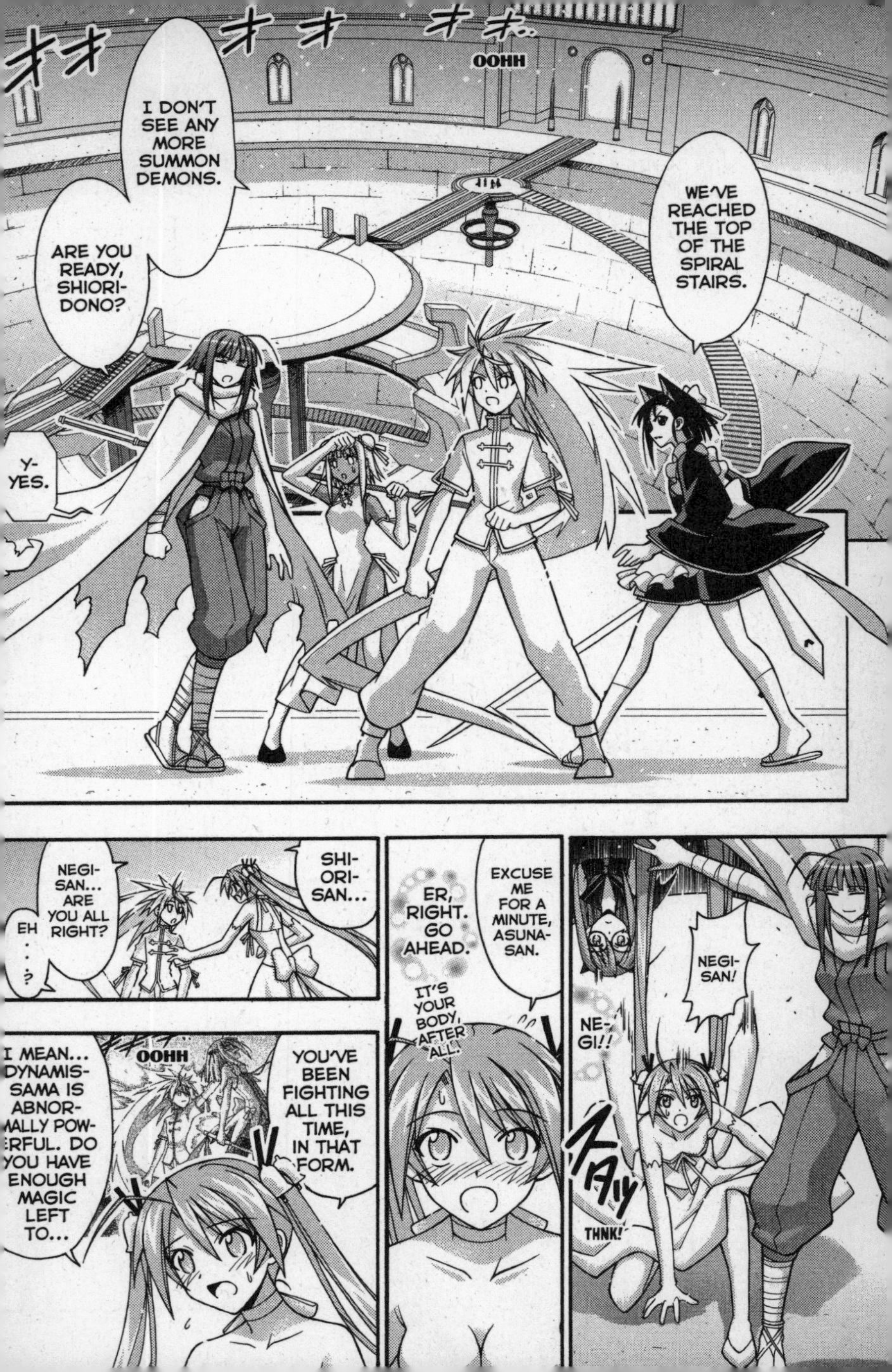
オオオオオ
OOHH
WE'VE REACHED THE TOP OF THE SPIRAL STAIRS.
I DON'T SEE ANY MORE SUMMON DEMONS.
ARE YOU READY, SHIORI-DONO?
Y-YES.
SHI-ORI-SAN...
NEGI-SAN... ARE YOU ALL RIGHT?
EH...?
YOU'VE BEEN FIGHTING ALL THIS TIME, IN THAT FORM.
OOHH
I MEAN... DYNAMIS-SAMA IS ABNORMALLY POWERFUL. DO YOU HAVE ENOUGH MAGIC LEFT TO...
EXCUSE ME FOR A MINUTE, ASUNA-SAN.
ER, RIGHT. GO AHEAD.
IT'S YOUR BODY, AFTER ALL.
NEGI-SAN!
NE-GI!!
THNK!

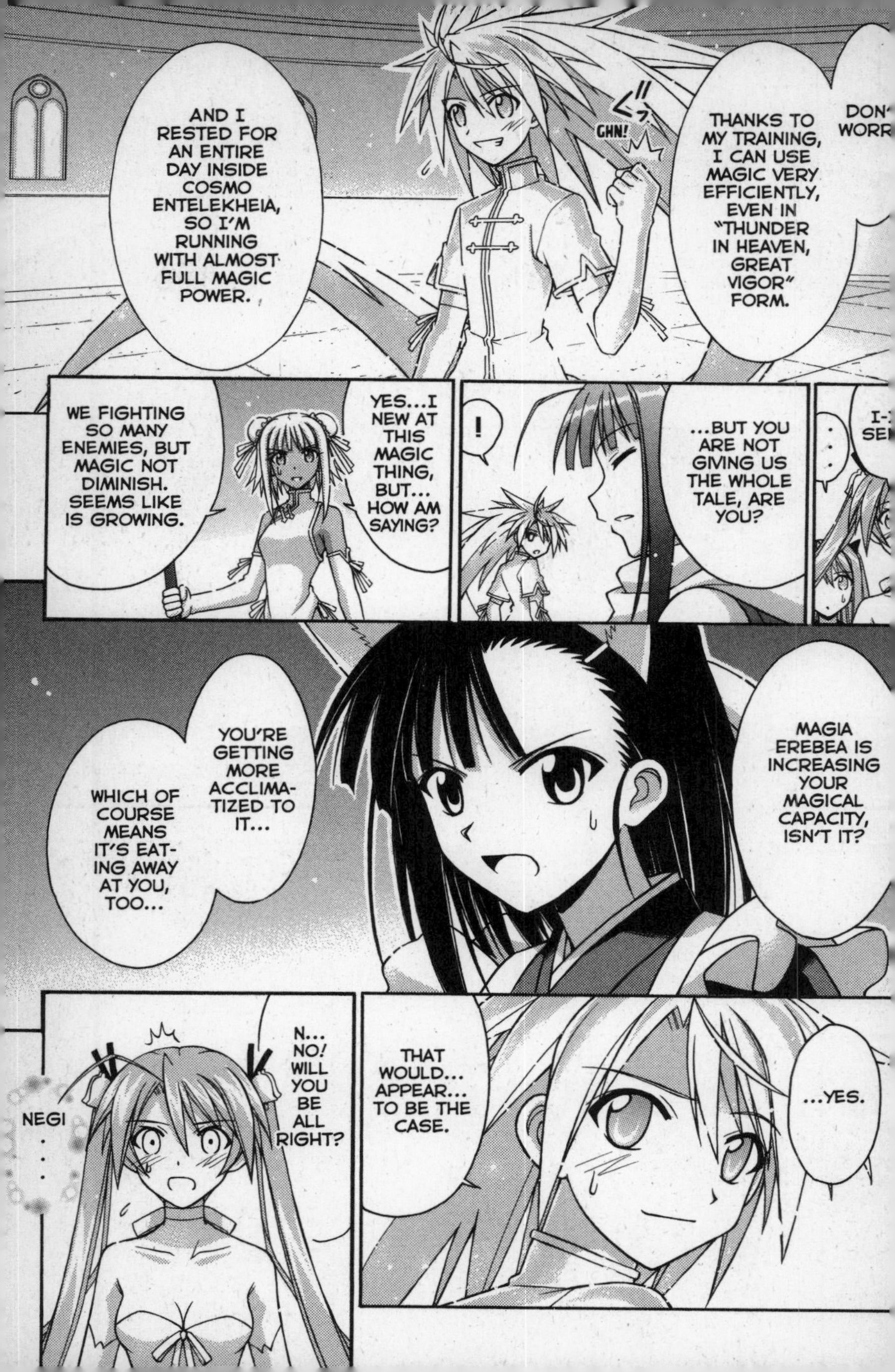
DON' WORR
THANKS TO MY TRAINING, I CAN USE MAGIC VERY EFFICIENTLY, EVEN IN "THUNDER IN HEAVEN, GREAT VIGOR" FORM.
GHN!
AND I RESTED FOR AN ENTIRE DAY INSIDE COSMO ENTELEKHEIA, SO I'M RUNNING WITH ALMOST FULL MAGIC POWER.
. . .
...BUT YOU ARE NOT GIVING US THE WHOLE TALE, ARE YOU?
!
YES...I NEW AT THIS MAGIC THING, BUT... HOW AM SAYING?
WE FIGHTING SO MANY ENEMIES, BUT MAGIC NOT DIMINISH. SEEMS LIKE IS GROWING.
MAGIA EREBEA IS INCREASING YOUR MAGICAL CAPACITY, ISN'T IT?
YOU'RE GETTING MORE ACCLIMATIZED TO IT...
WHICH OF COURSE MEANS IT'S EATING AWAY AT YOU, TOO...
...YES.
THAT WOULD... APPEAR... TO BE THE CASE.
N... NO! WILL YOU BE ALL RIGHT?
NEGI . . .

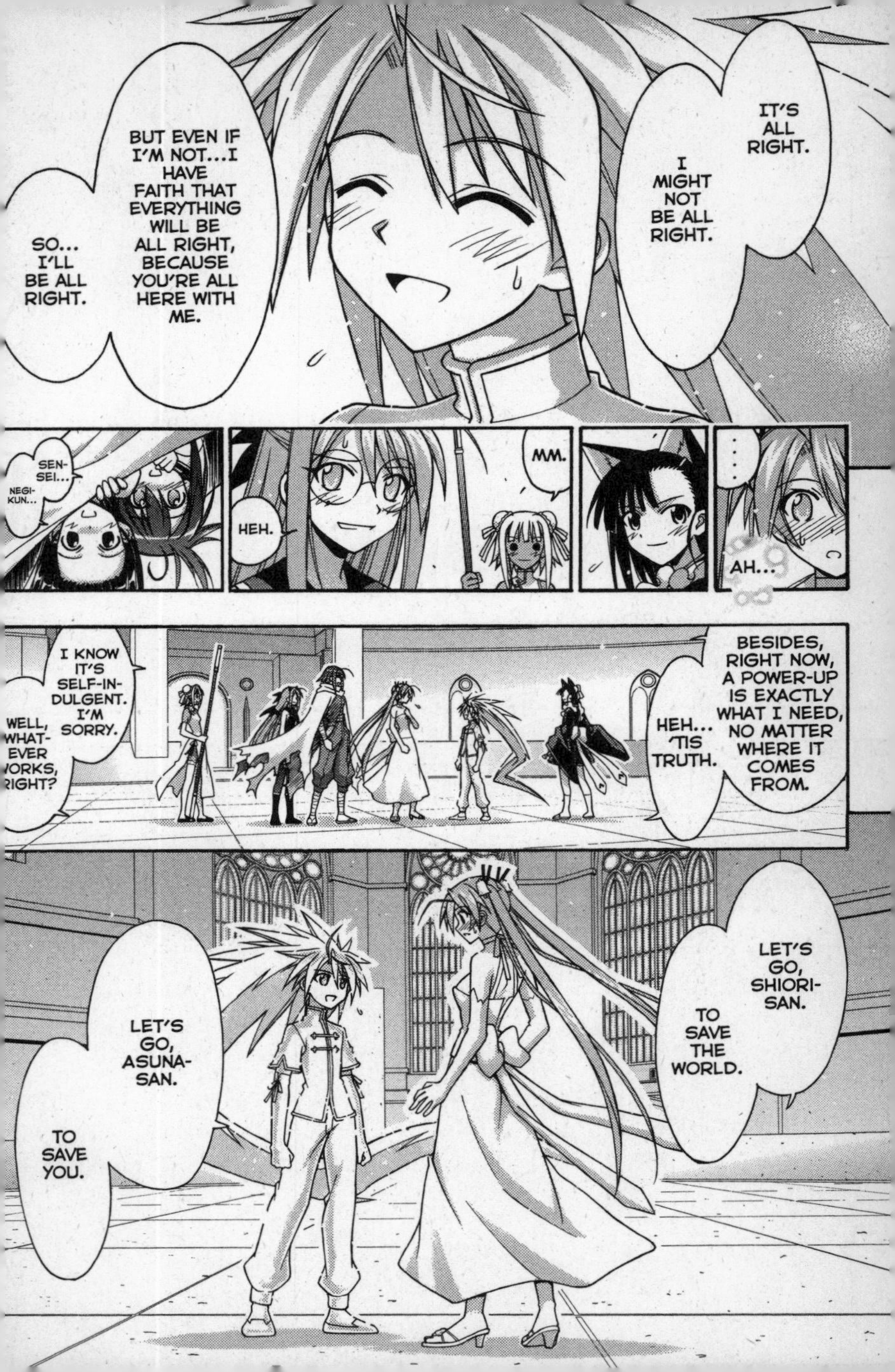
IT'S ALL RIGHT.
I MIGHT NOT BE ALL RIGHT.
BUT EVEN IF I'M NOT...I HAVE FAITH THAT EVERYTHING WILL BE ALL RIGHT, BECAUSE YOU'RE ALL HERE WITH ME.
SO... I'LL BE ALL RIGHT.
...
AH...
MM.
HEH.
SEN-SEI...
NEGI-KUN...
BESIDES, RIGHT NOW, A POWER-UP IS EXACTLY WHAT I NEED, NO MATTER WHERE IT COMES FROM.
HEH... 'TIS TRUTH.
I KNOW IT'S SELF-INDULGENT. I'M SORRY.
WELL, WHAT-EVER WORKS, RIGHT?
LET'S GO, SHIORI-SAN.
TO SAVE THE WORLD.
LET'S GO, ASUNA-SAN.
TO SAVE YOU.

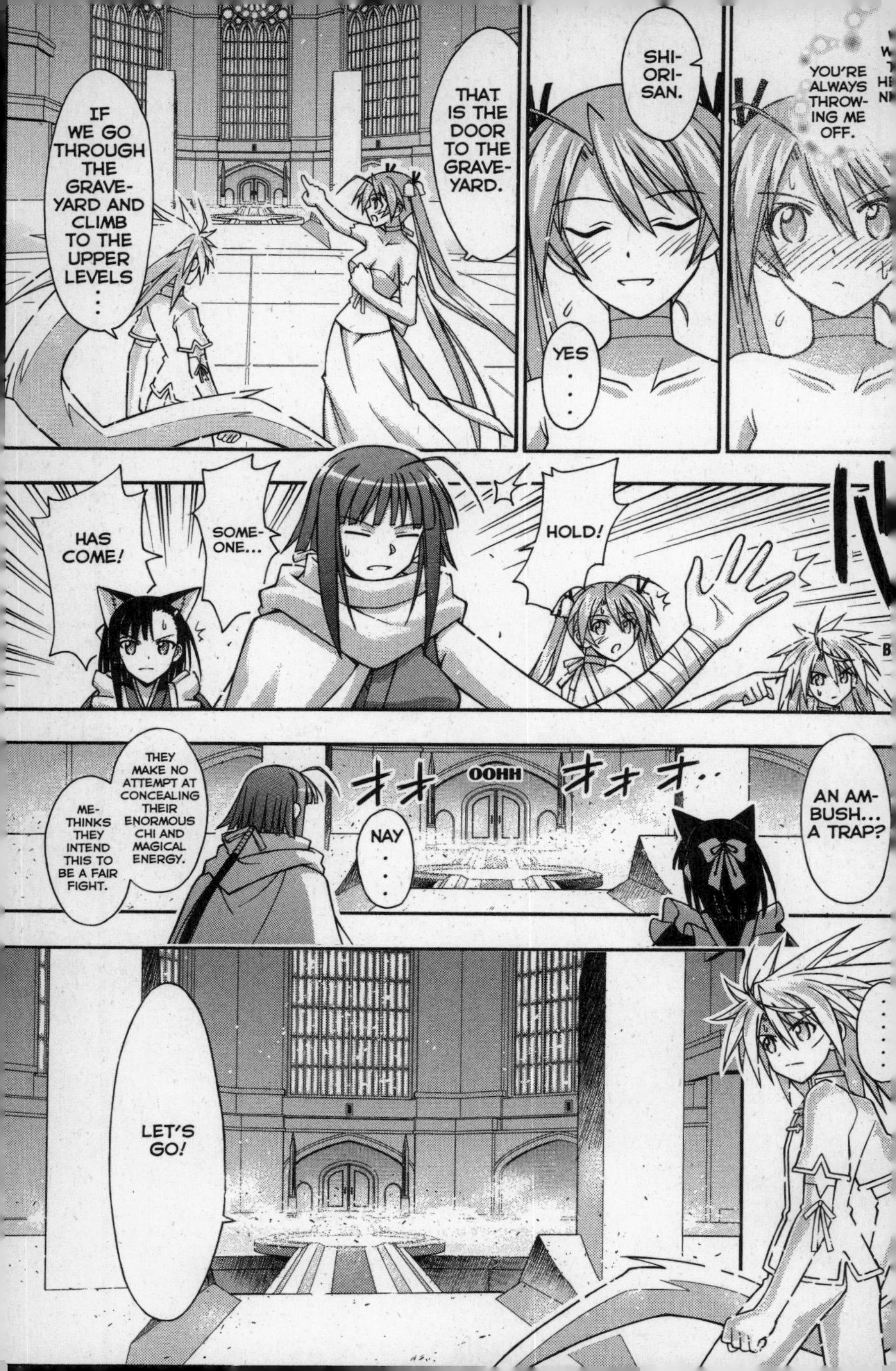
YOU'RE ALWAYS THROWING ME OFF.
SHI-ORI-SAN.
YES . . .
THAT IS THE DOOR TO THE GRAVE-YARD.
IF WE GO THROUGH THE GRAVE-YARD AND CLIMB TO THE UPPER LEVELS . . .
HOLD!
SOME-ONE...
HAS COME!
AN AM-BUSH... A TRAP?
OOHH
NAY . . .
THEY MAKE NO ATTEMPT AT CONCEALING THEIR ENORMOUS CHI AND MAGICAL ENERGY.
ME-THINKS THEY INTEND THIS TO BE A FAIR FIGHT.
LET'S GO!

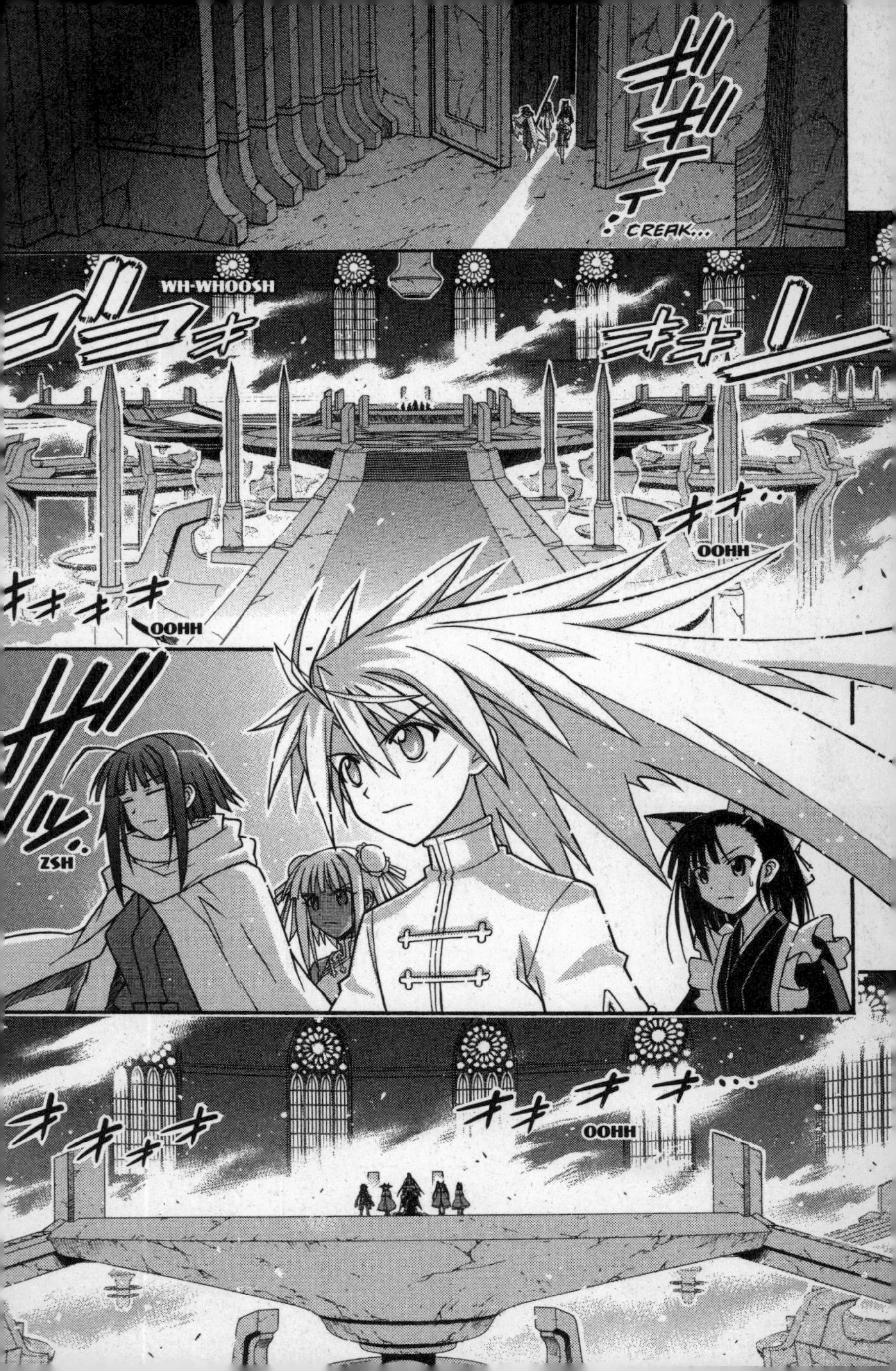
CREAK...
WH-WHOOSH
OOHH
OOHH
ZSH
OOHH

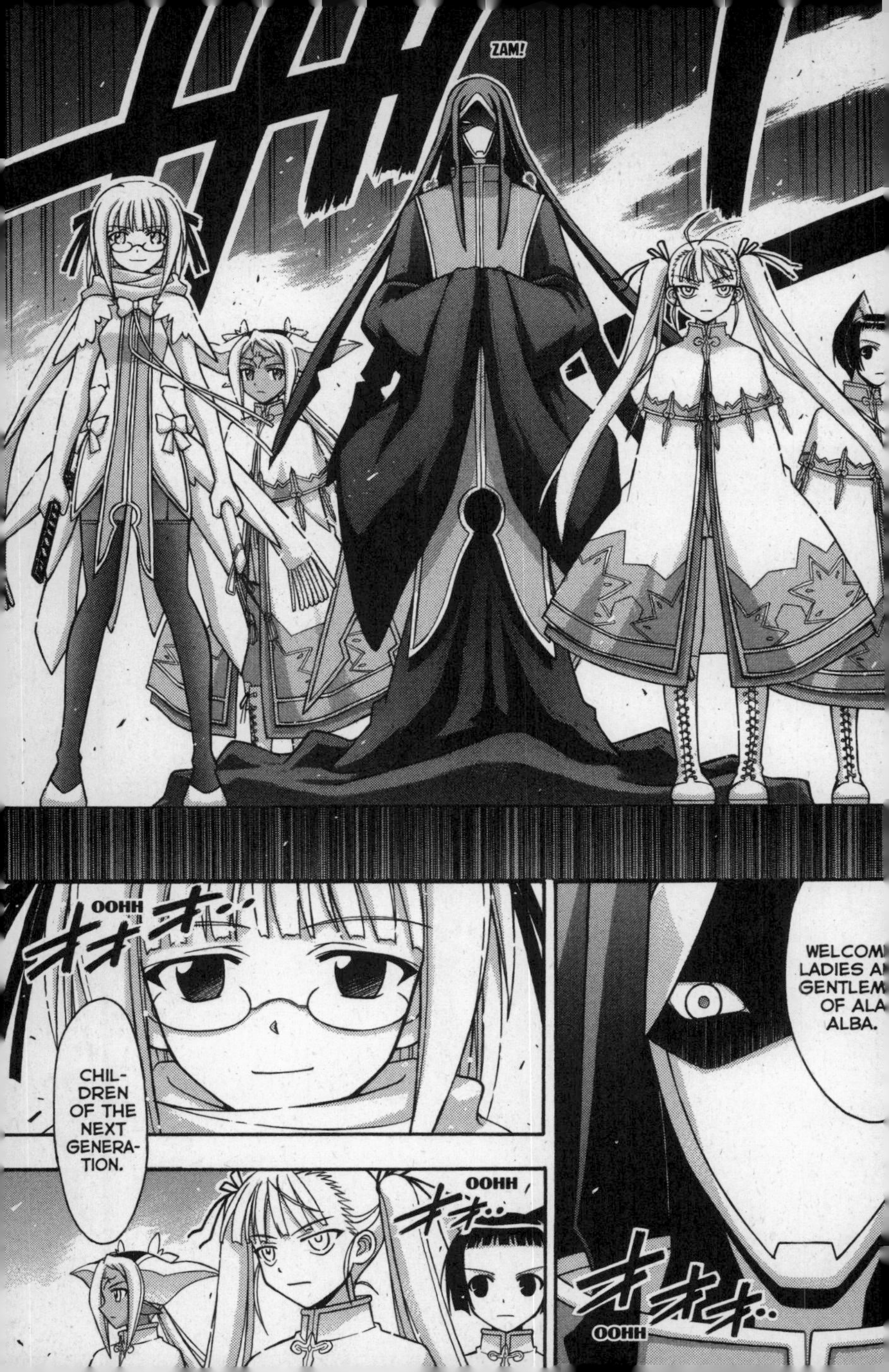
ZAM!
WELCOM LADIES A GENTLEM OF ALA ALBA.
OOHH
OOHH
CHIL-DREN OF THE NEXT GENERA-TION.
OOHH

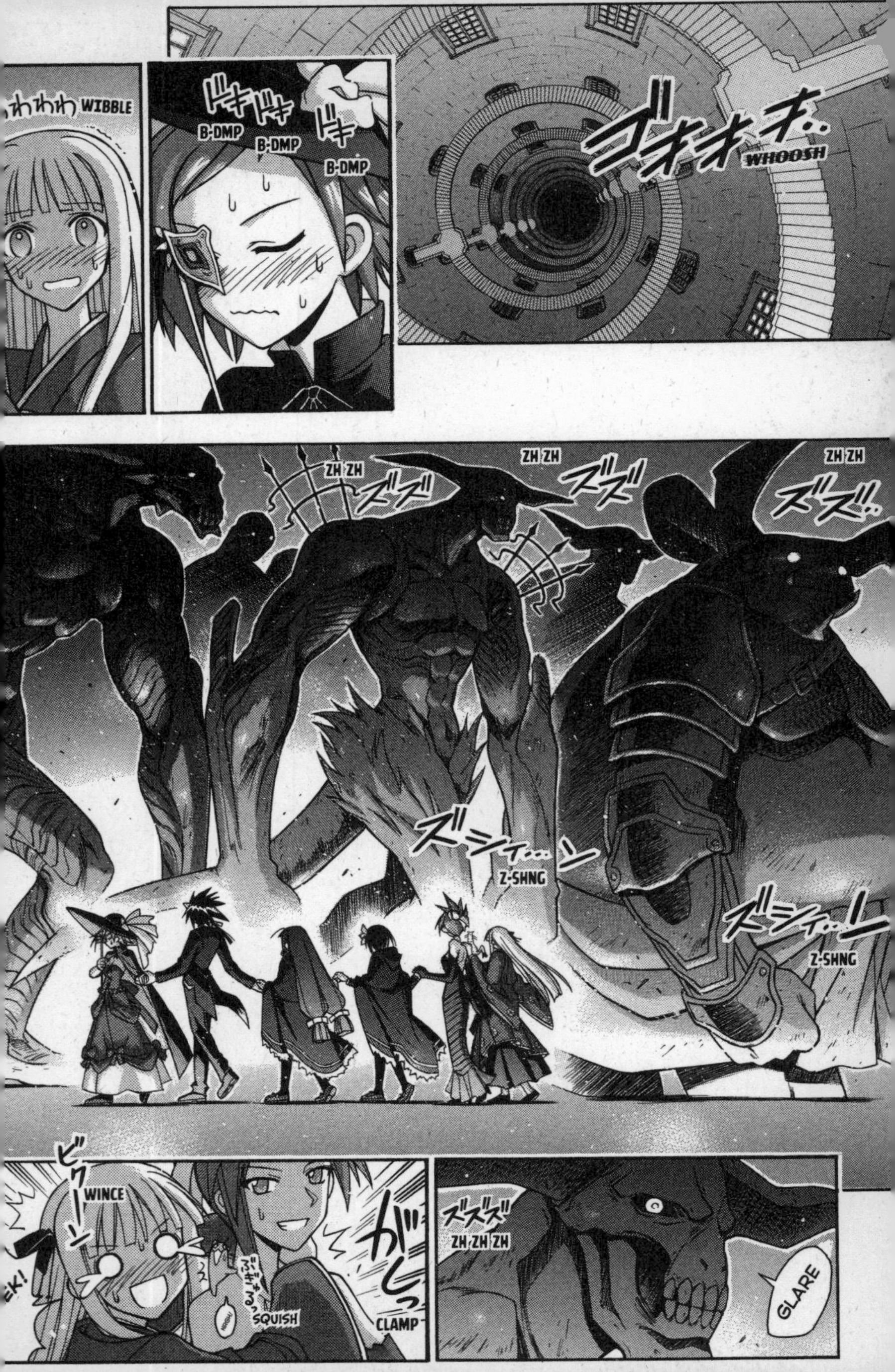
ゴオォォ…
WHOOSH
ドキドキ
B-DMP
B-DMP
ドキ
B-DMP
わわわ WIBBLE
ズズ!!
ZH ZH
ズズ
ZH ZH
ズズ
ZH ZH
ズシィ…ン
Z-SHNG
ズシィ…ン
Z-SHNG
ズズズ
ZH ZH ZH
GLARE
がしっ
CLAMP
ぶぎゅるっ
SQUISH
ビクーン
WINCE

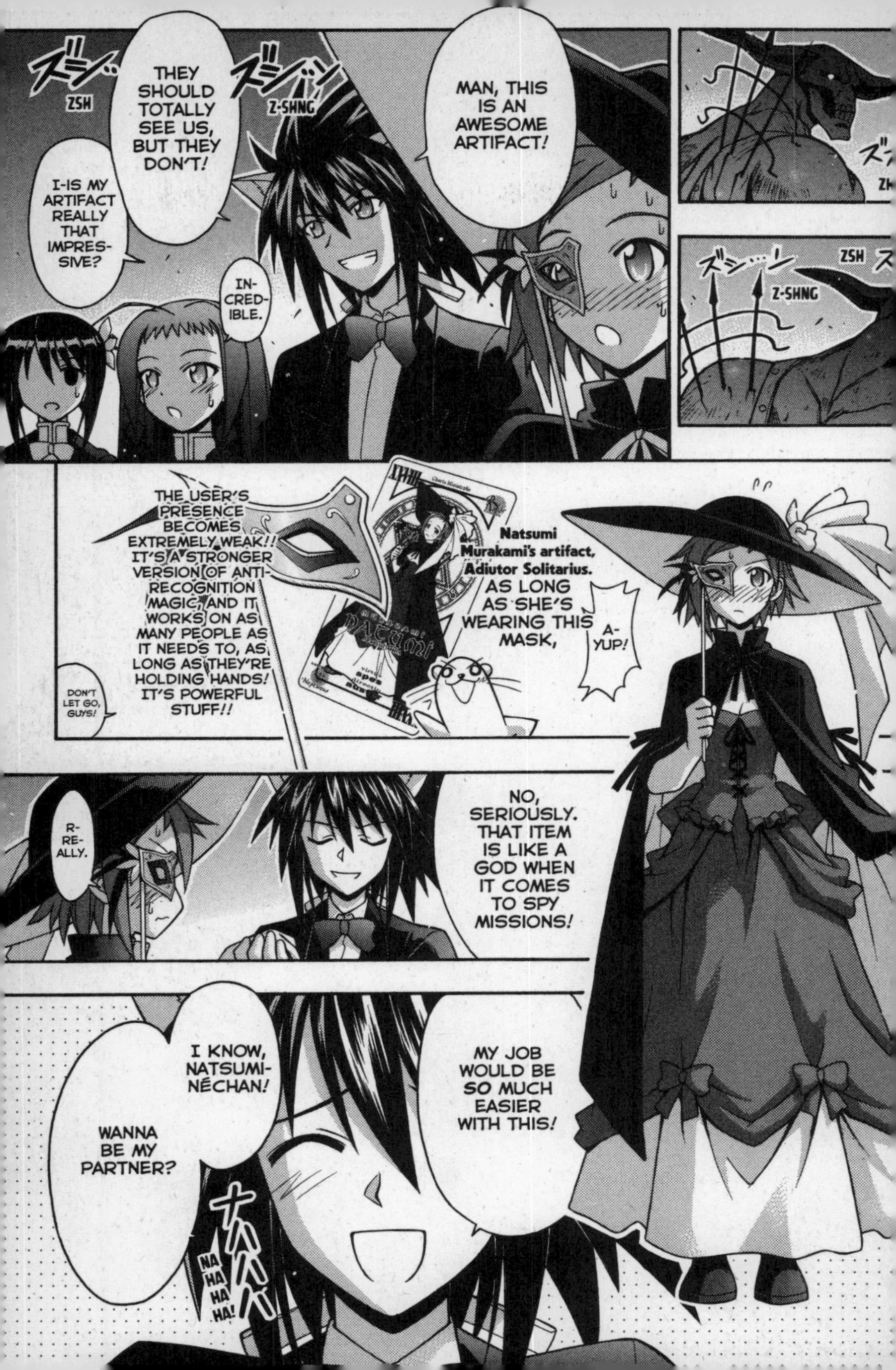
ZH
ZSH
Z-SHNG
MAN, THIS IS AN AWESOME ARTIFACT!
Z-SHNG
THEY SHOULD TOTALLY SEE US, BUT THEY DON'T!
ZSH
I-IS MY ARTIFACT REALLY THAT IMPRESSIVE?
INCREDIBLE.
Natsumi Murakami's artifact, Adiutor Solitarius. AS LONG AS SHE'S WEARING THIS MASK,
A-YUP!
THE USER'S PRESENCE BECOMES EXTREMELY WEAK!! IT'S A STRONGER VERSION OF ANTI-RECOGNITION MAGIC, AND IT WORKS ON AS MANY PEOPLE AS IT NEEDS TO, AS LONG AS THEY'RE HOLDING HANDS! IT'S POWERFUL STUFF!!
DON'T LET GO, GUYS!
NO, SERIOUSLY. THAT ITEM IS LIKE A GOD WHEN IT COMES TO SPY MISSIONS!
R-REALLY.
MY JOB WOULD BE SO MUCH EASIER WITH THIS!
I KNOW, NATSUMI-NÉCHAN!
WANNA BE MY PARTNER?
NA HA HA HA!

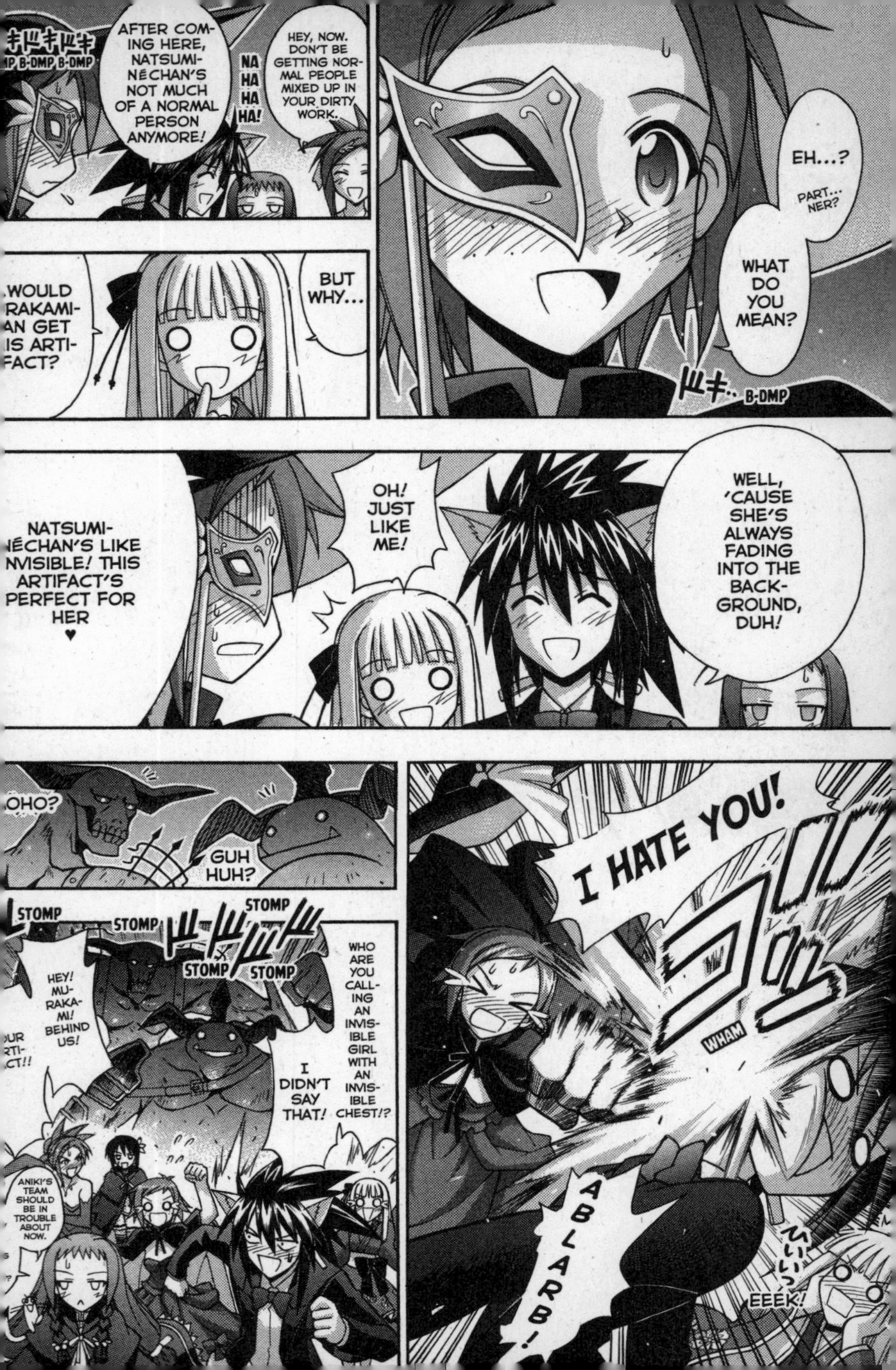
EH...?
PART... NER?
WHAT DO YOU MEAN?
B-DMP
HEY, NOW. DON'T BE GETTING NORMAL PEOPLE MIXED UP IN YOUR DIRTY WORK.
NA HA HA HA!
AFTER COMING HERE, NATSUMI-NÉCHAN'S NOT MUCH OF A NORMAL PERSON ANYMORE!
B-DMP B-DMP
BUT WHY...
.WOULD RAKAMI-AN GET IS ARTIFACT?
WELL, 'CAUSE SHE'S ALWAYS FADING INTO THE BACKGROUND, DUH!
OH! JUST LIKE ME!
NATSUMI-NÉCHAN'S LIKE NVISIBLE! THIS ARTIFACT'S PERFECT FOR HER ♥
I HATE YOU!
WHAM
ABLARB!
EEEK!
GUH HUH?
OHO?
STOMP STOMP STOMP STOMP STOMP STOMP
WHO ARE YOU CALLING AN INVISIBLE GIRL WITH AN INVISIBLE CHEST!?
I DIDN'T SAY THAT!
HEY! MURAKAMI! BEHIND US!
OUR RTI-CT!!
ANIKI'S TEAM SHOULD BE IN TROUBLE ABOUT NOW.

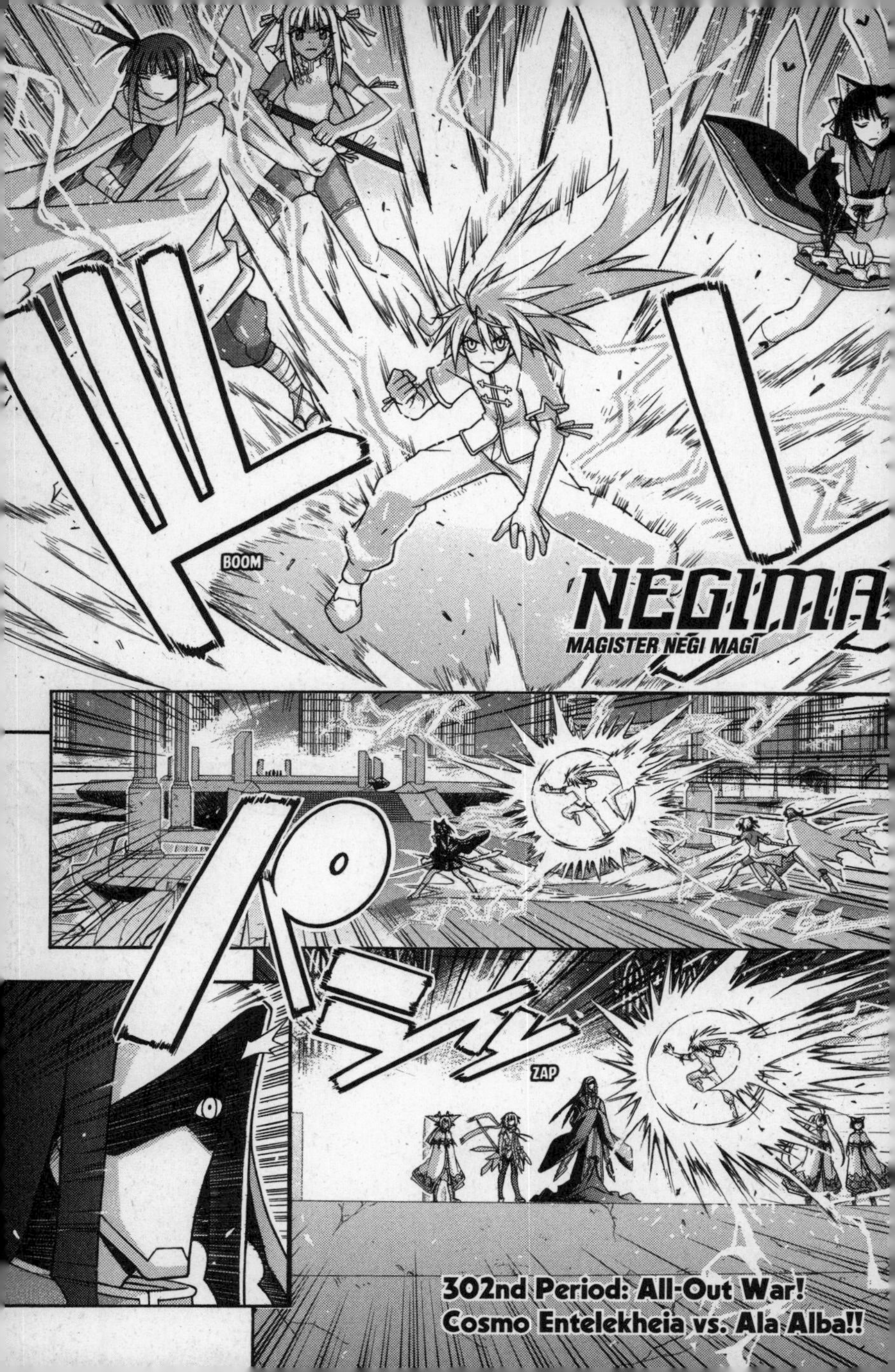
BOOM
NEGIMA
MAGISTER NEGI MAGI
ZAP
302nd Period: All-Out War!
Cosmo Entelekheia vs. Ala Alba!!

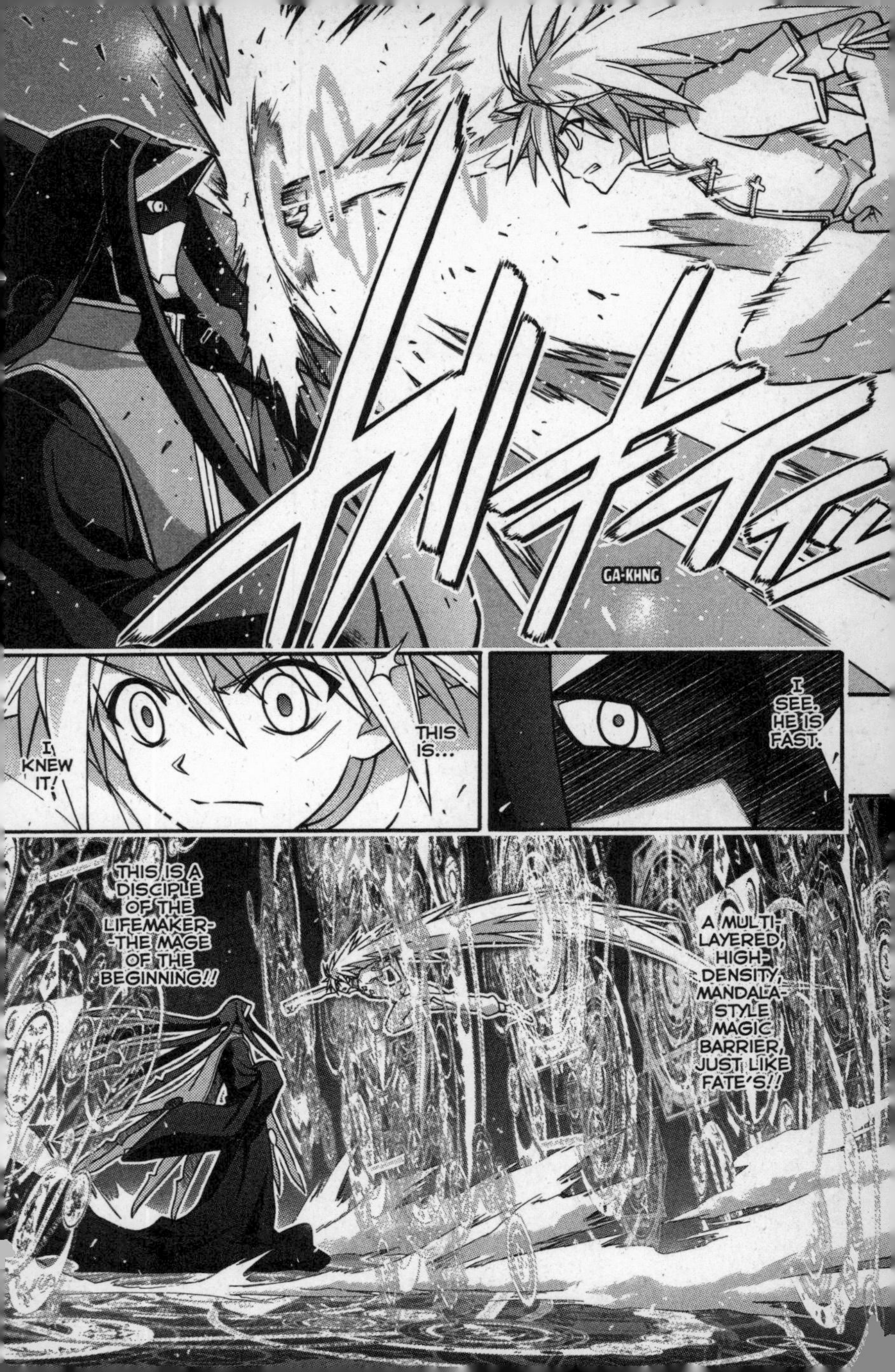
GA-KHNG
I SEE. HE IS FAST.
THIS IS...
I KNEW IT!
A MULTI-LAYERED, HIGH-DENSITY, MANDALA-STYLE MAGIC BARRIER, JUST LIKE FATE'S!!
THIS IS A DISCIPLE OF THE LIFEMAKER-THE MAGE OF THE BEGINNING!!

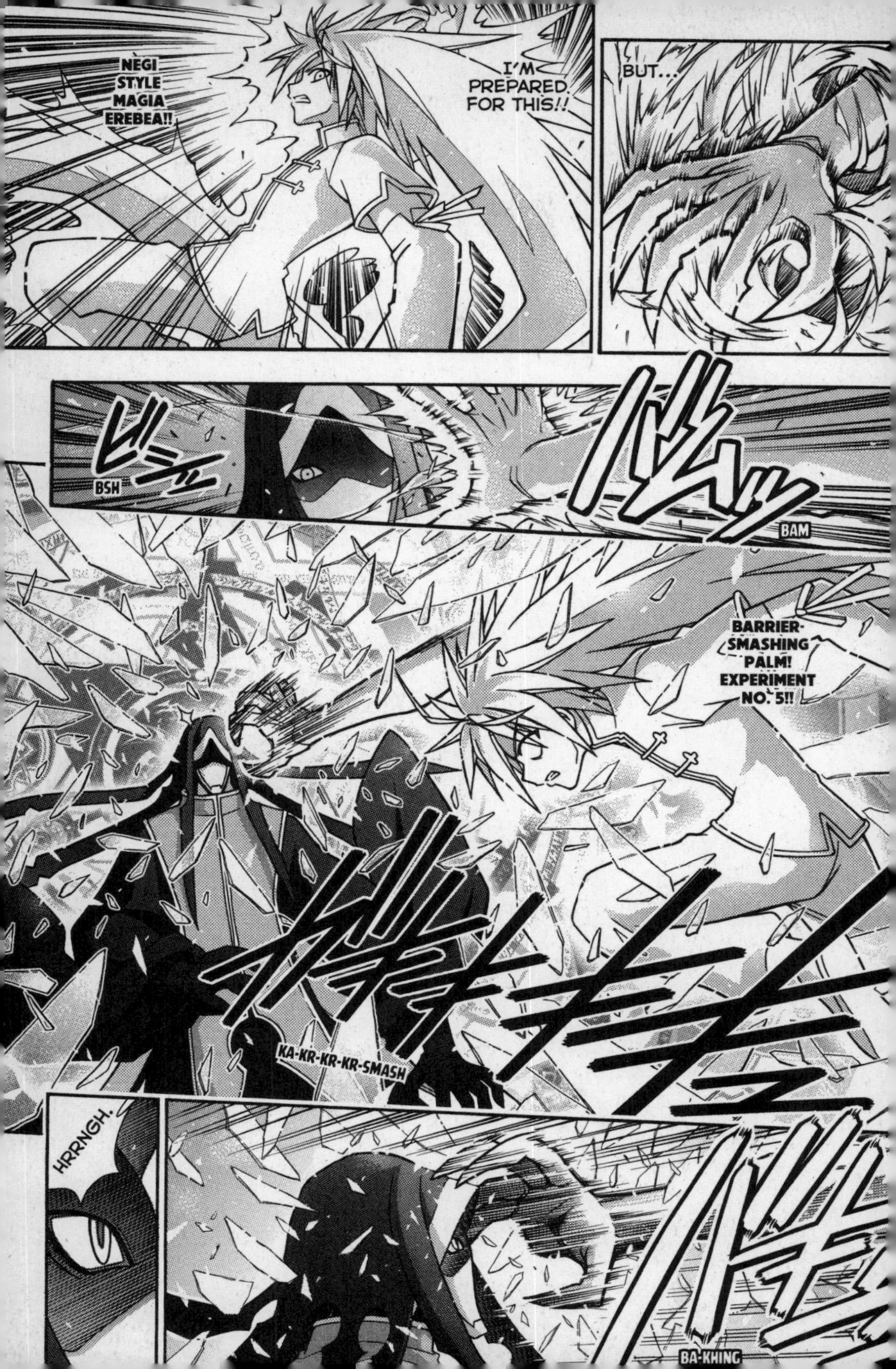
BUT...
I'M PREPARED FOR THIS!!
NEGI STYLE MAGIA EREBEA!!
BAM
BSH
BARRIER-SMASHING PALM! EXPERIMENT NO. 5!!
KA-KR-KR-KR-SMASH
BA-KHING
HRRNGH.

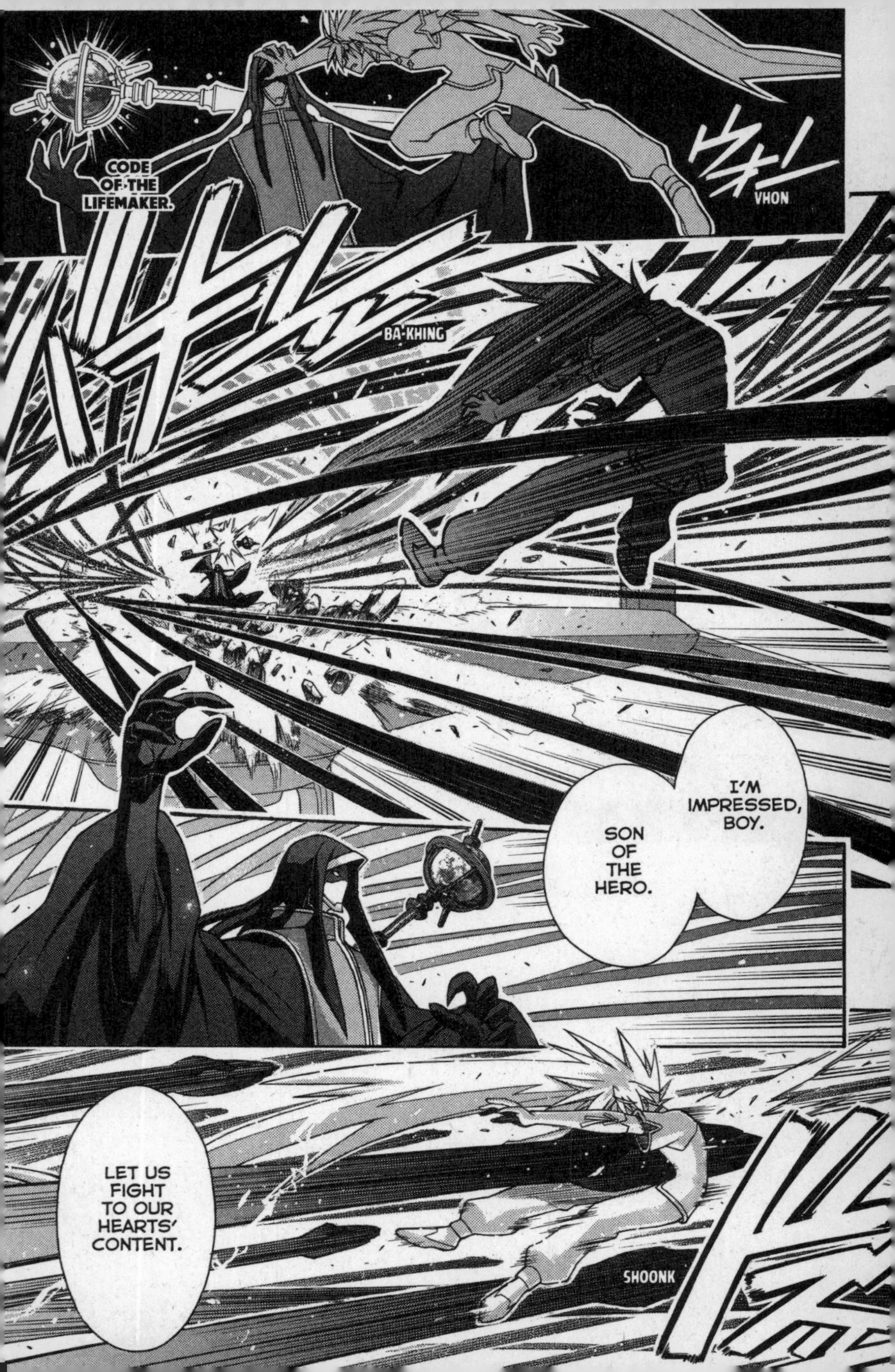
VHON
CODE OF THE LIFEMAKER.
BA-KHING
I'M IMPRESSED, BOY.
SON OF THE HERO.
SHOONK
LET US FIGHT TO OUR HEARTS' CONTENT.

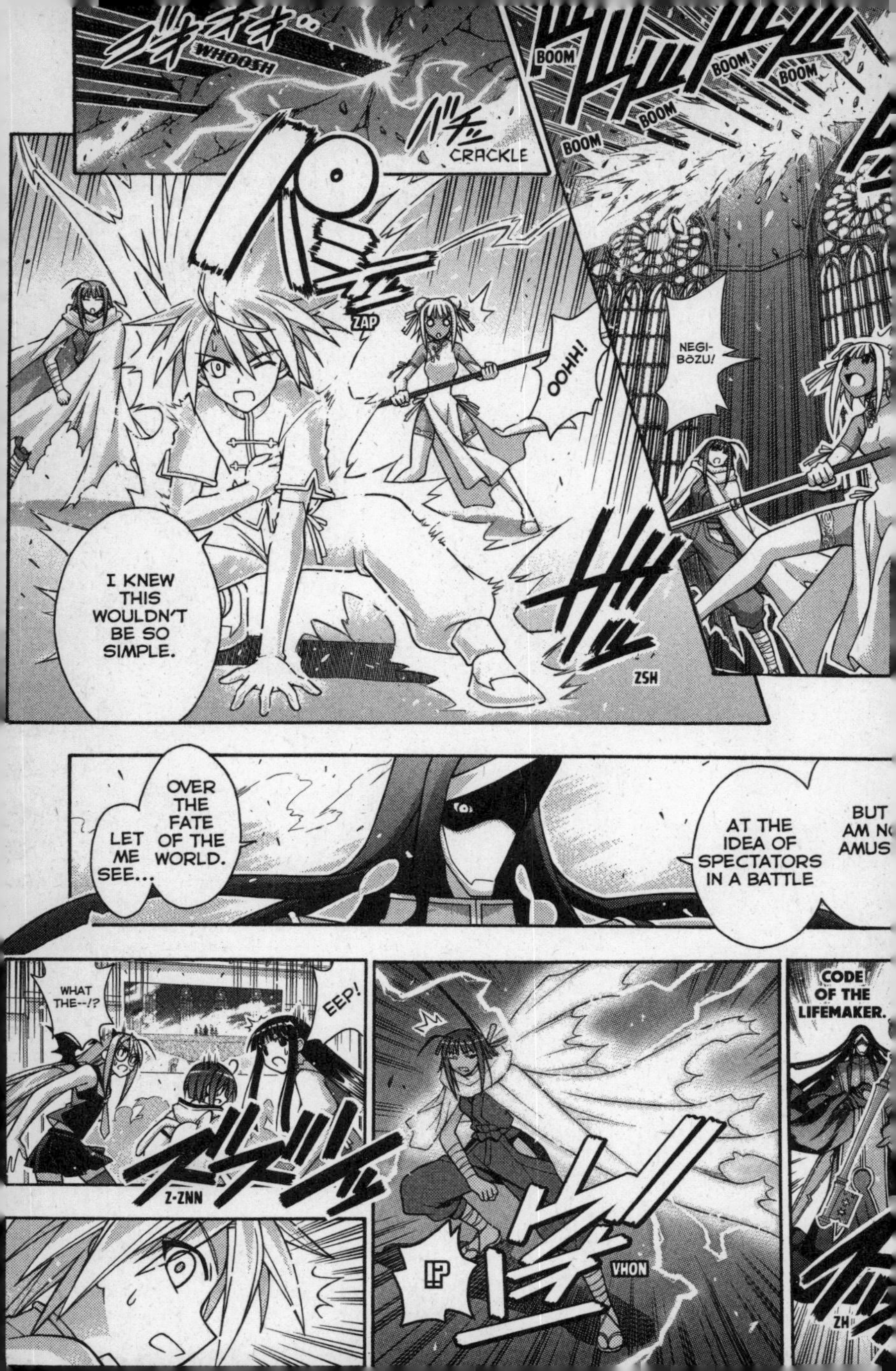

BOOM
BOOM
BOOM
BOOM
BOOM
BOOM
WHOOSH
CRACKLE
NEGI-BŌZU!
ZAP
OOHH!
I KNEW THIS WOULDN'T BE SO SIMPLE.
ZSH
BUT AM N AMUS
AT THE IDEA OF SPECTATORS IN A BATTLE
OVER THE FATE OF THE WORLD.
LET ME SEE...
CODE OF THE LIFEMAKER.
ZH
VHON
!?
WHAT THE--!?
EEP!
Z-ZNN

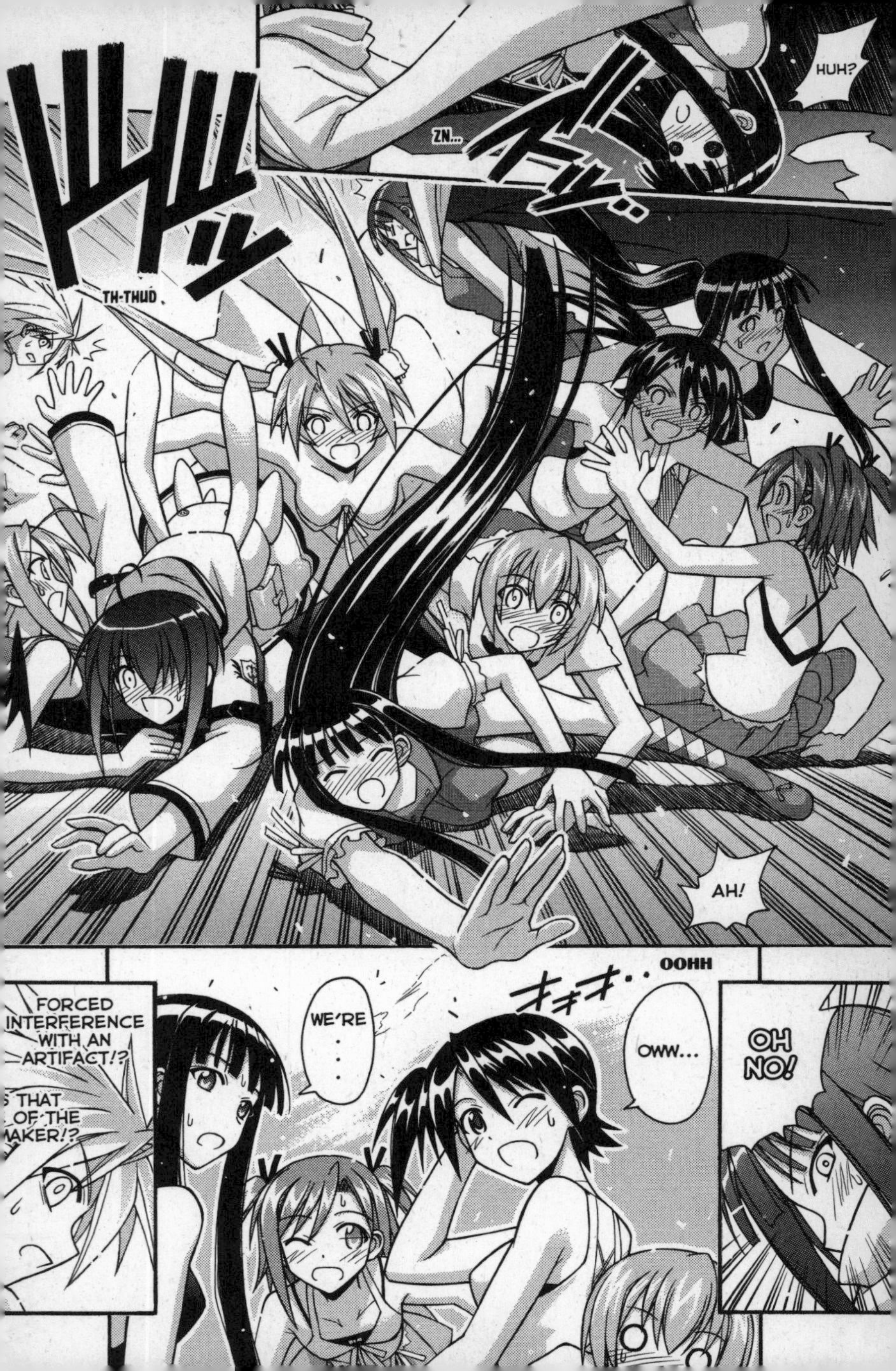
HUH?
ZN...
TH-THUD
AH!
OH NO!
OOHH
OWW...
WE'RE . . .
FORCED INTERFERENCE WITH AN ARTIFACT!?
S THAT OF THE MAKER!?

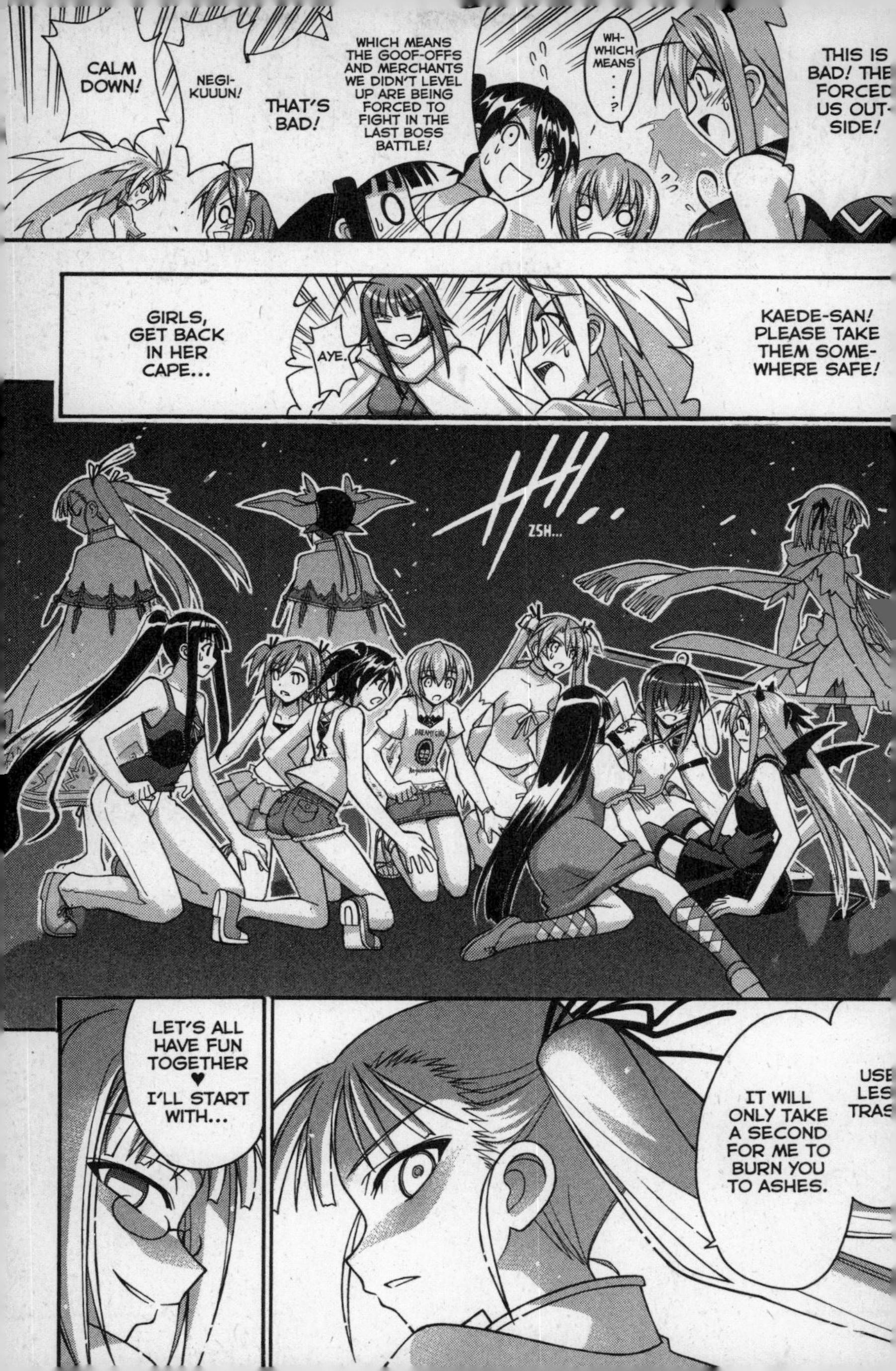
THIS IS BAD! THE FORCED US OUT-SIDE!
WH-WHICH MEANS . . . ?
WHICH MEANS THE GOOF-OFFS AND MERCHANTS WE DIDN'T LEVEL UP ARE BEING FORCED TO FIGHT IN THE LAST BOSS BATTLE!
THAT'S BAD!
NEGI-KUUUN!
CALM DOWN!
KAEDE-SAN! PLEASE TAKE THEM SOME-WHERE SAFE!
AYE.
GIRLS, GET BACK IN HER CAPE...
ZSH...
USE LES TRAS
IT WILL ONLY TAKE A SECOND FOR ME TO BURN YOU TO ASHES.
LET'S ALL HAVE FUN TOGETHER ♥ I'LL START WITH...

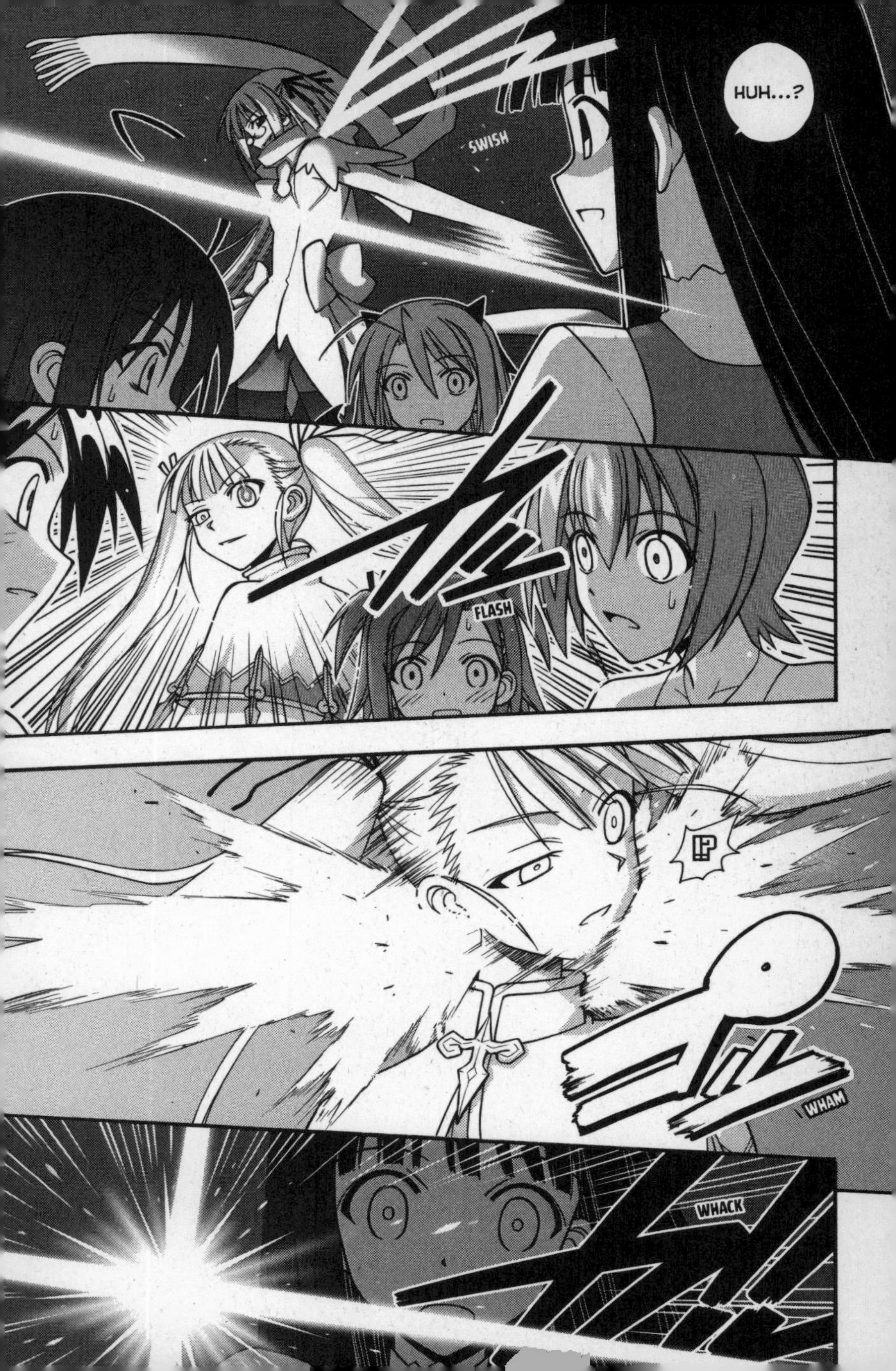
HUH...?
SWISH
FLASH
!?
WHAM
WHACK

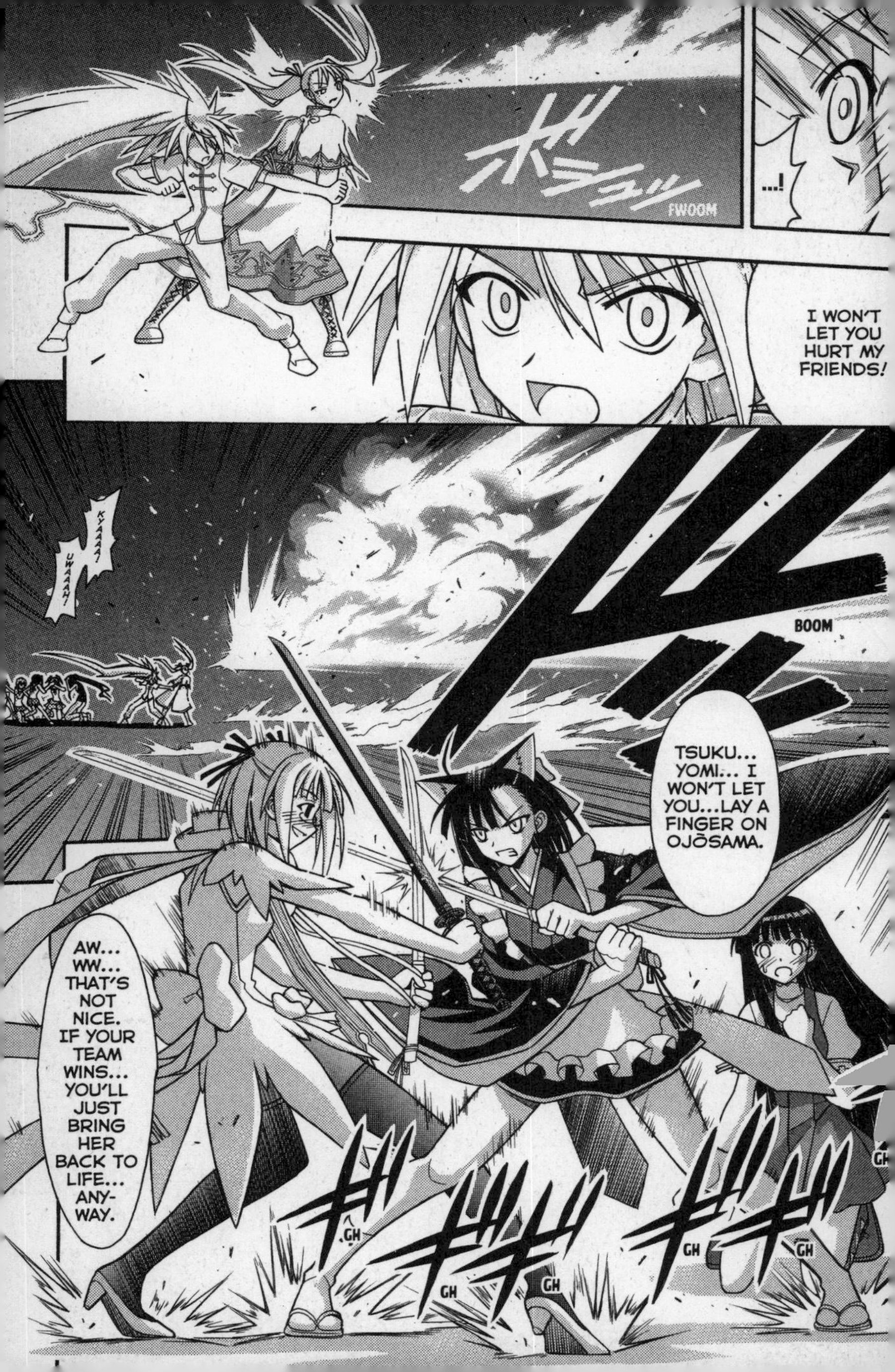
...!
FWOOM
I WON'T LET YOU HURT MY FRIENDS!
BOOM
KYAAAA!
UWAAAH!
TSUKU... YOMI... I WON'T LET YOU...LAY A FINGER ON OJŌSAMA.
AW... WW... THAT'S NOT NICE. IF YOUR TEAM WINS... YOU'LL JUST BRING HER BACK TO LIFE... ANYWAY.
GH
GH
GH
GH
GH
GH

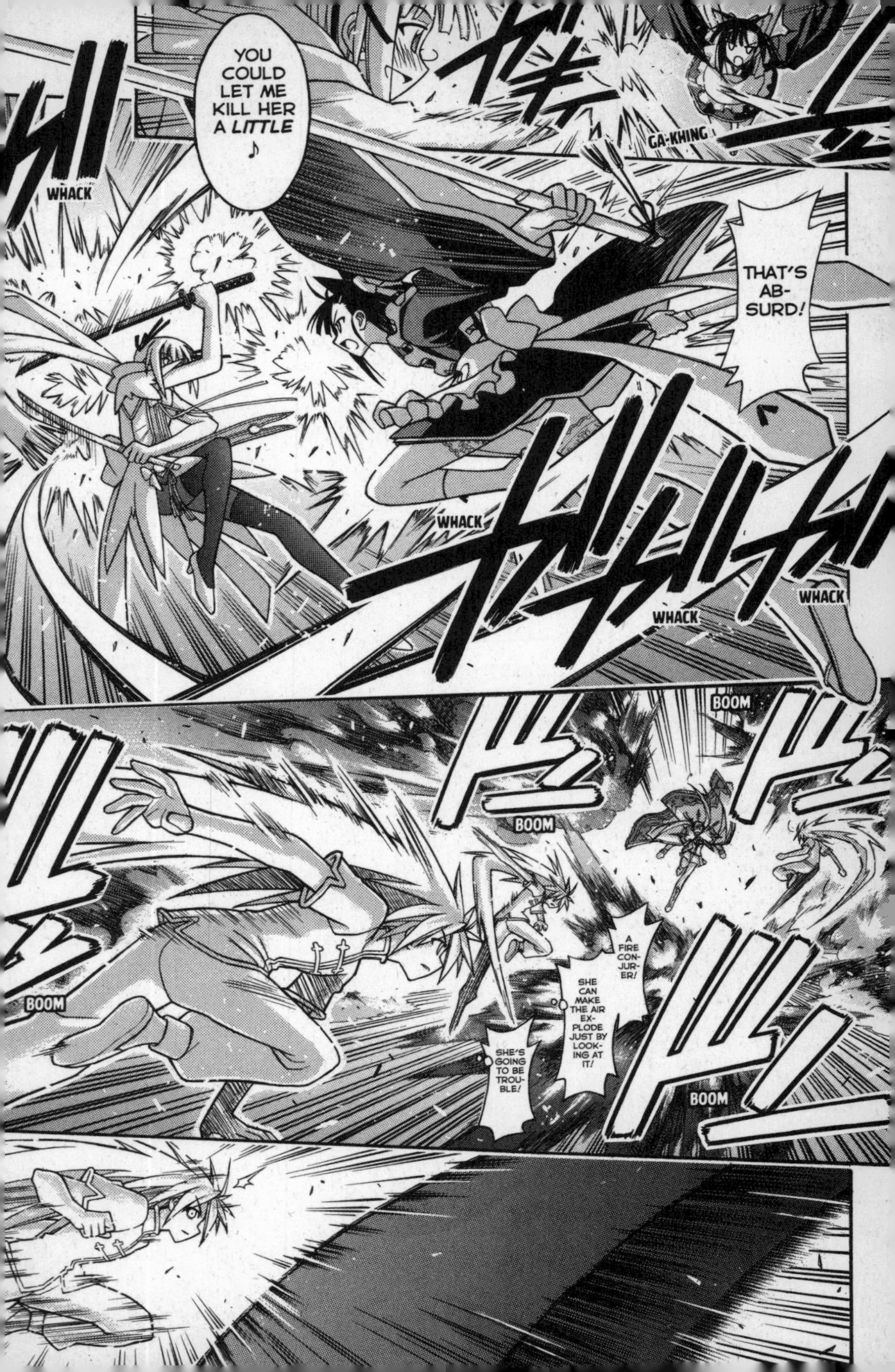
GA-KHING
THAT'S AB-SURD!
YOU COULD LET ME KILL HER A *LITTLE* ♪
WHACK
WHACK
WHACK
WHACK
BOOM
BOOM
A FIRE CON-JUR-ER!
SHE CAN MAKE THE AIR EX-PLODE JUST BY LOOK-ING AT IT!
SHE'S GOING TO BE TROU-BLE!
BOOM
BOOM

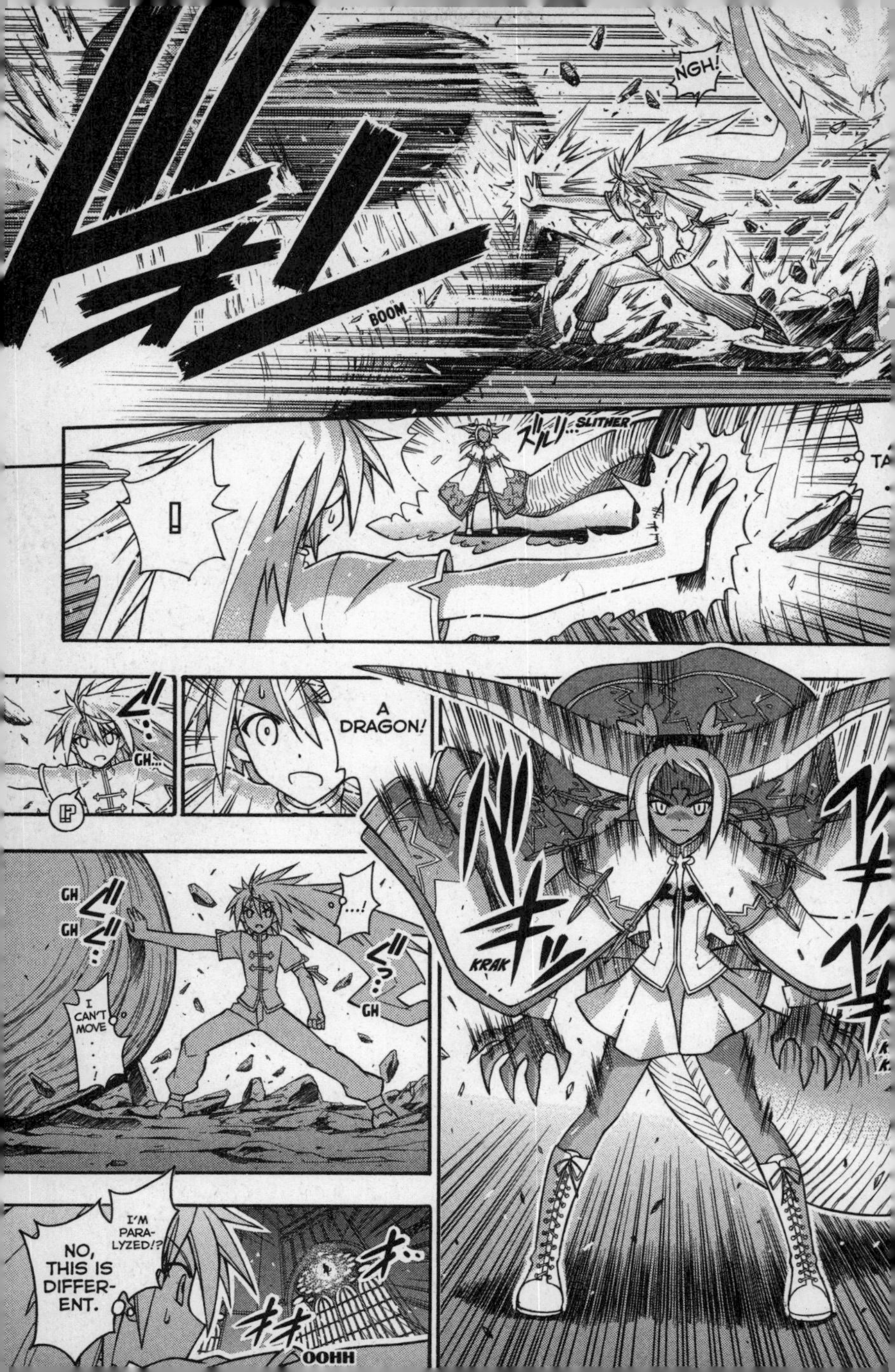
NGH!
BOOM
SLITHER
TA
!
KRAK
A DRAGON!
GH...
!?
...!
GH
GH
GH
I CAN'T MOVE
I'M PARALYZED!?
NO, THIS IS DIFFERENT.
OOHH

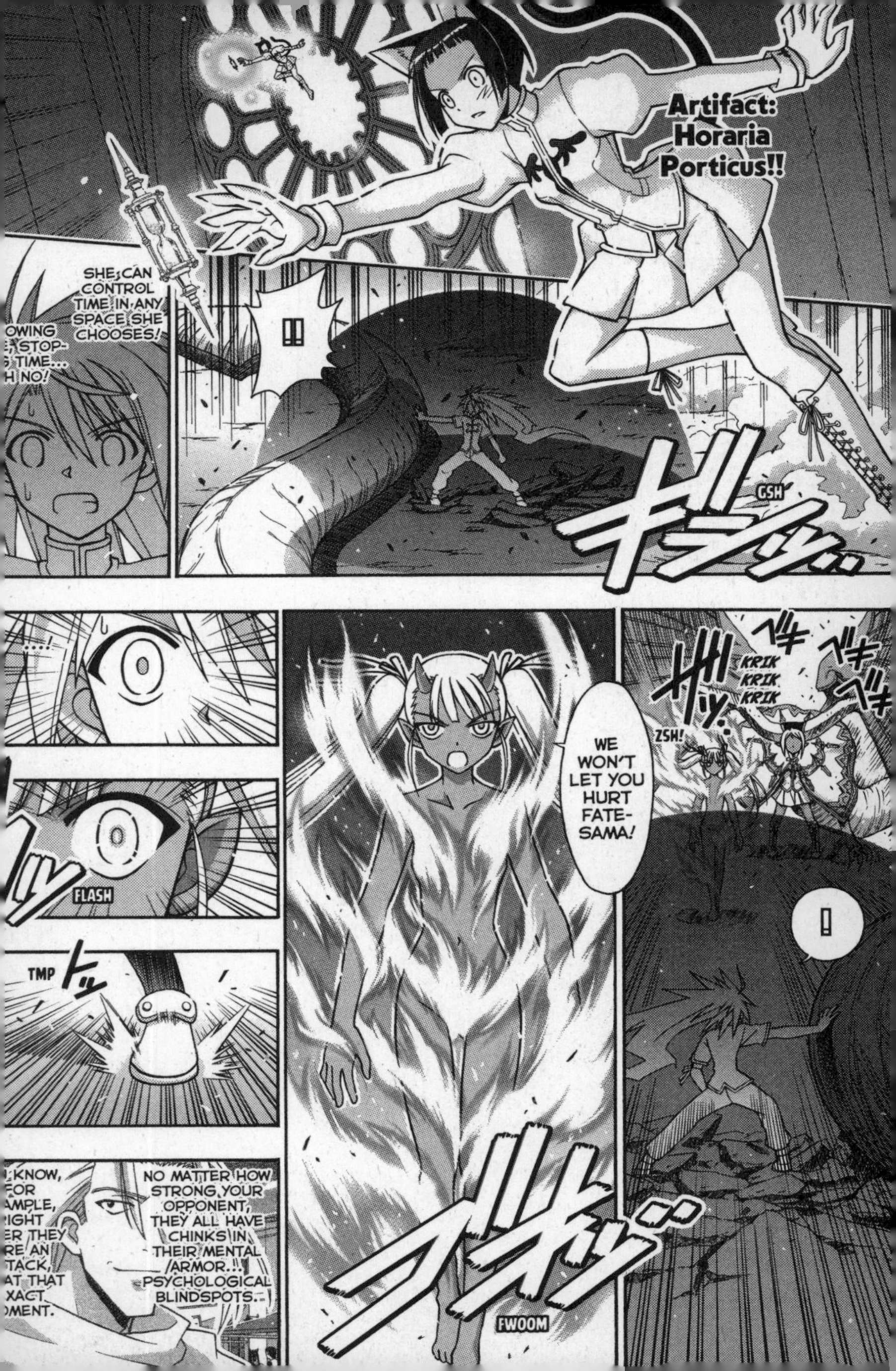

Artifact: Horaria Porticus!!
!!
GSH
SHE CAN CONTROL TIME IN ANY SPACE SHE CHOOSES!
OWING E, STOP- G TIME... H NO!
KRIK KRIK KRIK
ZSH!
!
WE WON'T LET YOU HURT FATE-SAMA!
FWOOM
...!
FLASH
TMP
NO MATTER HOW STRONG YOUR OPPONENT, THEY ALL HAVE CHINKS IN THEIR MENTAL ARMOR... PSYCHOLOGICAL BLINDSPOTS.
I KNOW, FOR AMPLE, RIGHT ER THEY RE AN TACK, AT THAT XACT OMENT.

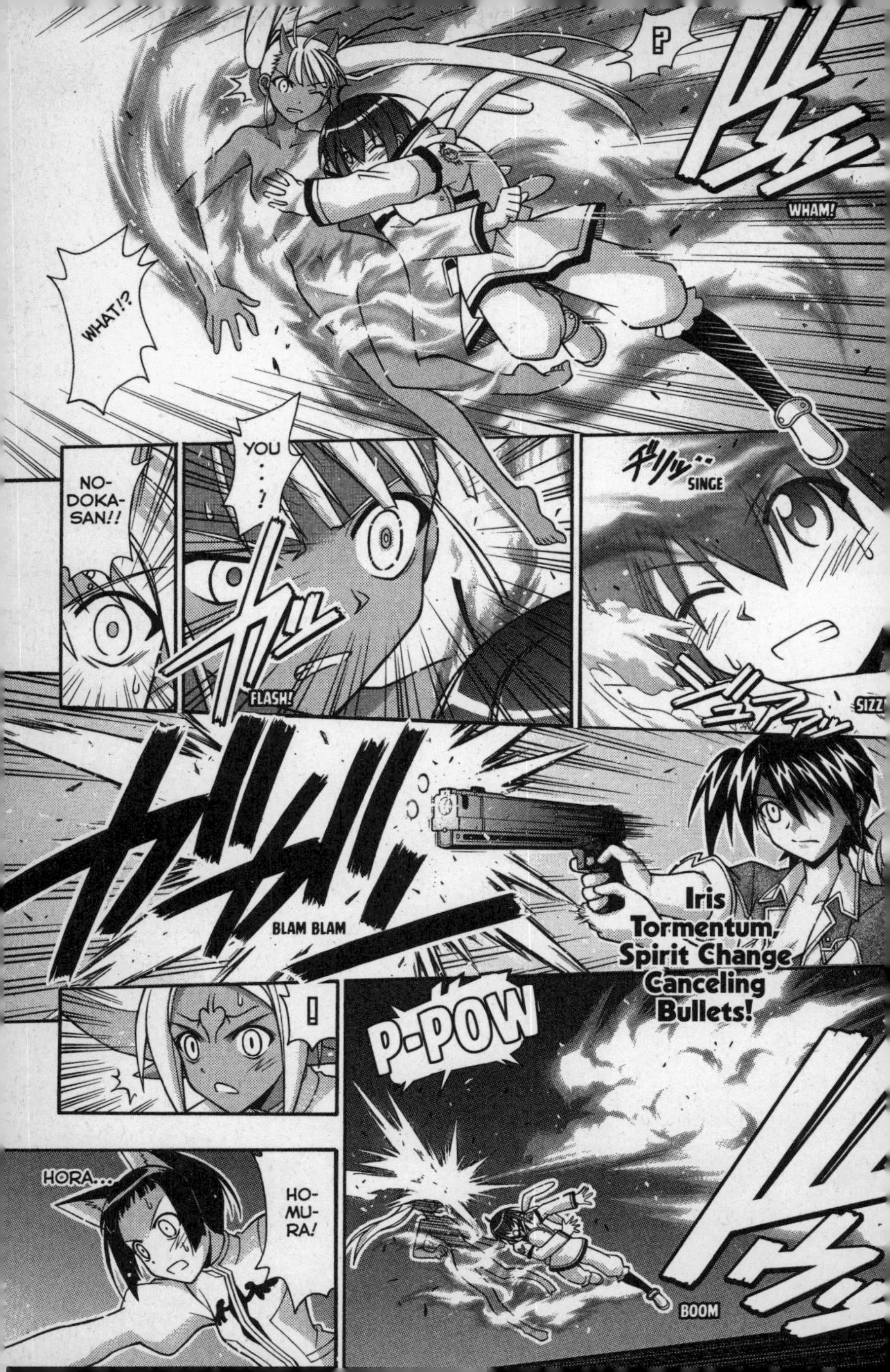

?
WHAM!
WHAT!?
SINGE
SIZZ
YOU...!
FLASH!
NO-DOKA-SAN!!
Iris Tormentum, Spirit Change Canceling Bullets!
BLAM BLAM
P-POW
BOOM
!
HORA...
HO-MU-RA!

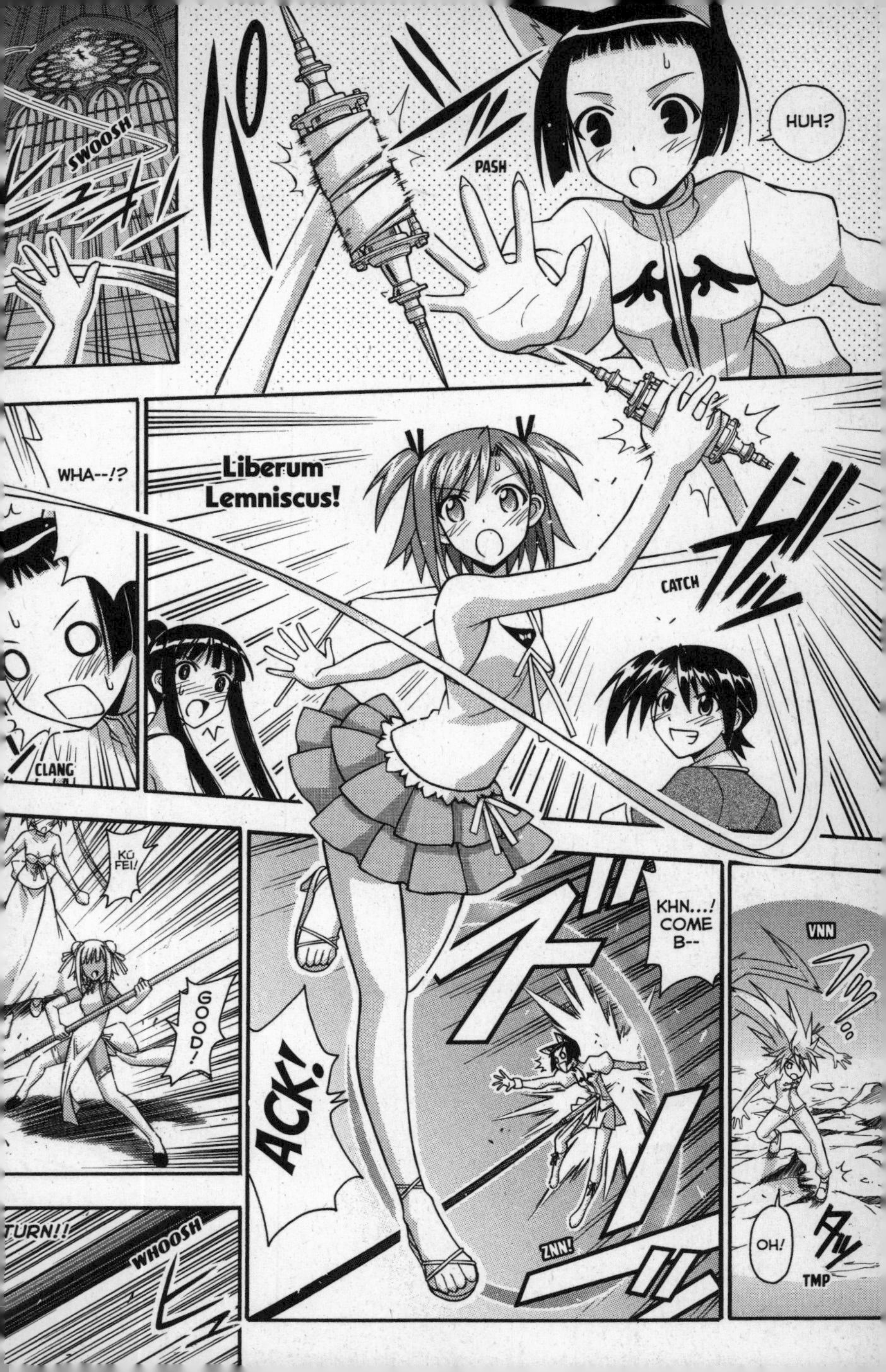
HUH?
PASH
SWOOSH
CATCH
Liberum Lemniscus!
WHA--!?
CLANG
VNN
OH!
TMP
KHN...! COME B--
ZNN!
ACK!
KŪ FEI!
GOOD!
TURN!!
WHOOSH

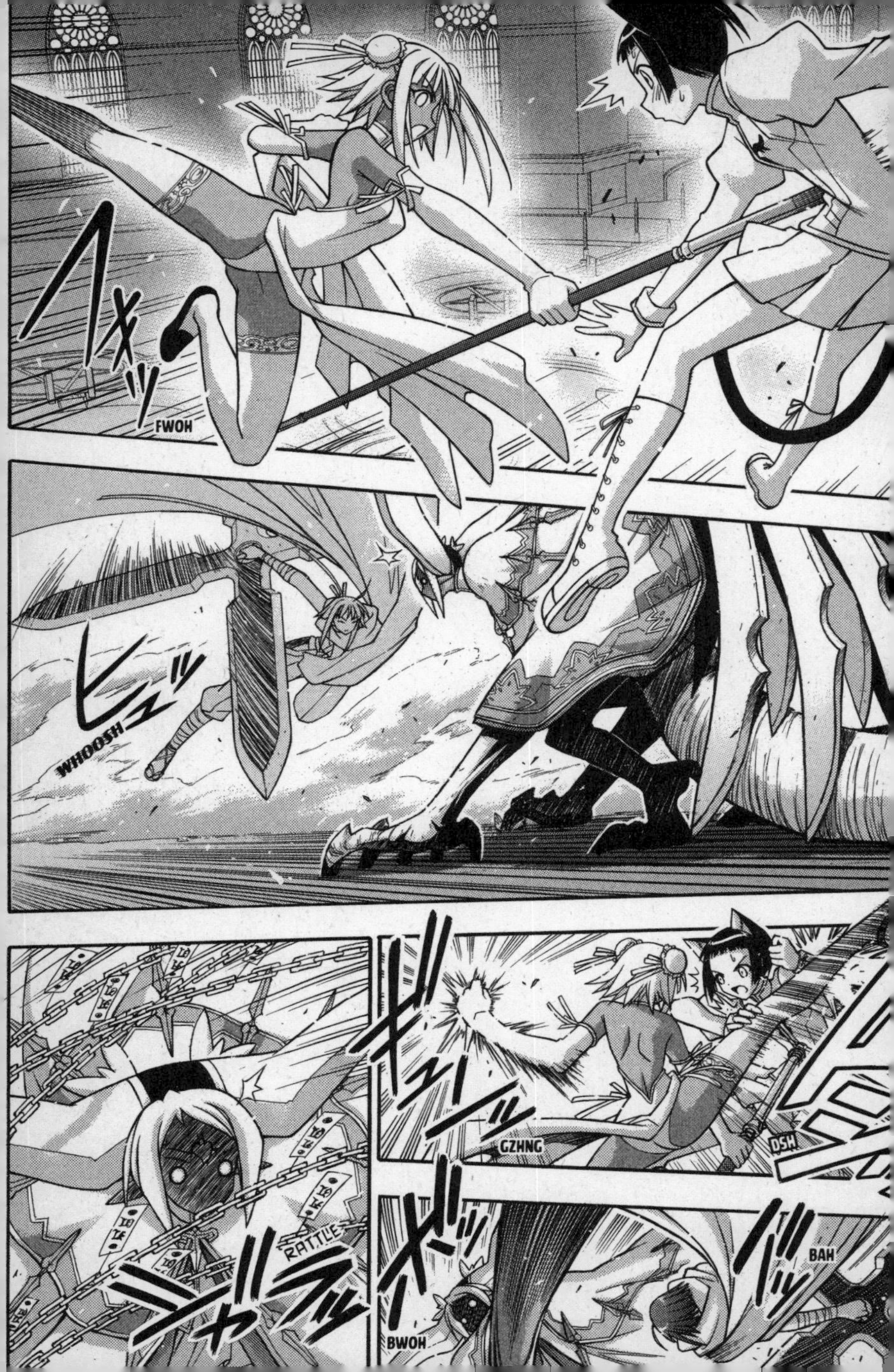
FWOH
WHOOSH
GZHNG
DSH
BAH
BWOH
RATTLE

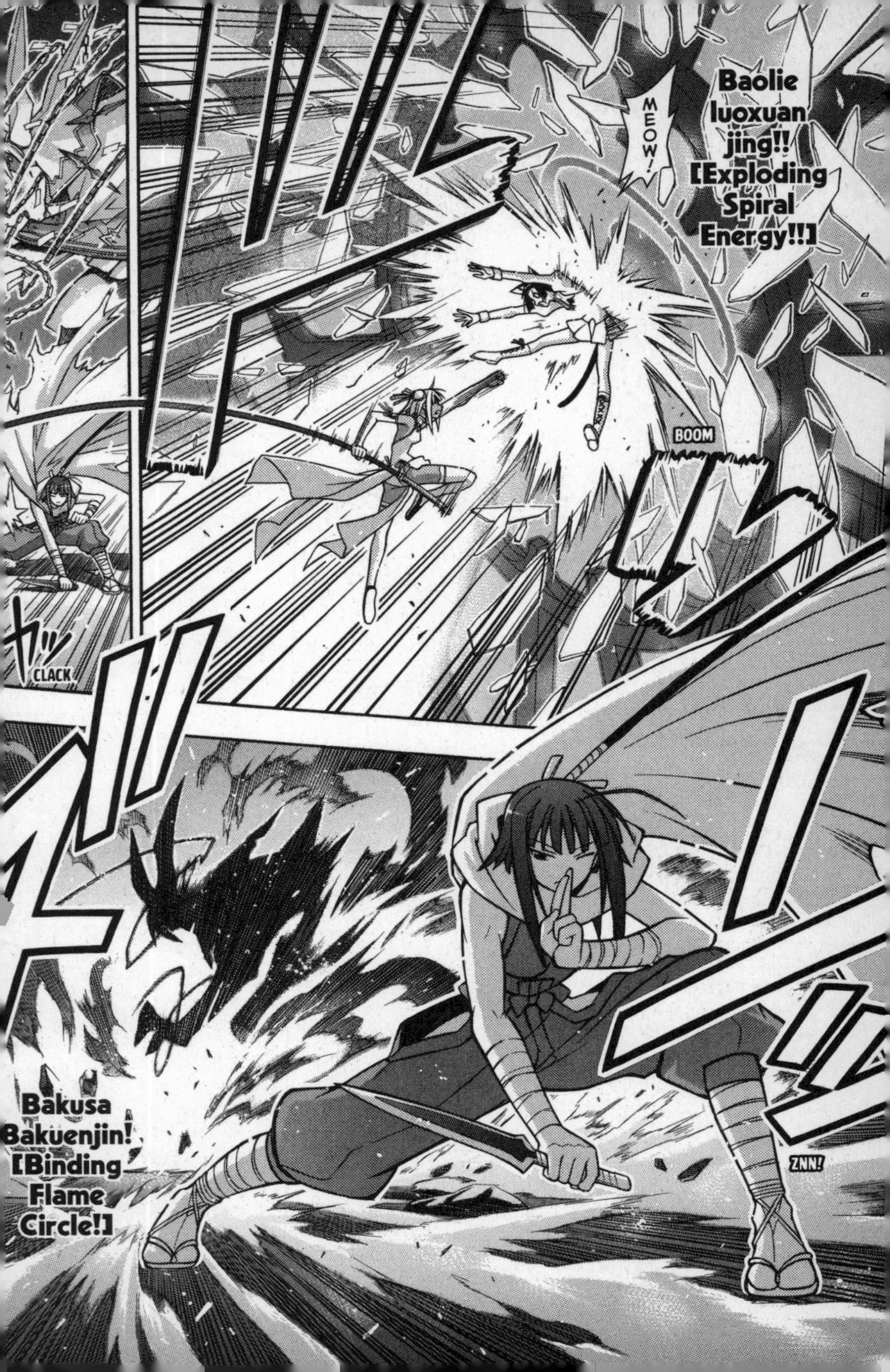
Baolie luoxuan jing!! [Exploding Spiral Energy!!]
MEOW!
BOOM
CLACK
ZNN!
Bakusa Bakuenjin! [Binding Flame Circle!]

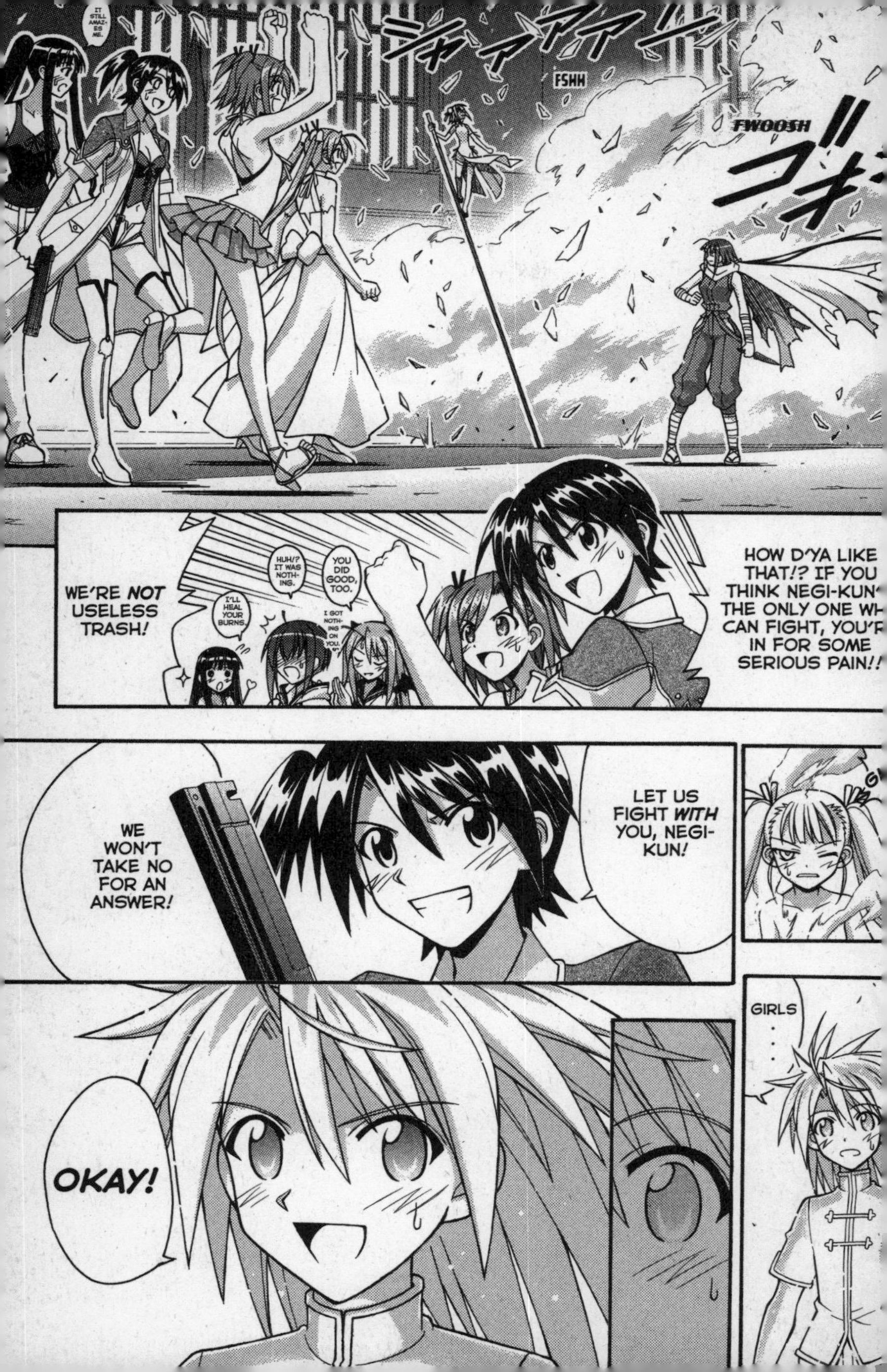
FWOOSH
FSHH
IT STILL AMAZES ME.
HOW D'YA LIKE THAT!? IF YOU THINK NEGI-KUN' THE ONLY ONE WH CAN FIGHT, YOU'R IN FOR SOME SERIOUS PAIN!!
YOU DID GOOD, TOO.
HUH!? IT WAS NOTHING.
I GOT NOTHING ON YOU.
I'LL HEAL YOUR BURNS.
WE'RE *NOT* USELESS TRASH!
LET US FIGHT *WITH* YOU, NEGI-KUN!
WE WON'T TAKE NO FOR AN ANSWER!
GIRLS . . .
OKAY!

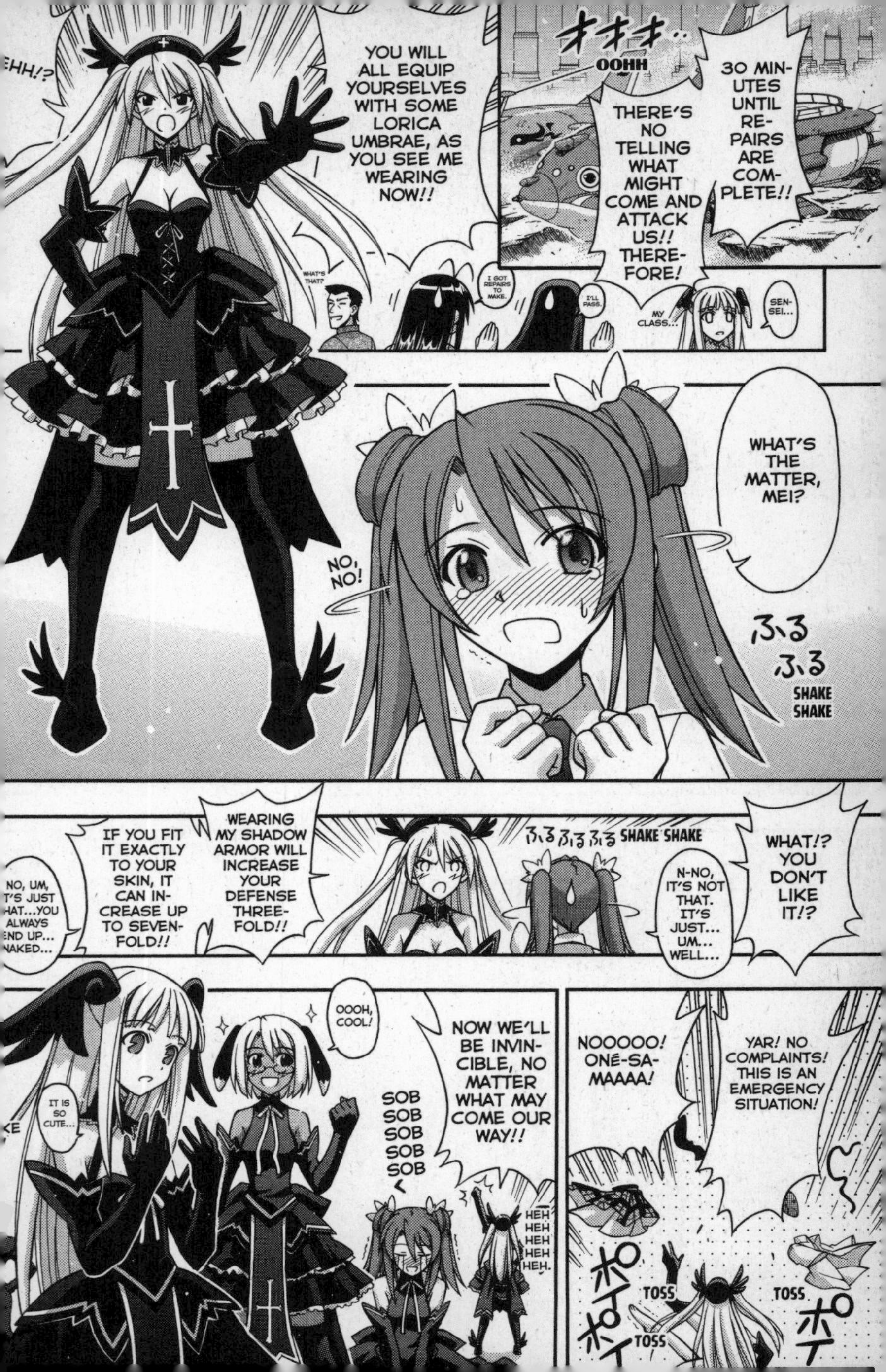
オオオ..
OOHH
30 MIN-UTES UNTIL RE-PAIRS ARE COM-PLETE!!
THERE'S NO TELLING WHAT MIGHT COME AND ATTACK US!! THEREFORE!
YOU WILL ALL EQUIP YOURSELVES WITH SOME LORICA UMBRAE, AS YOU SEE ME WEARING NOW!!
EHH!?
SEN-SEI...
MY CLASS...
I'LL PASS.
I GOT REPAIRS TO MAKE.
WHAT'S THAT?
WHAT'S THE MATTER, MEI?
ふるふる
SHAKE SHAKE
NO, NO!
WHAT!? YOU DON'T LIKE IT!?
N-NO, IT'S NOT THAT. IT'S JUST... UM... WELL...
ふるふるふる SHAKE SHAKE
WEARING MY SHADOW ARMOR WILL INCREASE YOUR DEFENSE THREE-FOLD!!
IF YOU FIT IT EXACTLY TO YOUR SKIN, IT CAN IN-CREASE UP TO SEVEN-FOLD!!
NO, UM, T'S JUST HAT...YOU ALWAYS END UP... NAKED...
YAR! NO COMPLAINTS! THIS IS AN EMERGENCY SITUATION!
NOOOOO! ONÉ-SA-MAAAAA!
ポイ
TOSS
ポイ
TOSS
ポイ
TOSS
NOW WE'LL BE INVIN-CIBLE, NO MATTER WHAT MAY COME OUR WAY!!
OOOH, COOL!
SOB SOB SOB SOB SOB
HEH HEH HEH HEH HEH.
IT IS SO CUTE...

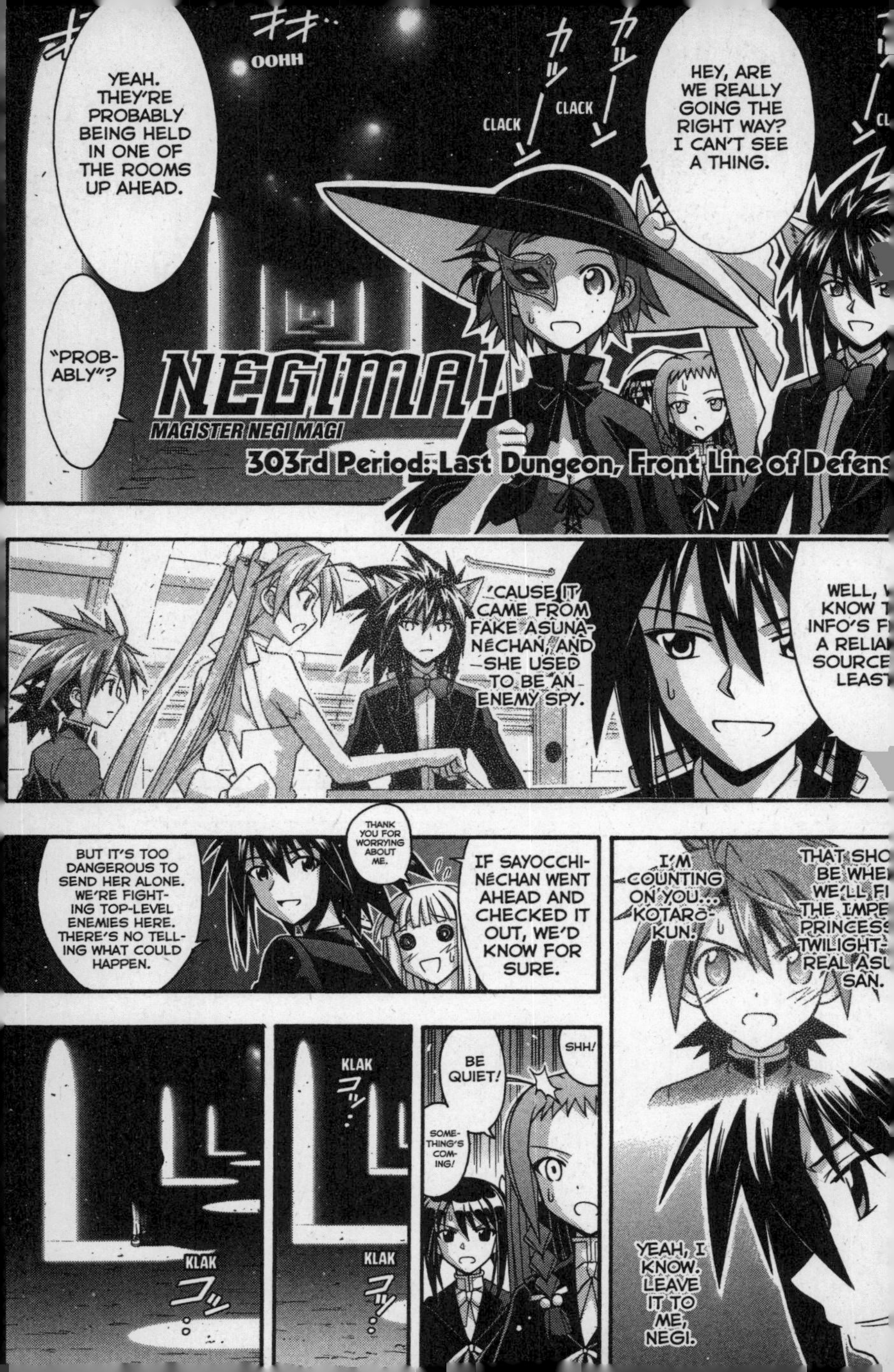
CLACK
CLACK
HEY, ARE WE REALLY GOING THE RIGHT WAY? I CAN'T SEE A THING.
OOHH
YEAH. THEY'RE PROBABLY BEING HELD IN ONE OF THE ROOMS UP AHEAD.
"PROBABLY"?
NEGIMA!
MAGISTER NEGI MAGI
303rd Period: Last Dungeon, Front Line of Defens
WELL, W KNOW T INFO'S F A RELIAB SOURCE LEAST
'CAUSE IT CAME FROM FAKE ASUNA-NÉCHAN, AND SHE USED TO BE AN ENEMY SPY.
THAT SHO BE WHE WE'LL FI THE IMPE PRINCESS TWILIGHT- REAL ASU SAN.
I'M COUNTING ON YOU... KOTARŌ-KUN.
YEAH, I KNOW. LEAVE IT TO ME, NEGI.
IF SAYOCCHI-NÉCHAN WENT AHEAD AND CHECKED IT OUT, WE'D KNOW FOR SURE.
THANK YOU FOR WORRYING ABOUT ME.
BUT IT'S TOO DANGEROUS TO SEND HER ALONE. WE'RE FIGHTING TOP-LEVEL ENEMIES HERE. THERE'S NO TELLING WHAT COULD HAPPEN.
SHH!
BE QUIET!
SOMETHING'S COMING!
KLAK
KLAK
KLAK
KLAK

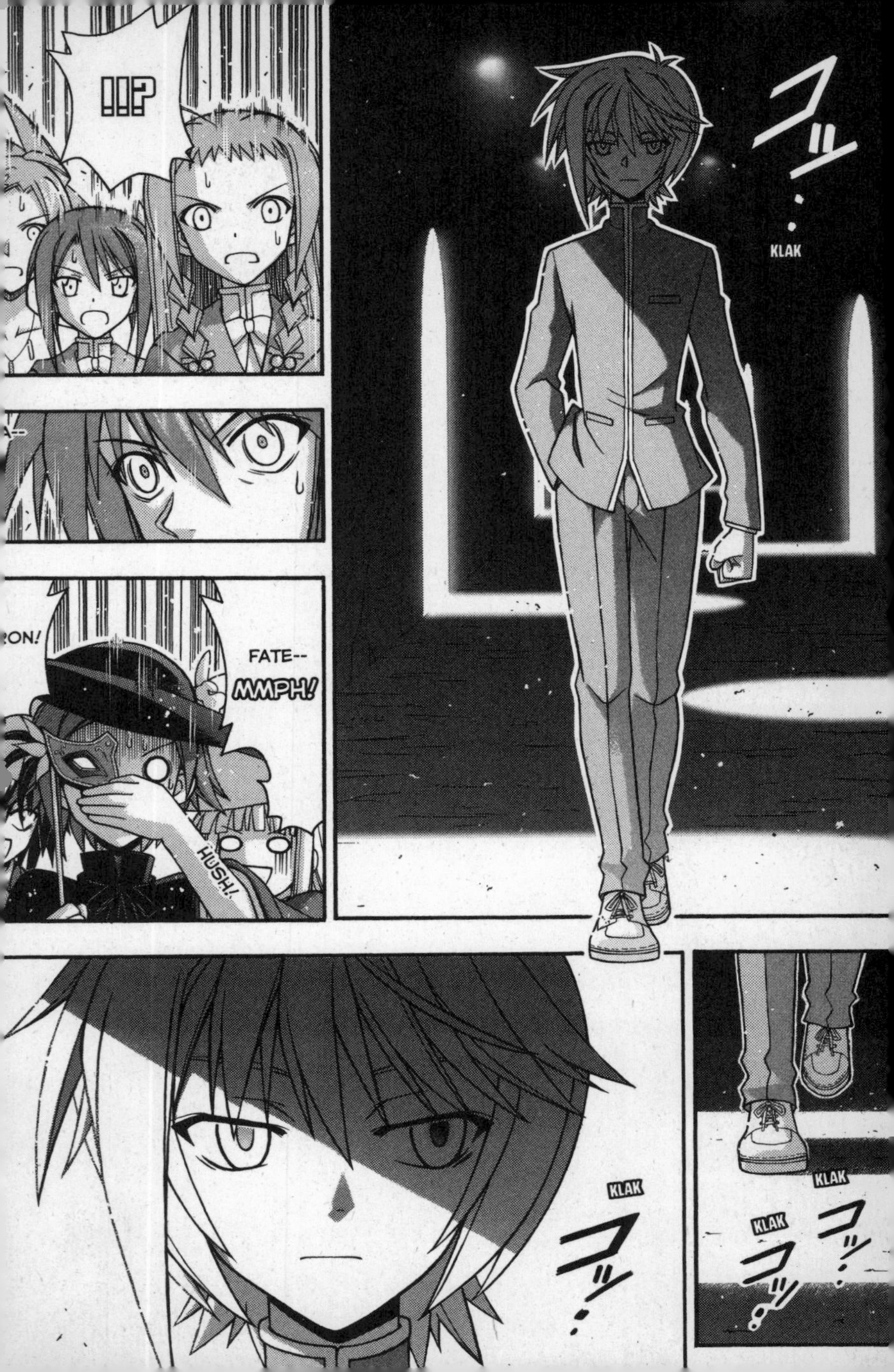
コッ…
KLAK
!!?
FATE--
MMPH!
HUSH!
KLAK
コッ…
KLAK
コッ…
KLAK
コッ…

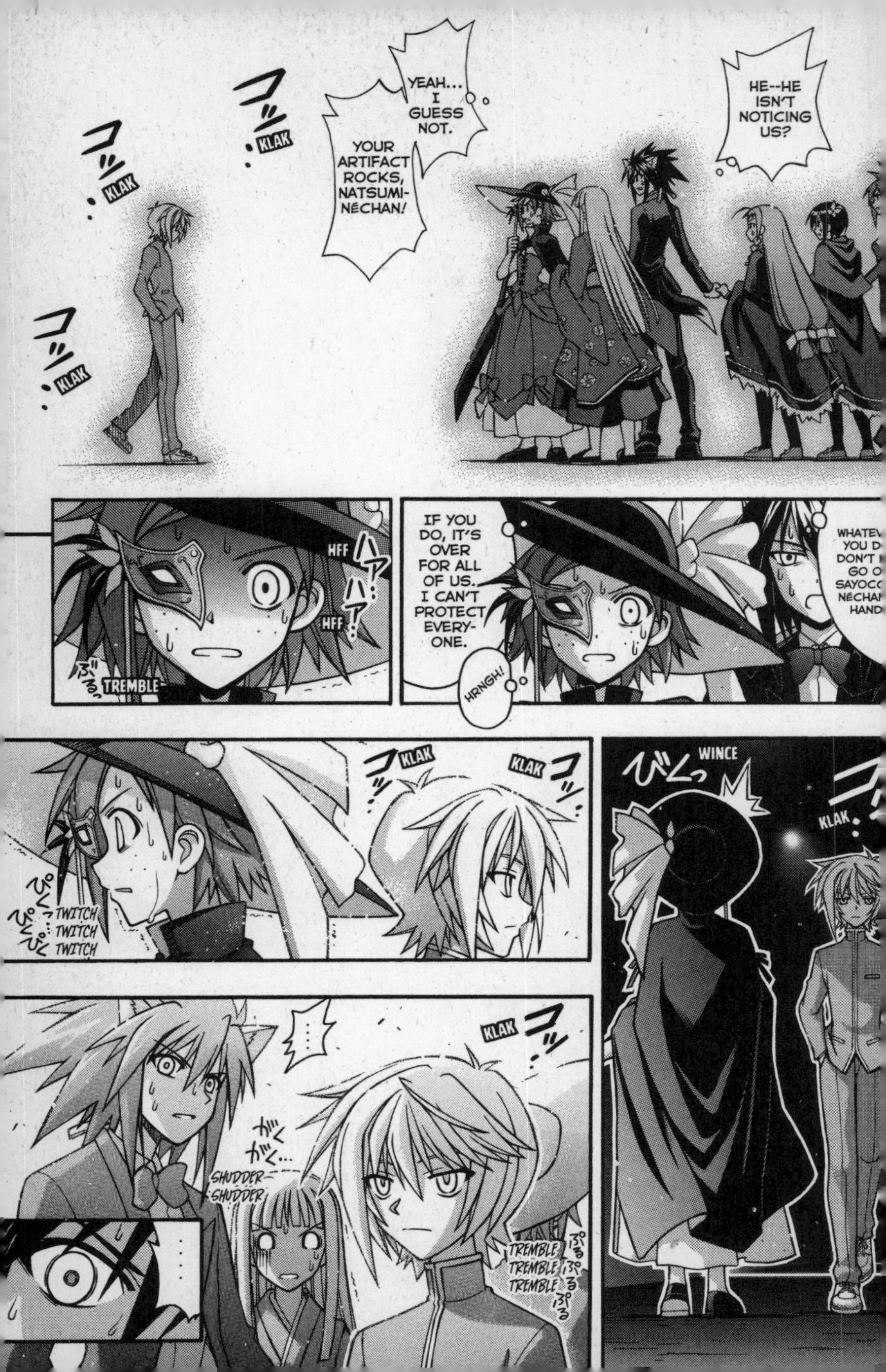
HE--HE ISN'T NOTICING US?
YEAH... I GUESS NOT.
YOUR ARTIFACT ROCKS, NATSUMI-NÉCHAN!
KLAK
KLAK
KLAK
WHATEV
YOU D
DON'T
GO O
SAYOC
NÉCHAN
HAND
IF YOU DO, IT'S OVER FOR ALL OF US. I CAN'T PROTECT EVERY-ONE.
HRNGH!
HFF
HFF
TREMBLE
WINCE
KLAK
KLAK
KLAK
TWITCH
TWITCH
TWITCH
...
KLAK
SHUDDER
SHUDDER
TREMBLE
TREMBLE
TREMBLE
...

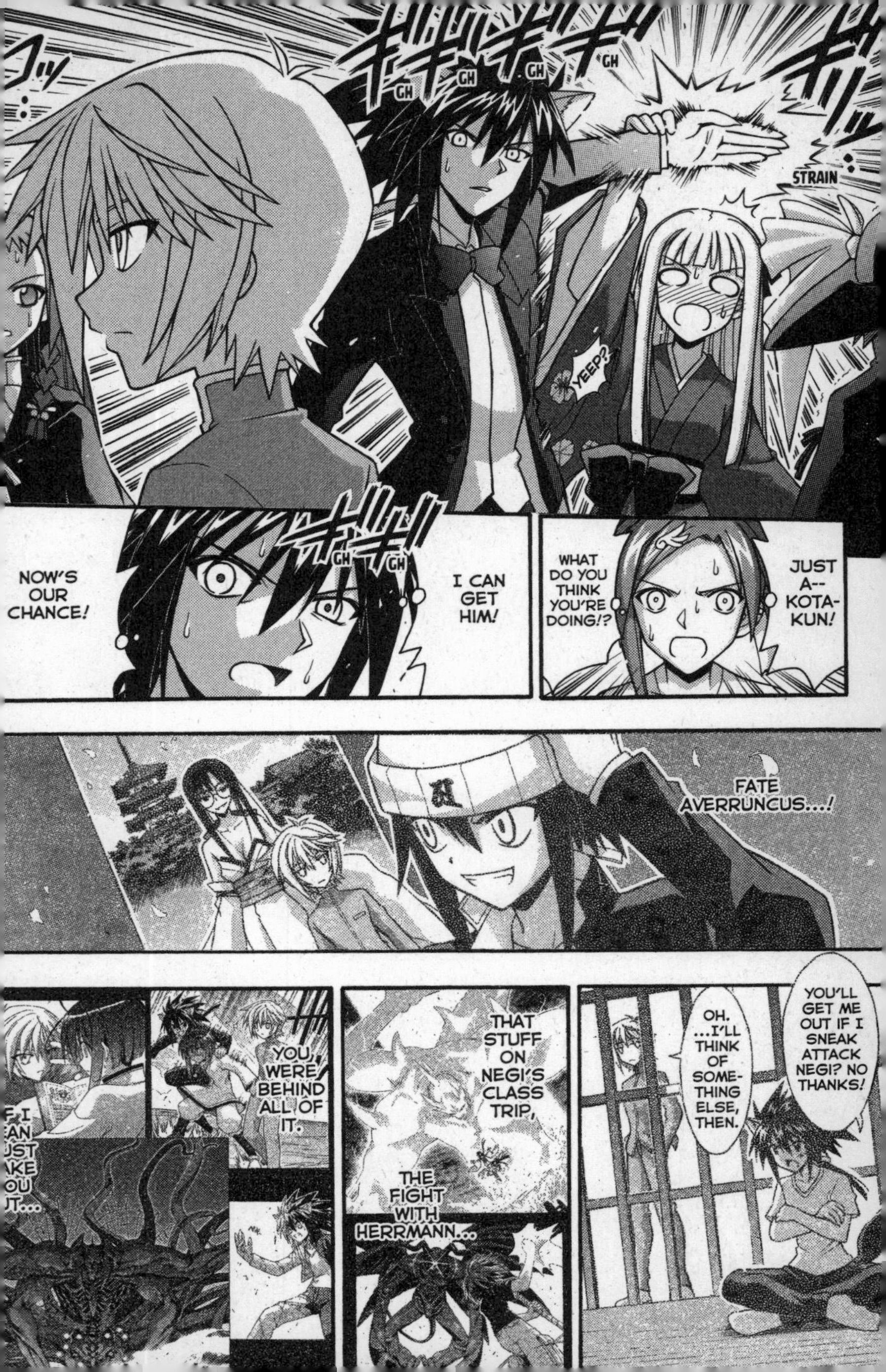
GH
GH
GH
GH
STRAIN
YEEP?
JUST A-- KOTA-KUN!
WHAT DO YOU THINK YOU'RE DOING!?
GH
GH
I CAN GET HIM!
NOW'S OUR CHANCE!
FATE AVERRUNCUS...!
YOU'LL GET ME OUT IF I SNEAK ATTACK NEGI? NO THANKS!
OH. ...I'LL THINK OF SOME-THING ELSE, THEN.
THAT STUFF ON NEGI'S CLASS TRIP,
THE FIGHT WITH HERRMANN...
YOU WERE BEHIND ALL OF IT.

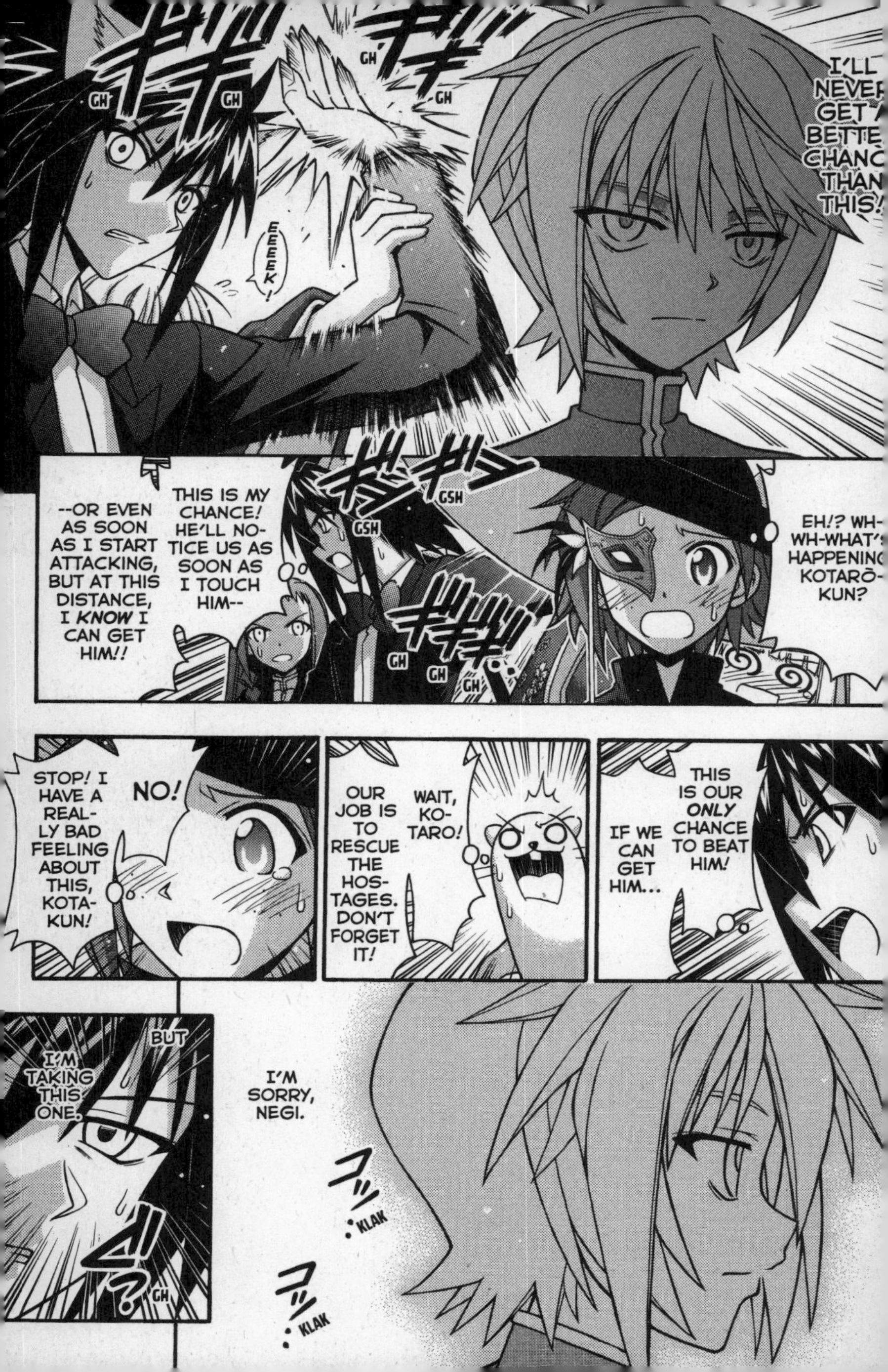
I'LL NEVER GET A BETTER CHANCE THAN THIS!
GH
GH
GH
GH
EEEEK!
EH!? WH-WH-WHAT'S HAPPENING KOTARŌ-KUN?
GSH
GSH
THIS IS MY CHANCE! HE'LL NOTICE US AS SOON AS I TOUCH HIM--
--OR EVEN AS SOON AS I START ATTACKING, BUT AT THIS DISTANCE, I KNOW I CAN GET HIM!!
GH
GH
GH
THIS IS OUR ONLY CHANCE TO BEAT HIM!
IF WE CAN GET HIM...
WAIT, KOTARO!
OUR JOB IS TO RESCUE THE HOSTAGES. DON'T FORGET IT!
NO!
STOP! I HAVE A REALLY BAD FEELING ABOUT THIS, KOTA-KUN!
KLAK
KLAK
I'M SORRY, NEGI.
BUT I'M TAKING THIS ONE.
GH

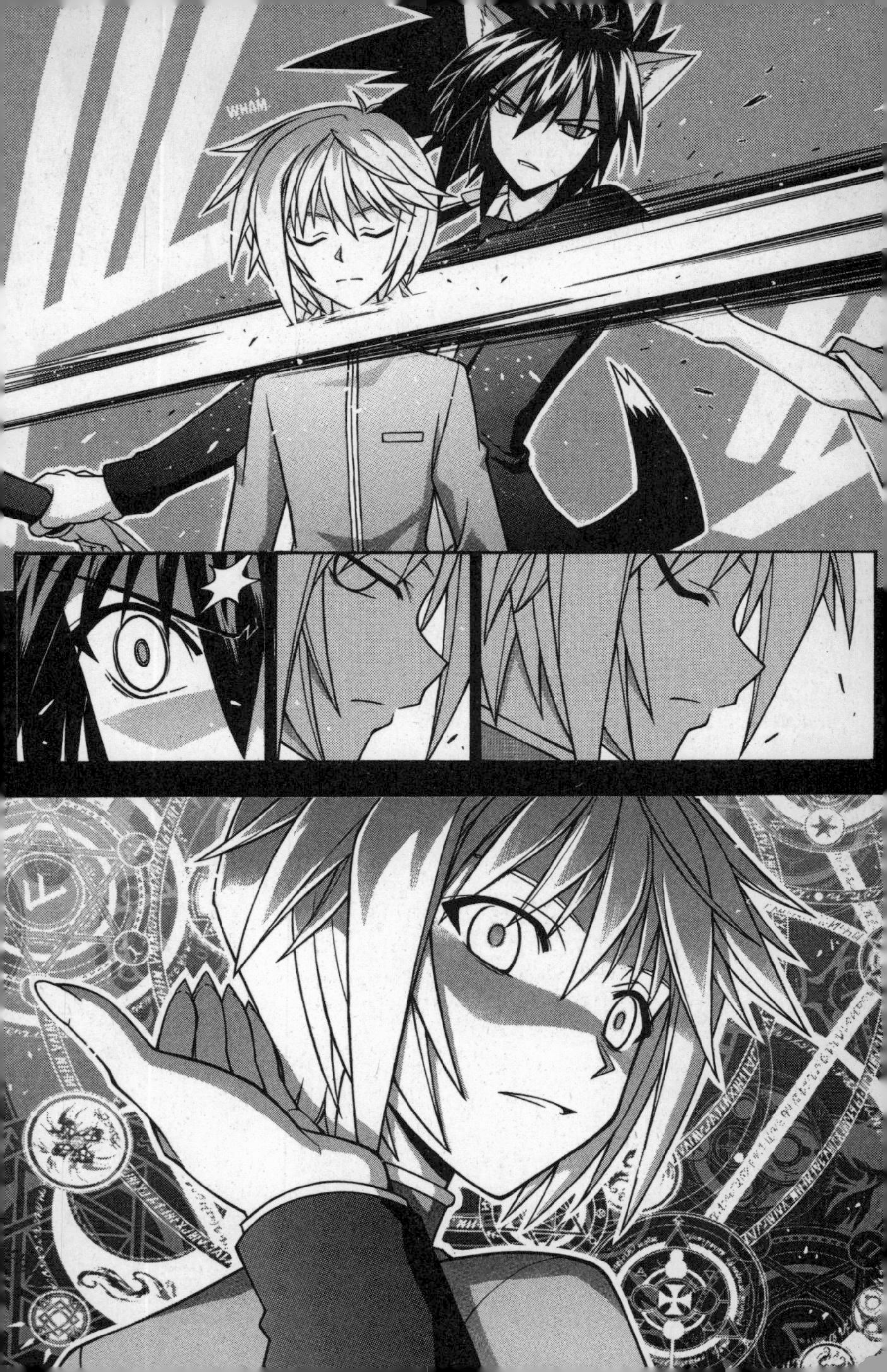
WHAM

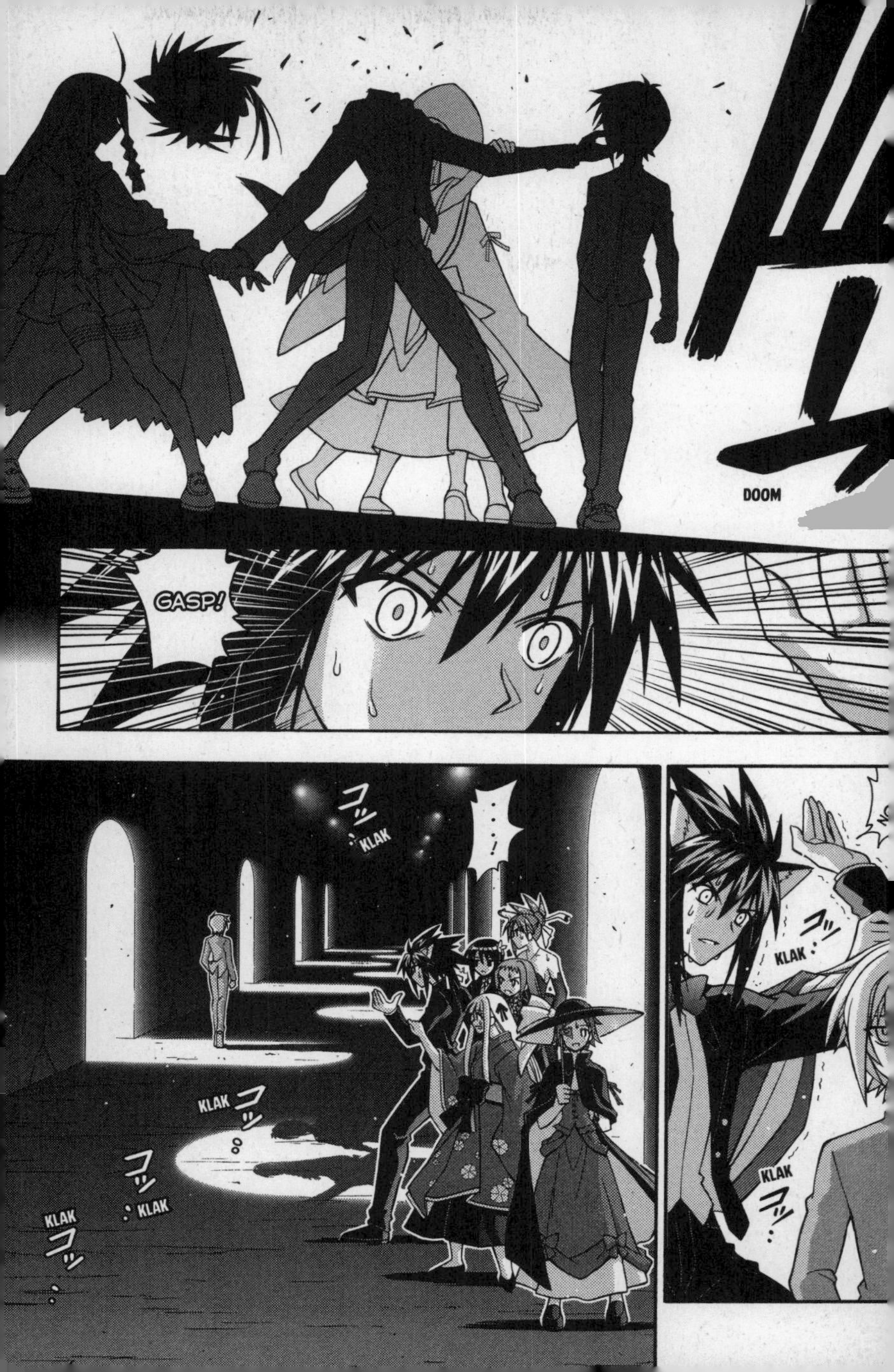

DOOM
GASP!
コッ
KLAK
KLAK
コッ
コッ
KLAK
...!
KLAK
コッ
コッ
KLAK
KLAK
コッ

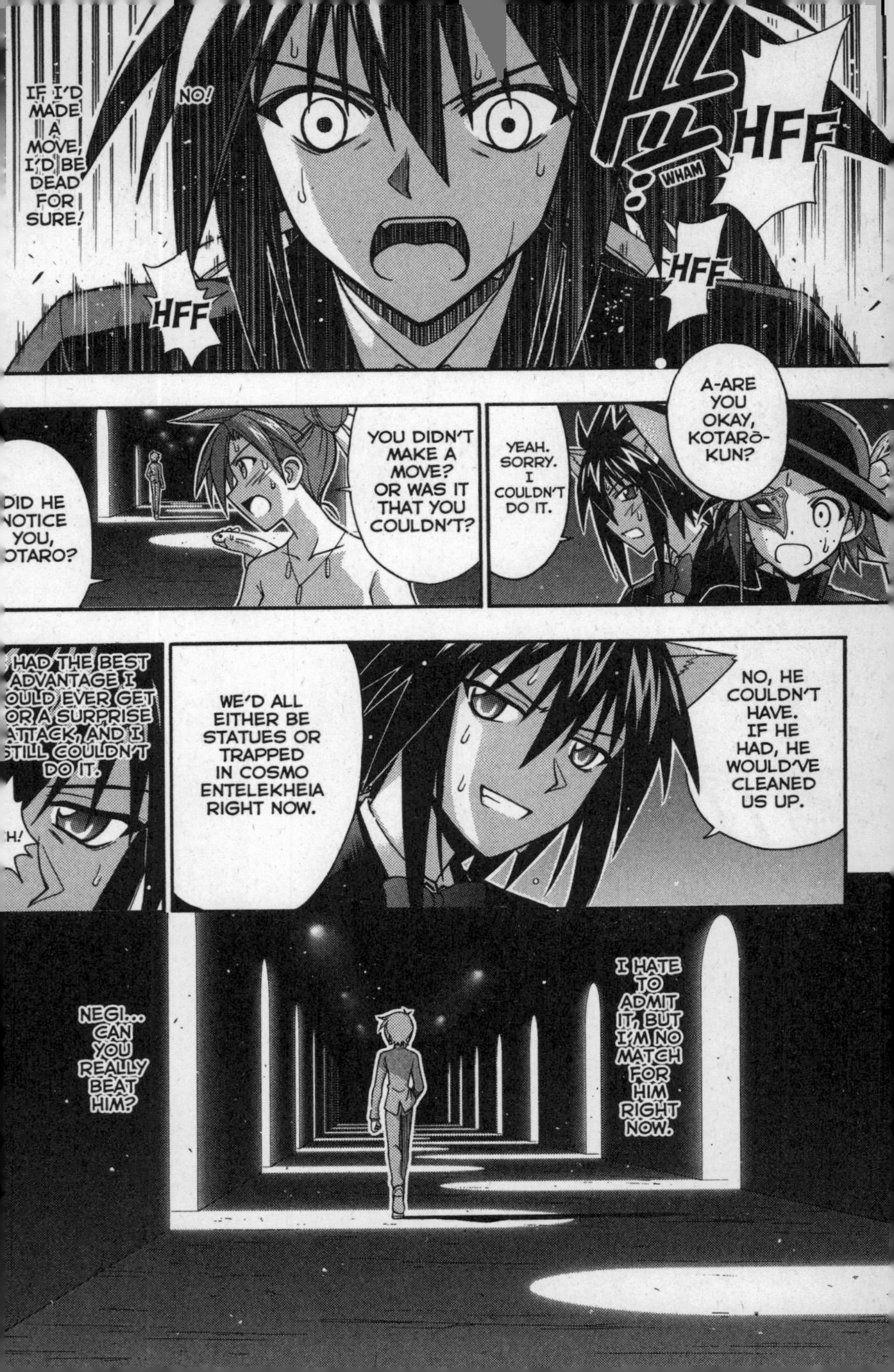
HFF
WHAM
HFF
NO!
IF I'D MADE A MOVE, I'D BE DEAD FOR SURE!
HFF
A-ARE YOU OKAY, KOTARŌ-KUN?
YEAH. SORRY. I COULDN'T DO IT.
YOU DIDN'T MAKE A MOVE? OR WAS IT THAT YOU COULDN'T?
DID HE NOTICE YOU, OTARO?
NO, HE COULDN'T HAVE. IF HE HAD, HE WOULD'VE CLEANED US UP.
WE'D ALL EITHER BE STATUES OR TRAPPED IN COSMO ENTELEKHEIA RIGHT NOW.
HAD THE BEST ADVANTAGE I OULD EVER GET OR A SURPRISE ATTACK, AND I STILL COULDN'T DO IT.
H!
I HATE TO ADMIT IT, BUT I'M NO MATCH FOR HIM RIGHT NOW.
NEGI... CAN YOU REALLY BEAT HIM?

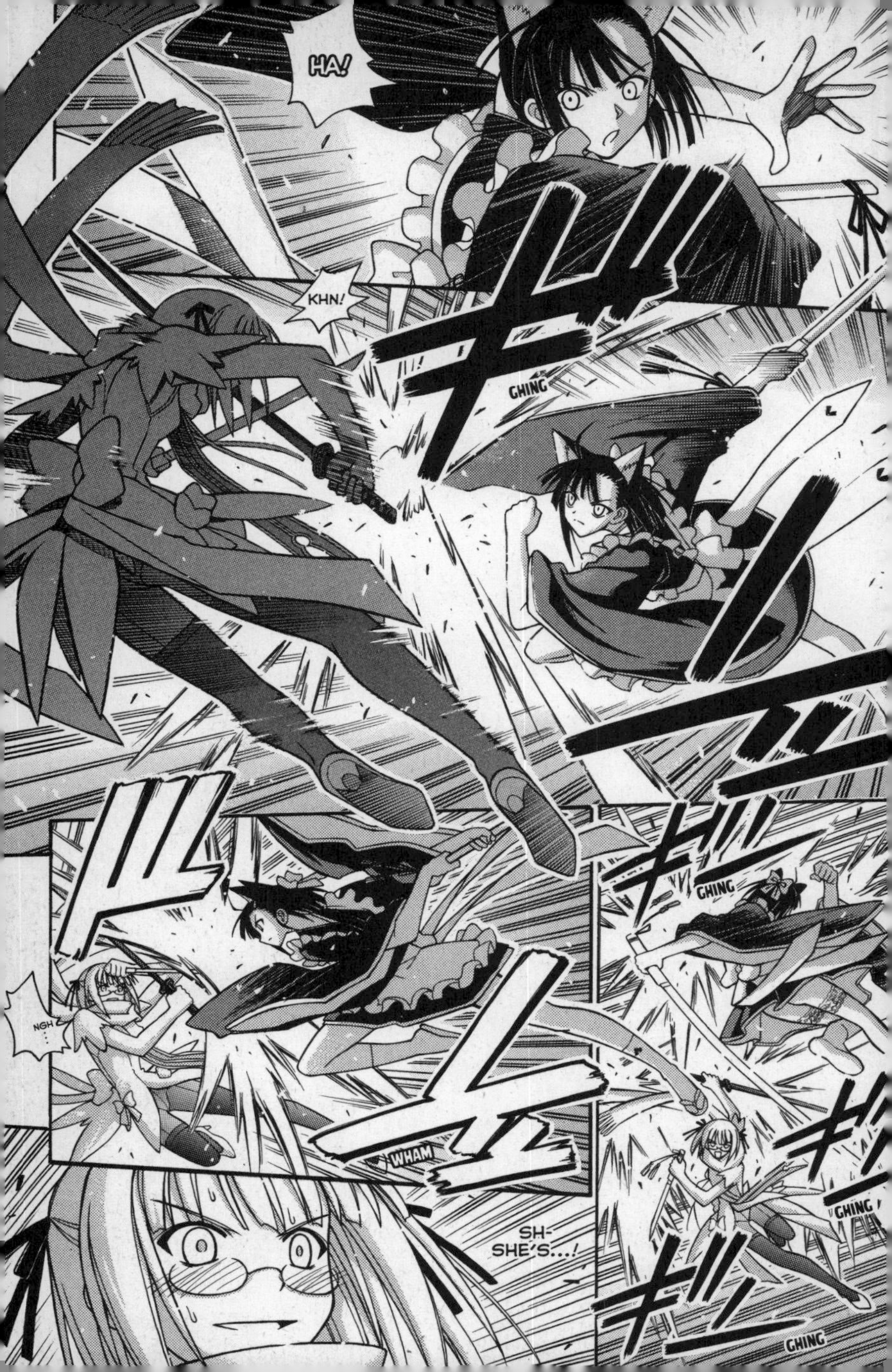
HA!
KHN!
GHING
GHING
GHING
GHING
NGH...
WHAM
SH- SHE'S...!

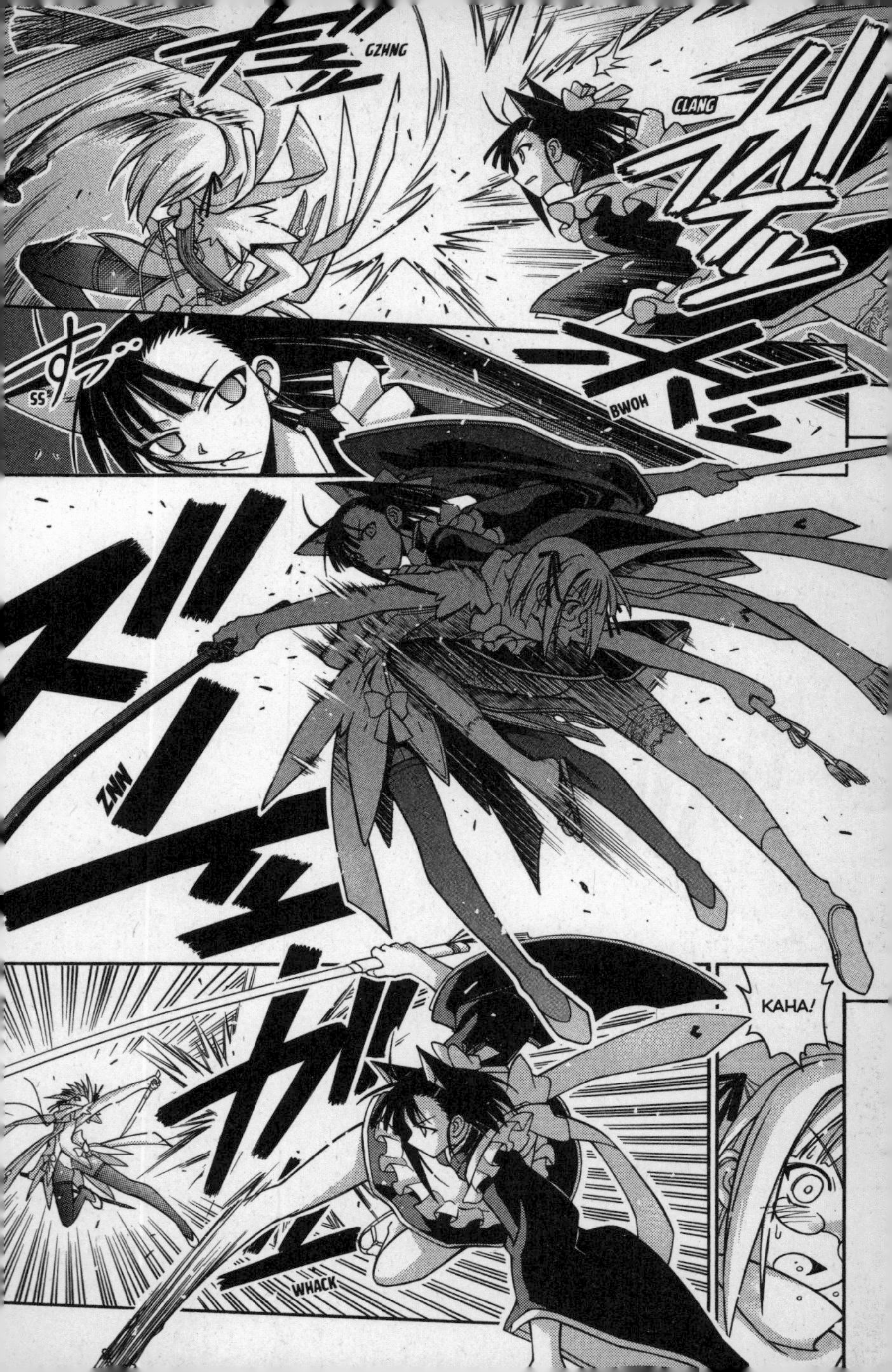
CLANG
GZHNG
BWOH
SS
ZNN
KAHA!
WHACK

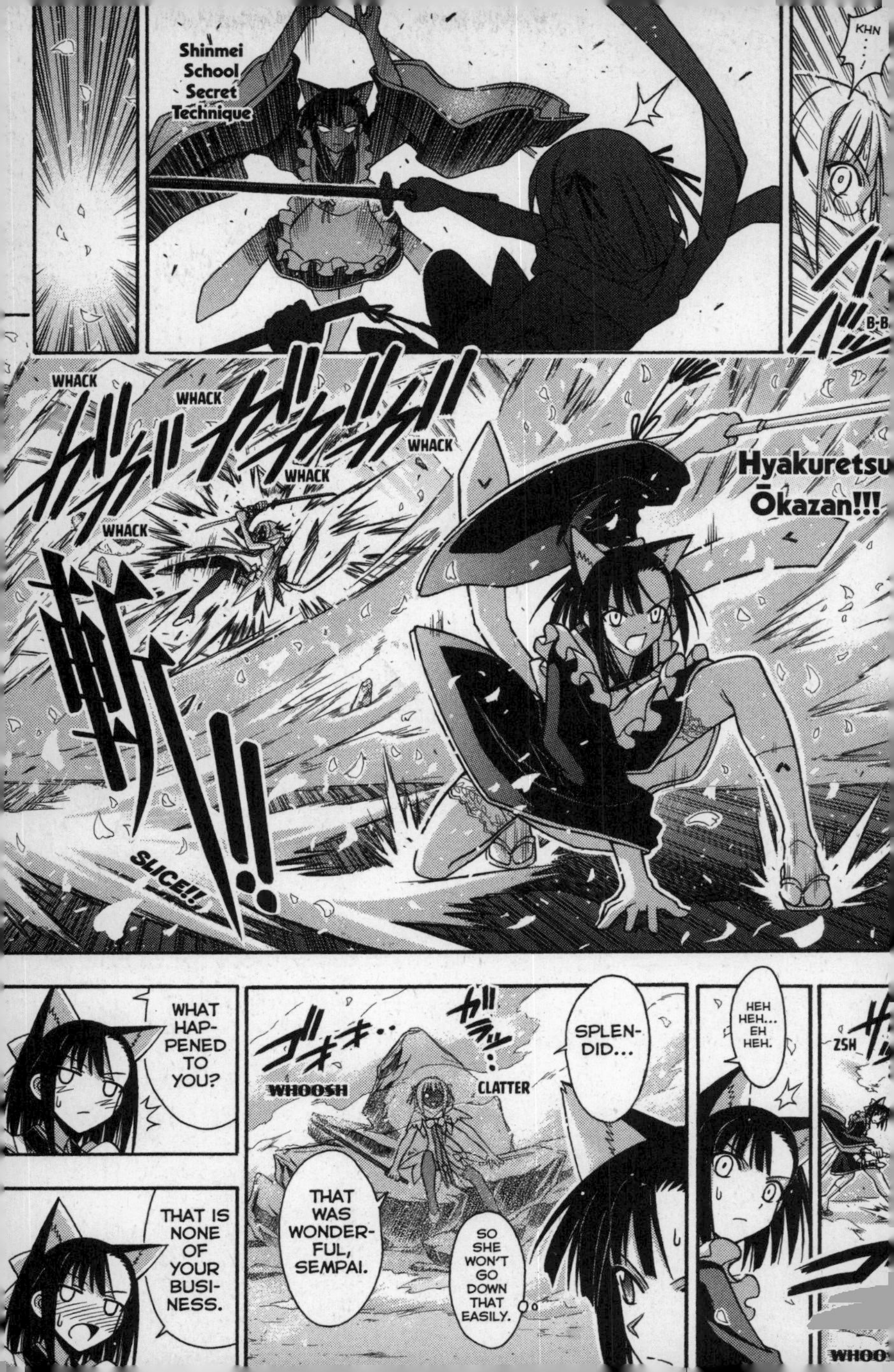

KHN...!
B-B...
Shinmei School Secret Technique
Hyakuretsu Ōkazan!!!
WHACK
WHACK
WHACK
WHACK
WHACK
SLICE!!
ZSH
WHOO
HEH HEH... EH HEH.
SPLEND-ID...
CLATTER
WHOOSH
THAT WAS WONDER-FUL, SEMPAI.
SO SHE WON'T GO DOWN THAT EASILY.
WHAT HAP-PENED TO YOU?
THAT IS NONE OF YOUR BUSI-NESS.

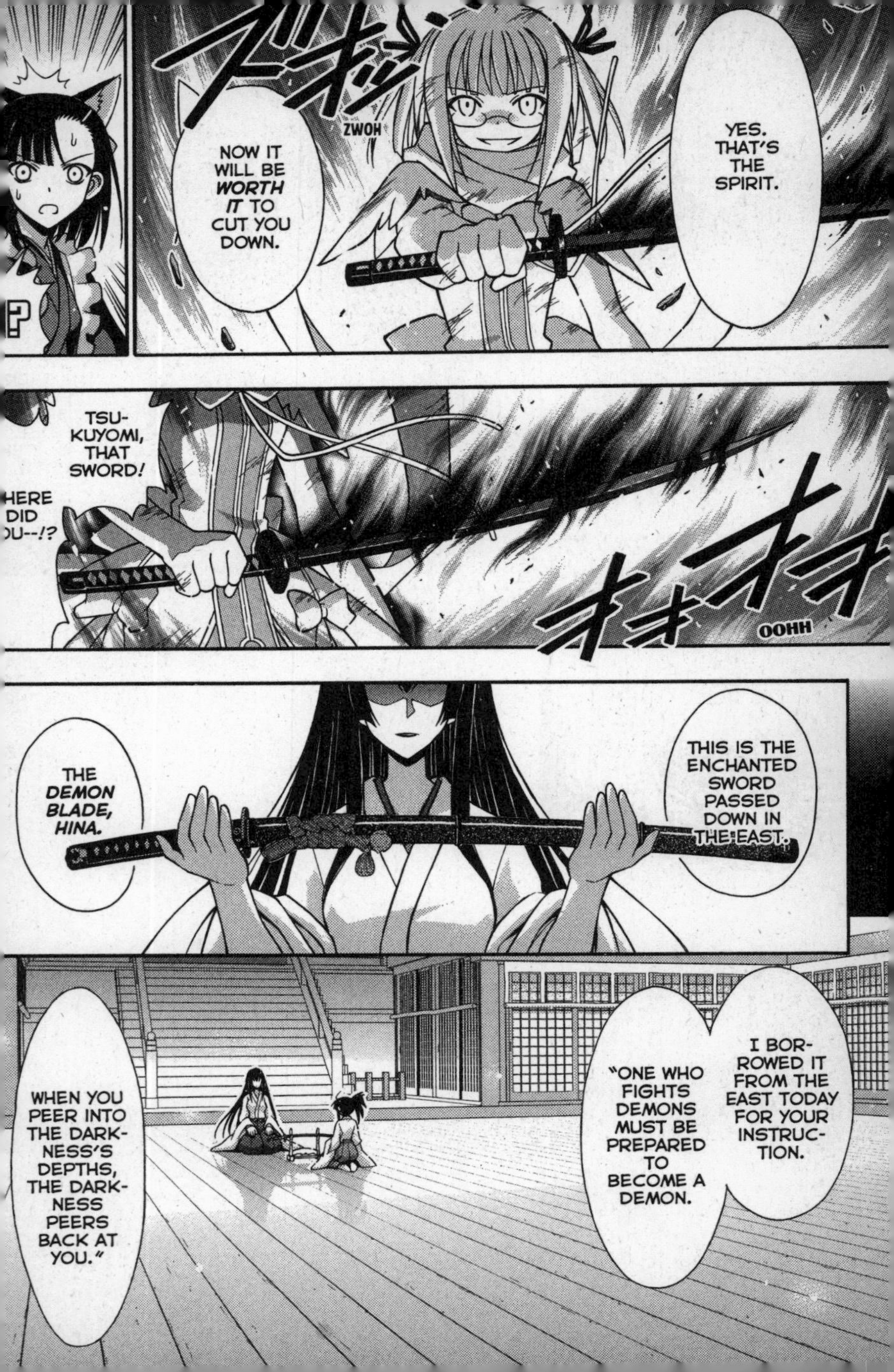
YES. THAT'S THE SPIRIT.
ZWOH
NOW IT WILL BE *WORTH IT* TO CUT YOU DOWN.
!?
OOHH
TSU-KUYOMI, THAT SWORD!
HERE DID OU--!?
THIS IS THE ENCHANTED SWORD PASSED DOWN IN THE EAST.
THE *DEMON BLADE, HINA.*
I BOR-ROWED IT FROM THE EAST TODAY FOR YOUR INSTRUC-TION.
"ONE WHO FIGHTS DEMONS MUST BE PREPARED TO BECOME A DEMON.
WHEN YOU PEER INTO THE DARK-NESS'S DEPTHS, THE DARK-NESS PEERS BACK AT YOU."

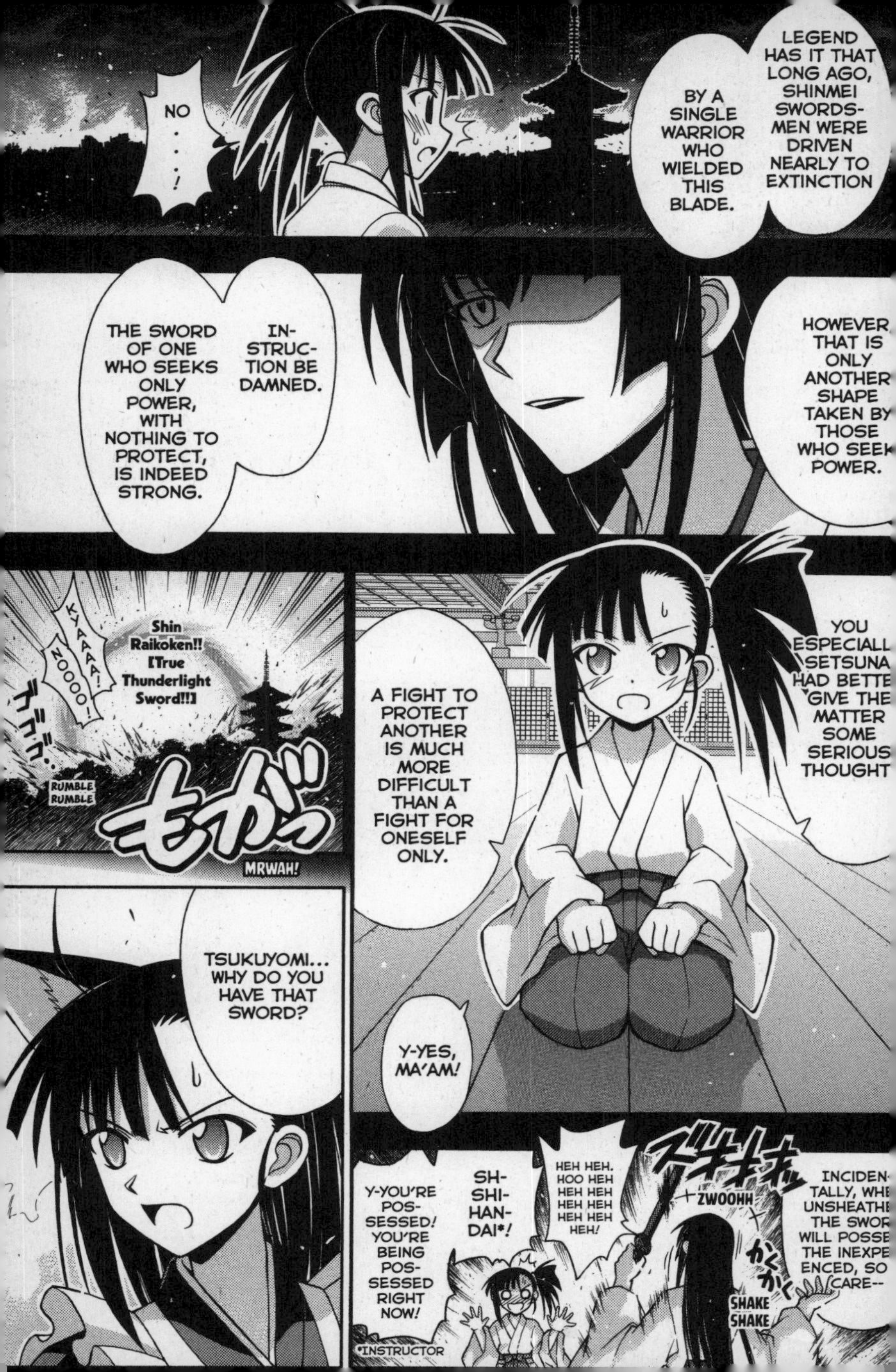
LEGEND HAS IT THAT LONG AGO, SHINMEI SWORDS-MEN WERE DRIVEN NEARLY TO EXTINCTION
BY A SINGLE WARRIOR WHO WIELDED THIS BLADE.
NO...!
HOWEVER, THAT IS ONLY ANOTHER SHAPE TAKEN BY THOSE WHO SEEK POWER.
IN-STRUC-TION BE DAMNED.
THE SWORD OF ONE WHO SEEKS ONLY POWER, WITH NOTHING TO PROTECT, IS INDEED STRONG.
YOU ESPECIALL SETSUNA HAD BETTE GIVE THE MATTER SOME SERIOUS THOUGHT
A FIGHT TO PROTECT ANOTHER IS MUCH MORE DIFFICULT THAN A FIGHT FOR ONESELF ONLY.
Y-YES, MA'AM!
INCIDEN-TALLY, WHE UNSHEATHE THE SWOR WILL POSSE THE INEXPE ENCED, SO CARE--
ZWOOHH
SHAKE SHAKE
HEH HEH. HOO HEH HEH HEH HEH HEH HEH HEH HEH!
SH-SHI-HAN-DAI*!
Y-YOU'RE POS-SESSED! YOU'RE BEING POS-SESSED RIGHT NOW!
*INSTRUCTOR
KYAAAA!
NOOOOO!
Shin Raikoken!! [True Thunderlight Sword!!]
RUMBLE RUMBLE
もがっ
MRWAH!
TSUKUYOMI... WHY DO YOU HAVE THAT SWORD?

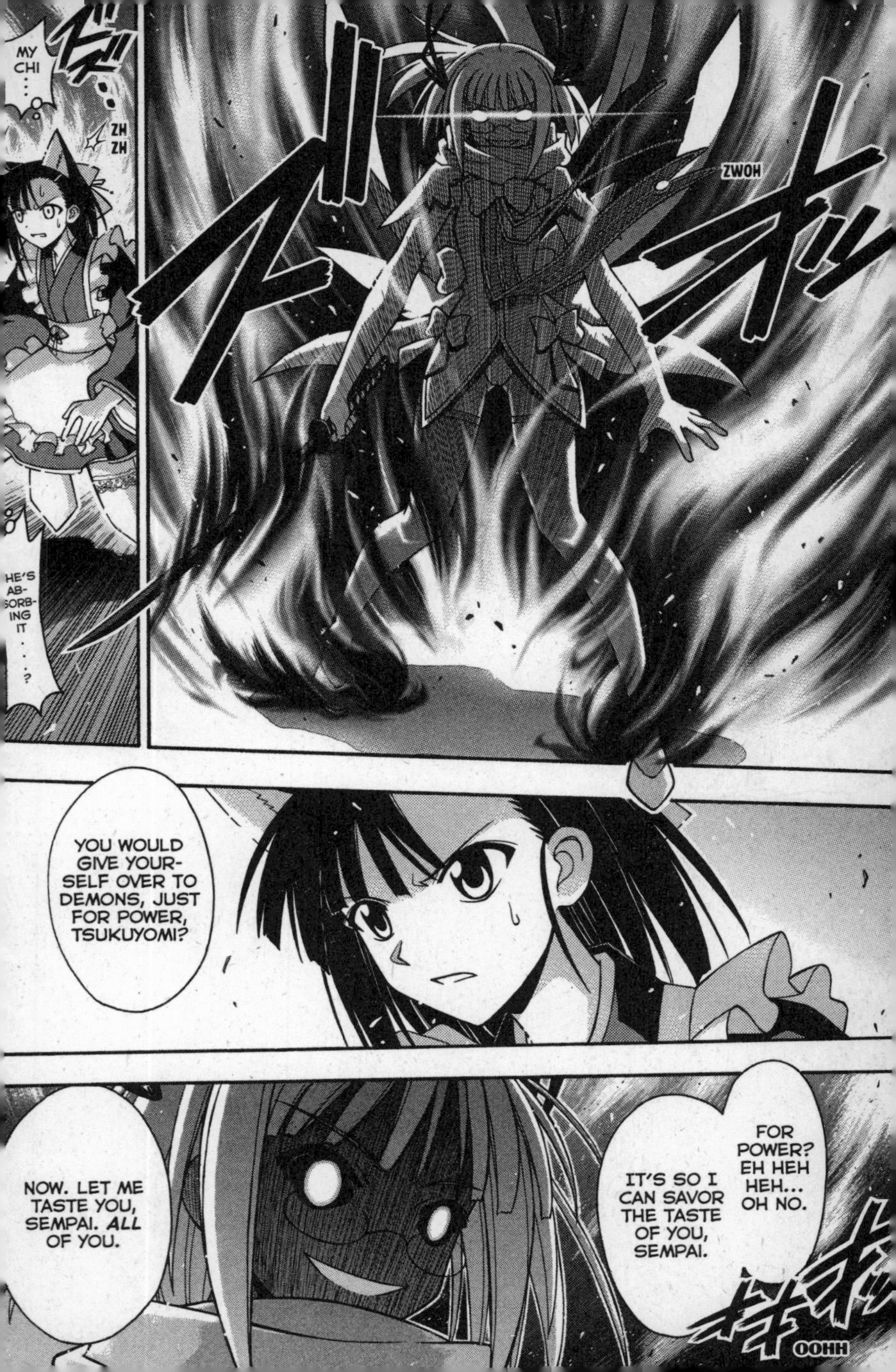
ZWOH
MY CHI . . .
ZH ZH
HE'S AB-SORB-ING IT . . . ?
YOU WOULD GIVE YOUR-SELF OVER TO DEMONS, JUST FOR POWER, TSUKUYOMI?
FOR POWER? EH HEH HEH... OH NO.
IT'S SO I CAN SAVOR THE TASTE OF YOU, SEMPAI.
NOW. LET ME TASTE YOU, SEMPAI. *ALL* OF YOU.
OOHH

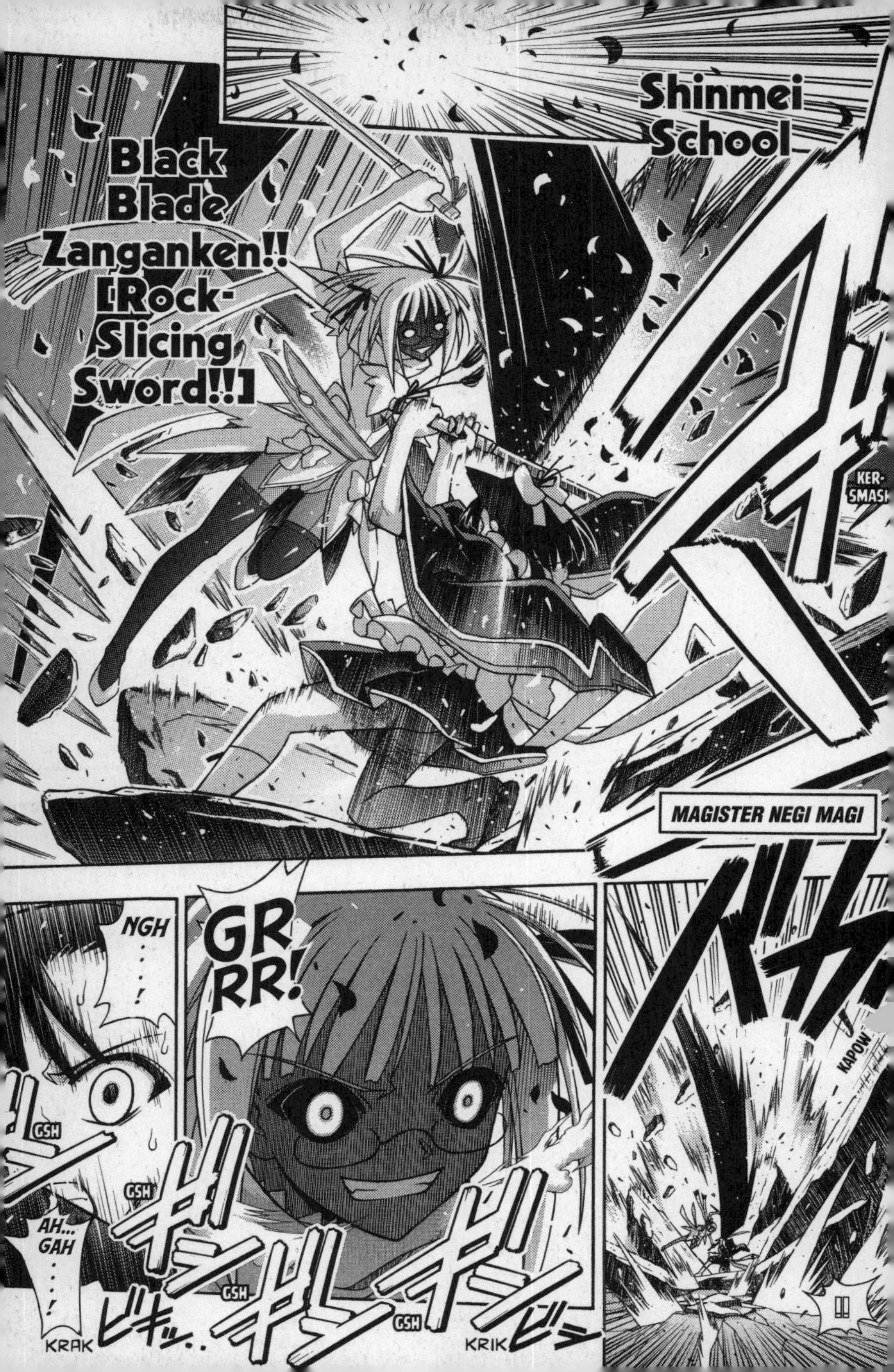
Shinmei School
Black Blade Zanganken!! [Rock-Slicing Sword!!]
KER-SMASH
MAGISTER NEGI MAGI
KAPOW
!!
GR RR!
GSH
GSH
KRIK
NGH...!
GSH
AH... GAH...!
KRAK

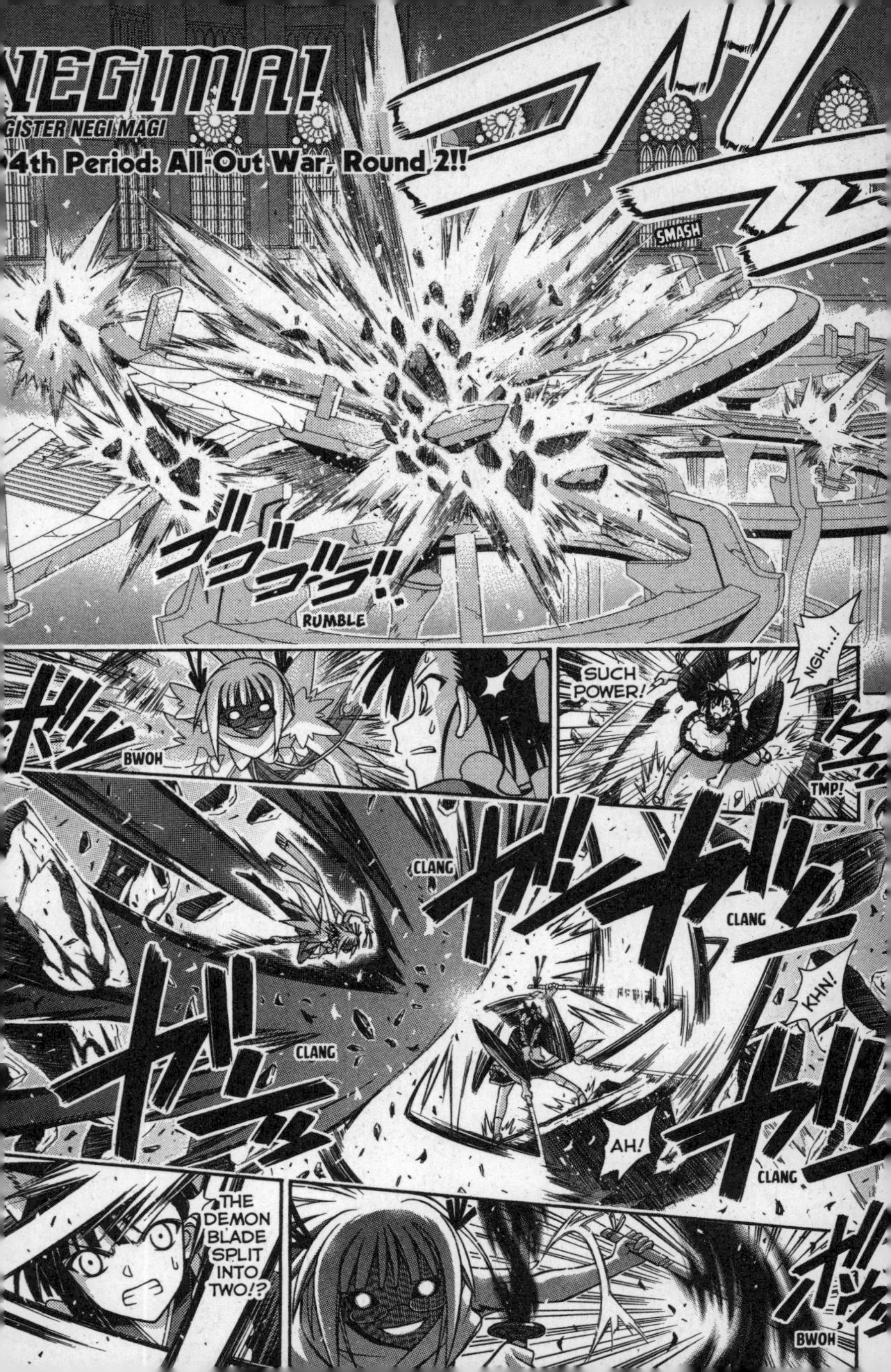
NEGIMA!
GISTER NEGI MAGI
4th Period: All-Out War, Round 2!!
SMASH
RUMBLE
SUCH POWER!
NGH...!
TMP!
BWOH
CLANG
KHN!
CLANG
AH!
CLANG
CLANG
BWOH
THE DEMON BLADE SPLIT INTO TWO!?

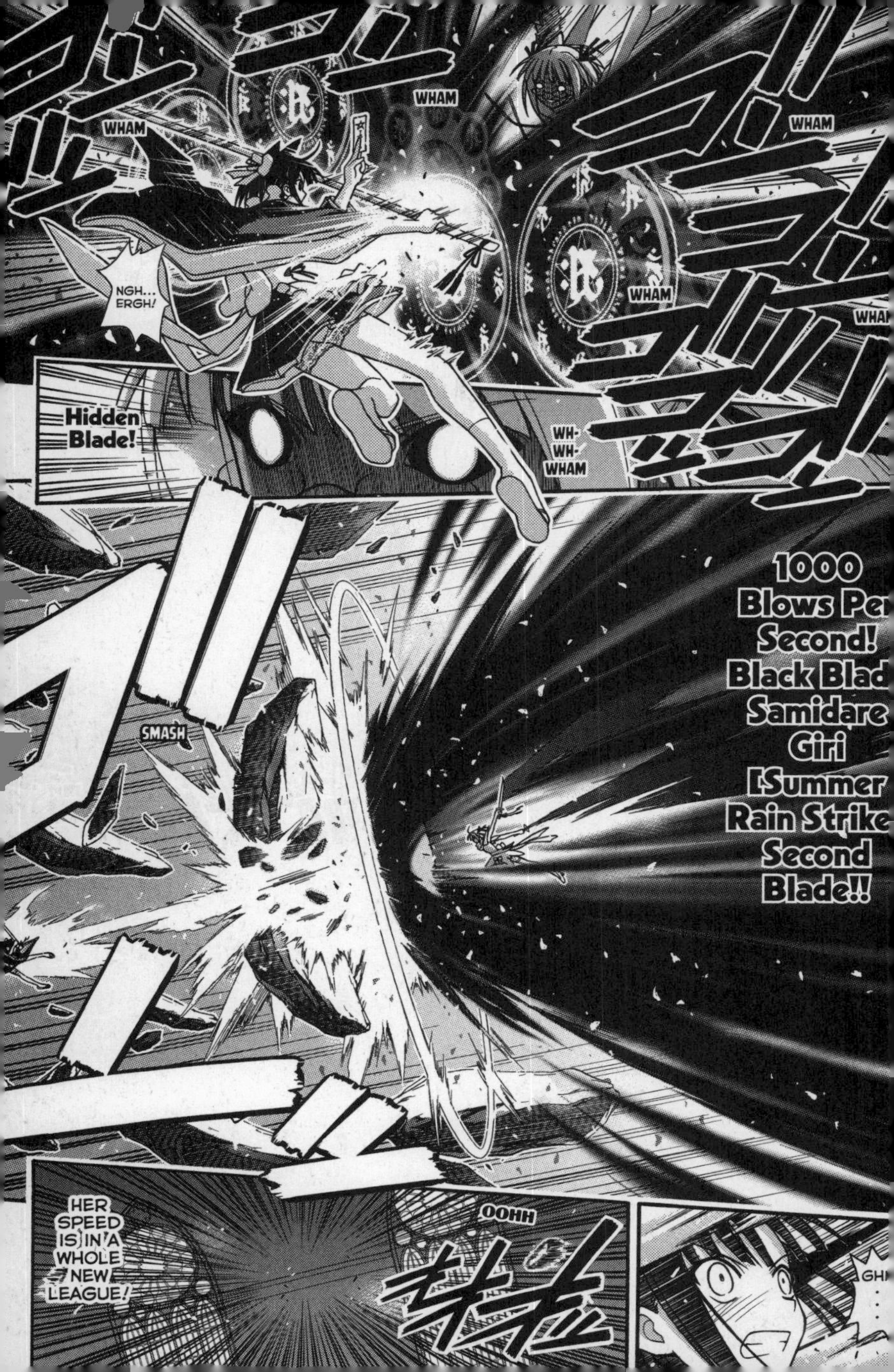

WHAM
WHAM
WHAM
WHAM
WHAM
NGH... ERGH!
WH- WH- WHAM
Hidden Blade!
1000 Blows Per Second! Black Blad Samidare Giri [Summer Rain Strike Second Blade!!
SMASH
GH...
OOHH
HER SPEED IS IN A WHOLE NEW LEAGUE!

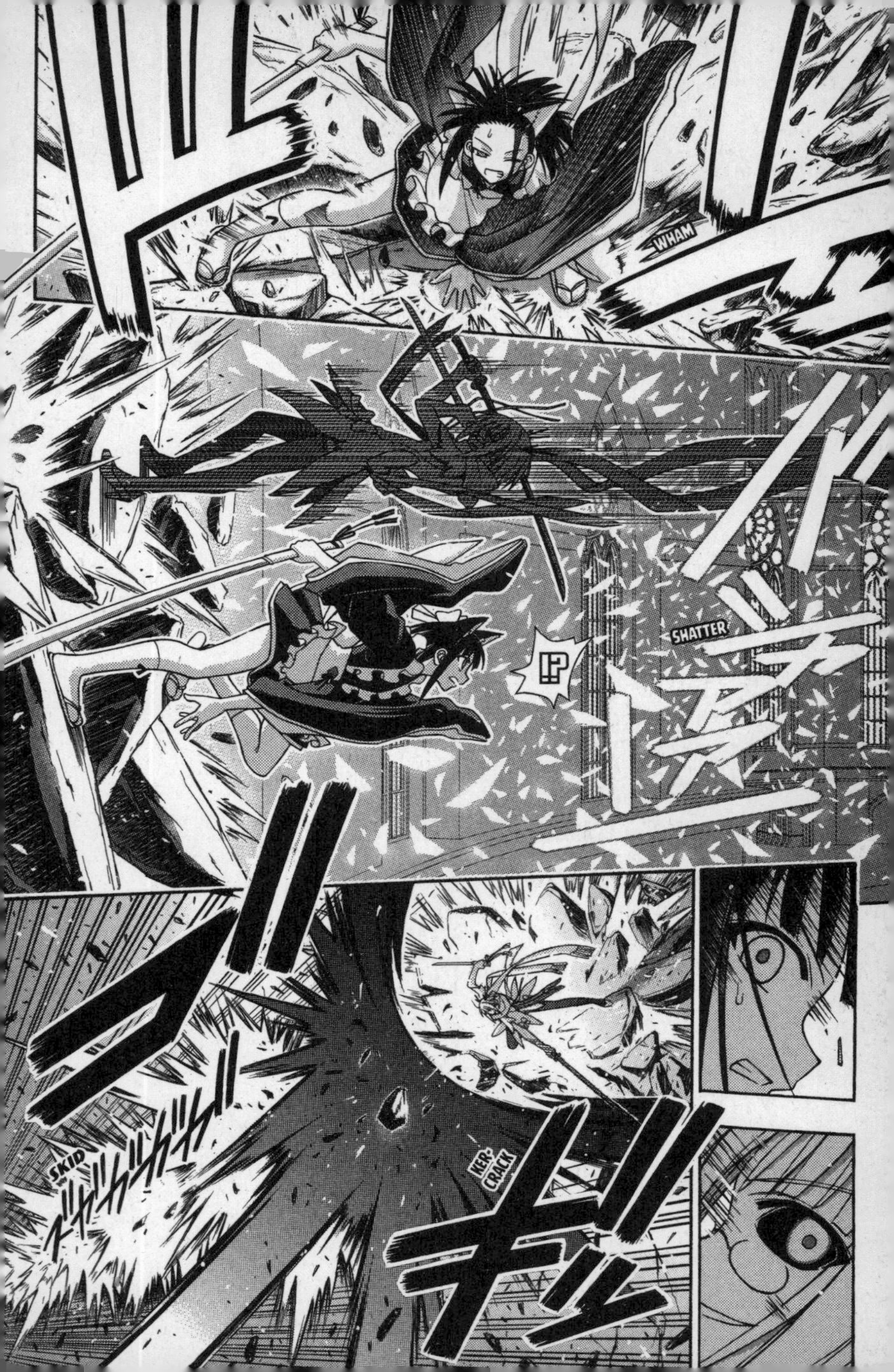
WHAM
SHATTER
!?
KER-CRACK
SKID

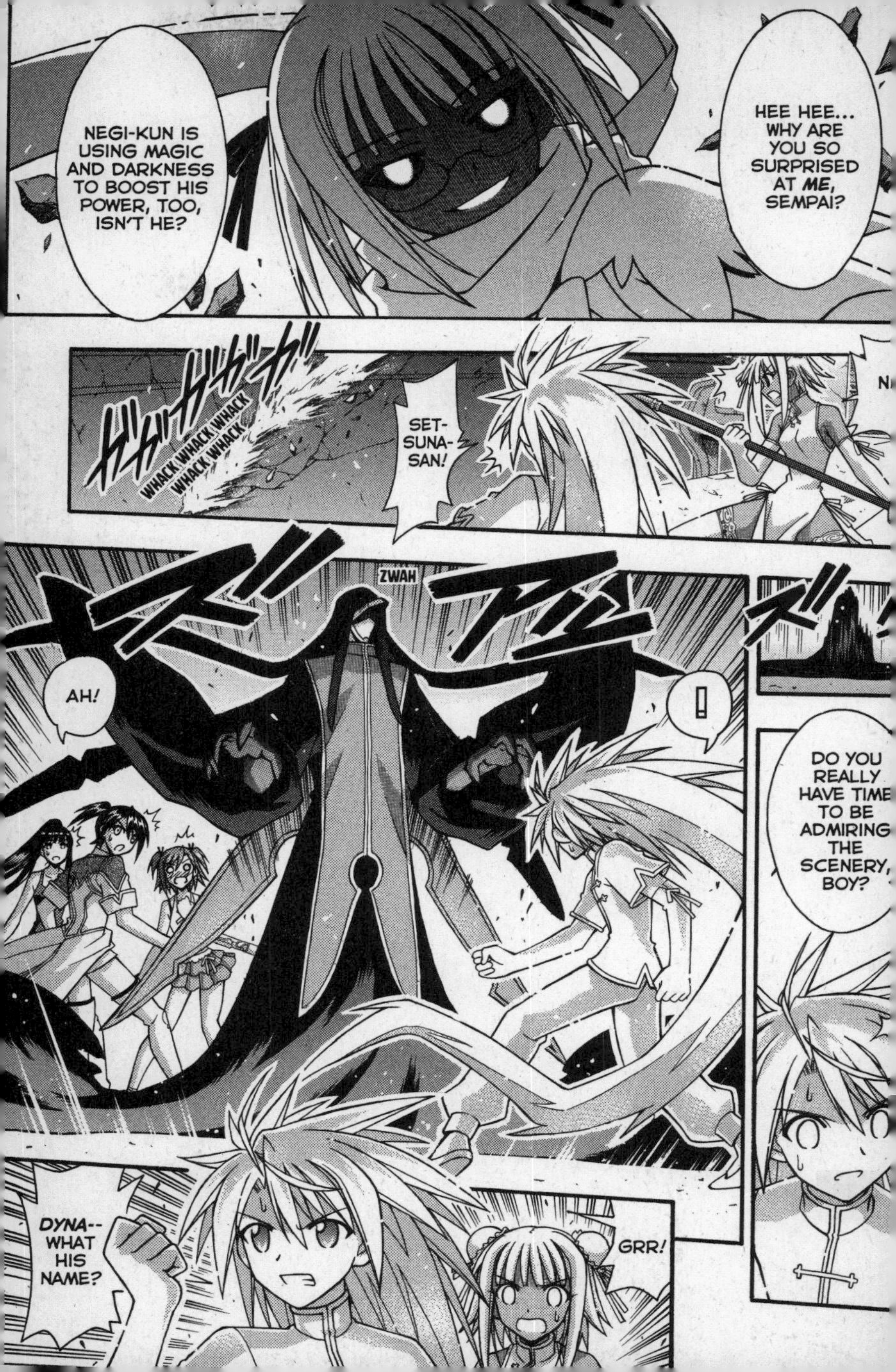
HEE HEE... WHY ARE YOU SO SURPRISED AT *ME*, SEMPAI?
NEGI-KUN IS USING MAGIC AND DARKNESS TO BOOST HIS POWER, TOO, ISN'T HE?
SET-SUNA-SAN!
WHACK WHACK WHACK WHACK
ZWAH
!
AH!
DO YOU REALLY HAVE TIME TO BE ADMIRING THE SCENERY, BOY?
GRR!
DYNA-- WHAT HIS NAME?

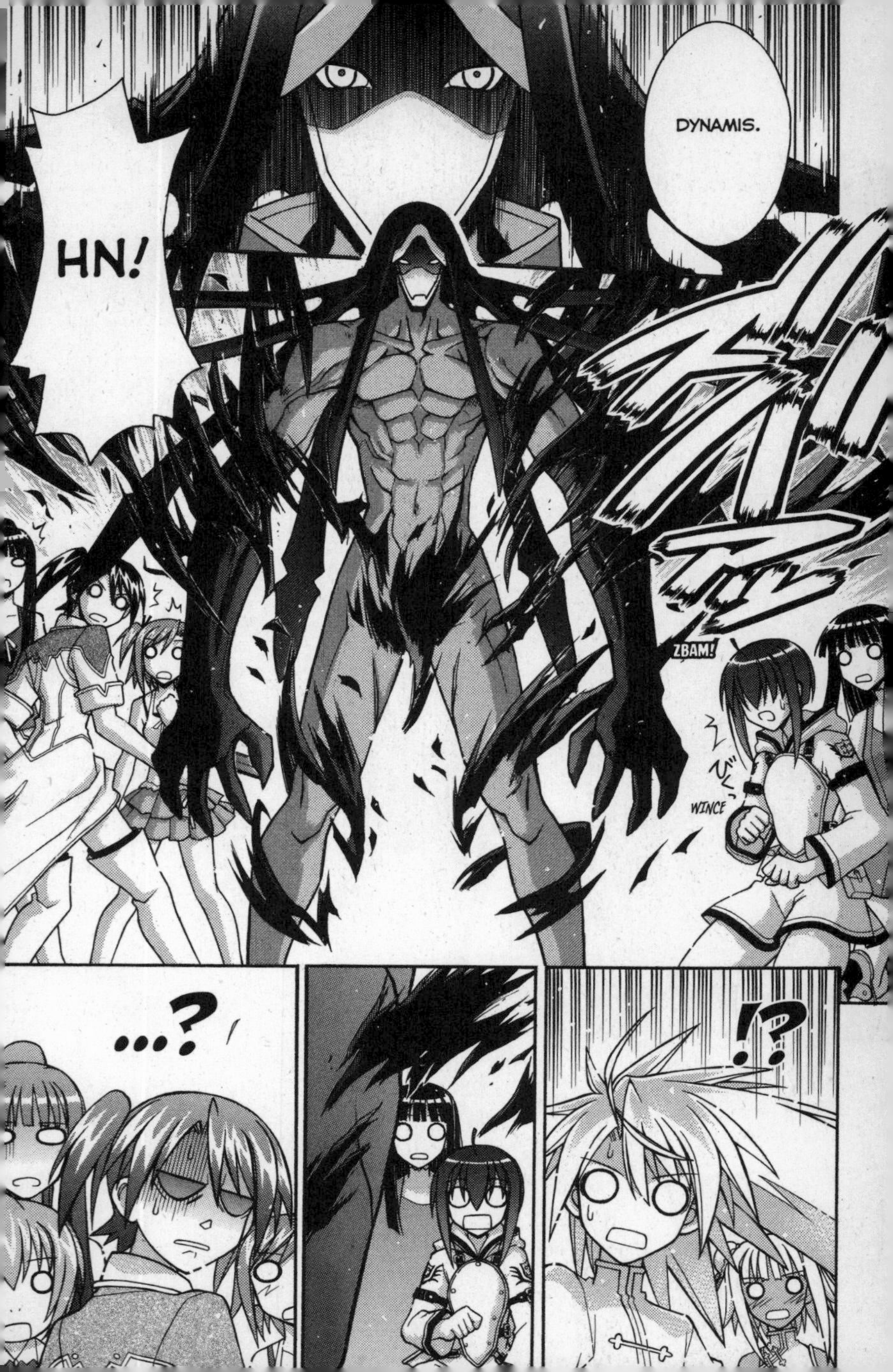
DYNAMIS.
HN!
ZBAM!
WINCE
!?
...?

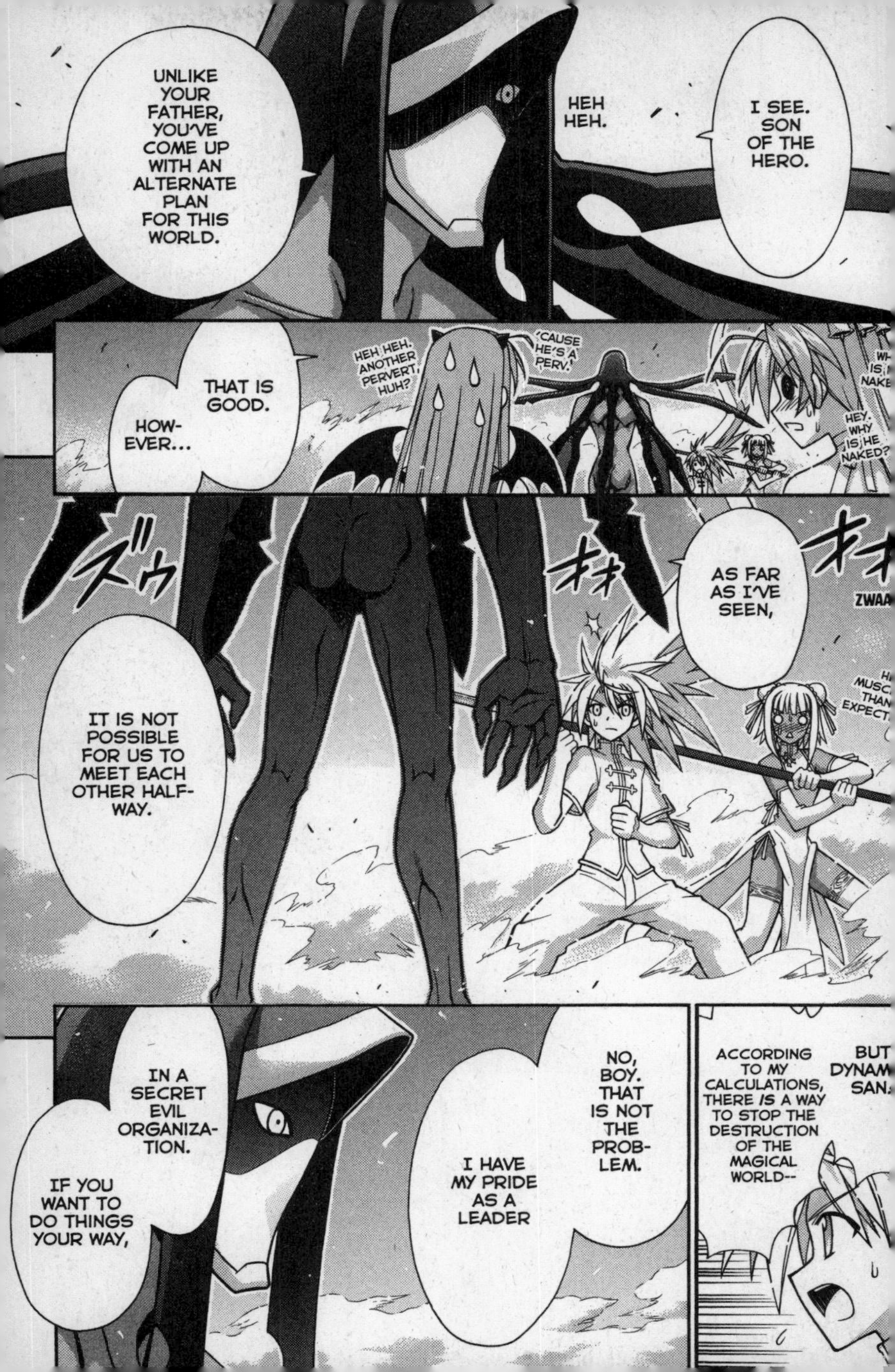

I SEE. SON OF THE HERO.
HEH HEH.
UNLIKE YOUR FATHER, YOU'VE COME UP WITH AN ALTERNATE PLAN FOR THIS WORLD.
HEY. WHY IS HE NAKED?
'CAUSE HE'S A PERV.
HEH HEH. ANOTHER PERVERT, HUH?
THAT IS GOOD.
HOW-EVER...
オオ
AS FAR AS I'VE SEEN,
オオ
ズゥ
IT IS NOT POSSIBLE FOR US TO MEET EACH OTHER HALF-WAY.
ACCORDING TO MY CALCULATIONS, THERE *IS* A WAY TO STOP THE DESTRUCTION OF THE MAGICAL WORLD--
NO, BOY. THAT IS NOT THE PROBLEM.
I HAVE MY PRIDE AS A LEADER
IN A SECRET EVIL ORGANIZA-TION.
IF YOU WANT TO DO THINGS YOUR WAY,

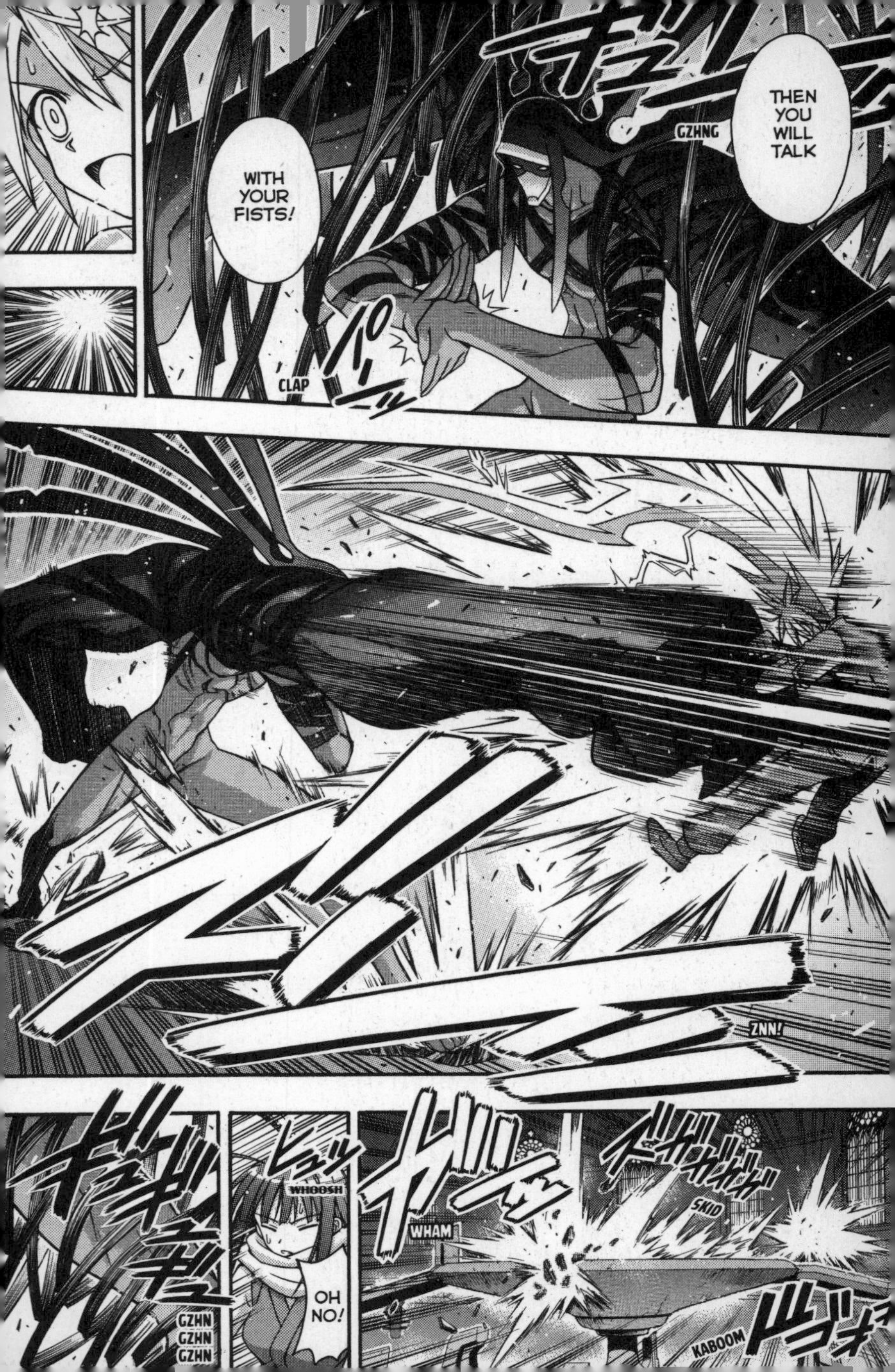
THEN YOU WILL TALK
GZHNG
WITH YOUR FISTS!
CLAP
ZNN!
SKID
WHAM
KABOOM
WHOOSH
OH NO!
GZHN
GZHN
GZHN

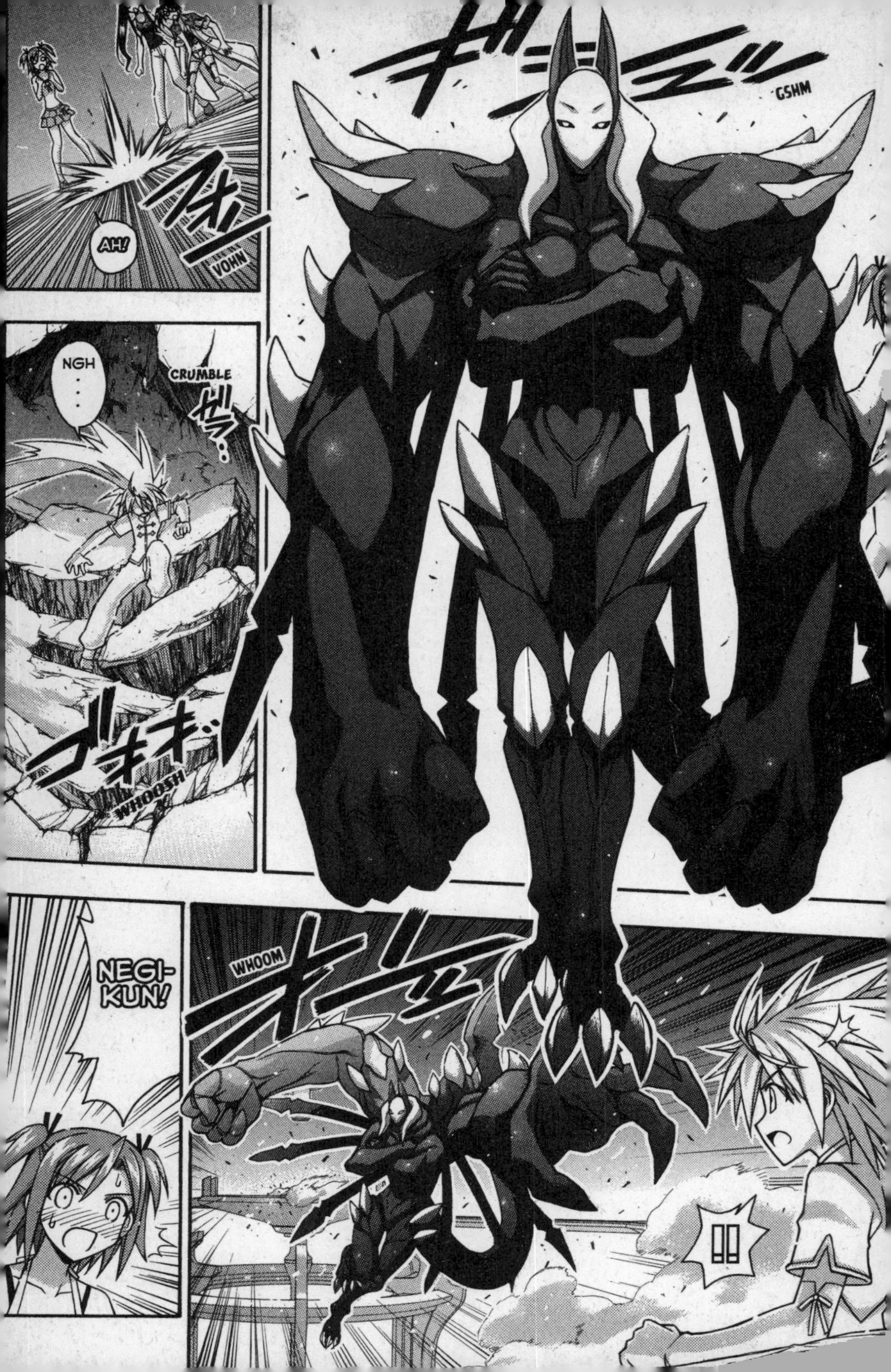

GSHM
AH!
VOHN
NGH...
CRUMBLE
WHOOSH
WHOOM
!!
NEGI-KUN!

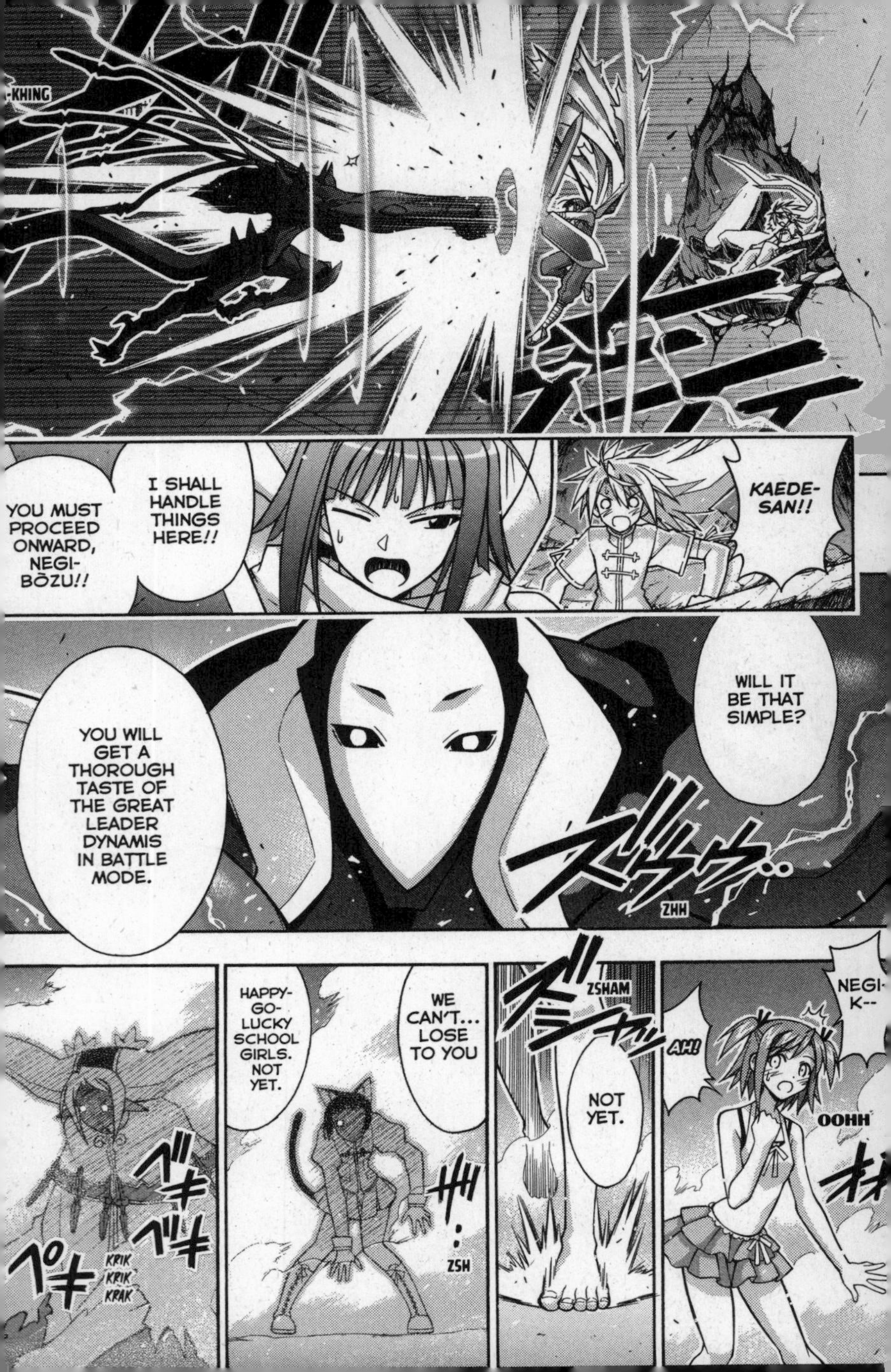
-KHING
KAEDE-SAN!!
I SHALL HANDLE THINGS HERE!!
YOU MUST PROCEED ONWARD, NEGI-BŌZU!!
WILL IT BE THAT SIMPLE?
YOU WILL GET A THOROUGH TASTE OF THE GREAT LEADER DYNAMIS IN BATTLE MODE.
ZHH
NEGI-K--
AH!
OOHH
ZSHAM
NOT YET.
WE CAN'T... LOSE TO YOU
HAPPY-GO-LUCKY SCHOOL GIRLS. NOT YET.
ZSH
KRIK KRIK KRAK

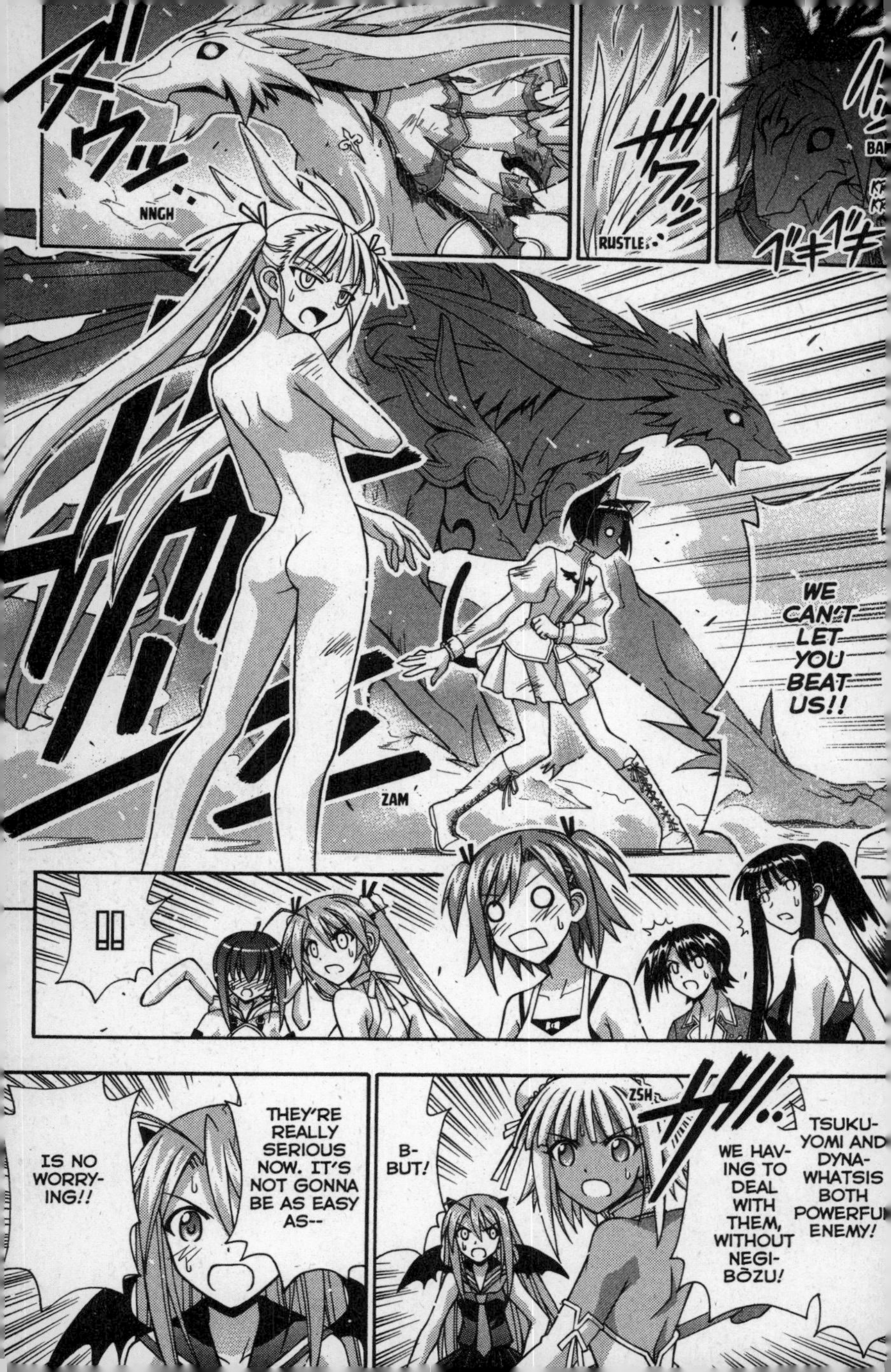
RUSTLE
NNGH
WE CAN'T LET YOU BEAT US!!
ZAM
!!
TSUKU-YOMI AND DYNA-WHATSIS BOTH POWERFU ENEMY!
WE HAVING TO DEAL WITH THEM, WITHOUT NEGI-BŌZU!
ZSH
B-BUT!
THEY'RE REALLY SERIOUS NOW. IT'S NOT GONNA BE AS EASY AS--
IS NO WORRYING!!

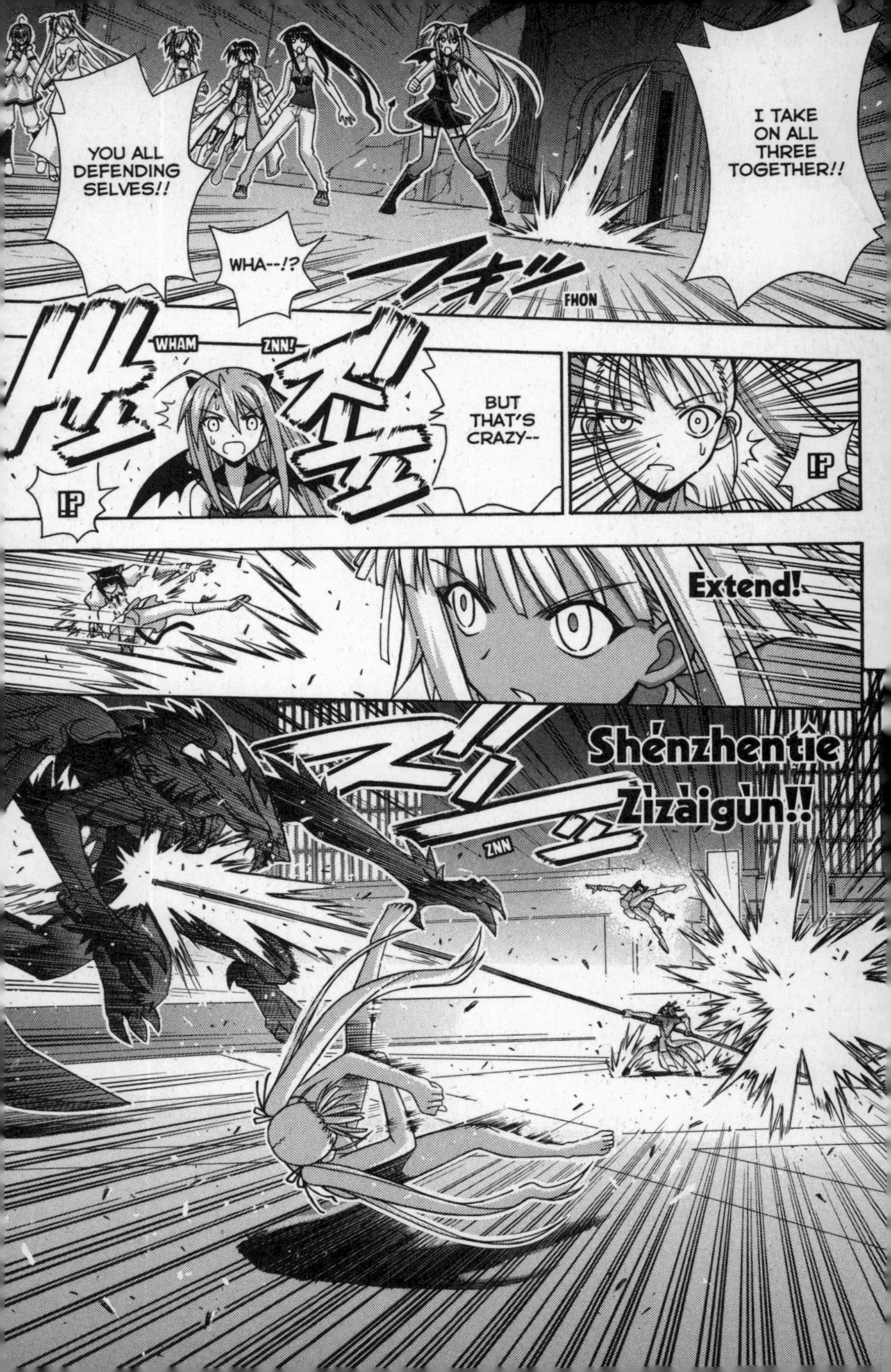
I TAKE ON ALL THREE TOGETHER!!
YOU ALL DEFENDING SELVES!!
WHA--!?
FHON
!?
BUT THAT'S CRAZY--
ZNN!
WHAM
!?
Extend!
Shénzhentie Zìzàigùn!!
ZNN

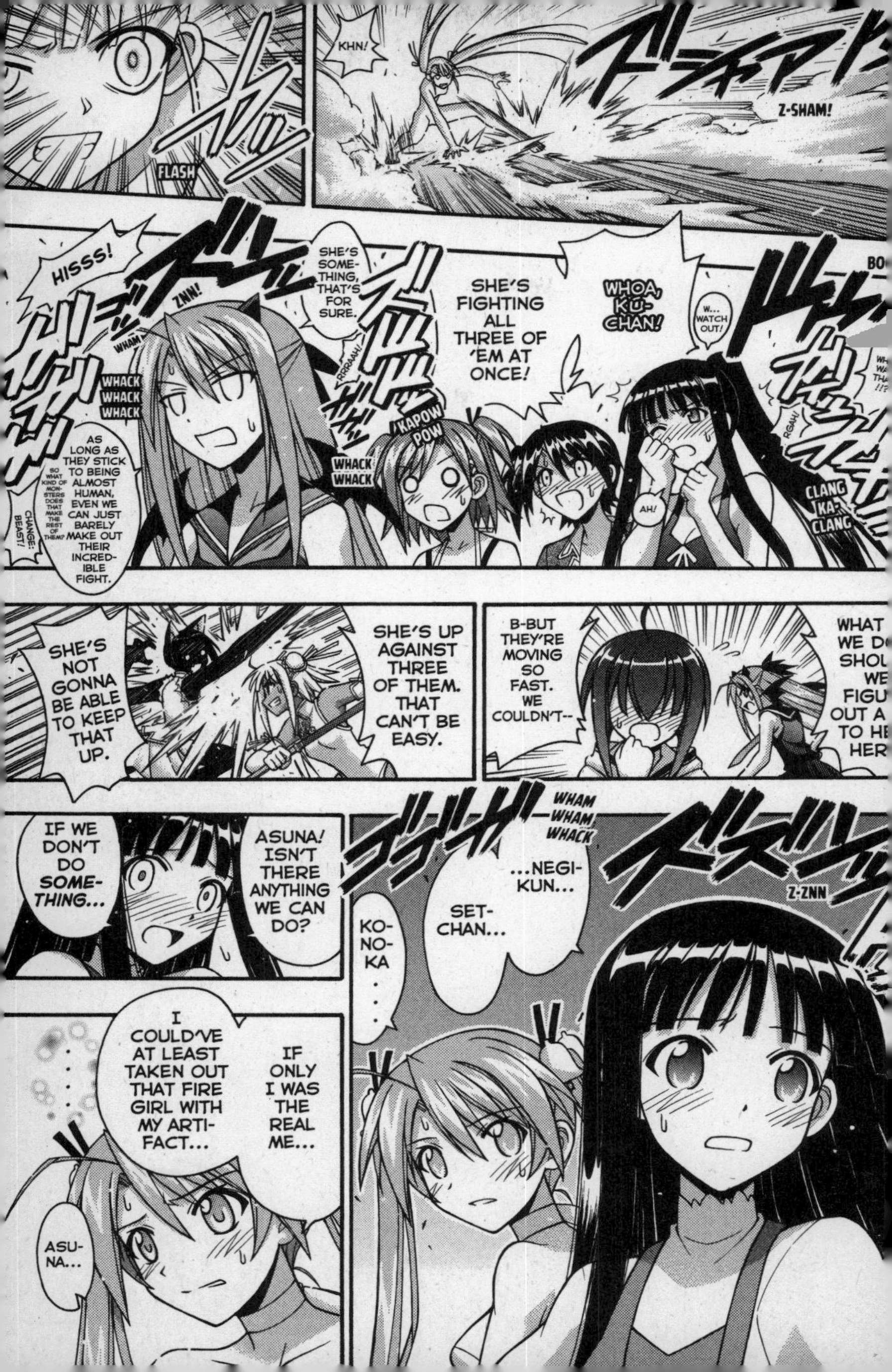

KHN!
Z-SHAM!
FLASH
BOO
W... WATCH OUT!
RGAH!
CLANG KA-CLANG
WHOA, KU-CHAN!
AH!
SHE'S FIGHTING ALL THREE OF 'EM AT ONCE!
SHE'S SOMETHING, THAT'S FOR SURE.
RRRAAH!
KAPOW POW
WHACK WHACK
ZNN!
HISSS!
WHAM
WHACK WHACK WHACK
AS LONG AS THEY STICK TO BEING ALMOST HUMAN, EVEN WE CAN JUST BARELY MAKE OUT THEIR INCREDIBLE FIGHT.
SO WHAT KIND OF MONSTERS DOES THAT MAKE THE REST OF THEM?
CHANGE: BEAST!
WHAT WE DO SHOU WE FIGU OUT A TO HE HER
B-BUT THEY'RE MOVING SO FAST. WE COULDN'T--
SHE'S UP AGAINST THREE OF THEM. THAT CAN'T BE EASY.
SHE'S NOT GONNA BE ABLE TO KEEP THAT UP.
WHAM WHAM WHACK
Z-ZNN
...NEGI-KUN...
SET-CHAN...
KO-NO-KA...
ASUNA! ISN'T THERE ANYTHING WE CAN DO?
IF WE DON'T DO SOMETHING...
IF ONLY I WAS THE REAL ME...
I COULD'VE AT LEAST TAKEN OUT THAT FIRE GIRL WITH MY ARTIFACT...
ASUNA...

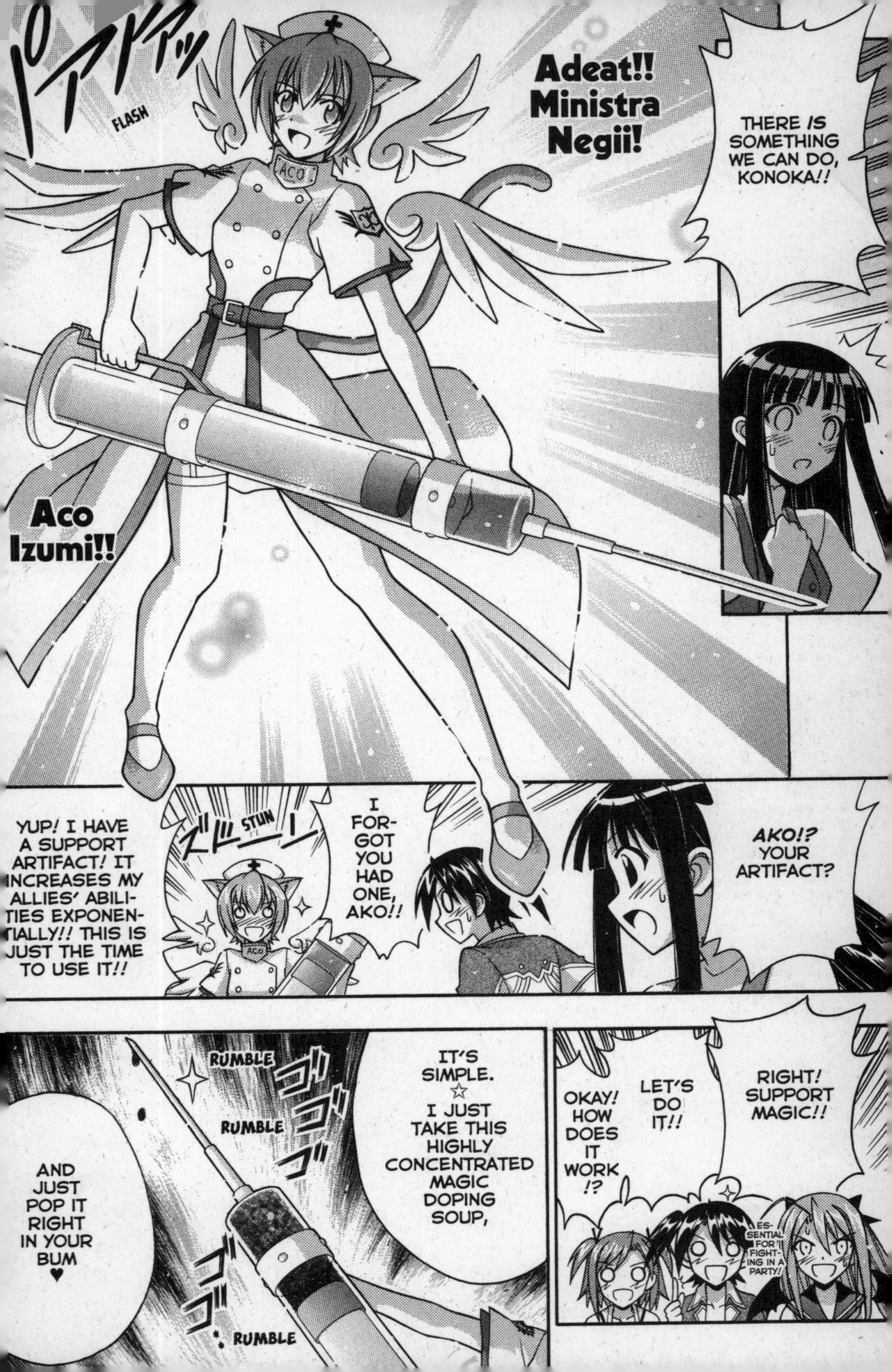
THERE IS SOMETHING WE CAN DO, KONOKA!!
Adeat!! Ministra Negii!
FLASH
Aco Izumi!!
AKO!? YOUR ARTIFACT?
I FORGOT YOU HAD ONE, AKO!!
STUN
YUP! I HAVE A SUPPORT ARTIFACT! IT INCREASES MY ALLIES' ABILITIES EXPONENTIALLY!! THIS IS JUST THE TIME TO USE IT!!
RIGHT! SUPPORT MAGIC!!
LET'S DO IT!!
OKAY! HOW DOES IT WORK!?
ESSENTIAL FOR FIGHTING IN A PARTY!
IT'S SIMPLE. ☆ I JUST TAKE THIS HIGHLY CONCENTRATED MAGIC DOPING SOUP,
RUMBLE
RUMBLE
RUMBLE
AND JUST POP IT RIGHT IN YOUR BUM ♥

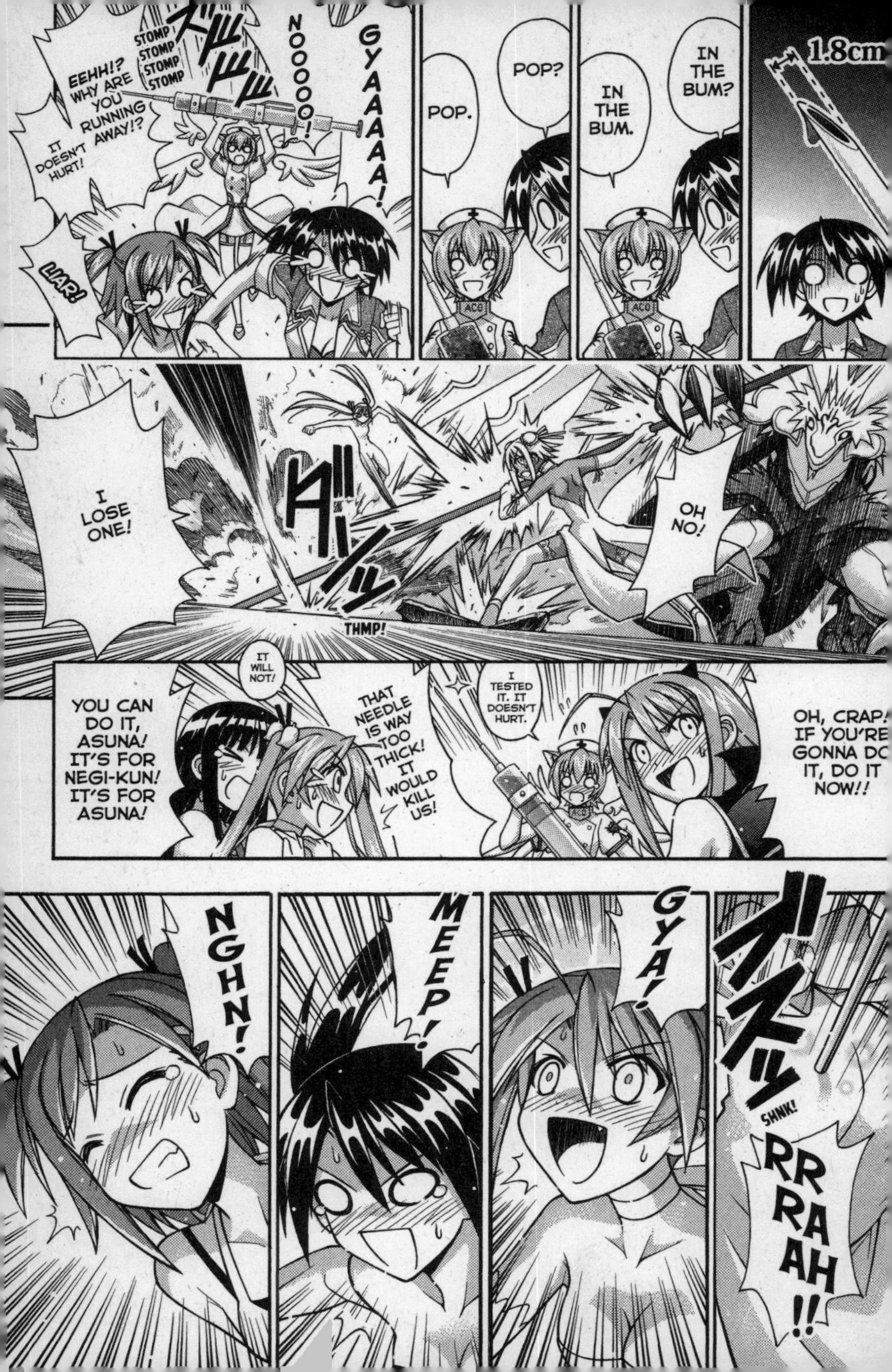

1.8cm
IN THE BUM?
IN THE BUM.
POP?
POP.
GYAAAAAA!
NOOOOOO!
STOMP STOMP STOMP STOMP
EEHH!? WHY ARE YOU RUNNING AWAY!?
IT DOESN'T HURT!
LIAR!
OH NO!
THMP!
I LOSE ONE!
OH, CRAP! IF YOU'RE GONNA DO IT, DO IT NOW!!
I TESTED IT. IT DOESN'T HURT.
THAT NEEDLE IS WAY TOO THICK! IT WOULD KILL US!
IT WILL NOT!
YOU CAN DO IT, ASUNA! IT'S FOR NEGI-KUN! IT'S FOR ASUNA!
SHNK!
RRRAAH!!
GYA!
MEEP!
NGHN!

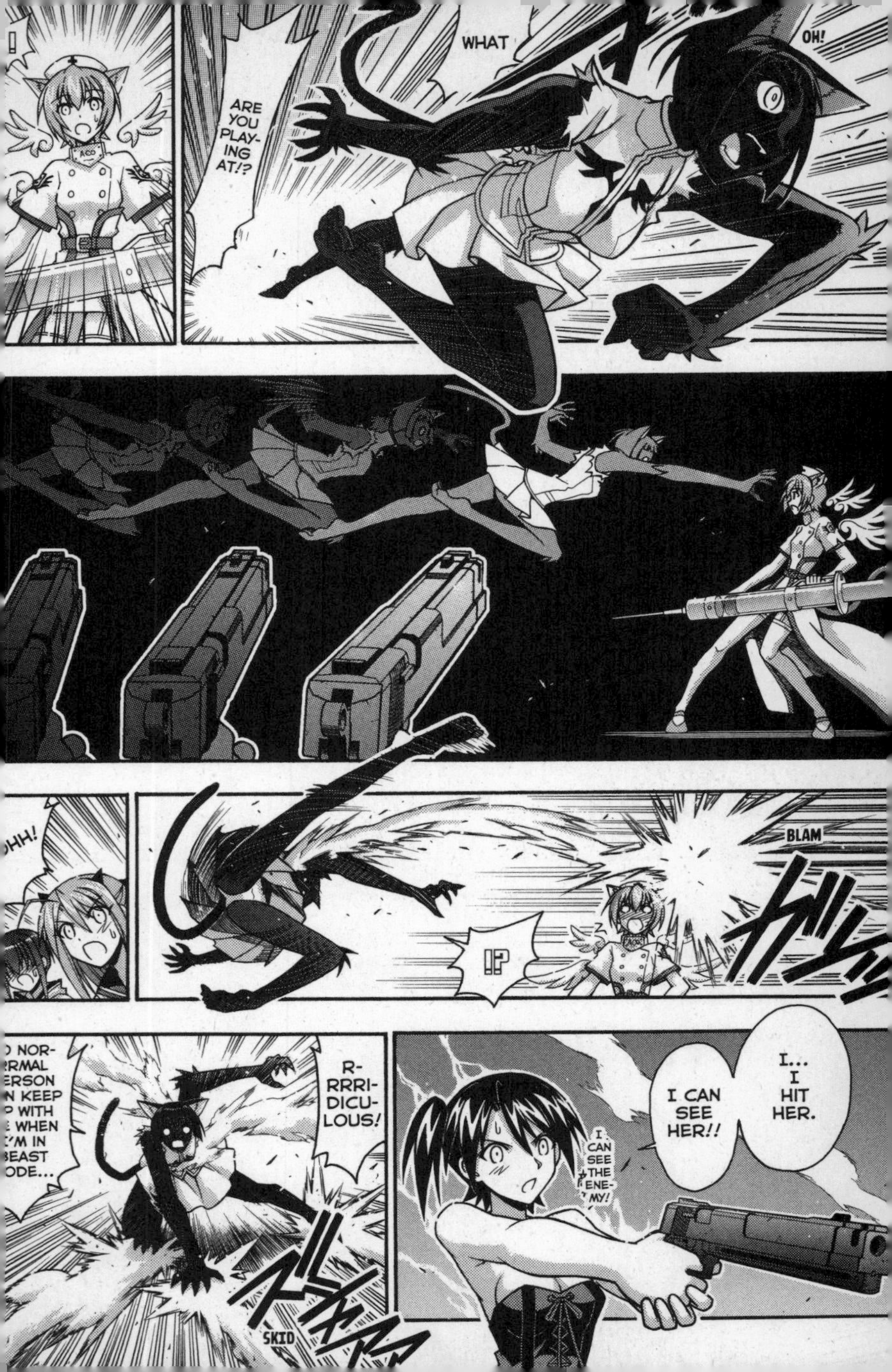
OH!
WHAT ARE YOU PLAYING AT!?
!
BLAM
!?
HH!
I... I HIT HER.
I CAN SEE HER!!
I CAN SEE THE ENEMY!
R-RRRI-DICULOUS!
D NOR-RRMAL ERSON N KEEP P WITH E WHEN I'M IN BEAST ODE...
SKID

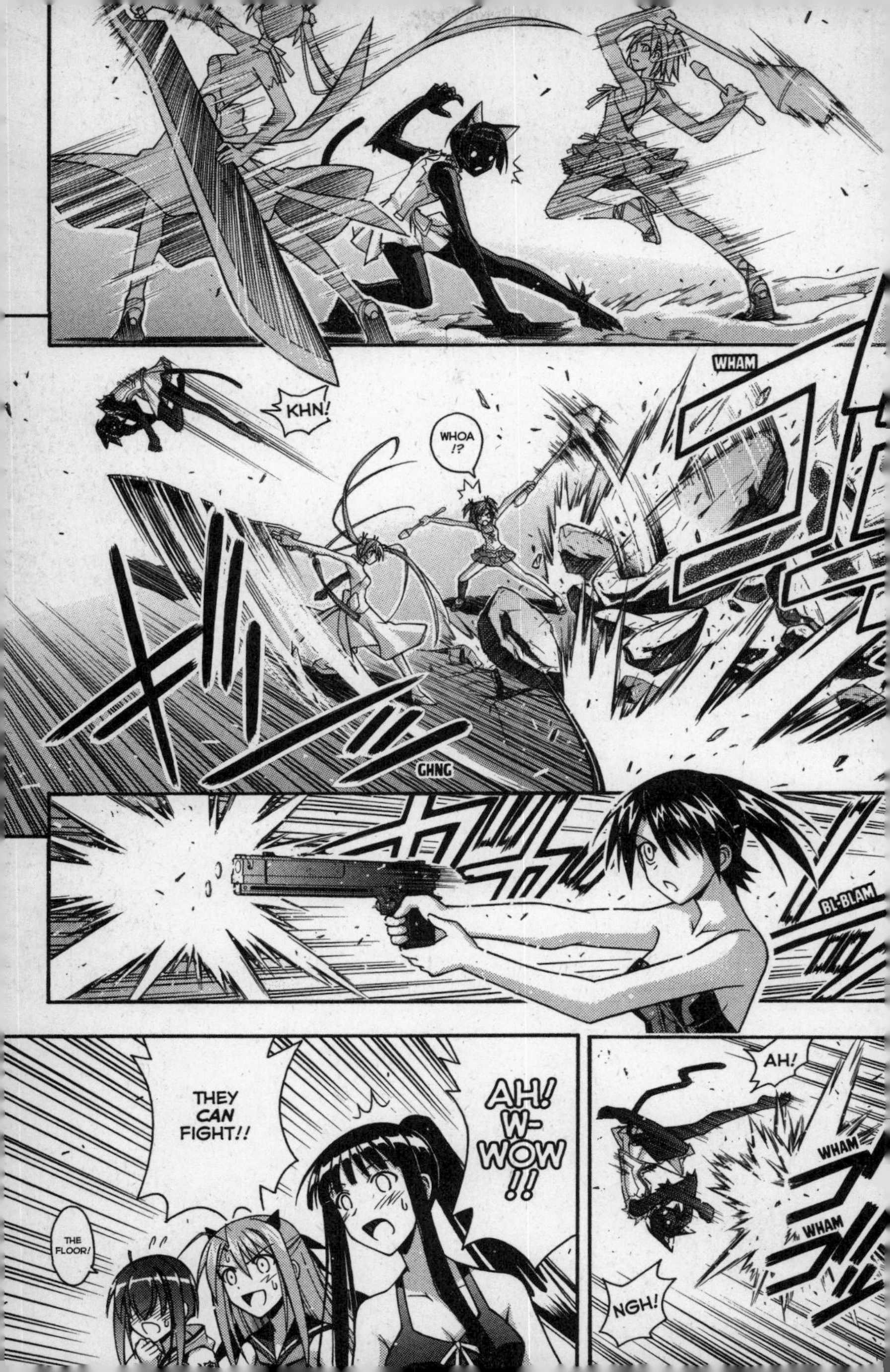
WHAM
WHOA !?
KHN!
GHNG
BL-BLAM
AH!
WHAM
WHAM
NGH!
AH! W-WOW!!
THEY *CAN* FIGHT!!
THE FLOOR!

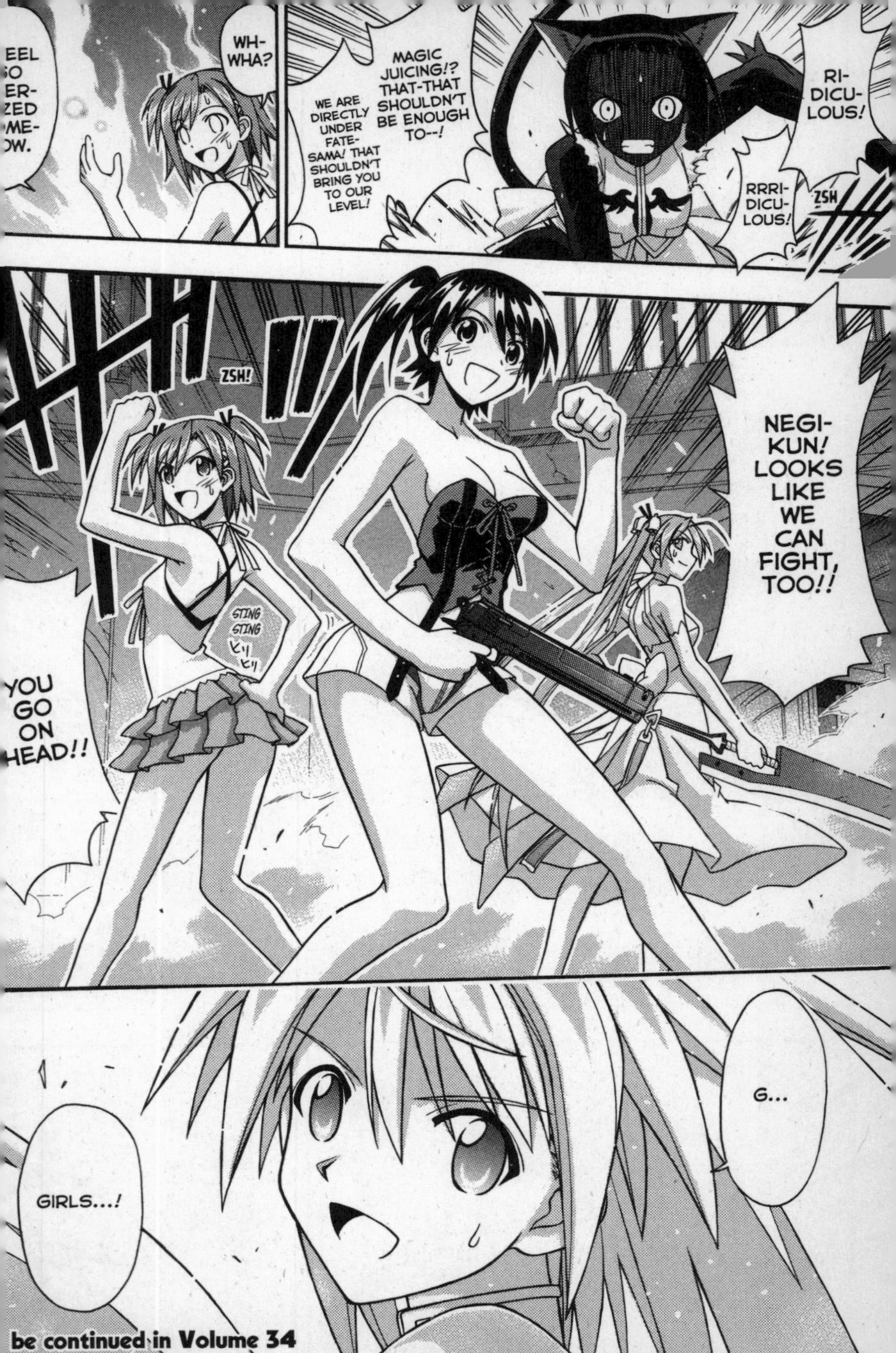
RI-DICU-LOUS!
RRRI-DICU-LOUS!
ZSH
MAGIC JUICING!? THAT-THAT SHOULDN'T BE ENOUGH TO--!
WE ARE DIRECTLY UNDER FATE-SAMA! THAT SHOULDN'T BRING YOU TO OUR LEVEL!
WH-WHA?
EEL SO ER-ZED ME-OW.
NEGI-KUN! LOOKS LIKE WE CAN FIGHT, TOO!!
ZSH!
STING STING ピリ ピリ
YOU GO ON HEAD!!
G...
GIRLS...!

be continued in Volume 34

-STAFF-

Ken Akamatsu

Takashi Takemoto

Kenichi Nakamura

Keiichi Yamashita

Tohru Mitsuhashi

Yuichi Yoshida

Susumu Kuwabara

Thanks to
Ran Ayanaga

あけまして
おめでとうございます

2回目の投稿からすみませんレイ一ヲみて
おりましてきました！
32巻の最後 おどろきました！！
雨で…サンが折れって感じく(笑)
個人的にはが好きです。
セーラー服サム
私、見たい方です！
赤松先生、
がんばって下さい♪

by Miyuki

家守割！

こんにちは！
中2の男子です。
今回で2回目
の投稿となります。
1回目の時は向
すごくゴキゲンで
まったんなことより、
キャ！！は友達から教えて
貰って、読みめめ、今やは
お違より 早く最新号を
買うほどですww
これからも 連載て
下さい！！

のせて そらえると
うれしいです！

▲ A HEARTWARMING
NEGI.

▲ THIS IS A
GOOD ZAZIE.

SHE'S SO
FULL OF LIFE. ▶

2011年

明けまして
おめでとうございます

**NEGIMA!
FAN ART CORNER**
AS ALWAYS, THANK YOU
FOR ALL YOUR FAN ART
AND LETTERS! WE'RE
A LITTLE SAD THAT WE
HAVEN'T GOT MANY
DRAWINGS OF NEW
CHARACTERS LATELY
(LAUGH). TO ALL OF YOU
THINKING, "I HAVEN'T
SENT IN ANY FAN ART YET
♪" PLEASE SEND SOME
IN! NOW, LET'S HAVE A
LOOK ♪

TEXT BY MAX

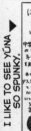

I LIKE TO SEE YŪNA
SO SPUNKY. ▶

はじめまして 赤松先生♡

初投稿となりるリョーク♀
は赤松和彦のファンです。

中学生の ころウス
ネギ！
いつも
ネギまには
神気と 元気を
もらってます

神気って
廊下生徒
バスケ部で
顔とが良くて
いつもネギ
に元気を
貰ってます
高校一年生です

『元気は最強！』 『元気が最優先！』

▲ HER EAR IS
DROOPING.

▲ THIS ONE REALLY
BRINGS OUT THE
MOÉ.

あけまして！です！

イラストでは一回
です！秋ですね
ネギ、栞も見れて
うれしいです！
ネギまには
ブラりして
あります
おねえさん
色んな気持ち
になります
それでは！

♪。DEBIRUのルア♪

▲ SHE'S WEARING
HER BADGE!

あけまして
おめでとうご
ざいます、

メイたん！(笑)

えんたところに
とうそです！！
ネギまも川実し
でおねるですが
ているキ
またメちルむ

メイ！！
LOVE(笑)

▲ THIS MEI IS
ADORABLE.

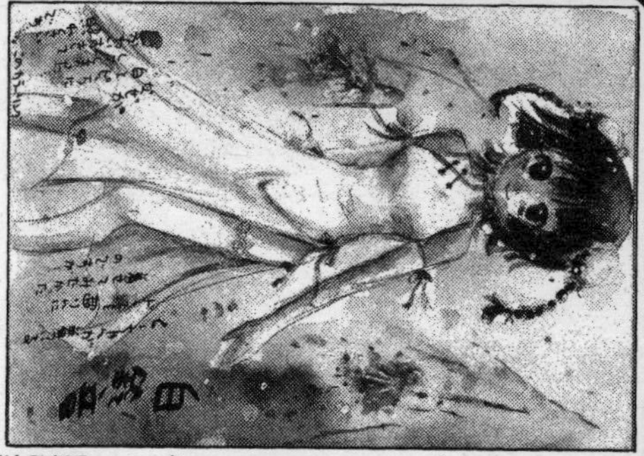

▲ THE PALE COLOR SCHEME IS BEAUTIFUL.

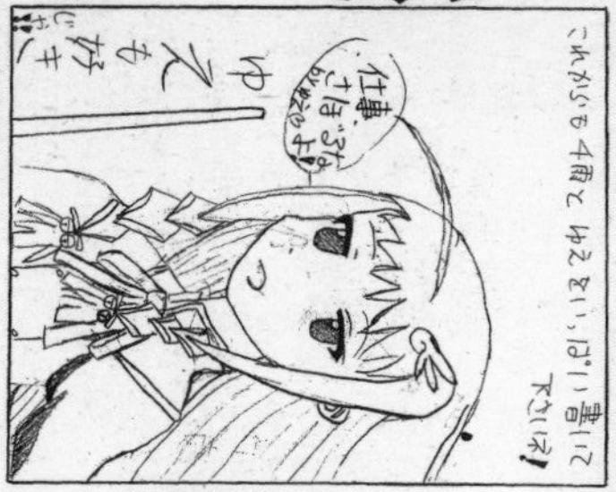
これからも4両とゆえをいっぱい書いて下さいネ!
仕事さぼるなよ!
ゆえも好き

▲ IT'S NICE TO HAVE SOMEONE TELL US NOT TO SLACK OFF SO COOLLY.

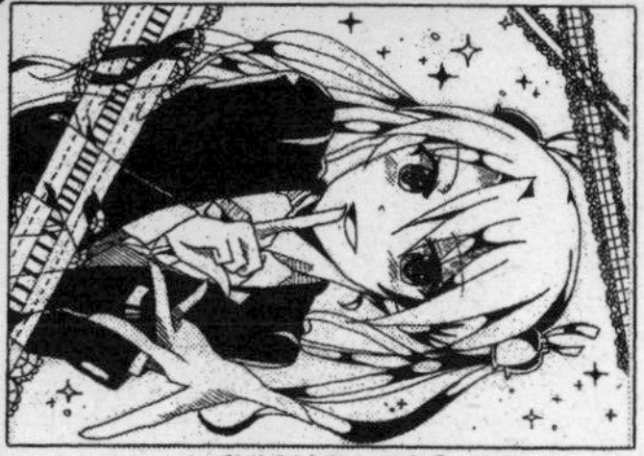

▲ SHE LOOKS LIKE A MAGICAL GIRL HEROINE ♪

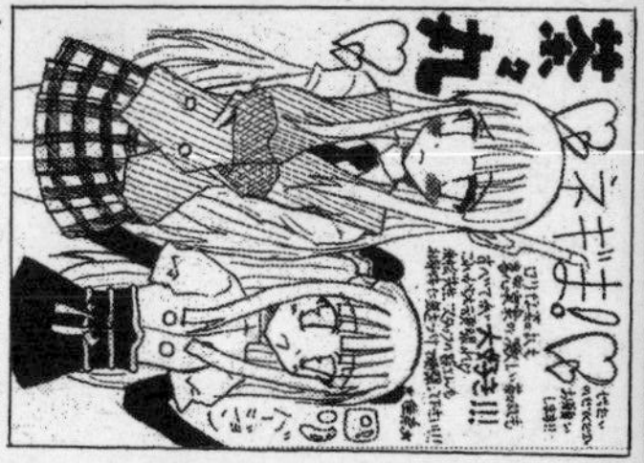
茶々丸
ネギま!

▲ I REALLY LIKE CHACHAMARU'S EXPRESSIONS HERE.

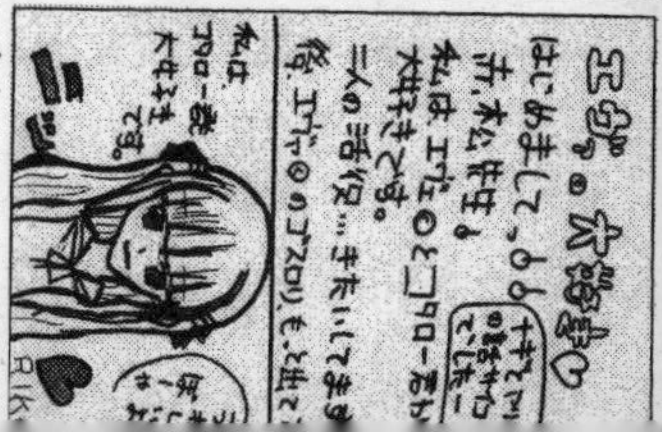
はじめまして。
赤松先生。
私はコタロー君大好きです。

▲ SUCH A CUTE MASTER!

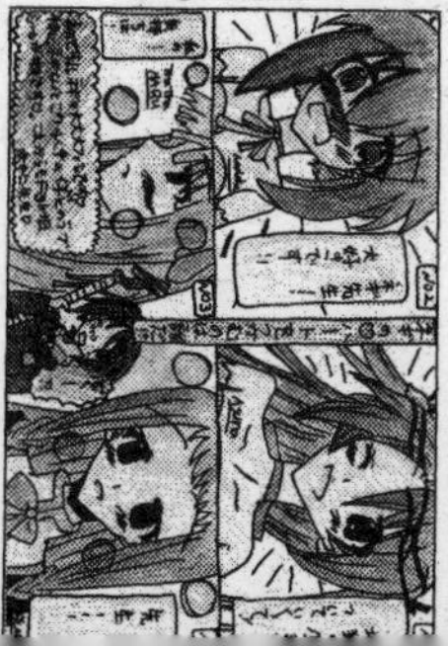

▲ EVERYBODY LOVES NEGI-KUN.

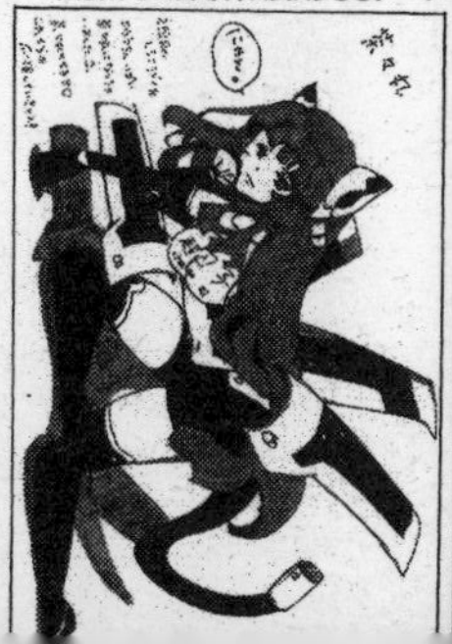

▲ CHACHAMARU AT MAXIMUM UNEARTHLINESS.

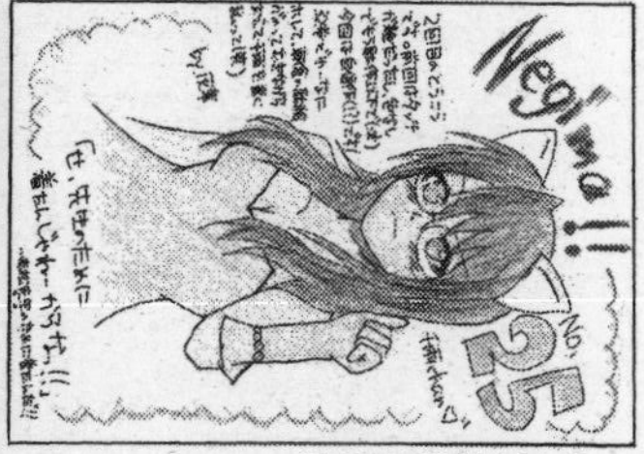
Negima!!
No. 25

▲ A KITTY POSE.

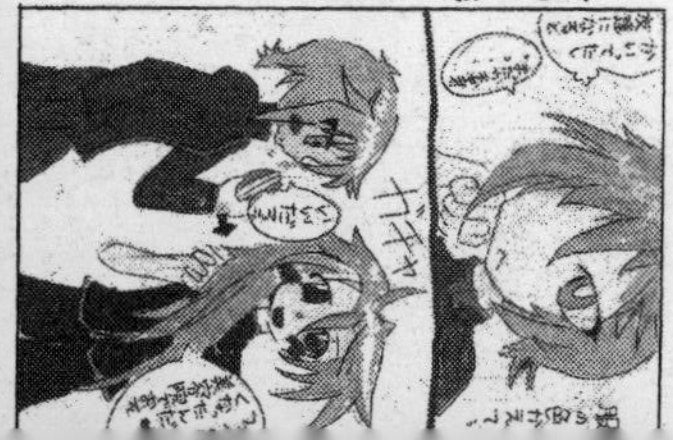
ガチャ

▲ ARE THEY LOVERS!? (LAUGH)

NEGI MA!

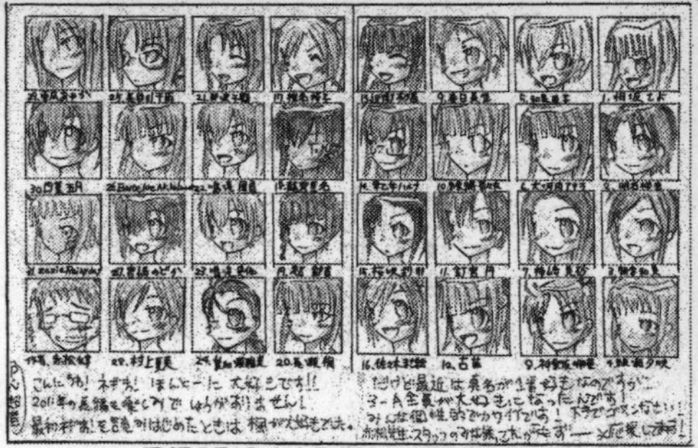

▲ THERE'S AN EXTRA PERSON MIXED IN THERE.

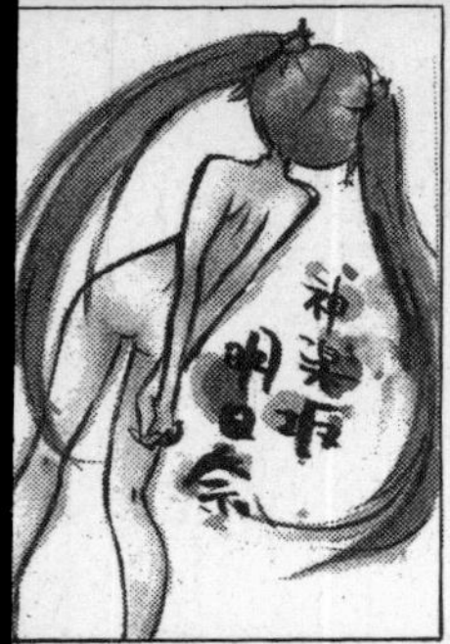

神楽坂明日菜

◀ B-DMP! (LAUGH)

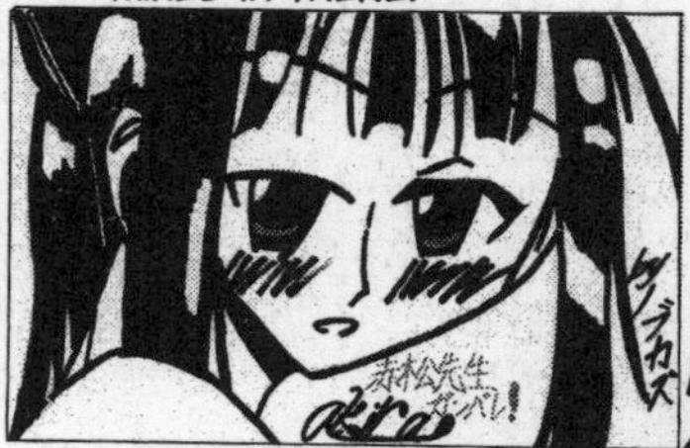

赤松先生ガンバレ!

▲ IS SHE LOOKING UP AT ME? (LAUGH)

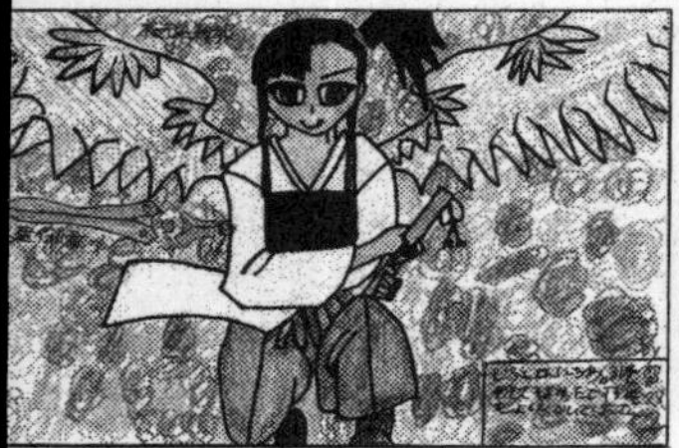

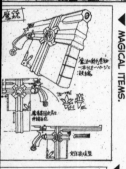

◀ THAT'S HER NEW ARTIFACT.

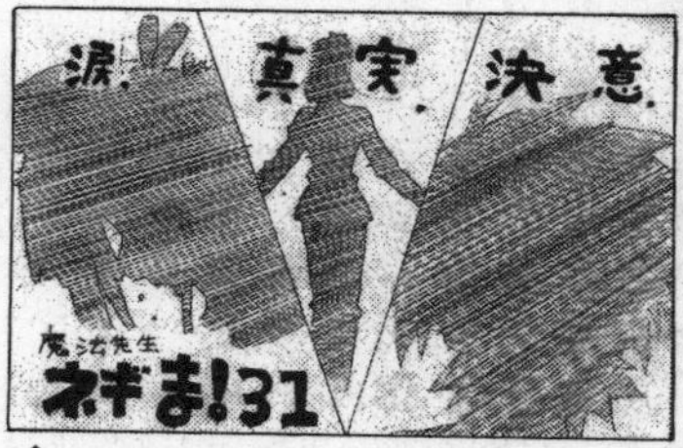

涙、
真実、
決意
魔法先生
ネギま!31

▲ S-SILHOUETTES! (LAUGH)

シ、シルエット!(笑)

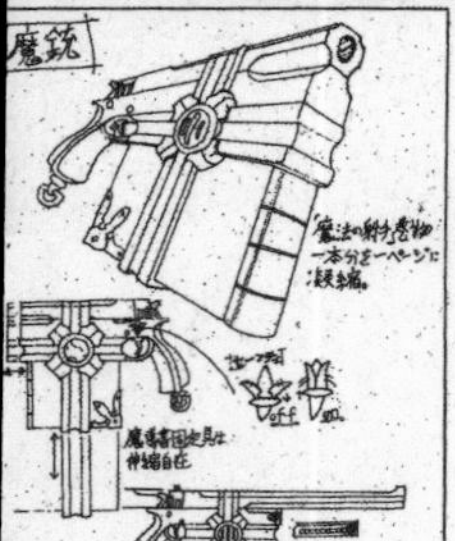

魔銃

◀ MAGICAL ITEMS.

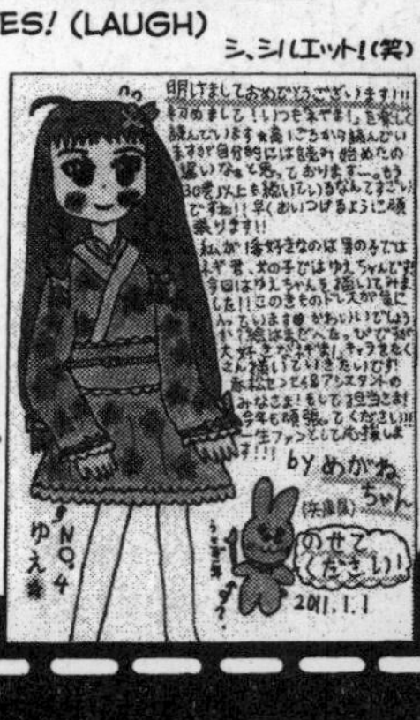

by めがねちゃん
のせてください!
2011.1.1

▶ HER KIMONO IS SO CUTE!

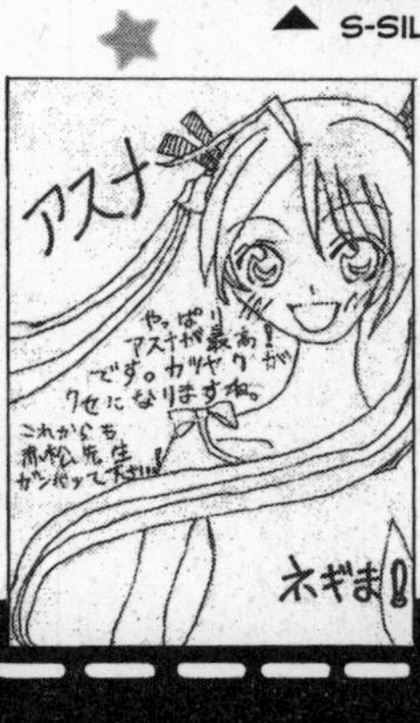

アスナ
ネギま!

◀ ASUNA IS RADIANT!

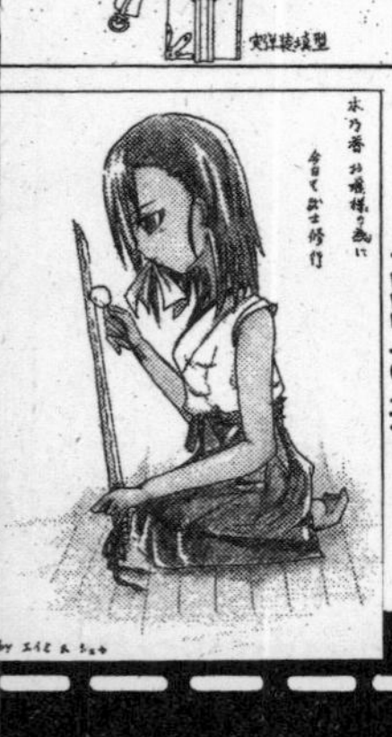

◀ IT HAS A REAL WARRIOR FEEL TO IT.

THIS VOLUME'S

MOST DRAWN CHARACTER!

Nagi Springfield & Arika Anarchia Entheofushia

Ranking

MAGISTER NEGI MAGI

次はフェイト書きま〜す
NAGI SPRINGFUIELDES

第1位
1st Place

THIS NAGI IS ALL BEAT UP, BUT HE'S SO COOL! (BY THE WAY, IT'S SPELLED "SPRINGFIELD.") SEND US MORE ART ♥

THANK YOU FOR ALL THE NEW YEAR'S CARDS, EVERYONE!! I HOPE YOU'LL KEEP READING THIS YEAR!! (AKAMATSU)

あけましておめでとうございます。
初投稿です
ネギま!

第2位
2nd Place

ASUNA LOOKS LIKE SHE'S A PART OF THE FAMILY, BUT THERE'S NO DEFINITIVE PROOF OF THAT YET. (LAUGH) BUT THANK YOU ♥

3rd Place
第3位

YOU'VE REALLY CAPTURED THE KINDNESS IN ARIKA'S EYES. THEY'RE SO IN LOVE!

アリカ
赤松先生コンニチワ♪
初めての投稿です。
私は、アリカとナギが好きです♪
先生がんばっ♪
by N.M
ナギ

Negima! 3-D Backgrounds Explanation Corner

...We say, but this time we will be focusing on the 3-D props that appear in the story.

It's been a long time since our last 3-D Explanation Corner. And because it's been so long, there are plenty of backgrounds that haven't been introduced. But this time, I specifically chose to present only props. I call it the "Even this stuff is in 3-D!" feature (laugh).

Artifacts

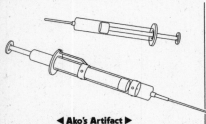

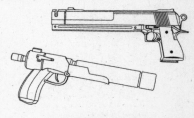

◄ Ako's Artifact ►

There have been two different versions of this artifact. The top picture shows the normal version, and the bottom shows the powered-up version. It enhances all kinds of abilities, but shaped like that, not many people would be interested in using it (laugh).

◄ Yūna's Artifact ►

This is the Iris Tormentum and the magic gun she's been using since the school festival. The former is a revised 3-D model of a Desert Eagle, and the latter is one of the guns from Negi's room that we just used as-is.

◄ Makie's Artifact ►

We call them artifacts, but they look like regular old gymnastics batons (laugh). But if she attacks with the big one, or with a lot at once, that could be pretty powerful.

◄ Code of the Lifemaker ►

Technically not an artifact, but since we're here.... The line drawing is 3-D of course, but sometimes we use the computer for the sheen as well. Furthermore, the globe(?) is added via Photoshop, so it's always facing the same way (laugh).

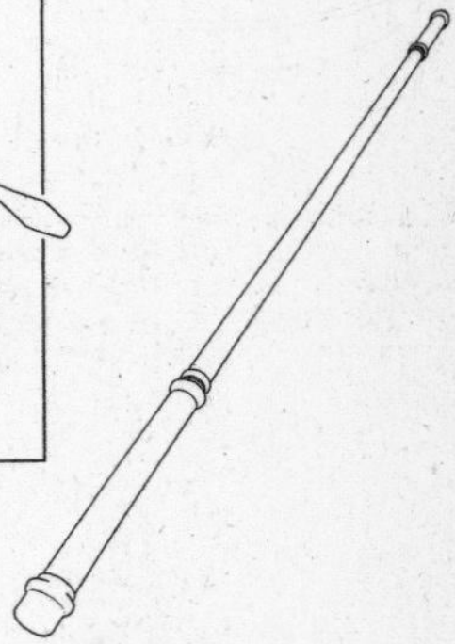

◄ Kū Fei's Artifact ►

In smaller panels, we often draw this by hand, but generally the Shénzhentîe Zìzàigùn is 3-D. She can change its length at will, of course, and she can also make it bend. Incidentally, it's very easy to make cylindrical objects.

Airships

They're way too big to be classified as "props,"
but they're not backgrounds, so... (^_^;)

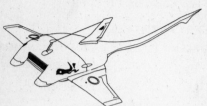

The FLYING
MANTA JOHNNY
◄ ►

Johnny-san's flying cargo
fish. We made it in our spare
time, so the details are kind of
half-hearted. We draw more in
when it shows up in the story.

Composite
Fleet Ships
◄ ►

We drew these by hand at first, but
we started doing them in 3-D when
the fleet made its charge in the last
volume. It's quite a spectacle to see
a lot of them lined up together.

Miscellaneous

There are miscellaneous props, including some things that we're
not really sure we needed to make (laugh).

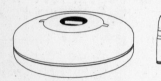

Gravity Mines
and Bullets
◄ ►

These are the special Chao-brand mines and
bullets that showed up in this volume. We make a lot weapon
type things in 3-D, but I don't think we're going to use
these particular ones anymore (laugh).

Desert Eagle
◄ ►

Tatsumiya has used this gun frequently
up to this point, but its 3-D-ification was
surprisingly recent. It even has writing
on the side like it's supposed to.

Starbooks Cup
◄ ►

We even make stuff like this in
3-D. But even after we went
to all the trouble of designing
a logo, it didn't show up in the
story (laugh).

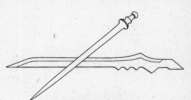

Fate's Weapon
◄ ►

There are a lot of swords and javelin-
type things in this series, so we need to
make them in 3-D, or we'll be in trouble.
But even in 3-D, it's pretty hard to line
them up with the drawings (laugh).

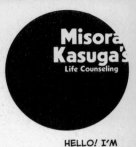

Misora Kasuga's

Life Counseling

HELLO! I'M THE NUN-IN-TRAINING, MISORA KASUGA. THIS CORNER WAS VERY POPULAR IN THE LAST VOLUME, SO HERE IT IS AGAIN, "MISORA KASUGA'S LIFE COUNSELING." WE HAVE A LOT OF CLASSMATES FROM 3-A HERE AS ADVISORS THIS TIME, SO LET'S SOLVE A TON OF PROBLEMS!!

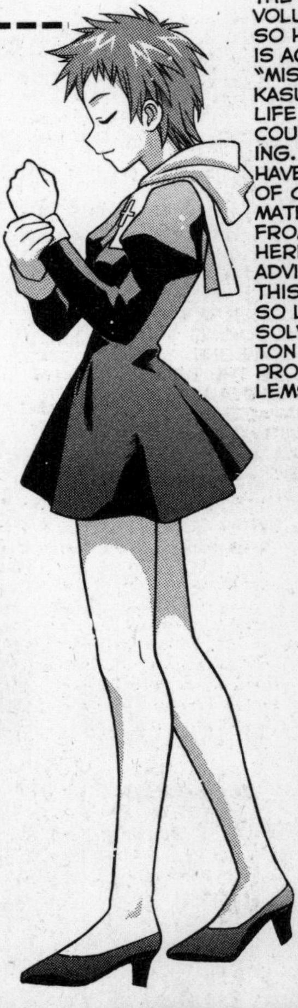

■ I DON'T LIKE CURRY VERY MUCH; IF I DON'T DO SOMETHING ABOUT IT, I'LL SPEND MY WHOLE LIFE UNABLE TO GO TO INDIA. ...HOW CAN I LEARN TO LIKE CURRY? (RINA SATŌ, VOICE OF NEGI)

★ YOU DON'T LIKE CURRY? THAT'S UNUSUAL. HEAD CHEF OF 3-A, SATSUKI YOTSUBA-SAN, WHAT DO YOU THINK?

YOTSUBA: (IF YOU CAN FIGURE OUT WHICH SPICES YOU DON'T LIKE, THEN YOU CAN MAKE IT WITHOUT THEM, BUT...)

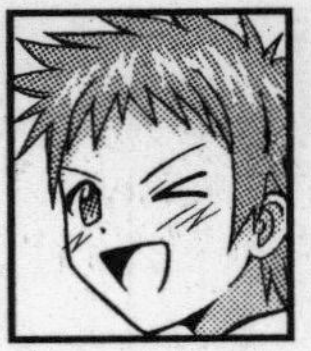

★ I SEE. BUT I BET SHE HATES EVERYTHING ABOUT CURRY. SO I THINK YOU COULD ALSO TRY MIXING IT IN ICE CREAM! OR SOAKING IT IN LIQUOR! OR NEVER GOING TO INDIA! AND THAT SHOULD BE FINE. OKAY, NEXT!

■ NEGI: "M-MISORA-SAN. I DON'T THINK YOU SHOULD START THE CORNER WITH SUCH HALF-HEARTED ADVICE.... (><)"

■ I DRAW WAY TOO MANY HOT GUYS, SO BEFORE I EVEN REALIZED IT, I'VE RAISED THE BAR SO HIGH THAT MY STRIKE ZONE IS AS SMALL AS A NEEDLE'S EYE. CAN SOMEONE LIKE ME FIND A BOYFRIEND AND GET MARRIED? INCIDENTALLY, MY IDEAL HUSBAND WOULD BE THE SINGER-SONGWRITER MASAHARU FUKUYAMA-SAN. (MAYU SHINJŌ, MANGA ARTIST)

★ MASAHARU FUKUYAMA... GOOD CHOICE. FELLOW MANGA ARTIST, HARUNA SAOTOME-SAN. ANY THOUGHTS?

PARU: "I'VE HAD EXPERIENCE WITH DRAWING ONLY HOT GUYS. JUST THINK OF THE MILITARY COMMANDERS FROM THE WARRING STATES ERA. THEY ALWAYS GET DRAWN AS HOT YOUNG GUYS, BUT THERE'S NO WAY THEY ACTUALLY ALL WERE! (LAUGH)"

★ AH! IT'S AKAMATSU-SENSEI! WHAT DO YOU THINK OF THIS PROBLEM?

AKAMATSU: "I HAVE EXPERIENCE DRAWING ONLY BEAUTIFUL YOUNG GIRLS, TOO. BUT WELL, IF A MANGA ARTIST DOESN'T CHASE AFTER THEIR IDEALS, THEY CAN'T GIVE DREAMS TO THEIR READERS. YOU'RE FINE JUST THE WAY YOU ARE!"

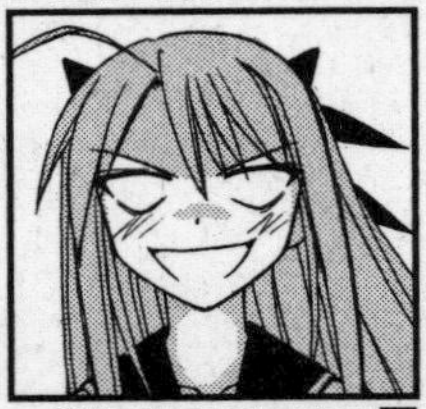

■ MY FAVORITE NET IDOL CHIU-SAN HASN'T UPDATED HER HOMEPAGE IN FOREVER. I'M WORRIED THAT SOMETHING HAPPENED TO HER. IS CHIU-SAN DOING OKAY? (ADACHI)

★ NO. SHE'S NOT (LAUGH). BUT IT SEEMS LIKE SHE'S PRETTY HAPPY THESE DAYS.

"WH-WHO'RE YOU CALLING HAPPY!?"

■ IN MIDDLE SCHOOL, THERE WAS A GIRL WHO TOLD ME SHE LIKES ME, AND I POLITELY TURNED HER DOWN. BUT NOW, I'M STARTING TO LIKE HER. WHAT SHOULD I DO? (EXAM STUDENT A)

★ SEEMS PRETTY HOPELESS. YOU'RE GOOD WITH MATTERS OF THE HEART, KAKIZAKI-SAN. WHAT ARE YOUR THOUGHTS?

I-I DON'T KNOW ABOUT THAT...

KAKIZAKI: "HMM, YOU MUST BE PRETTY GOOD-LOOKING IF THE GIRL CAME TO YOU FIRST. YOU'RE DEFINITELY HER TYPE, SO THERE'S NO NEED FOR YOU TO GIVE UP. AND WELL, THERE'S NOTHING BETTER THAN HAVING A LOT OF BOYFRIENDS, SO I THINK THE TWO OF YOU WILL BE GOING OUT IN NO TIME."

■ I'VE ALWAYS BEEN VERY SHY, AND WHEN I'M AROUND SOMEONE I'M MEETING FOR THE FIRST TIME, I START TO ACT UNUSUALLY RUDE.... HOW CAN I FIX MY SHYNESS? (SORA)

★ THE QUEEN OF TSUNDERE, CHISAME-SAN! ANY IDEAS?

CHISAME: "WH-WHO ARE YOU CALLING THE QUEEN OF TSUNDERE!? I'M JUST--!"

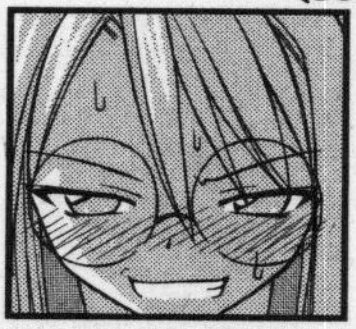

■ I'M A COLLEGE STUDENT MAJORING IN SCIENCE AND TECHNOLOGY, BUT I'M THINKING OF TAKING A CLASS ON PHILOSOPHY SO I CAN GET TO KNOW MY BELOVED YUE-SAN A LITTLE BETTER. BUT THEY ONLY OFFER IT AT THE SAME TIME AS A CLASS I NEED FOR MY MAJOR... (CRY). WHICH ONE SHOULD I TAKE? (SWEEP-GOPHER ☆ KMB)

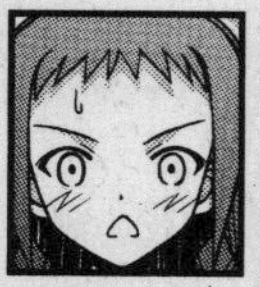

★ WHAT DO YOU THINK, YUE? YOU SHOULD GO OUT WITH HIM.

YUE: "I-I DON'T REALLY FOLLOW WHAT YOU'RE SAYING, BUT I THINK A GENERAL EDUCATION CLASS ON PHILOSOPHY WOULD MAINLY FOCUS ON ITS HISTORY. SO IF YOU WANT TO GET DEEPER INTO PHILOSOPHY, I DON'T THINK THERE WOULD BE ANYTHING WRONG WITH STUDYING IT INDEPENDENTLY."

■ MY BAND MEMBERS WON'T HELP ME DECIDE WHICH SONG TO COVER. HOW CAN I GET THEM ALL TO BE MORE PROACTIVE? (SEPIA YAMADA)

★ WHAT DO THE MEMBERS OF DEKOPIN ROCKET THINK?

KAKIZAKI: "IF IT'S AN ALL-MALE BAND, ADDING A FEMALE VOCALIST SHOULD DO THE TRICK."

KUGIMIYA: "BUT EVENTUALLY, WOULDN'T THAT JUST MAKE THEM ALL FIGHT *MORE?*"

SAKURAKO: "I KNOW, I KNOW! YOU SHOULD DO A DEKOPIN ROCKET SONG! (^^)"

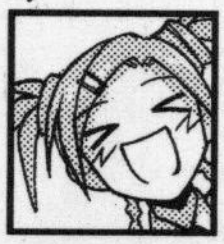

■ LATELY, I LOVE TWO-DIMENSIONAL GIRLS SO MUCH THAT I CAN'T BRING MYSELF TO LIKE THREE-DIMENSIONAL WOMEN. HOW CAN I START LIKING 3-D WOMEN? (MAZAKURA)

★ LET'S CONSULT OUR RESIDENT LOVER OF 2-D ONLY, AKAMATSU-SENSEI.

AKAMATSU: "WHO'RE YOU CALLING--!? ...DON'T JUMP RIGHT INTO THE THIRD DIMENSION. TAKE BABY STEPS, AND WORK ON THE 2.5TH DIMENSION. IN OTHER WORDS, TRY LOOKING AT SOMEONE *INSIDE* THE TWO-DIMENSIONAL CHARACTER, LIKE BY GOING TO A VOICE ACTRESS'S LIVE CONCERT.

■ I REALLY LOVE THE ARCH DEMON GREATSWORD (A SWORD BASED ON *NEGIMA!*) IN MONSTER HUNTER PORTABLE 3RD, BUT WHEN I'M WATCHING THE SPECIAL EFFECT, I GET ATTACKED. SHOULD I FOCUS ON HUNTING, OR SHOULD I JUST ENJOY FEELING LIKE ASUNA? (NYORA)

★ WHAT DO YOU THINK, ASUNA?

ASUNA: "HMM, I THINK YOU SHOULD ENJOY FEELING LIKE ASUNA--THE STRONG, ADORABLE, LOVED-BY-ALL ASUNA."

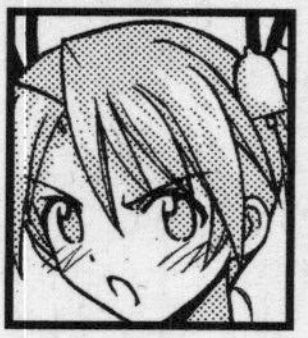

NEGI: "I-I THINK SO, TOO...(^^;)"

ASUNA: "THAT SOUNDED A LITTLE *FORCED,* DONCHA THINK?"

■ THERE'S A GIRL WHO WAS IN MY CLASS A LONG TIME AGO, AND I'M THINKING OF TELLING HER I LIKE HER WHEN SPRING STARTS. WE GOT ALONG REALLY WELL BACK THEN, BUT I HAVEN'T SPOKEN TO HER IN THREE YEARS, SO IT'S HARD TO TAKE THE PLUNGE. WHAT SHOULD I DO? (KAWAK)

★ WHAT DO YOU THINK, SAKURAZAKI-SAN?

SETSUNA: "EH...? UM, IF IT WAS ONLY THREE YEARS, THEN I BELIEVE HER MEMORIES FROM WHEN YOU WERE FRIENDS WILL COME RIGHT BACK TO HER, AND YOU'LL BE ABLE TO TALK AGAIN."

★ OH? YOU REALLY THINK SO?

SETSUNA: "Y-YES... I'M SURE THE GIRL...

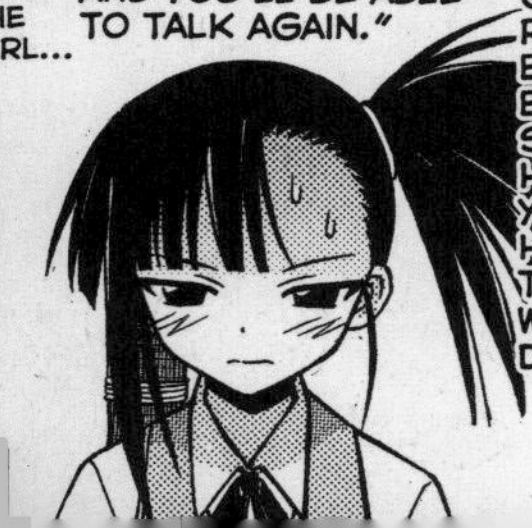

...WOULD BE HAPPY TO TALK TO YOU. I WISH YOU THE BEST OF LUCK."

■ I'M A GIRL, BUT I LIKE A GIRL! MISORA-CHAN, WHAT SHOULD I DO? (KOKOTA)

★ WHAT DO YOU THINK, SAKURAZAKI-SAN?

SETSUNA: "EH...? WELL, I THINK IT MAY BE BEST NOT TO WORRY TOO MUCH, AND JUST BE TRUE TO YOUR FEELINGS..."

★ ARE *YOU* TRUE TO YOUR FEELINGS, SAKURAZAKI-SAN?

SETSUNA: "ERK..."

■ I'M SO WORRIED ABOUT KONOKA AND SETSUNA'S FUTURE, I CAN'T SLEEP AT NIGHT. THEY MADE A PACTIO, BUT IS IT ALL RIGHT TO ASSUME THAT THEY'RE GOING TO GET MARRIED? (NEKOKO)

★ WELL, SAKURAZAKI-SAN?

SETSUNA: (WH-WHY DO I FEEL LIKE YOU'RE GANGING UP ON ME...?)

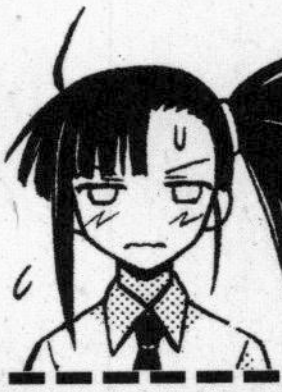

■ I'M STUDYING FOR ENTRANCE EXAMS. I HAVE AN EXAM FOR A PRIVATE COLLEGE COMING UP IN A WEEK, BUT YESTERDAY, I FELL DOWN THE STAIRS AND CUT MY LEG. DID SOMEONE PUT A CURSE ON ME? OR IS THIS A SOME KIND OF A SIGN FROM THE HEAVENS? (DICTIONARY'S LOVER)

★ IF IT'S FOR A PRIVATE COLLEGE, YOU DON'T HAVE TO WORRY ABOUT THE CENTER TEST* CUT-OFF, RIGHT? WHAT DO YOU THINK, HAKASE?

*NATIONAL CENTER TEST FOR UNIVERSITY ADMISSIONS, SIMILAR TO THE SATS.

HAKASE: "THERE ARE PRIVATE COLLEGES THAT USE THE CENTER TEST, TOO. BUT THIS PERSON IS TOO CONFUSED BY UNSCIENTIFIC PHENOMENA. THERE IS NO SUCH THING AS CURSES!"

★ SO WHAT DO YOU CALL THE STUFF EVANGELINE-SAN DOES?

■ *NEGIMA!* IS ALWAYS RELEASED WITH A LIMITED EDITION VERSION AND A NORMAL VERSION WITH A DIFFERENT COVER. I DON'T KNOW WHICH ONE TO BUY. WHAT SHOULD I DO? (HATAHATA)

★ PLEASE, BUY BOTH.

■ ASUNA WAS GOING TO BE MY BRIDE ONCE, BUT THESE DAYS, I'M SO IN LOVE WITH RIT-CHAN FROM *K-ON!* THAT I FIND IT HARD TO GO ON LIVING. DOES THIS MAKE ME UNFAITHFUL? (ZEROJI)

★ AT LEAST GO WITH COLLET-SAN INSTEAD. THEY'RE CONNECTED ON THE INSIDE*.

RIT-CHAN AND COLLET ARE BOTH VOICED BY SATOMI SATŌ.

■ WHEN I GO TO KARAOKE WITH SOMEONE WHO'S NOT AN ANIME OTAKU, I DON'T SING ANYTHING... (KOKO)

★ THERE ARE A LOT OF ANIME THEME SONGS THESE DAYS THAT HAVE NOTHING TO DO WITH WHAT HAPPENS IN THE ANIME. IF YOU SING A TON OF THOSE SONGS, I'M SURE YOU'LL BE ABLE TO OPEN UP EVENTUALLY!

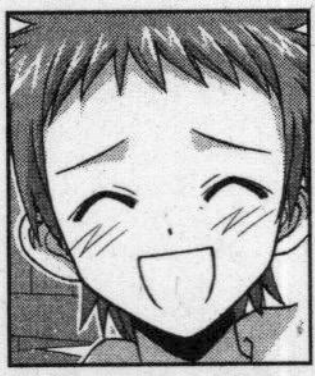

■ Dear Misora-san, I have fallen in love with a vampire girl. How can I make out with her without being bitten? (Marshall D. Teach)

★ NN? WHAT'S 「make out」*

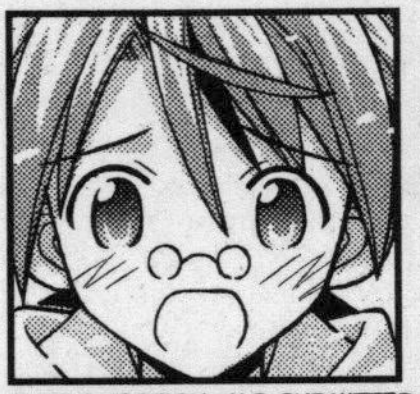

*THIS QUESTION WAS SUBMITTED IN ENGLISH, AND MANY OF 3-A ARE PROBABLY UNFAMILIAR WITH THAT PARTICULAR EXPRESSION.

NEGI: "UM, HOW SHOULD I SAY THIS? IT'S LIKE... *ICHATSUKU*? I'M SORRY."

ASUNA: "WHAT ARE *YOU* APOLOGIZING FOR? HEY, SOMEBODY TRANSLATE THIS."

KAKIZAKI: "WHAT'S WRONG WITH PLAY BITES? KEH HEH HEH..."

■ I'M A GUY, BUT MY CLUB (THE MANGA CLUB) IS FULL OF GIRLS (><). I DON'T KNOW WHAT TO TALK TO THEM ABOUT. (PARUPARU)

★ WHAT THE HECK? WHAT DO YOU THINK, PARU-SAN?

PARU: "IF YOU PLAY THE PART OF THE 'TIMID, OVERWHELMED BOY,' THE GIRLS WILL GO CRAZY OVER YOU."

■ EVA...I MEAN, MASTER, IS ALWAYS TALKING ABOUT "NO MATTER HOW DIRTY YOU GET," BUT WHEN I'M DEPRESSED, I HAVE A HARD TIME LETTING GO OF IT.... I TEND TO HOLD ON TO IT FOR A LONG TIME. HOW CAN I BE MORE LIKE MASTER AND NEGI-SENSEI? PLEASE TELL ME, MASTER! (YŪSHI)

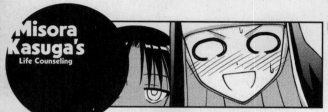

Misora Kasuga's
Life Counseling

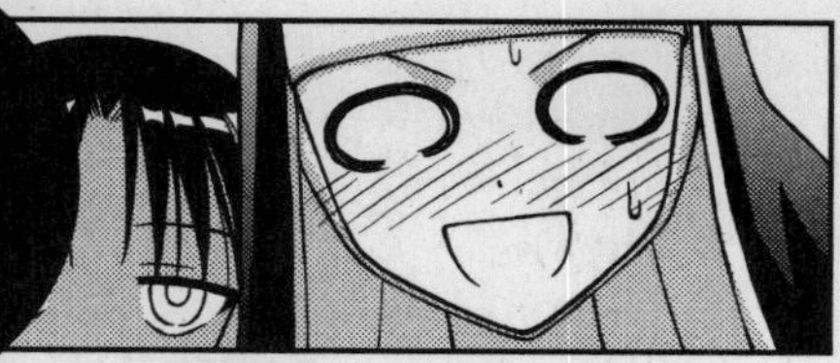

★ I D
KNO
IF IT
A G
IDEA
BE
EVA
LINE
NEG
KUN
(LAL

■ THERE'S THIS GIRL ON MY MIND LATELY... YOU KNOW THE GIRL ON THE TRACK TEAM, WHO LIKES PRACTICAL JOKES, AND IS A NUN...? THE GIRL WHO'S ALWAYS NEXT TO HER IS JUST SO CUTE, I CAN'T STAND IT. YOU'RE HER FRIEND. PLEASE TALK TO HER FOR ME! (RYŌ)

■ Y--!★

★ MY DOG ADAM IS ALWAYS CAUSING ME PROBLEMS BY ESCAPING FROM HIS DOGHOUSE. THE OTHER DAY, I ENDED UP CHASING HIM AROUND FOR ALMOST HALF AN HOUR, TRYING TO CATCH HIM. DO YOU THINK YOU COULD LEND ME YOUR ARTIFACT SOMETIME, MISORA-SAN? (GOMA-TAMAGO)

★ UM, I'M PRETTY SURE ONLY THE ARTIFACT'S OWNER CAN USE IT.

NEGI: "WITH MY 'MILLE VINCULA,' THEN OTHER PEOPLE CAN GET THE ABILITIES AND EFFECTS OF SOMEONE'S ARTIFACT."

■ AKAMATSU-SENSEI. I WANT NODOKA MIYAZAKI AND YŪNA AKASHI'S AUTOGRAPHS. HOW CAN I GET YOUR AUTOGRAPH, AKAMATSU-SENSEI? (LILAC)

★ JUST WHOSE AUTOGRAPH ARE YOU AFTER?

■ I'VE GAINED 6KG (13LBS.) IN THE LAST SIX MONTHS. HOW CAN I LOSE WEIGHT? (YANAGI)

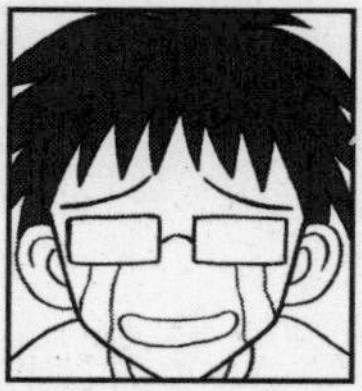

★ LET'S ASK AKAMATSU-SENSEI, WHO LOST 7KG (15.5LBS.) BY CLIMBING ON AND OFF A STEPPING STOOL!!

AKAMATSU: "EH...? UM, I THINK CLIMBING ON AND OFF A STEPPING STOOL MIGHT BE EFFECTIVE."

■ I'M TERRIBLE AT FIGHTING GAMES. HOW CAN I GET BETTER? I WOULD LIKE TO ASK MAHORA'S NUMBER ONE GAMER, EVA-SAMA. (RYŪ NO.26)

★ WELL?

EVA: "HMM... FIGHTING GAMES THESE DAYS ALL HAVE THE SAME COMMANDS; THEY'RE SO BORING. BUT ANYWAY, START BY PRACTICING YOUR BEST COMBO."

★ CHAO LINGSHEN'S NAME IS PRONOUNCED CHAO LINGSHEN, BUT MY CHINESE FRIEND SAID IT SHOULD BE CHAO LI-YING. IS IT MANDARIN OR SHANGHAINESE? IT BOTHERS ME SO MUCH I CAN'T SLEEP AT NIGHT. (RUMAP) ■

■ SERIOUSLY!? WELL, WHAT SAY YOU, AKAMATSU-SENSEI?

AKAMATSU: "IN THIS CASE, WE ASSUME THAT IT WILL BE PRONOUNCED 'CHAO LINGSHEN,' IN THE FUTURE. ACTUALLY, MY ASSISTANT M WHO DECIDED ON HER NAME HAD A BIT OF A MISUNDERSTANDING, SO...."

★ I JUST ENTERED HIGH SCHOOL, BUT IT'S STILL LOOKING LIKE THE ONLY ONE WHO WILL GIVE ME CHOCOLATE THIS VALENTINE'S DAY IS GOING TO BE MY MOM! PLEASE TELL ME WHAT KIND OF GUY MAKES GIRLS WANT TO GIVE HIM CHOCOLATE! (ZAKI-SAN)

■ HMMM, A GUY WHO'S HOT... AND RICH?

ASUNA: "... MISORA-CHAN. I THINK YOU'RE GETTING SICK OF THIS."

★ WHAT WILL I DO I-I-IF MY CONCERN GETS PUBLISHED IN A ***NEGIMA!*** GRAPHIC NOVEL? (NML27)

■ HERE IT IS! CONGRATULATIONS!

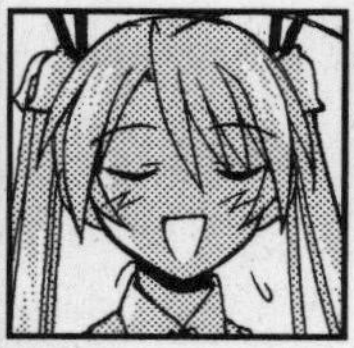

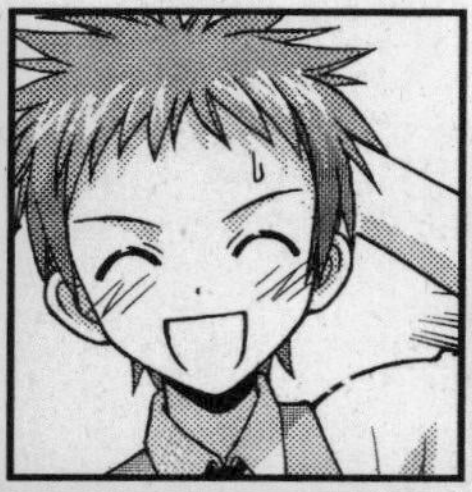

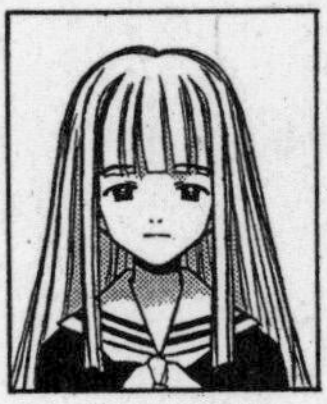

1. SAYO AISAKA

1940 ~

Don't change her seat

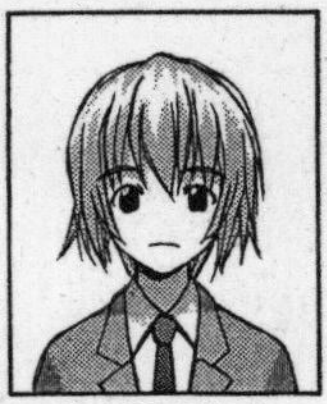

5. AKO IZUMI

Nurse's office aide, soccer team (non-school activity)

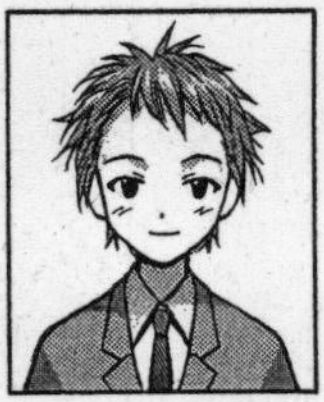

9. MISORA KASUGA

Track & field

Headmaster's granddaughter

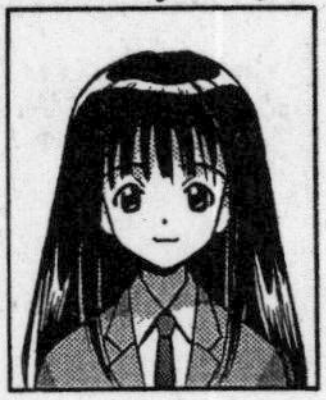

13. KONOKA KONOE

Secretary, fortune-telling club, library exploration club

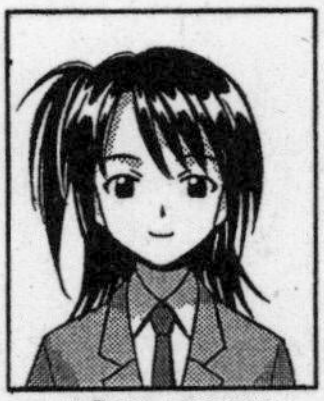

2. YŪNA AKASHI

Basketball team

Professor Akashi's daughter

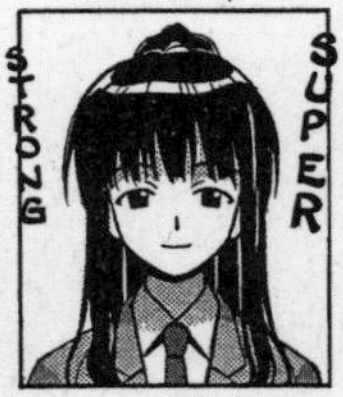

STRONG
SUPER

6. AKIRA ŌKOCHI

Swim team

VERY KIND

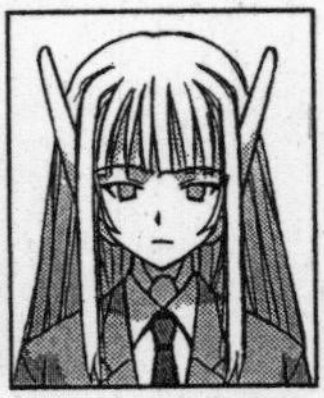

10. CHACHAMARU KARAKURI

Tea ceremony club, go club

In case of emergency, call engineering (ext. A00-7796)

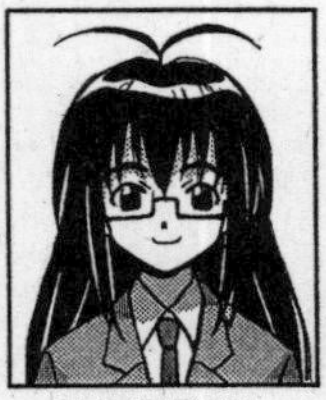

14. HARUNA SAOTOME

Manga club, library exploration club

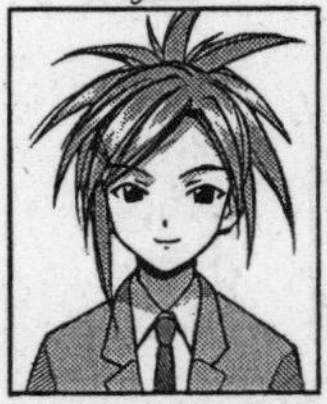

3. KAZUMI ASAKURA

School newspaper

Mahora News (ext.B09-3780)

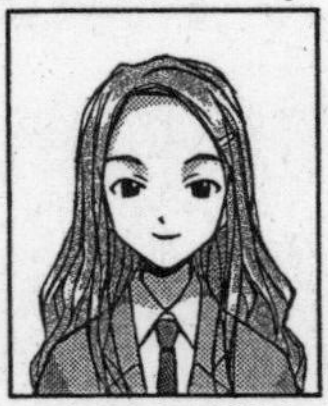

7. MISA KAKIZAKI

Cheerleader, chorus

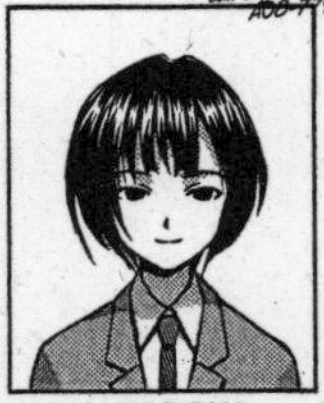

11. MADOKA KUGIMIYA

Cheerleader

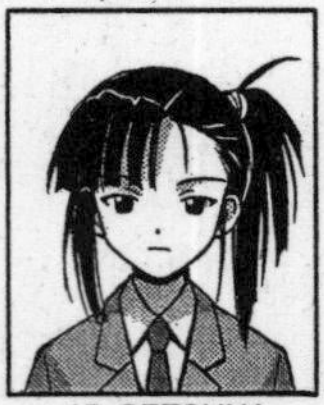

15. SETSUNA SAKURAZAKI

Kendo club

Kyoto Shinmei School

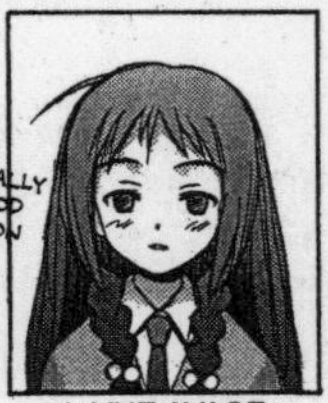

4. YUE AYASE

Kids' lit. club, philosophy club, library exploration club

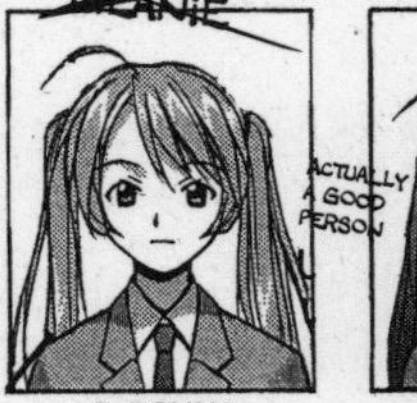

ACTUALLY A GOOD PERSON

8. ASUNA KAGURAZAKA

AMAZING KICK

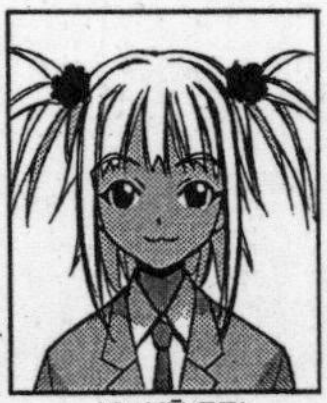

12. KŪ FEI

Chinese martial arts club

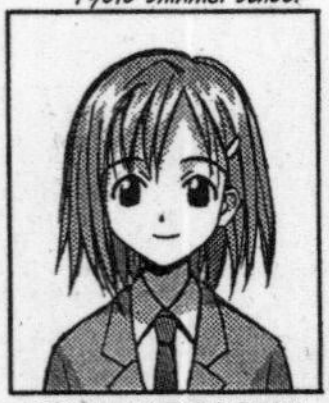

16. MAKIE SASAKI

Gymnastics

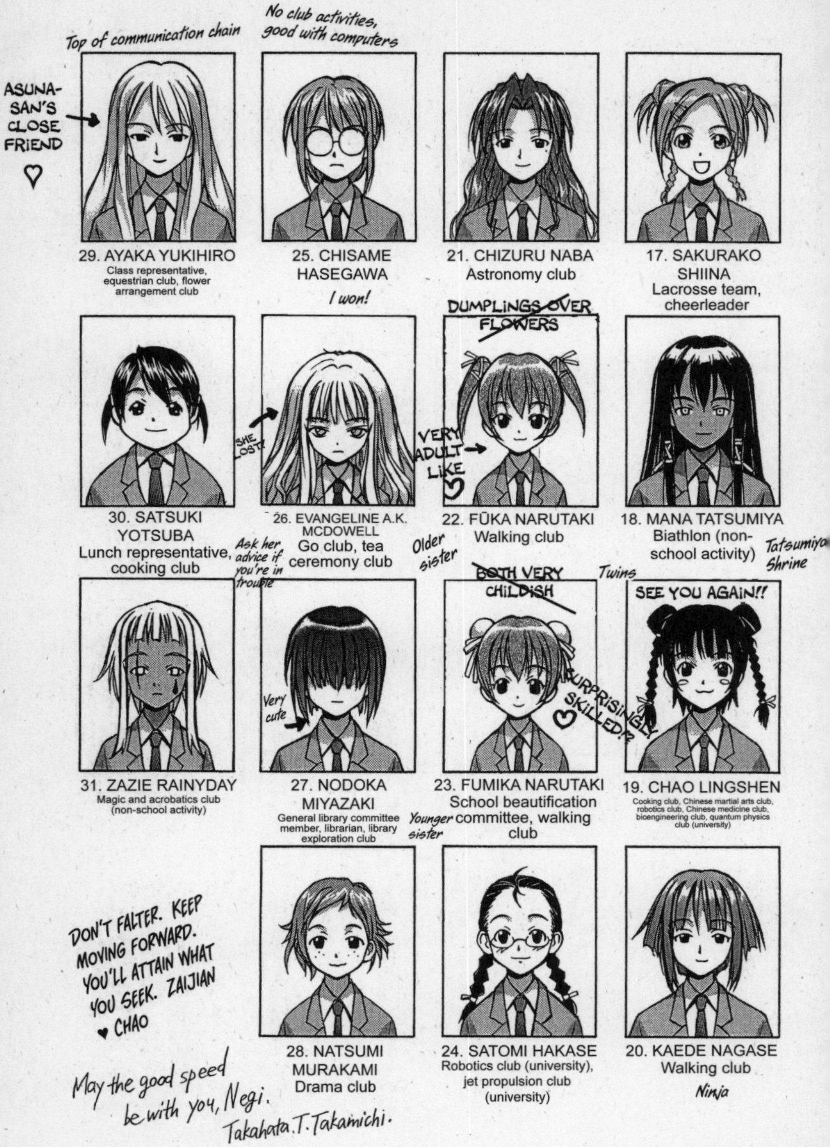
17. SAKURAKO SHIINA
Lacrosse team, cheerleader
21. CHIZURU NABA
Astronomy club
No club activities, good with computers
25. CHISAME HASEGAWA
I won!
Top of communication chain
ASUNA-SAN'S CLOSE FRIEND ♡
29. AYAKA YUKIHIRO
Class representative, equestrian club, flower arrangement club
Tatsumiya Shrine
18. MANA TATSUMIYA
Biathlon (non-school activity)
DUMPLINGS OVER FLOWERS
VERY ADULT LIKE ♡
Older sister
22. FŪKA NARUTAKI
Walking club
SHE LOST!!
26. EVANGELINE A.K. MCDOWELL
Go club, tea ceremony club
Ask her advice if you're in trouble
30. SATSUKI YOTSUBA
Lunch representative, cooking club
Twins
SEE YOU AGAIN!!
19. CHAO LINGSHEN
Cooking club, Chinese martial arts club, robotics club, Chinese medicine club, bioengineering club, quantum physics club (university)
BOTH VERY CHILDISH
SURPRISINGLY SKILLED!?
23. FUMIKA NARUTAKI
School beautification committee, walking club
Younger sister
Very cute
27. NODOKA MIYAZAKI
General library committee member, librarian, library exploration club
31. ZAZIE RAINYDAY
Magic and acrobatics club (non-school activity)
20. KAEDE NAGASE
Walking club
Ninja
24. SATOMI HAKASE
Robotics club (university), jet propulsion club (university)
28. NATSUMI MURAKAMI
Drama club
DON'T FALTER. KEEP MOVING FORWARD. YOU'LL ATTAIN WHAT YOU SEEK. ZAIJIAN ♥ CHAO
May the good speed be with you, Negi.
Takahata.T.Takamichi.

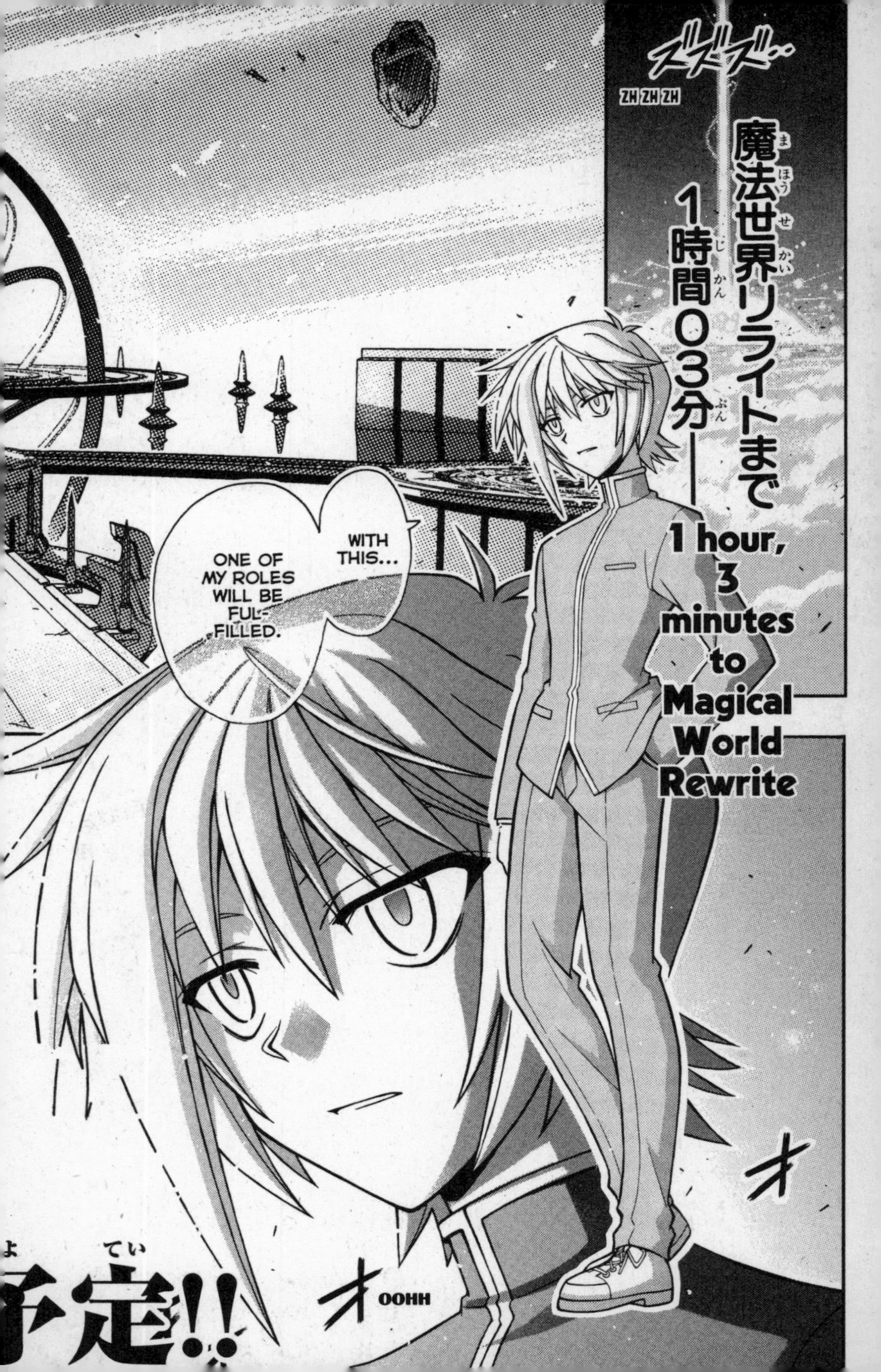
ズズズ…
ZH ZH ZH
魔法世界リライトまで1時間03分──
1 hour, 3 minutes to Magical World Rewrite
WITH THIS... ONE OF MY ROLES WILL BE FUL-FILLED.
オ
オ OOHH
予定!!

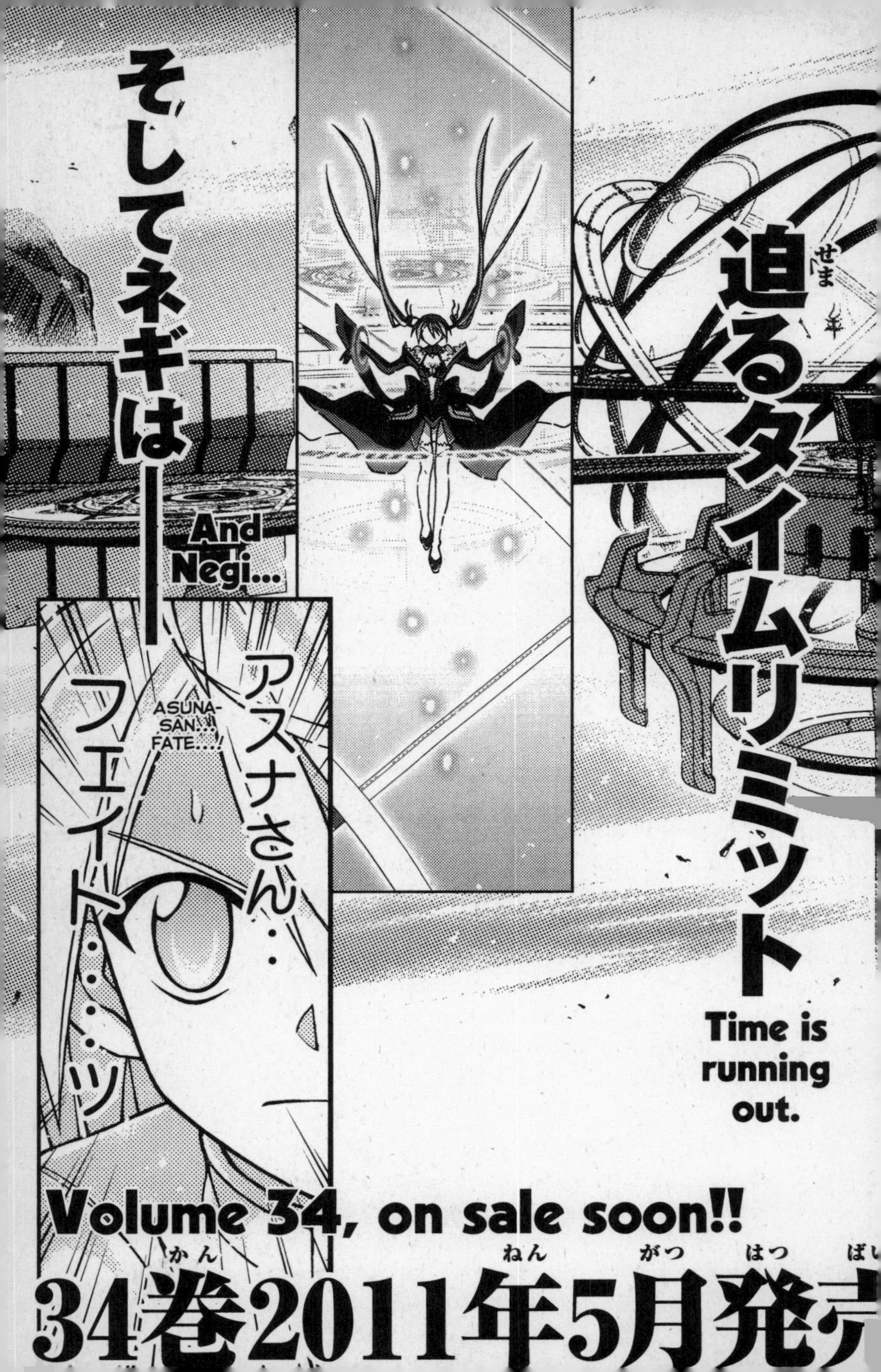

迫る(せま)タイムリミット
Time is running out.
そしてネギは――
And Negi...
アスナさん・・・フェイト・・・ッ
ASUNA-SAN...! FATE...!
Volume 34, on sale soon!!
34巻(かん)2011年(ねん)5月(がつ)発売(はつばい)

Translation Notes

Japanese is a tricky language for most Westerners, and translation is often more art than science. For your edification and reading pleasure, here are notes on some of the places where we could have gone in a different direction with our translation of the work, or where a Japanese cultural reference is used.

Summer homework, page 22

As long-term readers may remember, the start of the Japanese school year is in April. Japanese students do get a long summer break (about a month), but it comes in the middle of the year, along with a lot of homework to do in the students' free time.

Chao Lingshen's English, page 30

Hardcore Negima! fans may be aware that, in the Japanese version of the manga, Kū Fei ends her sentences with -*aru*. This is a common trick used in Japanese manga to indicate that a character is from China, and hasn't quite gotten the hang of the language, like how an American (like the translators of this manga) might incorrectly add *da* to the end of sentences when not used to speaking Japanese. That's why -*aru* is often translated into broken English. During the school festival, this trait wasn't nearly as prominent in Chao as it is in Kū, although she did have a bit of an accent. Perhaps in this alternate universe, she focused her superbrain more on things other than the Japanese language, because now she is using the -*aru* accent about as much as Kū. That, or Akamatsu-sensei didn't have time to accurately recreate her speech pattern. Either way, remember that being unfamiliar with a language doesn't make her any less intelligent. If languages were easy to learn, you would all be reading this manga in Japanese, and we would be out of a job.

Goof-offs and merchants, page 129

These are two character classes in the *Dragon Quest* video game series. They're not the most beneficial members of a battle party (and the Goof-off can be very difficult to use), so they tend to be left out. That being the case, by the time the player gets to the last boss, they would be far too weak to stand a chance in battle.

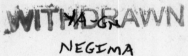

MAGN
NEGIMA
401-4190

Negima! volume 33 is a work of fiction. Names, characters, places, and incidents are the products of the author's imagination or are used fictitiously. Any resemblance to actual events, locales, or persons, living or dead, is entirely coincidental.

A Kodansha Comics Trade Paperback Original

Negima! volume 33 copyright © 2011 Ken Akamatsu
English translation copyright © 2012 Ken Akamatsu

Published in the United States by Kodansha Comics, an imprint of Kodansha USA Publishing, LLC, New York.

Publication rights arranged through Kodansha Ltd., Tokyo.

First published in Japan in 2011 by Kodansha Ltd., Tokyo, as *Maho sensei Negima!*, volume 33

ISBN 978-1-61262-115-9

Printed in the United States of America

www.kodanshacomics.com

9 8 7 6 5 4 3 2 1

Translator/Adapter: Alethea Nibley and Athena Nibley
Lettering: Scott O. Brown

3 1916 00401 4190

3/12

TOMARE!

[STOP!]

You're going the wrong way!

Manga is a completely different type of reading experience.

To start at the *beginning*, go to the *end*!

FRANKLIN PARK LIBRARY
WITHDRAWN PARK, IL

That's right! Authentic manga is read the traditional Japanese way—from right to left. Exactly the *opposite* of how American books are read. It's easy to follow: Just go to the other end of the book, and read each page—and each panel—from the right side to the left side, starting at the top right. Now you're experiencing manga as it was meant to be!